Authors
& Artists
for Young
Adults

ISSN 1040-5682

Authors & Artists for Young Adults

VOLUME 37

GALE GROUP

Detroit
New York
San Francisco
London
Boston
Woodbridge, CT

Scot Peacock, *Managing Editor, Literature Product*
Mark Scott, *Publisher, Literature Product*

Alan Hedblad, *Managing Editor*
Susan Trosky, *Literature Content Coordinator*

Marie Lazzari, Thomas McMahon, *Editors;* Katy Balcer, Sara Constantakis,
Kristen Dorsch, Shayla Hawkins, Arlene M. Johnson, Simone Sobel, *Associate Editors;*
Joshua Kondek, *Technical Training Specialist*

Victoria B. Cariappa, *Research Manager*
Tracie A. Richardson, *Project Coordinator*
Andrew Guy Malonis, Gary J. Oudersluys, Cheryl L. Warnock, *Research Specialists*
Tamara C. Nott, *Research Associate,* Tim Lehnerer, *Research Assistant*

Maria Franklin, *Permissions Manager*
Edna Hedblad, *Permissions Specialist*
Shalice Shah, *Permissions Associate*

Mary Beth Trimper, *Manager, Composition and Prepress*
Carolyn A. Roney, *Composition Specialist*

Dorothy Maki, *Manager, Manufacturing*
Stacy L. Melson, *Buyer*

Randy Bassett, *Image Database Supervisor*
Michael Logusz, *Graphic Artist*
Robert Duncan, *Imaging Specialist*
Pamela A. Reed, *Imaging Coordinator*
Dean Dauphinais, Robyn V. Young, *Senior Image Editors*
Kelly A. Quin, *Image Editor*

Library of Congress Catalog Card Number 89-641100
ISBN 0-7876-4670-9
ISSN 1040-5682

10 9 8 7 6 5 4 3 2 1

Printed in the United States of America

Authors and Artists for Young Adults

TEEN BOARD ADVISORS

Contents

Introduction

Authors and Artists for Young Adults is a reference series designed to serve the needs of middle school, junior high, and high school students interested in creative artists. Originally inspired by the need to bridge the gap between Gale's *Something about the Author,* created for children, and *Contemporary Authors,* intended for older students and adults, *Authors and Artists for Young Adults* has been expanded to cover not only an international scope of authors, but also a wide variety of other artists.

Although the emphasis of the series remains on the writer for young adults, we recognize that these readers have diverse interests covering a wide range of reading levels. The series therefore contains not only those creative artists who are of high interest to young adults, including cartoonists, photographers, music composers, bestselling authors of adult novels, media directors, producers, and performers, but also literary and artistic figures studied in academic curricula, such as influential novelists, playwrights, poets, and painters. The goal of *Authors and Artists for Young Adults* is to present this great diversity of creative artists in a format that is entertaining, informative, and understandable to the young adult reader.

Entry Format

Each volume of *Authors and Artists for Young Adults* will furnish in-depth coverage of twenty to twenty-five authors and artists. The typical entry consists of:

—A detailed biographical section that includes date of birth, marriage, children, education, and addresses.

—A comprehensive bibliography or filmography including publishers, producers, and years.

—Adaptations into other media forms.

—Works in progress.

—A distinctive essay featuring comments on an artist's life, career, artistic intentions, world views, and controversies.

—References for further reading.

—Extensive illustrations, photographs, movie stills, cartoons, book covers, and other relevant visual material.

A cumulative index to featured authors and artists appears in each volume.

Compilation Methods

The editors of *Authors and Artists for Young Adults* make every effort to secure information directly from the authors and artists through personal correspondence and interviews. Sketches on living authors and artists are sent to the biographee for review prior to publication. Any sketches not personally reviewed by biographees or their representatives are marked with an asterisk (*).

Highlights of Forthcoming Volumes

Among the authors and artists planned for future volumes are:

Berenice Abbott	Edward Gorey	Gloria Naylor
Mitch Albom	Adele Griffin	I. M. Pei
Amelia Atwater-Rhodes	Duane Hanson	Marsha Qualey
Miriam Bat-Ami	Will Hobbs	Rick Reilly
Gary L. Blackwood	Kimberly Willis Holt	Diego Rivera
Lewis Carroll	Nalo Hopkinson	Charles Schulz
Chris Crutcher	William Joyce	Martin Scorcese
Fedor Dostoevsky	C. S. Lewis	William Sleator
David Drake	Janet Lunn	Andrew Lloyd Webber
Jean Ferris	Mark Mathabane	Orson Welles
Shelby Foote	Peter Matthiessen	June Rae Wood
Jack Gantos	Lurlene McDaniel	Lois-Ann Yamanaka

Contact the Editor

We encourage our readers to examine the entire *AAYA* series. Please write and tell us if we can make *AAYA* even more helpful to you. Give your comments and suggestions to the editor:

BY MAIL: The Editor, *Authors and Artists for Young Adults,* 27500 Drake Rd., Farmington Hills, MI 48331-3535.

BY TELEPHONE: (800) 347-GALE

Acknowledgments

Grateful acknowledgment is made to the following publishers, authors, and artists for their kind permission to reproduce copyrighted material.

K. A. APPLEGATE. Mattingly, David B., illustrator. From a jacket of *Animorphs: The Change (#13)* by K. A. Applegate. Apple Paperbacks, 1997. Jacket illustration copyright 1997 by Scholastic Inc. ANIMORPHS is a registered trademark of Scholastic Inc. Reproduced by permission. / Mattingly, David B., illustrator. From a cover of *Animorphs: The Arrival (#35)*, by K. A. Applegate. Scholastic Inc., 2000. Jacket illustration copyright 2000 by Scholastic Inc. ANIMORPHS is a registered trademark of Scholastic Inc. Reproduced by permission. / Spalenka, Greg, illustrator. From a cover of *Everworld: Fear the Fantastic*, by K. A. Applegate. Scholastic Inc., 2000. Jacket illustration copyright 2000 by Scholastic Inc. EVERWORLD is a registered trademark of Scholastic Inc. Reproduced by permission. / Applegate, K. A., photograph. AP/Wide World Photos. Reproduced by permission.

AVI. Catalanotto, Peter, illustrator. From a jacket of *Nothing but the Truth: A Documentary Novel*, by Avi. Orchard Books, 1991. Jacket illustration copyright 1991 by Peter Catalanotto. All rights reserved. Reproduced by permission of Orchard Books, New York. / Mitchell, Tracy, illustrator. From a cover of *What Do Fish Have to Do with Anything? And Other Stories*, by Avi. Candlewick Press, 1997. Illustration 1997 by Tracy Mitchell. Reproduced by permission of the publisher, Candlewick Press Inc., Cambridge, MA. / Mangiat, Jeff, illustrator. From a cover of *Who Stole The Wizard of Oz?*, by Avi. Knopf, 1997. Cover art copyright 1997 by Jeff Mangiat. Reproduced by permission of Alfred A. Knopf Children's Books, a division of Random House, Inc. / Long, Laurel, illustrator. From a jacket of *Midnight Magic*, by Avi. Scholastic Press, 1999. Jacket illustration copyright 1999 Laurel Long. Reproduced by permission of Scholastic Press, a division of Scholastic Inc. / Reed, Marcie, illustrator. From a cover of *Perloo the Bold*, by Avi. Scholastic Press, 1999. Jacket illustration copyright 1998 by Marcie Reed. Reproduced by permission of Scholastic Inc. / Avi, photograph by Jim Shea. AP/Wide World Photos. Reproduced by permission.

MARTHA BROOKS. Martin, Sean Francis. From a cover of *Paradise Cafe and Other Stories*, by Martha Brooks. Thistledown Press, 1988. Reproduced by permission. / Pederson, Judy, illustrator. From a cover of *Two Moons in August*, by Martha Brooks. Groundwood Books, 1991. Reproduced by permission of Douglas & McIntyre Ltd. / Desimini, Lisa, illustrator. From a jacket of *Traveling on into the Light and Other Stories*, by Martha Brooks. Orchard Books, 1994. Jacket illustration copyright 1994 by Lisa Desimini. All rights reserved. Reproduced by permission of Orchard Books, New York. / McLoughlin, Wayne, illustrator. From a jacket of *Bone Dance*, by Martha Brooks. Orchard Books, 1997. Jacket illustration copyright 1997 by Wayne McLoughlin. All rights reserved. Reproduced by permission of Orchard Books, New York. / Brooks, Martha, photograph. Groundwood/Douglas & McIntyre Books Ltd. Reproduced by permission.

J. M. COETZEE. Collier, John, illustrator. From a cover of *In the Heart of the Country*, by J. M. Coetzee. Penguin Books, 1982. Copyright 1976, 1977 by J. M. Coetzee. Reproduced by permission of Viking Penguin, a division of Penguin Putnam Inc. / Collier, John, illustrator. From a cover of *Waiting for the Barbarians*, by J. M. Coetzee. Penguin Books, 1982. Copyright 1980 by J. M. Coetzee. Reproduced by permission of Viking Penguin, a division of Penguin Putnam Inc. / Collier, John, illustrator. From a cover of *Life & Times of Michael K.*, by J. M. Coetzee. Penguin Books, 1985. Copyright 1983 by J. M. Coetzee. Reproduced by permission of Viking Penguin, a division of Penguin Putnam Inc. / Collier, John, illustrator. From a cover of *Foe*, by J. M. Coetzee. Penguin Books, 1987. Copyright 1986 by J. M. Coetzee. Reproduced by permission of Penguin Putnam Inc. / Collier, John, illustrator. From a cover of *The Master of Petersburg*, by J. M. Coetzee. Penguin Books, 1995. Copyright 1994 by J. M. Coetzee. Reproduced by permission of Viking Penguin, a division of Penguin Putnam Inc. / Coetzee, J. M., photograph by Jerry Bauer. Jerry Bauer. Reproduced by permission.

CHRISTOPHER PAUL CURTIS. From a jacket of *The Watsons Go to Birmingham--1963*, by Christopher Paul Curtis. Delacorte Press, 1995. Car photograph copyright 1995 FPG International. Left photograph copyright

1995 Rohn Engh/FPG International. Middle and right photographs copyright 1995 Paul Lewis. Reproduced by permission of Random House Children's Books, a division of Random House, Inc. / Norcia, Ernie, illustrator. From a cover of *Bud, Not Buddy,* by Christopher Paul Curtis. Delacorte Press, 1999. Cover illustration 1999 by Ernie Norcia. Reproduced by permission of Random House Children's Books, a division of Random House, Inc. / Curtis, Christopher Paul, photograph. Copyright 1995 Curtis Photographic. Reproduced by permission.

DAPHNE DU MAURIER. Laughton, Charles, with others, in the film *Jamaica Inn,* 1939, photograph. The Kobal Collection. Reproduced by permission. / Fontaine, Joan, and Laurence Olivier, in the film *Rebecca,* 1940, photograph. The Kobal Collection. Reproduced by permission. / Christie, Julie, and Hilary Mason, in the film *Don't Look Now,* 1973, photograph. The Kobal Collection. Reproduced by permission. / Scene from *The Birds,* photograph. Archive Photos, Inc. Reproduced by permission. / Du Maurier, Daphne, photograph. Popperfoto/Archive Photos, Inc. Reproduced by permission.

SUSAN FLETCHER. Guay, Rebecca, illustrator. From a cover of *The Dragon Chronicles: Flight of the Dragon Kyn,* by Susan Fletcher. Aladdin Paperbacks, 1997. Cover illustration copyright 1997 by Rebecca Guay. Reproduced by permission of Rebecca Guay. / Guay, Rebecca, illustrator. From a cover of *Dragon's Milk,* by Susan Fletcher. Aladdin Paperbacks, 1997. Cover illustration 1997 by Rebecca Guay. Reproduced by permission of Rebecca Guay. / Guay, Rebecca, illustrator. From a cover of *The Dragon Chronicles: Sign of the Dove,* by Susan Fletcher. Aladdin Paperbacks, 1999. Cover illustration 1999 by Rebecca Guay. Reproduced by permission of Rebecca Guay. / Fletcher, Susan, photograph by Liz Demott. Reproduced by permission of Susan Fletcher.

E. M. FORSTER. From a cover of *A Room with a View,* by E. M. Forster. Dover Publications, Inc., 1995. Copyright 1995 by Dover Publications, Inc. Reproduced by permission. / Davis, Judy, and Nigel Havers in the film *A Passage to India,* 1984, photograph. The Kobal Collection. Reproduced by permission. / From a movie still of *Howard's End,* with Emma Thompson as Margaret Schlegel and Anthony Hopkins as Henry Wilcox. Mayfair. The Kobal Collection. Reproduced by permission. / Forster, E. M., photograph. Archive Photos, Inc. Reproduced by permission.

PAULA FOX. Waldman, Neil, illustrator. From a jacket of *One-Eyed Cat,* by Paula Fox. Simon & Schuster Books for Young Readers, 1984. Jacket painting 1984 by Simon & Schuster, Inc. Reproduced by permission of Simon & Schuster Children's Publishing Division. / From a cover of *The Moonlight Man,* by Paula Fox. Laurel-Leaf Books, 1988. Reproduced by permission of Random House Children's Books, a division of Random House, Inc. / Hamanaka, Sheila, illustrator. From a jacket of *The Village by the Sea,* by Paula Fox. Orchard Books, 1988. Jacket illustration copyright 1988 by Sheila Hamanaka. All rights reserved. Reproduced by permission of Orchard Books, New York. / Popp, Wendy, illustrator. From a cover of *The Slave Dancer,* by Paula Fox. Yearling Books, 1991. Reproduced by permission of Dell Publishing, a division of Random House, Inc. / Norman, Elaine, illustrator. From a cover of *A Place Apart,* by Paula Fox. Farrar, Straus & Giroux, 1993. Copyright 1980 by Paula Fox. Cover art copyright 1993 by Elaine Norman. Reproduced by permission of Farrar, Straus and Giroux, LLC. / Fox, Paula, photograph. Jerry Bauer. Reproduced by permission.

ADELE GRIFFIN. Pedersen, Judy, illustrator. From a jacket of *Rainy Season,* by Adele Griffin. Houghton Mifflin Company, 1996. Jacket art 1996 by Judy Pedersen. Reproduced by permission of Houghton Mifflin Company. / Carroll, Jim, illustrator. From a jacket of *The Other Shepards,* by Adele Griffin. Hyperion Paperbacks for Children, 1997. Jacket illustration 1998 by Jim Carroll. Reproduced by permission of Hyperion Books for Children. / McCarty, Peter, illustrator. From a jacket of *Sons of Liberty,* by Adele Griffin. Hyperion Paperbacks for Children, 1997. Copyright 1997 by Adele Griffin. Jacket illustration 1997 by Peter McCarty. Reproduced by permission of Hyperion Books for Children. / Muna, R. J., photographer. From a jacket of *Dive,* by Adele Griffin. Hyperion Books for Children, 1999. Jacket photograph 1999 by R. J. Muna/Graphistock. Reproduced by permission of Disney Publishing, Inc., and Graphistock. / McMullan, Jim, illustrator. From a cover of *Split Just Right,* by Adele Griffin. Hyperion Paperbacks for Children, 1999. Copyright 1997 by Adele Griffin. Cover art 1997 by Jim McMullan. Reproduced by permission of Hyperion Books for Children. / Griffin, Adele, photograph. Reproduced by permission of Adele Griffin.

ROSA GUY. From a cover of *The Disappearance,* by Rosa Guy. Laurel-Leaf Books, 1992. Reproduced by permission of Dell Publishing, a division of Random House, Inc. / Waldman, Neil, illustrator. From a cover of *The Friends,* by Rosa Guy. Laurel-Leaf Books, 1996. Cover illustration 1992 by Neil Waldman. Reproduced by permission of Bantam Books, a division of Random House, Inc. / Guy, Rosa, photograph by Jerry Bauer. Jerry Bauer. Reproduced by permission.

LIBBY HATHORN. Hathorn, Libby, photograph. Reproduced by permission.

ALICE HOFFMAN. Marcellino, Fred, illustrator. From a cover of *Illumination Night,* by Alice Hoffman. Ballantine Books, 1988. Cover art Fred Marcellino. Reproduced by permission of Random House, Inc. / Bullock, Sandra, in the film *Practical Magic,* 1998, photograph. The Kobal Collection. Reproduced by permission. / Hoffman, Alice, photograph. Jerry Bauer. Reproduced by permission.

FRANCESS LANTZ. Cosale, Paul, illustrator. From a cover of *Spinach with Chocolate Sauce,* by Francess Lantz. Troll, 1997. Copyright 1997 by Troll Communications, L.L.C. Published by and reproduced with permission of Troll Communications L.L.C. / Gaadt, David, illustrator. From a cover of *Stepsister from the Planet Weird,* by Francess Lantz. Random House, Inc., 1997. Cover art copyright 1997 by David Gaadt. Reproduced by permission of Random House Children's Books, a division of Random House, Inc. / Lantz, Francess, photograph by John M. Landsberg. Reproduced by permission of Francess Lantz.

GAIL CARSON LEVINE. Elliott, Mark, illustrator. From a cover of *Ella Enchanted,* by Gail Carson Levine. HarperTrophy, 1998. Cover art 1997 by Mark Elliott. Cover 1998 by HarperCollins Publishers. Reproduced by permission. / Long, Loren, illustrator. From a jacket of *Dave at Night,* by Gail Carson Levine. HarperCollins Publishers, 1999. Jacket art 1999 by Loren Long. Reproduced by permission. / Elliott, Mark, illustrator. From a jacket of *The Fairy's Mistake,* by Gail Carson Levine. HarperCollins Publishers, 1999. Jacket art 1999 by Mark Elliott. Reproduced by permission. / Levine, Gail Carson, photograph. Reproduced by permission of Gail Carson Levine.

BEN MIKAELSEN. Wimmer, Mike, illustrator. From a cover of *Rescue Josh McGuire,* by Ben Mikaelsen. Hyperion Paperbacks for Children, 1993. Copyright 1991 by Ben Mikaelsen. Cover art 1993 by Mike Wimmer. Reproduced by permission of Hyperion Books for Children. / Velasquez, Eric, illustrator. From a cover of *Sparrow Hawk Red,* by Ben Mikaelsen. Hyperion Books for Children, 1994. Text 1993 by Ben Mikaelsen. Cover art 1993 by Eric Velasquez. Reproduced by permission of Hyperion Books for Children. / Mangiat, Jeff, illustrator. From a cover of *Stranded,* by Ben Mikaelsen. Hyperion Paperbacks, 1996. Text 1995 by Ben Mikaelsen. Cover art 1995 by Jeff Mangiat. Reproduced by permission of Hyperion Books for Children. / Brown, Dan, illustrator. From a cover of *Countdown,* by Ben Mikaelsen. Hyperion Books for Children, 1996. Text 1996 by Ben Mikaelsen. Cover art 1996 by Dan Brown. Reproduced by permission of Hyperion Books for Children. / Geerinck, Manuel, illustrator. From a jacket of *Petey,* by Ben Mikaelsen. Hyperion Books for Children, 1998. Jacket illustration 1998 by Manuel Geerinck. Reproduced by permission of Hyperion Books for Children. / Mikaelsen, Ben, photograph. Reproduced by permission.

HAYAO MIYAZAKI. "Princess Mononoke," standing in center, scene from Hayao Miyazaki's animated film, *Princess Mononoke,* photograph. Reuters Newmedia Inc./Corbis. Reproduced by permission. / Miyazaki, Hayao, at New York Film Festival. Corbis/Mitch Gerber. Reproduced by permission.

MICHAEL MORPURGO. Rane, Walter, illustrator. From a cover of *Why the Whales Came,* by Michael Morpurgo. Scholastic, Inc., 1990. Cover illustration copyright 1990 by Scholastic Inc. Reproduced by permission. / DiCesare, Joe, illustrator. From a cover of *Waiting for Anya,* by Michael Morpurgo. Puffin Books, 1997. Cover illustration copyright Joe DiCesare, 1997. Reproduced by permission of Puffin Books, a division of Penguin Putnam Inc.

THYLIAS MOSS. From a cover of *Rainbow Remnants in Rock Bottom Ghetto Sky,* by Thylias Moss. Persea Books, 1991. Reproduced by permission. / "The Last Judgment," painting by Hieronymous Bosch. From a cover of *Last Chance for the Tarzan Holler: Poems,* by Thylias Moss. Persea Books, 1998. Reproduced by permission. / Moss, Thylias, photograph by D. C. Goings. University of Michigan Photo Services. Reproduced by permission of Thylias Moss.

MELISSA SCOTT. Roberts, Tony, illustrator. From a cover of *Dreamships,* by Melissa Scott. TOR, A Tom Doherty Associates Book, 1992. Copyright 1992 by Melissa Scott. Reproduced by permission of St. Martin's Press, Inc. / Johnson, Kevin Eugene. From a cover of *Point of Hopes,* by Melissa Scott and Lisa A. Barnett.

Authors & Artists for Young Adults

K. A. Applegate

■ **Personal**

Born Katherine Applegate in 1956, in Michigan. *Hobbies and other interests:* Playing the cello, traveling, reading, gardening, her pet cats.

■ **Addresses**

Home—Illinois. *E-mail*—kaapplegate@scholastic.com. *Agent*—c/o Scholastic Inc., 555 Broadway, New York, NY 10012.

■ **Career**

Freelance writer.

■ **Writings**

"ANIMORPHS" SERIES; FOR JUVENILES; UNDER NAME K. A. APPLEGATE

The Invasion, Scholastic, 1996.
The Visitor, Scholastic, 1996.
The Encounter, Demco Media, 1996.
The Predator, Apple, 1996.

The Message, Scholastic, 1996.
The Andalite Chronicles, Scholastic, 1997.
The Capture, Scholastic, 1997.
The Stranger, Scholastic, 1997.
The Alien, Scholastic, 1997.
The Secret, Scholastic, 1997.
The Android, Scholastic, 1997.
The Forgotten, Scholastic, 1997.
The Reaction, Scholastic, 1997.
The Change, Scholastic, 1997.
The Hork-Bajir Chronicles, Scholastic, 1998.
The Unknown, Scholastic, 1998.
The Escape, Scholastic, 1998.
The Warning, Scholastic, 1998.
The Underground, Scholastic, 1998.
The Decision, Scholastic, 1998.
The Departure, Scholastic, 1998.
The Discovery, Scholastic, 1998.
The Threat, Demco Media, 1998.
The Solution, Demco Media, 1999.
The Pretender, Demco Media, 1999.
The Suspicion, Demco Media, 1999.
The Extreme, Little Apple, 1999.
The Attack, Apple, 1999.
The Exposed, Scholastic, 1999.
The Experiment, Scholastic, 1999.
The Sickness, Scholastic, 1999.
The Reunion, Apple, 1999.
The Conspiracy, Apple, 1999.
The Separation, Apple, 1999.
The Illusion, Apple, 1999.
The Prophecy, Scholastic, 1999.
The Proposal, Scholastic, 1999.
The Mutation, Scholastic, 1999.

The Weakness, Apple, 2000.
The Arrival, Apple, 2000.
The Hidden, Apple, 2000.
The Other, Apple, 2000.
The Familiar, Scholastic, 2000.
The Journey, Apple, 2000.
The Test, Apple, 2000.
The Unexpected, Scholastic, 2000.
The Revelation, Apple, 2000.
The Deception, Apple, 2000.
The Resistance, Apple, 2000.
The Ellinist Chronicles, Apple, 2000.

ANIMORPHS "MEGAMORPHS" SERIES

The Andalite's Gift, Scholastic, 1997.
Animorphs: In the Time of the Dinosaurs, Scholastic, 1998.
Elfangor's Secret, Apple, 1999.
Back to Before, Scholastic, 2000.

ANIMORPHS "ALTERNAMORPHS" SERIES

The First Journey, Scholastic, 1999.
The Next Passage, Apple, 2000.

"EVERWORLD" SERIES

Search for Senna, Scholastic, 1999.
Land of Loss, Scholastic, 1999.
Enter the Enchanted, Scholastic, 1999.
Realm of the Reaper, Scholastic, 1999.
Discover the Destroyer, Scholastic, 2000.
Fear the Fantastic, Scholastic, 2000.
Gateway to the Gods, Apple, 2000.
Brave the Betrayal, Scholastic, 2000.
Inside the Illusion, Apple, 2000.
Understand the Unknown, Scholastic, 2000.

"BOYFRIENDS AND GIRLFRIENDS" SERIES: REISSUED AS "MAKING OUT" SERIES

Zoey Fools Around, Harper, 1994, Flare, 1998.
Jake Finds Out, Flare, 1998.
Nina Won't Tell, Flare, 1998.
Ben's in Love, Flare, 1998.
What Zoey Saw, Flare, 1998.
Claire Gets Caught, Flare, 1998.
Lucas Gets Hurt, Flare, 1998.
Aisha Goes Wild, Avon, 1999.
Zoey Plays Games, Avon, 1999.
Nina Shapes Up, Camelot, 1999.
Ben Takes a Chance, Avon, 1999.
Claire Can't Lose, Flare, 1999.
Don't Tell Zoey, Flare, 1999.
Aaron Lets Go, Flare, 1999.
Who Loves Kate, Flare, 1999.
Lara Gets Even, Flare, 1999.

Two-Timing Aisha, Flare, 1999.
Zoey Speaks Out, Flare, 1999,
Kate Finds Love, Flare, 1999.
Never Trust Lara, Flare, 2000.
Trouble with Aaron, Flare, 2000.
Always Loving Zoey, Flare, 2000.
Lara Gets Lucky, Flare, 2000.
Now Zoey's Alone, Avon, 2000.
Don't Forget Lara, Avon, 2000.
Zoey's Broken Heart, Avon, 2000.
Falling for Claire, Avon, 2000.
Zoey Comes Home, Avon, 2000.

"SUMMER" SERIES

June Dreams, Archway, 1995.
July's Promise, Archway, 1995.
August Magic, Archway, 1995.
Beaches, Boys, and Betrayal, Archway, 1996.
Sand, Surf, and Secrets, Archway, 1996.
Rays, Romance, and Rivalry, Archway, 1996.
Christmas Special Edition, Archway, 1996.
Spring Break Reunion, Archway, 1996.

BY L. E. BLAIR; TEXT BY KATHERINE APPLEGATE

Horse Fever ("Girl Talk" series), Western Publishing (Racine, WI), 1991.
Family Rules ("Girl Talk" series), Western Publishing, 1991.
Randy's Big Dream, Western Publishing, 1992.
Randy and the Great Canoe Race, Western Publishing, 1992.
Randy and the Perfect Boy, Western Publishing, 1992.
Randy's Big Chance, Western Publishing, 1992.

OTHER

The Story of Two American Generals: Benjamin O. Davis, Jr., and Colin L. Powell (nonfiction), Dell, 1992.
Disney's The Little Mermaid: The Haunted Palace, illustrated by Philo Barnhart, Disney Press, 1993.
Disney's The Little Mermaid: King Triton, Beware!, illustrated by Philo Barnhart, Disney Press, 1993.
Disney's Christmas with All the Trimmings: Original Stories and Crafts from Mickey Mouse and Friends, illustrated by Phil Wilson, Disney Press, 1994.
The Boyfriend Mix-up, illustrated by Philo Barnhart, Disney Press, 1994.
Sharing Sam (novel), Bantam, c. 1995.
Disney's Tales from Agrabah: Seven Original Stories of Aladdin and Jasmine, illustrated by Fred Marvin and Jose Cardona, Disney Press, 1995.
(With Nicholas Stephens) *Disney's Climb Aboard if You Dare!: Stories from the Pirates of the Caribbean,*

illustrated by Roberta Collier-Morales, Disney Press, 1996.

Listen to My Heart ("Love Stories Super" series), Bantam, 1996.

Jack Rabbit and the Beanstalk (picture book), illustrated by Holly Hannon, Inchworm Press, 1997.

Escape (picture book; "Magic School Bus" series), Scholastic, 1998.

Also the author of many other juvenile novels, including installments in the "Sweet Valley Twin" series, the "Ocean City" series, the "Changes Romance" series, and Harlequin romances for adults.

■ Adaptations

The "Animorphs" books have been adapted as a television series for Nickelodeon.

■ Work in Progress

Further novels in the "Animorphs" and "Everworld" series.

■ Sidelights

Katherine Applegate, who also writes as K. A. Applegate, has authored more than one hundred books. While her publications include romances for the Harlequin line, she has aimed most of her writing at middle-grade readers, penning some titles for the popular "Sweet Valley Twins" series and authoring several books featuring Disney characters. Applegate's most successful venture in juvenile fiction, however, has been her creation of the "Animorphs" series. These books, about young adolescents given the power by aliens to "morph" themselves into various animals, have rivaled R. L. Stine's "Goosebumps" series in popularity.

Applegate has completed many titles either in the "Animorphs" series or related to it, such as the "Megamorphs" series wherein the characters take turns narrating chapters, and the "choose-your-own-adventure" "Alternamorphs" series. Writing in *Horn Book*, Christine Heppermann attributed the series' success to this: "Readers can take what they want from it—the animal info or the aliens or the realistic adolescent dilemmas of crushes and problem parents. They can skim over the rest." According to Sally Lodge in *Publishers Weekly*, by the late 1990s, the series "reside[d] at the top" of that publication's "children's paperback series bestseller list, where booksellers predict it [would] roost for the foreseeable future."

Tobias discovers he can morph into many different animals, not just a red-tailed hawk, in this installment of the "Animorphs" fantasy series.

The Origin of Animorphs

During an interview in *Publishers Weekly*, Applegate told Lodge where her idea for the "Animorphs" books came from. "I grew up loving animals and lived with the usual suburban menagerie of dogs, cats and gerbils," she confided. "I really wanted to find a way to get kids into the heads of various species and decided that a science-fiction premise was the way to do this." She worked up a plan for an entire series—which she initially called "The Changelings"—and submitted it, with rough drafts of chapters for several different novels, to Scholastic. Picked up by the publisher, Applegate's "Animorphs" series received heavy promotion from Scholastic, and the firm gave the books eye-catching, die-cut covers. But Jean Feiwel, a vice president at Scholastic, credited Applegate's skill in bringing to life the series' main concept with the success of

When the Andalites arrive on Earth, Ax must decide whether to remain with his friends the Animorphs or join the Andalites in this 2000 "Animorphs" novel.

"Animorphs." Feiwel explained to *Publishers Weekly* that the concept "is absolutely unbelievable but utterly possible. The notion of kids' morphing is also close to adolescent body changes in some ways. It is out of their control," the Scholastic staffer continued, "but becomes something quite fabulous— which is what you like to think happens in the process of growing up." Feiwel also noted that while the protagonists of "Animorphs" "may go off to defend the earth against aliens, at the end of the day they still have math homework to do."

One of the earliest novels in the "Animorphs" series, *The Message,* features a young woman named Cassie who is disturbed by strange messages in her dreams. Cassie eventually realizes that she is receiving a distress signal from the Andalites, the aliens that gave her and her friends morphic powers. She persuades her friends that they should change into dolphins in order to rescue their allies from an invading race of aliens, the Yeerks. Linda Bindner, reviewing *The Message* for *School Library Journal,* praised Cassie's portrayal, stating that "her struggles to come to terms with her decision are realistic and engaging." Bindner also judged that "the descriptions of becoming and living as dolphins and other animals are impressive."

Before embarking on the "Animorphs," Applegate authored a nonfiction work aimed at young people interested in the achievements of African Americans. *The Story of Two American Generals: Benjamin O. Davis, Jr., and Colin L. Powell* examines two African Americans who became pioneers in the United States Armed Forces. Sheilamae O'Hara, who critiqued the volume for *Booklist,* found it provided basic facts about its two subjects, and suggested that "libraries needing additional material on living black men of achievement may find it useful."

Popular Romance Series

Applegate was also selected to write the first novel in Harper's "Boyfriends and Girlfriends" series, later reissued as the "Making Out" series. This book, *Zoey Fools Around,* is composed of both a normal third-person narrative, and what a *Publishers Weekly* contributor described as "autobiographical fragments" from Zoey herself. Zoey, a senior in high school, has a long-time boyfriend named Jake; they live on a small island off the coast of Maine, where they are awaiting their graduation. The balance of the relationships between Zoey, Jake, and their circle of friends is upset when Lucas Cabral returns to their high school after spending two years in a juvenile facility because of his part in an alcohol-related accident that caused the death of Jake's older brother.

Zoey Fools Around also contains a subplot revolving around an African-American girl named Aisha, who is frightened of having a relationship with a boy who might prove to be her romantic destiny. Complicating matters further is Claire, who, in the words of a *Publishers Weekly* reviewer, "is more unhappy and confused than evil." The reviewer cited "better-than-average character development" in predicting that *Zoey Fools Around* would be "likely to hook its intended audience." The same cast of characters returns for more adventures in several additional titles in the series.

Another of Applegate's young adult efforts is *Sharing Sam.* In this novel, Alison is just starting to get to know Sam, the new guy who rides his own Harley Davidson motorcycle to their school in Florida,

If you enjoy the works of K. A. Applegate, you might want to check out the following books:

David Brin, *Startide Rising*, 1983.
Susan Cooper, *Silver on the Tree*, 1977.
David Drake, *Cross the Stars*, 1984.
Alan Dean Foster, *The Spoils of War*, 1993.
Rebecca Ore, *Becoming Alien*, 1987.

when she learns that her long-time best friend Izzy has developed brain cancer and has only a few months to live. When Izzy begins expressing interest in Sam, Alison decides to put her own desires on hold in favor of making her friend's last days as happy as possible. Alison manages to talk Sam into dating Izzy; meanwhile, Sam is dealing with the effects of the aging process on his much-loved grandfather and trying to face their inevitable parting. A contributor to *Publishers Weekly* praised *Sharing Sam* for the "thoughtful characterizations and the logical, not entirely strife-free way in which the premise is developed." Frances Bradburn, writing in *Booklist*, stated: "While adults will find the premise uncomfortable, teenage girls will be fascinated."

Applegate discussed with Lodge her feelings about writing for middle graders, calling her audience "the best readers on the planet. They are open-minded, imaginative and willing to embrace ideas." She also revealed that she enjoys the challenges presented to her by "Animorphs," because "a series writer has to develop plotting and pacing that become a well-oiled machine. You don't have the luxury of spending a year on a book and absolutely cannot indulge in writer's block. Yet I knew," Applegate continued, "I had to write in perfect language and choose just the right images, to make sure that my middle readers fell in love with the characters and returned again and again."

Applegate's most recent venture is the "Everworld" series. It mixes the fantasy of an alternative world where gods and wizards and all manner of mythical creatures abide, with the trials and tribulations of five present-day high schoolers. When the universe created by Earth's ancient immortals is invaded by creatures of myth that are not part of human tradition, the Norse god Loki recruits Senna Wales and her four friends from the real world. Discussing her new series on the Scholastic website, Applegate stated: "I felt it was time to come up with a follow-on, or companion series for "Animorphs." I knew I didn't want

In this sixth book of the "Everworld" series, Christopher, David, April, Jalil, and Senna find themselves helping the Greek god Zeus save Olympus from an evil alien god.

to do straight science fiction. I felt I should try my hand at fantasy, but I wanted contemporary characters. In other words, I didn't want the characters to belong in the fantasy environment, I wanted them to be from our own world. And I wanted them to continue to be part of the real world. So from there I just had to come up with a device to allow me to do that."

■ Works Cited

Applegate, Katherine, comments from Scholastic's Animorphs website at: http://scholastic.com/everworld/evqa.htm.

Bindner, Linda, review of *The Message, School Library Journal*, June, 1997, p. 114.

Bradburn, Frances, review of *Sharing Sam, Booklist,* March 15, 1995, p. 132.

Heppermann, Christine, "Invasion of the Animorphs," *Horn Book,* May, 1997, pp. 54-56.

Lodge, Sally, "Scholastic's Animorphs Series Has Legs," *Publishers Weekly,* November 3, 1997, p. 36.

O'Hara, Sheilamae, review of *The Story of Two American Generals: Benjamin O. Davis, Jr., and Colin L. Powell, Booklist,* April 15, 1992, p. 1532.

Review of *Search for Senna, Publishers Weekly,* June 21, 1999, pp. 69-70.

Review of *Sharing Sam, Publishers Weekly,* December 19, 1994, p. 55.

Review of *Zoey Fools Around, Publishers Weekly,* February 28, 1994, p. 89.

■ For More Information See

PERIODICALS

Booklist, January 1, 1996, p. 813.
Kliatt, March, 1995, p. 8; November, 1995, p. 21.
Publishers Weekly, July 10, 1995, p. 59; February 16, 1998, pp. 178-88.
School Librarian, August, 1997, p. 157.
Voice of Youth Advocates, February, 1996, p. 368; April, 1996, p. 21; April, 1997, p. 21; August, 2000, p. 182.

ON-LINE

The Animorphs Web site is located at http://www.scholastic.com/Animorphs/kaa.htm (June 24, 1999).*

Avi

1962-70; Lambeth Public Library, London, England, exchange program librarian, 1968; Trenton State College, Trenton, NJ, assistant professor and humanities librarian, 1970-86. Has also taught a variety of college courses pertaining to children's literature for Simmons College, UCLA extension, Wesleyan University, and Illinois Wesleyan. Visiting writer in schools across the United States and in Canada and Denmark, conducting workshops and seminars with children, parents and educators.

■ Member

Authors Guild.

■ Awards, Honors

Best Book list, British Book Council, 1973, for *Snail Tale: The Adventures of a Rather Small Snail*; Grants from New Jersey State Council on the Arts, 1974, 1976, and 1978; runner-up for Edgar Allan Poe Award, Mystery Writers of America, 1975, for *No More Magic*, 1979, for *Emily Upham's Revenge*, and 1984, for *Shadrach's Crossing*; Christopher Book Award, 1981, for *Encounter at Easton*; Children's Choice Award, International Reading Association, 1980, for *Man from the Sky*, and 1988, for *Romeo & Juliet—Together (& Alive) at Last*; Best Books, *School Library Journal*, 1980, for *Night Journeys*; Scott O'Dell Award for historical fiction, *Bulletin of the Center for Children's Books*, and Best Books for Young Adults, American Library Association (ALA), both 1984,

■ Personal

Full name is Avi Wortis; given name is pronounced "Ah-vee"; born December 23, 1937, in New York, NY; son of Joseph (a psychiatrist) and Helen (a social worker; maiden name Zunser) Wortis; married Joan Gabriner (a weaver), November 1, 1963 (divorced); married Coppelia Kahn (a professor of English); married Linda C. Wright (a businesswoman); children: Shaun Wortis, Kevin Wortis; stepchildren: Gabriel Kahn (second marriage), Hayden, Catherine, Robert, Jack Spina. *Education:* Attended Antioch University; University of Wisconsin-Madison, B.A., 1959, M.A., 1962; Columbia University, M.S.L.S., 1964.

■ Addresses

Home—Denver, CO. *Agent*—Gail Hochman, Brandt & Brandt, 1501 Broadway, New York, NY 10036.

■ Career

Writer, 1960—. New York Public Library, New York City, librarian in Performing Arts Research Center, both for *The Fighting Ground;* Best Books for Young Adults, ALA, 1986, Best Books, *School Library Journal,* 1987, Best Books of the Eighties, *Booklist,* 1988, Virginia Young Readers' Award, 1990, all for *Wolf Rider: A Tale of Terror;* Best Books, Library of Congress, 1989, for *Something Upstairs,* and 1990, for *The Man Who Was Poe;* Golden Kite Award, Society of Children's Book Writers and Illustrators, Best Books, *School Library Journal,* Editor's Choice, *Booklist,* and Books for the Teen Age, New York Public Library, all 1990, and Newbery Honor Book, ALA, Notable Book, ALA, *Boston Globe-Horn Book* Award, and Judy Lopez Memorial Award, all 1991, all for *The True Confessions of Charlotte Doyle;* Rhode Island Award, 1991, Volunteer State Award, 1991-92, Sunshine State Young Readers Award, 1992, all for *Something Upstairs: A Tale of Ghosts;* Notable Trade Book in the Field of Social Studies, National Council for the Social Studies and Children's Book Council (NCSS-CBC), Editor's Choice, *Booklist,* and Best Books, *Horn Book, School Library Journal,* and *Publishers Weekly,* all 1991, Newbery Honor Book, ALA, Honor Book, *Boston Globe-Horn Book,* Books for the Teen Age, New York Public Library, Blue Ribbon Book, *Bulletin of the Center for Children's Books,* Best Books, Library of Congress and Bank Street Teachers' College, all 1992, and Best YA's from the last twenty-five years, Young Adult Library Services Association (YALSA-ALA), 1994, all for *Nothing but the Truth;* One Hundred Titles for Reading and Sharing, New York Public Library, Editor's Choice, *Booklist,* and Best Books, *School Library Journal,* all 1992, Pick of the Lists, American Booksellers Association (ABA), and Notable Book, ALA, both 1993, all for *"Who Was That Masked Man, Anyway?";* Books for the Teen Age, New York Public Library, and Best Books for Young Adults, ALA, both 1993, both for *Blue Heron;* Books for the Teen Age, New York Public Library, 1994, for *City of Light/City of Dark;* Children's Books of the Year, Bank Street, and Pick of the Lists, ABA, both 1994, both for *The Bird, the Frog, and the Light;* Children's Books of the Year, Bank Street, Pick of the Lists, ABA, and Editor's Choice, *Booklist,* all 1994, and Notable Book, ALA, 1995, all for *The Barn;* Best Books, *School Library Journal, Booklist,* and New York Public Library, all 1995, and *Boston Globe/Horn Book* Award and Notable Book, ALA, 1996, all for *Poppy;* Notable Children's Book in the Language Arts, National Council of Teachers of English, 1997, for *When I Was Your Age;* Blue Ribbon Book, *Bulletin of the Center for Children's Books,* Notable Trade Book in the Field of Social Studies, NCSS-CBC, and Best Books for Young Adults, ALA, all 1997, all for *Beyond the*

Western Sea; Top 10 Fantasy Novels for Youth, *Booklist,* 1999, for *Perloo the Bold.*

■ Writings

Things That Sometimes Happen, illustrated by Jodi Robbin, Doubleday, 1970.

Snail Tale: The Adventures of a Rather Small Snail, illustrated by Tom Kindron, Pantheon, 1972.

No More Magic, Pantheon, 1975.

Captain Grey, illustrated by Charles Mikolaycak, Pantheon, 1977.

Emily Upham's Revenge; or, How Deadwood Dick Saved the Banker's Niece: A Massachusetts Adventure, illustrated by Paul O. Zelinsky, Pantheon, 1978.

Night Journeys, Pantheon, 1979.

Encounter at Easton (sequel to *Night Journeys*), Pantheon, 1980.

Man from the Sky, illustrated by David Weisner, Knopf, 1980.

History of Helpless Harry: To Which Is Added a Variety of Amusing and Entertaining Adventures, illustrated by Paul O. Zelinsky, Pantheon, 1980.

A Place Called Ugly, Pantheon, 1981.

Who Stole the Wizard of Oz?, illustrated by Derek James, Knopf, 1981.

Sometimes I Think I Hear My Name, Pantheon, 1982.

Shadrach's Crossing, Pantheon, 1983, reprinted as *Smuggler's Island,* Morrow, 1994.

S.O.R. Losers, Bradbury, 1984.

Devil's Race, Lippincott, 1984.

The Fighting Ground, Lippincott, 1984.

Bright Shadow, Bradbury, 1985.

Wolf Rider: A Tale of Terror, Bradbury, 1986.

Romeo & Juliet—Together (& Alive) at Last (sequel to *S.O.R. Losers*), Orchard, 1987, Avon, 1988.

Something Upstairs: A Tale of Ghosts, Orchard Books, 1988.

The Man Who Was Poe, Orchard Books, 1989.

The True Confessions of Charlotte Doyle, Orchard Books, 1990.

Windcatcher, Bradbury, 1991.

Nothing but the Truth, Orchard Books, 1991.

Blue Heron, Bradbury, 1992.

"Who Was That Masked Man, Anyway?", Orchard Books, 1992.

Punch With Judy, illustrated by Emily Lisker, Bradbury, 1993.

City of Light/City of Dark: A Comic Book Novel, Orchard Books, 1993.

The Bird, the Frog, and the Light: A Fable, illustrated by Matthew Henry, Orchard, 1994.

The Barn, Orchard, 1994.

Tom, Babette, & Simon: Three Tales of Transformation, illustrated by Alexi Natchev, Macmillan, 1995.

Poppy, illustrated by Brian Floca, Orchard, 1995.

Beyond the Western Sea, Book One: The Escape from Home, Orchard, 1996.

Beyond the Western Sea, Book Two: Lord Kirkle's Money, Orchard, 1996.

What Do Fish Have to Do with Anything?: And Other Stories, illustrated by Tracy Mitchell, Candlewick, 1997.

Finding Providence: The Story of Roger Williams, illustrated by James Watling, HarperCollins, 1997.

Poppy and Rye, illustrated by Brian Floca, Avon, 1998.

Perloo the Bold, illustrated by Marcie Reed, Scholastic, 1998.

Abigail Takes the Wheel, illustrated by Don Bolognese, HarperCollins, 1999.

Ragweed, illustrated by Brian Floca, Avon, 1999.

Midnight Magic, Scholastic, 1999.

(Editor) *Second Sight: Stories for a New Millenium*, Philomel, 1999.

Ereth's Birthday, illustrated by Brian Floca, HarperCollins, 2000.

Also author of numerous plays. Contributor to books, including *Performing Arts Resources, 1974*, edited by Ted Perry, Drama Book Publishers, 1975. Contributor to periodicals, including *New York Public Library Bulletin, Top of the News, Children's Literature in Education, Horn Book, ALAN Review, Journal of Youth Services in Libraries, Voice of Youth Advocates*, and *Writer*. Book reviewer for *Library Journal, School Library Journal*, and *Previews*, 1965-73.

Translations of Avi's books have been published in Germany, Austria, Denmark, Norway, Spain, Italy, and Japan.

■ Adaptations

Emily Upham's Revenge, Shadrach's Crossing, Something Upstairs, The Fighting Ground, The True Confessions of Charlotte Doyle, Nothing but the Truth, and *Read to Me* were produced on the radio programs "Read to Me," Maine Public Radio, and "Books Aloud," WWON-Rhode Island; *True Confessions of Charlotte Doyle, City of Light/City of Dark, Sometimes I Think I Hear My Name, Something Upstairs*, and *Night Journeys* have all been optioned for film; *Something Upstairs* was adapted as a play performed by Louisville (KY) Children's Theater, 1997; *Nothing but the Truth* was adapted for the stage by Ronn Smith and has been performed in numerous schools.

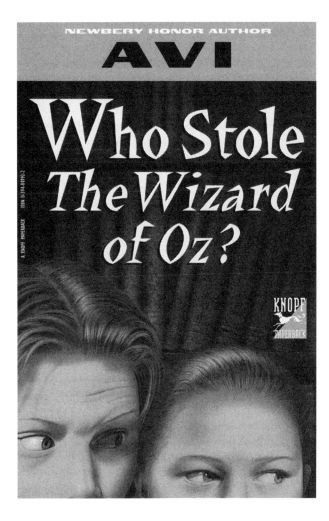

Twins Becky and Toby piece together clues to a secret treasure from a string of stolen children's books in Avi's suspenseful 1981 yarn.

A recording of *The Fighting Ground* was produced by Listening Library, *The Man Who was Poe* by Audio Bookshelf; many others of Avi's books have been recorded on audio cassette, including: *The Barn, Beyond the Western Sea, Blue Heron, Bright Shadow, Man from the Sky, Night Journeys, Perloo the Bold, Poppy, Poppy and Rye, Punch With Judy, Romeo & Juliet—Together (& Alive) at Last, Something Upstairs, Smuggler's Island, The True Confessions of Charlotte Doyle, What Do Fish Have to Do with Anything?, "Who Was That Masked Man, Anyway?,"* and *Wolf Rider*.

■ Work in Progress

The Good Dog, for DK Ink; *Prairie School*, for HarperCollins.

■ Sidelights

An inventive and prolific writer, Avi is well-known to critics, teachers, parents, and especially to young readers for his inviting, readable novels. Even reluctant readers are swept away by Avi's fast-paced, adventurous, and imaginative plots. Because he uses a variety of genres, such as mystery, adventure, historical, coming-of-age, and fantasy, to tell his stories, Avi broadens his audience with each new work. In a statement for *Twentieth-Century Children's Writers*, the talented author summarized his goals as a young adult novelist: "I try to write about complex issues—young people in an adult world—full of irony and contradiction, in a narrative style that relies heavily on suspense with a texture rich in emotion and imagery. I take a great deal of satisfaction in using popular forms—the adventure, the mystery, the thriller—so as to hold my reader with the sheer pleasure of a good story. At the same time I try to resolve my books with an ambiguity that compels engagement. In short, I want my readers to feel, to think, sometimes to laugh. But most of all I want them to enjoy a good read."

Born in Manhattan in 1937 and raised in Brooklyn, Avi comes from a long line of artists. His great-grandparents, a grandmother, an aunt, and his parents were writers, while two uncles were painters and another a composer. Many members of his close and extended family are active in the arts, including Avi's twin sister, who is also a writer. Avi's family was quite politically active in ways considered radical; they actively worked against racism, and for the rights of women and laborers, addressing concerns emanating from the Great Depression of the 1930s. The author once explained that his extended family comprised "a very strong art community and what this meant for me as a child was that there was always a kind of uproarious sense of debate. It was all a very affectionate sharing of ideas—arguing, but not arguing in anger, arguing about ideas."

Growing up, Avi was an avid reader. He experienced difficulties in writing, however, which eventually caused him to flunk out of one school. It was later discovered that he has a dysfunction known as dysgraphia, an impairment that causes him to reverse letters or misspell words. "One of my aunts said I could spell a four letter word wrong five ways," he once stated. "In a school environment, I was perceived as being sloppy and erratic, and not paying attention." Avi, however, kept writing and credits his family's emphasis on books for his perseverance. When papers came back to him covered in his teachers' red ink, he simply saved them, corrections and all.

Decides to Write

Just after junior high, despite his writing difficulties, Avi became fixed on becoming a writer. A tutor, hired by his parents to improve his spelling and writing skills, fed his interest in writing, as did his own avid reading habits. Avi claims he learned more from reading—everything from comic books and science magazines to histories, plays, and novels—than he learned in school. In a *Booklist* interview with Hazel Rochman, Avi said, "I love to write. No, let's start first, I love to read. No, start even before, I love stories. My strength as a writer is my strength as a reader."

When he reached college age, Avi enrolled in playwriting classes at Antioch University. "That's where I really started to write seriously," he once recalled. One of the plays Avi wrote in college won a contest and was published in a magazine. There were many other plays—"a trunkful of plays," said the author, "but I would say ninety-nine percent of them weren't very good."

After receiving his master's degree, Avi worked at a variety of jobs. Capitalizing on his experience as a playwright, he took a job in the theater collection of the New York Public library. This career move led to his interest in becoming a librarian. He enrolled in Columbia University's library science program and eventually became a librarian—a career that lasted twenty-five years. While a librarian, he continued to write. It wasn't until his two sons were born that he considered writing for a younger audience. Avi enjoyed telling his boys stories, and they enjoyed listening and participating in the storytelling process. Eventually Avi wrote some of his stories down, illustrated them, then submitted them to several publishers. In 1970, Doubleday accepted the text for one of his stories, *Things That Sometimes Happen*. Explaining his abbreviated pen name, Avi once explained that his agent called asking what name to put on the book cover, and without much thought Avi responded, ""just put Avi down" and that was the decision. Just like that."

Things That Sometimes Happen, a collection of "Very Short Stories for Very Young Readers," was designed with Avi's young sons in mind. For several years he continued to write children's stories geared to his sons' advancing reading levels, but he stated: "At a certain point they kept growing and I didn't. I hit a fallow period, and then I wrote *No More Magic.* Suddenly I felt "This is right! I'm writing novels and I love it." From then on I was committed to writing novels."

Popular Historical Novels

Avi has penned novels for many different genres. Because several of his early works, including *Captain Grey, Night Journeys,* and *Encounter at Easton,* are set in colonial America, he quickly earned a reputation as an historical novelist. Avi's 1984 novel *The Fighting Ground,* winner of the Scott O'Dell Award for historical fiction for children, presents one event-filled day in the life of Jonathan, a thirteen-year-old boy caught up in the Revolutionary War. The novel begins as Jonathan slips away from his family's New Jersey farm one morning in order to take part in a skirmish with the Hessians (German mercenary soldiers hired by the English). Jonathan sets out full of unquestioned hatred for the Hessians, the British, and the Americans who were loyal to the British— the Tories. He hopes for a chance to take part in the glory of battle. "O Lord, he said to himself, make it be a battle. With armies, big ones, and cannons and flags and drums and dress parades! Oh, he could, *would* fight. Good as his older brother. Maybe good as his pa. Better, maybe. O Lord, he said to himself, make it something *grand!*"

Avi portrays no grandeur in the war. Jonathan can barely carry his six-foot long musket, and has a worse time trying to understand the talk among the men with whom he marches. The small voluntary group's leader is a crude man who lies to the men and is said to be "overfond of killing." After a bloody and confusing skirmish, Jonathan is captured by three Hessians and briefly comes to understand them as individual human beings. Later, when he is called upon to be the brave soldier he had yearned to be, Jonathan's harrowing experience reveals the delusion behind his wish. The close of the novel brings the reader and Jonathan an understanding of what war means in human terms. *The Fighting Ground* was widely praised by critics, many of whom expressed sentiments similar to these from Zena Sutherland of *Bulletin of the Center for Children's Books,* who asserted: "[The novel] makes the war personal and immediate: not history or event, but experience; near and within oneself, and horrible."

More interested in telling a good story and providing a means of imagining and understanding the past than in teaching a specific historical fact, Avi's style is well-suited to the historical fiction genre.

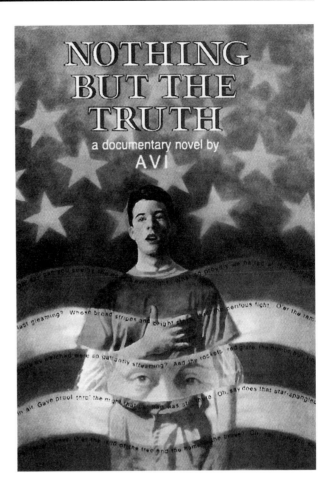

In this 1991 coming-of-age novel, Philip Malloy's small act of humming the national anthem during homeroom snowballs into a national media event.

"The historical novel is a curious construction," he once remarked. "It represents history but it's not truly accurate. It's a style." He elaborated in an interview with Jim Roginski in *Behind the Covers:* "Somewhere along the line, I can't explain where, I developed an understanding of history not as fact but as story. That you could look at a field and, with only a slight shift of your imagination, suddenly watch the battle that took place there. . . . You have to have a willingness to look beyond *things. . . .* Take the Battle of Bunker Hill during the Revolution. The leader of the American troops was Dr. Warren, who was killed during the battle. His body had been so dismembered and disemboweled, the only way he could be identified was by the nature of his teeth. And it was Paul Revere who did it. When you tell the story of war that way, a much stronger statement about how ghastly war really is, is made."

Taking readers back in time to pre-Civil War America, Avi combined elements of the historical novel, ghost story, and science fiction genres, to create *Something Upstairs: A Tale of Ghosts.* When the book's main character discovers the ghost of a murdered slave in the historic house his family recently moved into in Providence, Rhode Island, he travels back in time to the days of slave trading. There, the young man uncovers information about the murder and, perhaps more importantly, about the manner in which American history is collectively remembered. Although Avi was praised for his historical representation in this work, the author once declared that "the irony is that in those Providence books there is nothing historical at all; it's a kind of fantasy of my neighborhood." Like his narrator in *Something Upstairs*, Avi moved from Los Angeles to Providence; in fact, he moved into the historic house featured in this novel.

The Man Who Was Poe, Avi's fictionalized portrait of nineteenth-century writer Edgar Allan Poe, intertwines fiction and history on several levels. Historically, Poe went through a period of severe depression and poverty, aggravated by alcoholism during the two years preceding his death in 1849. Avi, whose novel focuses on this period, said he became fascinated with Poe because he was so extraordinary and yet such "a horrible man." In the novel, a young boy, Edmund, has recently immigrated to Providence from England with his aunt and twin sister in order to look for his missing mother. When both aunt and sister disappear, the penniless boy must elicit help from a stranger—who happens to be Edgar Allen Poe. Poe, noticing similarities between Edmund's story and his own life, detects material for his writing and agrees to help the boy. Between maddening bouts of drunkenness, Poe ingeniously finds a trail of clues to the family's disappearance. Edmund, who has been taught to defer to adults, alternates between awe of the great man's perceptive powers and despair at his madness.

Vividly reflecting the macabre tone of Poe's fiction, Avi portrays the old port city of Providence as a bleak and chaotic world in which compassion and moral order seem to have given way to violence and greed. The character Poe, with his morbid imagination, makes an apt detective in this realm until it becomes clear that he wants the "story" of Edmund's family to end tragically. Edmund's plight is a harsh one, relying on Poe as the only adult who can help him, while at the same time attempting to ensure that Poe's vision does not become a reality. Roger Sutton of the *Bulletin of the Center for Children's Books,* called the novel "a complex, atmospheric thriller." "Avi recreates the gloom of 1840s

Baltimore with a storyteller's ease," remarked Sutton, "blending drama, history, and mystery without a hint of pastiche or calculation. And, as in the best mystery stories, readers will be left in the end with both the comfort of puzzles solved and the unease of mysteries remaining."

Charlotte Doyle's Adventures

In another unique twist on the convention of historical novels, *The True Confessions of Charlotte Doyle* presents the unlikely story of a very proper thirteen-year-old girl who, as the sole passenger and only female on a transatlantic ship in 1832, becomes involved in a mutiny at sea. Holding her family's aristocratic views on social class and demeanor, Charlotte begins her voyage trusting only Captain Jaggery, whose fine manners and authoritative command remind her of her father. She is thus shocked to find that Jaggery is a viciously brutal shipmaster. This discovery, along with her growing fondness for members of the ship's crew, gradually leads Charlotte to question—and discard—the values of her privileged background. As she exchanges her finishing school wardrobe for a common sailor's garb and joins the crew in its work, she reveals the strength of her character, initially masked by her restrictive upbringing.

In the adventures that follow, including a mysterious murder, a storm, and a mutiny, Charlotte's reeducation and emancipation provide a new version of the conventionally male story of rugged individualism at sea. The multi-award-winning novel has received accolades from critics for its suspense, its evocation of life at sea, and particularly for the rich and believable narrative of its protagonist as she undergoes a tremendous change in outlook. The impact of Charlotte's liberation from social bonds and gender restrictions in *The True Confessions of Charlotte Doyle* has a powerful emotional effect on many of its readers. Avi once stated that "many people, mostly girls, and even adults," have told him of "bursting into tears" at the book's ending—tears of relief that Charlotte finds the freedom to realize herself as she chooses. In her *Five Owls* review of *The True Confessions of Charlotte Doyle,* Cathryn M. Mercier wrote that Charlotte's "struggle will fully engage readers, who will find themselves cheering the improbable but deeply satisfying conclusion." Avi addressed Ms. Mercier's contention of an "improbable conclusion" in his *Boston Globe-Horn Book* Award acceptance speech, in which he commented: "I am deeply grateful for the award you have given me today. But I hope you will understand me when I tell you that if the "improbable" life I wrote lives in someone's heart as a life *possible*, then I have already been given the greatest gift a writer can receive: a reader who takes my story and endows it with life by the grace of their own desire."

Other historical novels by Avi are *The Barn*, published in 1994, and the two-volume *Beyond the Western Sea*, published in 1996. Set in 1850s Oregon, *The Barn* features an intelligent nine-year-old boy named Ben who must return home from boarding school to care for his widowed, invalid father. Ben decides that he wants to fulfill his father's dream of building a barn on their farm. His brother and sister reluctantly agree to help, and after three long months, they finish the barn. That evening, though, their father dies in his sleep, never seeing the barn. While his brother and sister eventually move on, Ben stays on the farm with the memory of his father linked to the barn. Deeply affected by the novel, *Booklist*'s Hazel Rochman raved, "This small, beautiful historical novel has a timeless simplicity. It's the best thing he's done."

With *Beyond the Western Sea: The Escape from Home*, the first book in his Victorian-modeled series, Avi created an exciting cliffhanger with plenty of adventure and a cast of colorful characters. "While you actually do have to turn the pages for yourself here," wrote Roger Sutton of *Bulletin of the Center for Children's Books*, "the task soon feels like it's out of your hands as Avi's tense, twisting storytelling takes over." The story begins in 1850s Ireland during the potato famine, with Maura and Patrick O'Connell and their mother being forced out of their home by their relentless landlord, Lord Kirkle. Like many others during this infamous period, the O'Connells plan to sail to America to join their father. Mother, however, decides to stay behind, leaving the children on their own. Who should the children meet in Liverpool while en route but Sir Laurence Kirkle—the eleven-year-old son of Lord Kirkle. Laurence, they learn, is running away from his father. By book's end, Laurence is a stowaway facing big trouble. Mary M. Burns of *Horn Book* maintained: "The ending leaves one of the main characters "in dire straits," as the old-fashioned melodramas used to say, insuring that readers will be eagerly awaiting the promised sequel." As evidence of those eagerly awaiting readers, *Voice of Youth Advocates* contributor Kathleen Beck offered, "no sooner had *Escape from Home* been published than [a young library patron] was breathlessly requesting this sequel."

In all seven tales from this 1997 collection of short stories, Avi features strong young adult protagonists who help themselves and others make positive changes in their lives.

With the second installment, *Beyond the Western Sea, Book Two: Lord Kirkle's Money*, Avi transforms the first book into what Burns called a "blockbuster epic . . . totaling 675 pages." While readers of book two find that Laurence is safe, they also learn about the harsh realities and discrimination that the Irish-born characters face in America. Patrick and Maura discover that their father is dead, and each character learns to survive independently. Concluding her positive review of the "Beyond the Western Sea" series, *Horn Book*'s Burns declared, "an adventure in grand style, the story benefits from its historical foundation and skillful plotting."

Avi, although an enthusiastic reader of history, is by no means tied to the historical novel and delights in finding new ways to structure his stories. He once remarked, "People constantly ask, "How come you

Readers meet a shy rabbit-like creature named Perloo in Avi's 1999 fantasy novel.

keep changing styles?" I think that's a misquestion. Put it this way, "What makes you so fascinated with technique?" You know that there are a lot of ways to tell a story. To me that's just fun." With his extensive background in theater, it is no surprise that many of Avi's novels have roots in drama.

Injects Humor into His Works

In 1984, Avi published *S.O.R. Losers*, a funny contemporary novel about a group of unathletic boys forced by their school (based on Avi's high school in New York City) to form a soccer team. Opposing the time-honored school ethic that triumph in sports is the American way, the boys form their own opinions about winning at something that means little to them. In a team meeting, they take stock of who they are and why it's so important to everyone *else* that they should win their games. The narrator, who is the team's captain, sums it up: "Every one of us is

good at something. Right? Maybe more than one thing. The point is *other* things. . . . But I don't like sports. I'm not good at it. I don't enjoy it. So I say, so what? I mean if Saltz here writes a stinko poem—and he does all the time—do they yell at him? When was the last time Mr. Tillman came around and said, "Saltz, I *believe* in your being a poet!""

Avi makes a clear statement with his humor in *S.O.R. Losers*. He once remarked that he sees an irony in the American attitude toward education. "On the one hand, our culture likes to give a lot of lip service to support for kids, but on the other hand, I don't think the culture as a whole likes kids. And kids are caught in this contradiction. I ask teachers at conferences "How many of you have athletic trophies displayed in your schools?" You know how many raise their hands. And I ask, "How many of you have trophy displays for the best reader or writer?" Nobody raises their hands. And I say "What is it therefore that stands as the essential achievement in your school?" With test scores falling, we need to make kids better readers, but instead we're interested in a minority of kids, mostly males, whose primary focus is sports."

With its narrator's deadpan reporting of the fiascos of a consistently losing sports team, *S.O.R. Losers* does more than make a point—it's funny. *Horn Book* contributor Mary M. Burns, who called the novel "one of the funniest and most original sports sagas on record," particularly praised Avi's skill with comedic form. "Short, pithy chapters highlighting key events maintain the pace necessary for successful comedy. As in a Charlie Chaplin movie, emphasis is on individual episode—each distinct, yet organically related to an overall idea." Avi has written several other comic novels, including his sequel to *S.O.R. Losers*, *Romeo & Juliet—Together (& Alive) At Last*, and two well-received spoofs on nineteenth-century melodrama, *Emily Upham's Revenge* and *History of Helpless Harry*.

Pens Novels for Young Adults

Avi is also the author of several acclaimed contemporary coming-of-age novels, including *A Place Called Ugly* and *Sometimes I Think I Hear My Name*. His 1992 Newbery honor book, *Nothing but the Truth*, is the story of Philip Malloy and his battle with an English teacher, Miss Narwin. Kept off the track team with bad grades in English, Philip repeatedly breaks school rules by humming the national anthem along with the public address system in Miss Narwin's home room. Eventually, the principal suspends Philip from school. Because the school happens to be in the midst of elections, various self-interested members of the community exploit this story of a boy being suspended for his patriotism. Much to everyone's surprise, the incident in homeroom snowballs into a national media event that, in its frenzied patriotic rhetoric, thoroughly overshadows the true story about a good teacher's inability to reach a student, a young man's alienation, a community's disinterest in its children's needs, and a school system's hypocrisy.

Nothing but the Truth is a book without a narrator, relating its story through school memos, diary entries, letters, dialogues, newspaper articles, and radio talk show scripts. Presented without narrative bias, the story takes into account the differing points of view surrounding the incident, allowing the reader to root out the real problems leading to the incident. Avi explained that he got the idea for the structure of this novel from a form of theater that arose in the 1930s called "Living Newspapers"—dramatizations of issues and problems confronting American society presented through a "hodge podge" of document readings and dialogues.

Displaying Avi's obvious sympathy for the "outsider" position of adolescence is *Nothing but the Truth*'s main character, Philip Malloy. In all the national attention Philip receives as a patriotic hero, no one asks him what he feels or thinks, and no one seems to notice that he changes from a fairly happy and enthusiastic youth to a depressed and alienated adolescent. Philip's interest in *The Outsiders*, S. E. Hinton's novel about rival gangs of teenagers (written when Hinton was only seventeen years old), reveals that Philip would like to read about a world that looks like his own, with people experiencing problems like his. The Shakespeare plays assigned in school do not reach him. Avi once stated: "It's not an accident that in the last decades the book most read by young people is *The Outsiders*. I wish Stephen King's novels were taught in the schools, so that kids could respond to them and talk about them." Avi does not hesitate to set complexities and harsh truths before his readers because, he noted, these truths are already well-known to children. "I think writers like myself say to kids like this, "We affirm your sense of reality." We help frame it and give it recognition."

In his 1997 work *What Do Fish Have to Do with Anything?: And Other Stories*, Avi offers seven stories in which young adult protagonists realize the power they hold over their lives, as well as the lives of oth-

An unusual group of people—a servant boy, a princess, and a magician—team up to confront a ghost in their midst in this 1999 mystery.

ers. For example, in "What's Inside," a thirteen-year-old boy is able to convince his older cousin not to commit suicide. "Whether facing a domineering mother, divorced parents, or a reputation as the bad guy, the protagonists take positive steps forward," wrote *School Library Journal* contributor Carol A. Edwards. It is each individual's choice of good over bad, "the halo over the pitchfork, that makes these stories inspiring," added Edwards. *Booklist* reviewer Michael Cart praised the "authentic emotional insights that provide the surprises and right-on rites of passage."

Avi has also successfully penned fantasy fiction. *Poppy*, which received a *Boston Globe-Horn Book* Award in 1996, is an example of Avi's highly regarded fantasy writing. In this story two deer mice, Ragweed and Poppy, are about to marry when the self-proclaimed king of Dimwood Forest—an owl

If you enjoy the works of Avi, you might want to check out the following books and films:

James Lincoln Collier, *The Clock*, 1992.
Michael Morpurgo, *Twist of Gold*, 1993.
Jane Yolen, *The Wild Hunt*, 1995.
David Copperfield, a film adaptation of the novel by Charles Dickens, 1935.

named Mr. Ocax—eats Ragwood, supposedly as punishment for neglecting to seek his permission to marry. Although Mr. Ocax eats Ragwood, Poppy escapes. Soon, the other mice go to Mr. Ocax for permission to move to New House, where there is more food. He refuses their request, using Poppy's disobedience as an excuse, but Poppy suspects that Mr. Ocax has another motive for keeping the mice nearby and sets out to find it so she can save her family. Ann A. Flowers of *Horn Book* called *Poppy* "a tribute to the inquiring mind and the stout heart." *Bulletin of the Center for Children's Books* critic Roger Sutton wrote: "Sprightly but un-cute dialogue, suspenseful chapter endings, and swift shifts of perspective between Ocax and Poppy will make chapter-a-day readalouds cause for anticipation." Avi followed *Poppy* with the sequels *Poppy and Rye* and *Ragweed*.

Although writing on a full-time basis, Avi maintains regular interaction with children by traveling around the country, talking in schools about his work. "I think it's very important for me to keep these kids in front of my eyes. They're wonderfully interesting and they hold me to the reality of who they are." Avi once declared that children are passionate and honest readers who will either "swallow a book whole" if they like it, or drop it "like a hot potato" if they don't. In an article in *School Library Journal*, he provides a telling anecdote about his approach to children: "Being dysgraphic, with the standard history of frustration and anguish, I always ask to speak to the learning-disabled kids. They come in slowly, waiting for yet another pep talk, more instructions. Eyes cast down, they won't even look at me. Their anger glows. I don't say a thing. I lay out pages of my copy-edited manuscripts, which are covered with red marks. "Look here," I say, "see that spelling mistake. There, another spelling mistake. Looks like I forgot to put a capital letter there. Oops! Letter reversal." Their eyes lift. They are listening. And I am among friends."

■ Works Cited

Avi, *The Fighting Ground*, Lippincott, 1984.

Avi, *S.O.R. Losers*, Bradbury, 1984.

Avi (with Betty Miles), "School Visits: The Author's Viewpoint," *School Library Journal*, January, 1987, p. 21.

Avi, "All That Glitters," *Horn Book*, September-October, 1987, pp. 569-76.

Avi, autobiographical statement in *Twentieth-Century Children's Writers*, St. Martin's, 1989, pp. 45-46.

Avi, *Boston Globe-Horn Book* Award acceptance speech, *Horn Book*, January-February, 1992, pp. 24-27.

Beck, Kathleen, review of *Beyond the Western Sea, Book Two: Lord Kirkle's Money*, Voice of Youth Advocates, December, 1996, p. 267.

Burns, Mary M., review of *S.O.R. Losers*, Horn Book, January-February, 1985, p. 49.

Burns, Mary M., review of *Beyond the Western Sea, Book One: The Escape from Home*, Horn Book, July-August, 1996, p. 461.

Burns, Mary M., review of *Beyond the Western Sea, Book Two: Lord Kirkle's Money*, Horn Book, November-December, 1996, p. 731.

Cart, Michael, review of *Poppy*, Booklist, November 15, 1997, p. 557.

Cart, Michael, review of *What Do Fish Have to Do with Anything?: And Other Stories*, Booklist, November 15, 1997, p. 560.

Edwards, Carol A., review of *What Do Fish Have to Do with Anything?: And Other Stories*, School Library Journal, December, 1997, p. 120.

Review of *The Fighting Ground*, Bulletin of the Center for Children's Books, June, 1984, p. 180.

Flowers, Ann A., review of *Poppy*, Horn Book, January-February, 1996, p. 70.

Mercier, Cathryn M., review of *The True Confessions of Charlotte Doyle*, Five Owls, January-February, 1991, pp. 56-57.

Rochman, Hazel, "A Conversation with Avi," Booklist, January 15, 1992, p. 930.

Rochman, Hazel, "Focus: How to Build a Barn," Booklist, September 1, 1994, p. 40.

Roginski, Jim, *Behind the Covers: Interviews with Authors and Illustrators of Books for Children and Young Adults*, Libraries Unlimited, 1985, pp. 33-41.

Sutherland, Zena, review of *The Fighting Ground*, Bulletin of the Center for Children's Books, June, 1984, p. 180.

Sutton, Roger, review of *The Man Who Was Poe*, Bulletin of the Center for Children's Books, October, 1989, p. 27.

Sutton, Roger, review of *Poppy, Bulletin of the Center for Children's Books,* January, 1996, p. 154.

Sutton, Roger, review of *Beyond the Western Sea, Book One: The Escape from Home, Bulletin of the Center for Children's Books,* February, 1996, p. 183.

■ For More Information See

BOOKS

Bloom, Susan P. and Cathryn M. Mercier, *Presenting Avi,* Twayne, 1997.

Markham, Lois, *Avi,* Learning Works (Santa Barbara, CA), 1996.

PERIODICALS

Booklist, March 15, 1993, p. 1312; April 15, 1994, p. 1538; February 1, 1996, p. 930; February 1, 1997, p. 949; May 15, 1998, p. 1625; April 1, 1999, p. 1424.

Bulletin of the Center for Children's Books, October, 1992, p. 35; December, 1994, p. 120; March, 1997, p. 240; November, 1999, p. 83; December, 1999, p. 121.

Horn Book, January-February, 1989, p. 65; January-February, 1995, p. 57; January-February, 1997, pp. 40-43; March-April, 1999, p. 206.

Kirkus Reviews, October 1, 1993, p. 1268; September 15, 1995, p. 1346; October 15, 1999, p. 1638.

Publishers Weekly, September 14, 1990, p. 128; September 6, 1991, p. 105; September 5, 1994, p. 112; June 15, 1998, p. 60; May 10, 1999, p. 68; May 8, 2000, p. 222.

School Library Journal, April, 1994, p. 95; November, 1998, p. 116; May, 1999, p. 85.

Voice of Youth Advocates, April, 1992, p. 21; June, 1996, p. 92; December, 1999, p. 340.

Martha Brooks

■ Personal

Born July 15, 1944, in Ninette, Manitoba, Canada; daughter of Alfred Leroy (a thoracic surgeon) and Theodis (a nurse; maiden name, Marteinsson) Paine; married Brian Brooks (an owner and operator of an advertising and public relations firm), August 26, 1967; children: Kirsten. *Education:* St. Michael's Academy, Brandon, Manitoba, 1962.

■ Addresses

Home—58-361 Westwood Dr., Winnipeg, Manitoba, Canada R3K 1G4.

■ Career

Writer, 1972; creative writing teacher in junior and senior high schools, through the Artist in the Schools program of the Manitoba Arts Council, beginning in early 1980s. Has also worked as a model, secretary, mentor to young writers, and a jazz singer.

■ Awards, Honors

Vicky Metcalf Award, shortlisting for Governor General's Award for Children's Literature, 1988, and *Boston Globe/Horn Book* Honor Book Award, 1991, all for *Paradise Cafe and Other Stories;* Chalmers Canadian Children's Play Award, 1991, for *Andrew's Tree;* Best Book for Young Adults selection, American Library Association, for *Two Moons in August;* Best Book for Young Adults selection and Best Books for Reluctant Readers selection, American Library Association, both for *Traveling on into the Light and Other Stories;* Best Book of the Year selection, American Library Association, 1997, Ruth Schwartz Award, and CLA Young Adult Canadian Book of the Year, 1998, all for *Bone Dance;* Mr. Christie's Book Award, 1999, for *Being with Henry.*

■ Writings

FOR YOUNG ADULTS

Paradise Cafe and Other Stories, Thistledown Press, 1988, Little, Brown, 1990.

Two Moons in August, Groundwood Books, 1991, Little, Brown, 1992.

Traveling on into the Light and Other Stories, Orchard, 1994.

Bone Dance, Orchard, 1997.

Being with Henry, DK Inc., 2000.

OTHER

A Hill for Looking, Queenston House, 1982.

Moonlight Sonata (play), produced at Prairie Theater Exchange, Winnipeg, Manitoba, Canada, 1994.

(With Maureen Hunter) *I Met a Bully on a Hill* (play; produced across Canada), Scirocco Drama, 1995.

Andrew's Tree (play; produced across Canada), Scirocco Drama, 1995.

Also author, with Sandra Birdsell and David Gillies, of the play *A Prairie Boy's Winter*.

■ Work in Progress

"Another book which, at the moment of this writing, is gathering power at the edge of dreamtime."

■ Sidelights

Canadian author Martha Brooks has penned award-winning short stories and several powerful novels for young readers, as well as several plays, all of which deal with the universal themes of love and loss. Her finely drawn characters learn to deal with the trials life sends their way and grow because of such trials. Brooks's first collection of short stories, *Paradise Cafe and Other Stories*, was nominated for the prestigious Governor General's Award for Children's Literature in Canada, and "is a significant title in Canadian Young Adult literature for its 1988 publication signaled a rebirth of the short story collection as a legitimate vehicle for adolescents' recreational reading," according to Dave Jenkinson writing in *St. James Guide to Young Adult Writers*.

Brooks is known for tautly drawn stories and novels in which "each word is carefully chosen" to build "quietly eloquent sentences weaving a richly textured story that will appeal to introspective readers," as Judy Sasges described Brooks's fiction in Voice of Youth Advocates. In an interview for *Authors and Artists for Young Adults* (*AAYA*), Brooks described her work as "cross-generational fiction." The author went on to note, "I have to say that I do like the defining description, Young Adult Author. Right away, that has the propensity for limiting my readership. I'm really at a cross-roads with my writing. It would be so easy to tip over to the other side, in other words to write for a (much larger) adult audience. But I still feel that what I am doing is important in recording young adult experience, and in sharing with that audience. As well, there are some of us who dare to redefine the borders of our chosen art form and I think that's what I'm doing, along with other good people who refuse to stay put and do the same thing over and over again."

Five teenagers struggle to understand the meaning of family love in Brooks' 1988 story collection.

Brooks once explained that her fiction "is about that particular time in life when the senses are sharp and life is bewildering and pain and love have very blurry borders. What is important is that I try to be true to the characters I invent—listening to them, letting them tell their stories, and respecting the lives they live on the page as they face the realities of love, death, family turmoil, exploitation, addiction. I always keep in mind, though, the aspects of healing and hope because life is full of possibilities." Such instances of healing and hope are sprinkled throughout the stories in the collections *Paradise Cafe* and *Traveling on into the Light*, as well as in Brooks's three novels, *Two Moons in August, Bone Dance,* and *Being with Henry.*

Canadian Roots

Born in a rural community in Manitoba, Canada, Brooks grew up in a medical household. Her parents both worked at a tuberculosis (TB) sanatorium in southern Manitoba, and she came of age "on the lyrically beautiful grounds" of the sanatorium, as she told *AAYA*, living in "the sprawling red-roofed superintendent's residence. Hills rose above our house, and hills rolled away below to the shores of long green Pelican Lake. That was long ago, but my husband and I now spend most summer weekends at our cottage on that lake. The landscape of my youth still guides me spiritually, appearing as forceful entity in all of my fiction, but most specially in *Bone Dance*. Its latest incarnation is Heron Lake country in the final chapters of *Being with Henry*."

When her older sister left for college, Brooks, only nine at the time and was left with few playmates. As

Even though their mother died a year ago, sixteen-year-old Sidonie and her older sister, Bobbi, continue to sort out their grief in this 1991 novel.

a result, she turned to the patients at the sanatorium and to the staff, becoming a classically precocious child. "Children who grow up to be artists very often have unusual beginnings," Brooks once noted, "so these were mine—surrounded by people who were fighting to cure, or be cured of, a life-threatening disease. I, too, was not well. I suffered from recurring bouts with pneumonia as a child. All of these things made me an early and keen observer of human behavior; I had an "old" way of looking at the world before I reached adulthood."

Brooks married an advertising and public relations professional in 1967, and moved to Winnipeg, Manitoba. With the birth of her daughter Kirsten, she turned her hand to a long-time dream: becoming an author. However, for the first ten years that she was writing, editors were uninterested in her work. Finally in 1982 came her first publication, *A Hill for Looking*, but it was another six years before her next publication, the award-winning *Paradise Cafe*. This collection of fourteen stories deals with all varieties of love, from that of a boy for his dying pet in "A Boy and His Dog," to first love in "Dying for Love," in which Ardis feels humiliated when her love is not returned by the best looking boy in class. In another tale, "The Crystal Stars Have Just Begun to Shine," teenage Deirdre plays matchmaker between her lonely father and the checkout woman at the local grocery. In "Like Lauren Bacall," Donalda relives the crush she once felt for her cousin and discovers that it was pure fantasy on her part. A retarded boy becomes part of a farm family in "The Way Things Are," and a girl is jilted because she is from the wrong side of the tracks in "King of the Roller Rink." Brooks used her own background to powerful effect in this first collection: many of the stories are set at a tuberculosis sanatorium, while others find their settings at an abandoned house, a roller rink, or the Paradise Cafe of the title.

Each of the stories in *Paradise Cafe* "packs an emotional wallop," according to Jenkinson, and none are longer than ten or eleven pages, making them a perfect fit for classroom reading. One of the most powerful is "A Boy and His Dog," which in 1988 won the Vicky Metcalf Short Story Award from the Canadian Authors Association. Buddy's dog Alphonse has been a beloved pet and companion since the boy was an infant, and now he learns that his dog is dying of cancer. "I'm fourteen going on fifteen and he's thirteen going on ninety-four," Buddy muses as he analyzes the unfairness of his pet's imminent death. Cynthia L. Beatty, writing in *Voice of Youth Advocates*, found this story "Especially

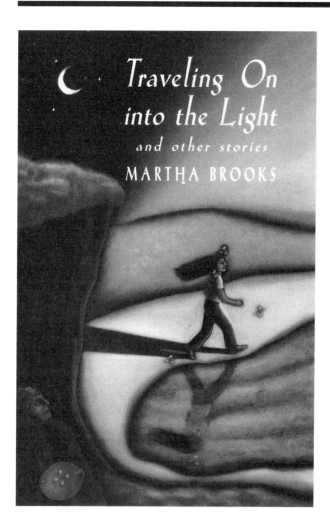

Traveling On into the Light and other stories
MARTHA BROOKS

A variety of teenage characters, many in search of love or acceptance, fills the pages of Brooks' 1994 collection of short stories.

touching." Beatty also commented, "There is enough variety in the stories for almost anyone to find several of interest." "The cast is diverse," noted Betsy Hearne in the *Bulletin of the Center for Children's Books,* "including French, Indian, and black characters. All share the pain and triumph of maturation with which young adult readers can identify." Reviewing the title in *Canadian Materials,* Gail Lennon felt that the stories could prove useful in a creative writing program because of their "excellent diction and use of figurative speech." Lennon went on to conclude, "It is among the best short story collections I have read in a long time!"

Brooks once recalled that the inspiration she had for her award-winning story in the collection. "How a story, for instance, like "A Boy and His Dog" begins to be born is usually with a first line. "My dog is old and he farts a lot." I woke up one night with that

line running through my head. It was a pretty funny line. It also contained a conflict, a necessary ingredient. It was sad, suggesting the theme, again, of love and loss. Within the first paragraph I had the voice of Buddy telling about his dog, Alphonse. The end result is of a boy's despairing over the unfairness of the death of Alphonse."

From Short Stories to Novels and Back

With her next work, *Two Moons in August,* Brooks turned to the novel format to tell the story of two girls in rural Manitoba in the summer of 1959 dealing with their grief over the loss of their mother. Sidonie's sixteenth birthday is approaching, as is the first anniversary of her mother's death. Sidonie's older sister Bobbi, back from college, escapes her sadness by taking on the role of boss, while her father has largely abandoned his daughters, throwing himself into his work at the local TB hospital. Sidonie is longing for the comfort of someone, anyone. Enter Kieran McMorran, the next door neighbor's son, who forms an attachment with Sidonie, helping her to work through her own grief. In the process, Kieran's problems also surface, and the two help each other toward a healing.

Ellen Ramsay, reviewing the novel in *School Library Journal,* felt that all the characters "are realistic individuals who develop credible insight and self-understanding over the course of the story." Ramsay concluded that *Two Moons in August* was a book that "belongs on the shelf with the few but essential novels that are both intelligently written and appealing to YA audiences." *Horn Book* reviewer Nancy Vasilakis commented that Brooks once again "explores the minute nuances" of love in a story which has the "sultry dog-day atmosphere of late summer." Vasilakis praised Brooks for the "leisurely" manner in which she let her story develop, "investing a wealth of meaning in the most trivial actions." Vasilakis added, "By the end of the novel, all the members of this sad family have acknowlededged the need to exorcise the ghosts of the past.... An introspective, multidimensional narrative 'mixing memory with desire'—to quote Eliot's famous lines—with resounding effect." Peter Carver, reviewing *Two Moons in August* for *Quill and Quire,* felt that Brooks took up the challenge to chart the emotional territory of teens "with artfulness and insight." Carver further noted, "Martha Brooks conveys, with great skill, the cross-currents of feeling and behaviour that swirl around teenagers as they come of age. . . . Taken with her much admired *Par-*

adise Cafe, this new book confirms Martha Brooks is an eloquent writer of young-adult fiction."

Reading Affects Writing

Brooks credits her love of reading in part for her abilities as a writer. "I recently spoke in a telephone interview with grades nine to twelve students who were reading at a grade one to two level," Brooks told *AAYA* in her interview. "They had, in groups, with the help of their dedicated teacher, read some of my short stories. Their questions were thoughtful, as were my answers. They liked my writing because it is realistic. None of them had ever read an entire novel. I am re-reading *Anna Karenina.* Books open the world for us in a way that nothing else can. My experience with reading flows into my art, my life, my relationships with people. Reading allows me to intimately engage in the living experience of history, in the heartbeat and profound humanity of others whose experiences are vastly different from my own, in the exploration of landscapes where I have never been and may never have the opportunity to go, in the flowering of thought that may transform me and thus allow me to offer that gift of transformation to the life of someone else."

Brooks next found such possibilities for transformation in short stories. Annette Goldsmith of *Quill and Quire,* found *Traveling on into the Light and Other Stories,* Brooks's 1994 book of stories, a "memorable collection . . . snapshots of young people yearning for love, acceptance, and explanations." The collection consists of ten stories and a novella, "Moonlight Sonata," later adapted for a play. The adolescents here deal with more complex issues than those in Brooks's initial collection, and thus the stories themselves are also longer. Sidonie, from *Two Moons in August,* makes an appearance here, in "Sunday at Sidonie's," narrated from her boyfriend Kieran's point of view, and in "All the Stars in the Universe" and "A Wedding," both narrated by Sidonie. Told in the first person, the stories in this collection variously explore sexuality, deal with the death of a parent, or focus on survival. Lindsay looks for real love in the midst of artificiality in "Where Has Romance Gone"; Donald is accused of drug trafficking when an artistic creation is mistaken for a joint in "The Tiniest Guitar in the World"; runaway Laker is not wanted by his pregnant mother and stepfather in "The Kindness of Strangers"; a babysitter comes close to having an affair with the father of the child she is taking care of in "You've Always Been So

Good to Me"; and, in the title story, Sam has difficulties dealing with his father's male lover.

"Martha Brooks balances ... sadness with hope," commented reviewer Annette Goldsmith, while *Booklist*'s Hazel Rochman noted, "It's the honesty about conflicting emotions and viewpoints that give this collection its power." Rochman also observed that, as with Brooks's first collection of stories, *Traveling on into the Light* also has an assortment of narrative voices which "show a remarkable range or young men and women across class and setting." "The young-adult protagonists in this taut, carefully crafted collection ... are struggling to make connections to keep their bearings under the strains of rejection, betrayal, or death," commented *Horn Book*'s Vasilakis. While Vasilakis felt the inclusion of three stories dealing with Sidonie and Kieran "somewhat incongruously placed here," she observed that the collection as a whole "is piercingly direct in its depiction of young people struggling to find their way into adulthood." *Publishers Weekly* also found the collection "[m]oving and memorable," and that it demonstrated "a profound understanding of sorrow and joy."

Brooks has written two further novels, *Bone Dance,* published in 1997, and *Being with Henry,* published in 2000. In the former title, Alexandra meets a young man who shares her Native Canadian heritage when she inherits a cabin on a lake from her father. Together, the two deal with the spirits that haunt them both. Jenkinson, writing in *St. James Guide to Young Adult Writers,* remarked that *Bone Dance* "possesses a remarkable and engaging Yin-Yang quality." The reviewer was referring to the two halves of the story: seventeen-year-old Alexandra or Alex of Dene heritage, and eighteen-year-old Lonny, of Metis heritage. What brings the two together is a piece of property Alex inherits from her absent and undependable father. The property is a piece of unspoiled lakefront that had been in Lonny's family for generations, but which was sold to finance Lonny's education. The two meet at this disputed bit of property, both carrying emotional baggage, both needing to work through the spirits haunting their earlier lives. Alex must put to rest her resentment for the white father she never knew; Lonny attempts to deal with fears that he caused his mother's death as a child when he dug up sacred bones at an Indian burial site.

"Each character in *Bone Dance* is beautifully drawn, intelligent, and completely believable," commented Judy Sasges in *Voice of Youth Advocates. Quill and*

A pair of teenagers, Alexandra and Lonny, find they have two things in common: a piece of land in rural Manitoba and the spirits who haunt and guide them both.

Quire reviewer Teresa Toten noted, "This novel beautifully captures the drift and dance of two teenagers whose lives are embraced by spirits of the dead.... Read it and weep. But read it." Cheryl Archer described the novel in *Canadian Materials* as the "enchanting and spiritual journey of two [teenagers] who must confront their ghosts of memory and mysterious visions." Archer concluded, "This is a fine novel that will leave readers embracing nature and honouring the spirits of the ancestors. Another splendid book by award-winning Manitoba author Martha Brooks."

Brooks's novel *Being with Henry* is an adaptation of her earlier short story, "The Kindness of Strangers," which deals with Laker's adventures when he is forced out of his home by a bullying stepfather. "The story was one which my readers, both young and old, most fretted over," Brooks told *AAYA*. "The final scene upset them. Runaway Laker Wyatt makes his fateful wrenching phone call home, then he and his newfound friend, the elderly Henry Olsen, are left sitting silently together at Henry's kitchen table. A frequently asked question was "Why would Laker Wyatt's mother reject him so cruelly—how could any mother do that to her son?" A twelve-year-old reader, who had found, mirrored back, his own sad relationship with his mother, asked me with direct poignancy, "What will happen to him?""

Being with Henry is an answer to the question. In the novel, Laker's earlier life is detailed, and then out on his own, he strikes up an unexpected friendship with a frail but determined old man. Brooks told *AAYA* that the novel follows Laker's journey "to redefine his notion of family, loyalty and acceptance." Such a theme of love lost and love found fits neatly into the arc of Brooks's works.

"I see love and loss so much more clearly than I did when I was twenty, or thirty, or even forty," Brooks concluded for *AAYA*. "And since that is the subject I write about, along with those other great themes such as forgiveness and regret and redemption, I bring a lifetime of observation to my subject. Old truths were never truer, like the adage about history repeating itself. Give me any seventeen-year-old, now, or in the past, or in the future, and I will tell you that this is a person who carries a burning terrible secret that no one will ever understand or forgive. So they think."

■ **Works Cited**

Archer, Cheryl, review of *Bone People*, *Canadian Materials*, October 17, 1997.

Beatty, Cynthia L., review of *Paradise Cafe and Other Stories*, *Voice of Youth Advocates*, February, 1991, p. 350.

Brooks, Martha, *Paradise Cafe and Other Stories*, Little, Brown, 1990.

If you enjoy the works of Martha Brooks, you might want to check out the following books:

C. S. Adler, *The Lump in the Middle*, 1989.
Sharon Creech, *Walk Two Moons*, 1994.
Norman Fox Mazer, *Out of Control*, 1993.

Brooks, Martha, interview with J. Sydney Jones for *Authors and Artists for Young Adults,* conducted March 28, 2000.

Carver, Peter, review of *Two Moons in August, Quill and Quire,* November, 1991, pp. 24-25.

Goldsmith, Annette, review of *Traveling on into the Light, Quill and Quire,* October, 1994, p. 38.

Hearne, Betsy, review of *Paradise Cafe and Other Stories, Bulletin of the Center for Children's Books,* December, 1990, pp. 79-80.

Jenkinson, Dave, "Brooks, Martha," *St. James Guide to Young Writers,* 2nd edition, St. James Press, 1999.

Lennon, Gail, review of *Paradise Cafe and Other Stories, Canadian Materials,* March, 1989.

Ramsay, Ellen, review of *Two Moons in August, School Library Journal,* March, 1992, p. 256.

Rochman, Hazel, review of *Traveling on into the Light and Other Stories, Booklist,* August, 1994, p. 2039.

Sasges, Judy, review of *Bone Dance, Voice of Youth Advocates,* December, 1997, pp. 313-14.

Toten, Teresa, review of *Bone Dance, Quill and Quire,* November, 1997, p. 44.

Review of *Traveling on into the Light and Other Stories, Publishers Weekly,* October 31, 1994, p. 64.

Vasilakis, Nancy, review of *Two Moons in August, Horn Book,* March-April, 1992, p. 208.

Vasilakis, Nancy, review of *Traveling on into the Light, Horn Book,* January-February, 1995, p. 62.

■ For More Information See

PERIODICALS

Booklist, September 15, 1997, p. 330; September 15, 1998, p. 220.

English Journal, November, 1995, p. 98.

Horn Book, November-December, 1997, p. 677.

Maclean's, November 10, 1997, p. 70.

Publishers Weekly, September 15, 1997, p. 78.

School Library Journal, December, 1990, p. 20; August, 1994, p. 168; November, 1997, p. 330.

Wilson Library Bulletin, February, 1995, p. 98.

ON-LINE

Martha Brooks's personal Web site is located at http://www.marthabrooks.com.

—Sketch by J. Sydney Jones

J. M. Coetzee

■ Personal

Born February 9, 1940, in Cape Town, South Africa; son of Zachariah (an attorney) and Vera (a schoolteacher) Coetzee; married, 1963 (divorced, 1980); children: Nicholas, Gisela. *Education:* University of Cape Town, B.A., 1960, M.A., 1963; University of Texas, Austin, Ph.D., 1969.

■ Addresses

Home—P.O. Box 92, Rondebosch, Cape Province 7700, South Africa. *Agent*—Peter Lampack, 551 Fifth Ave., New York, NY 10017.

■ Career

International Business Machines (IBM), London, England, applications programmer, 1962-63; International Computers, Bracknell, Berkshire, England, systems programmer, 1964-65; State University of New York at Buffalo, assistant professor, 1968-71, Butler Professor of English, 1984, 1986; University of Cape Town, Cape Town, South Africa, lecturer in English, 1972-82, professor of general literature, 1983—; Johns Hopkins University, Hinkley Professor of English, 1986, 1989; Harvard University, visiting professor of English, 1991.

■ Member

International Comparative Literature Association, Modern Language Association of America.

■ Awards, Honors

CNA Literary Award, 1977, for *In the Heart of the Country;* CNA Literary Award, James Tait Black Memorial Prize, and Geoffrey Faber Award, all 1980, all for *Waiting for the Barbarians;* CNA Literary Award, Booker-McConnell Prize, and Prix Femina Etranger, all 1984, all for *The Life and Times of Michael K;* D. Litt., University of Strathclyde, Glasgow, 1985; Jerusalem Prize for the Freedom of the Individual in Society, 1987; *Irish Times* International Fiction Prize, 1995, for *The Master of Petersburg;* Booker-McConnell Prize, 1999, for *Disgrace;* Life Fellow, University of Cape Town.

■ Writings

NOVELS

Dusklands (contains two novellas, *The Vietnam Project* and *The Narrative of Jacobus Coetzee*), Ravan Press (Johannesburg), 1974, Penguin Books (New York City), 1985.

From the Heart of the Country, Harper (New York City), 1977, published in England as *In the Heart of the Country,* Secker & Warburg, 1977.
Waiting for the Barbarians, Secker & Warburg, 1980, Penguin Books, 1982.
Life and Times of Michael K., Secker & Warburg, 1983, Viking (New York City), 1984.
Foe, Viking, 1987.
Age of Iron, Random House (New York City), 1990.
The Master of Petersburg, Viking, 1994.
Disgrace, Viking, 1999.

OTHER

(Translator) Marcellus Emants, *A Posthumous Confession,* Twayne (Boston), 1976.
(Translator) Wilma Stockenstroem, *The Expedition to the Baobab Tree,* Faber, 1983.
(Editor with Andre Brink) *A Land Apart: A Contemporary South African Reader,* Viking, 1987.
White Writing: On the Culture of Letters in South Africa (essays), Yale University Press (New Haven, CT), 1988.
Doubling the Point: Essays and Interviews, edited by David Attwell, Harvard University Press (Cambridge, MA), 1992.
(With Graham Swift, John Lanchester, and Ian Jack) *Food: The Vital Stuff,* Penguin, 1995.
Giving Offense: Essays on Censorship, University of Chicago Press (Chicago), 1996.
Boyhood: Scenes from Provincial Life, Viking, 1997.
(With Bill Reichblum) *What is Realism?* Bennington College (Bennington, VT), 1997.
(With Amy Gutmann) *The Lives of Animals,* Princeton University Press, 1999.

Contributor of reviews to *New York Review of Books.*

■ **Adaptations**

An adaptation of *In the Heart of the Country* was filmed as *Dust,* by ICA (Great Britain), 1986.

■ **Sidelights**

"When some men suffer unjustly . . . it is the fate of those who witness their suffering to suffer the shame of it." This observation by the Magistrate in J. M. Coetzee's 1980 novel, *Waiting for the Barbarians,* may well serve as an epigraph to the body of work by this South African writer, the first author ever to win Britain's prestigious Booker Prize twice. In 1983, he was honored by the prize committee for his apocalyptic *Life and Times of Michael K.* In 1999, he

again received the prize for *Disgrace,* a novel about shame and responsibility in post-apartheid South Africa. Coetzee's prose is trim, elegant, enigmatic; David Attwell in his critical study, *J.M. Coetzee: South Africa and the Politics of Writing,* called it "postmodern metafiction." Growing up during the brutal years of South African apartheid, Coetzee deals with the issues of the day, but in an oblique, symbolic, and, at times fable-like manner. There is no easy dialectic in a Coetzee book; no white hats and black hats by which to tell villain and hero. Often using his native South Africa as a backdrop, Coetzee explores the implications of oppressive societies on the lives of their inhabitants. Tales such as *Waiting for the Barbarians* and *Life and Times of Michael K* are novels which, according to Maureen Nicholson writing in *West Coast Review,* "subtly examined brutal actions in what appeared to be an allegorized South Africa."

Nicholson further commented, "[Coetzee's] writing in these novels was moving, convincing and frank. . . . Mutilation, obsession, jealousy, oppression and madness—issues at the distraught heart of Coetzee's writing—could, presented in his spare prose, make the reader sicken with recognition and realization." Writing in *Southern Humanities Review,* Ashton Nichols described Coetzee as "an archaeologist of the imagination, an excavator of language who testifies to the powers and weaknesses of the words he discovers." Nichols pointed to works of fiction by Coetzee such as *Dusklands, In the Heart of the Country, Waiting for the Barbarians,* and *Life and Times of Michael K,* as providing "sparse, rich allegories of the South African system and, more widely, of all forms of injustice." Comparisons to Kafka abound, and indeed, as Michael Scrogin pointed out in *The Christian Century,* Coetzee "has fashioned a method of storytelling that is closer to classical myth than to modern realism. . . . Like Kafka, Coetzee often sets his work in unspecified or unnamed locations, or else in the distant past or not-too-distant future." Avoiding the particulars of South Africa's regime of terror in most of his fiction, Coetzee has created tales with a more powerful, universal message.

Afrikaner by Name Only

John Michael Coetzee was born in Cape Town, South Africa, in 1940, the son of an Afrikaner father and an English mother. On his father's side he was descended from Dutch settlers who came to Africa in the seventeenth century, and on both sides he had grandparents who were farmers. During the Second

World War, with his father away in the military, Coetzee, his younger brother, and his mother lived in a rented room in the town of Prince Albert. They were "surviving," as Coetzee wrote in his memoir, *Boyhood: Scenes from Provincial Life*, "on the six pounds a month his father remitted from the Government General's Distress Fund." Writing of himself in the third person, Coetzee continued: "Of Prince Albert he remembers only the whine of mosquitoes in the long hot nights, and his mother walking to and from in her petticoat, sweat standing out on her skin, her heavy, fleshy legs crisscrossed with varicose veins, trying to soothe his baby brother . . . ." During this time there was little contact with his father's family, which owned a farm only a couple of hours away. Once the father returned from the war, the family moved to provincial Worcester, in a new housing estate at 12 Poplar Avenue, with "identical" houses "set in red clay earth where nothing grows, separated by wire fences," according to Coetzee. Coetzee's father, who practiced law until 1937, was in difficult financial circumstances, working for Standard Canners. His mother railed against the provincial conditions of the Karoo, the huge desert plateau of Cape Province, badly wanting to return to Cape Town.

Coetzee attended grammar school in Worcester, where he was a hard worker, earning firsts, but was secretly appalled at the barbaric form of punishment meted out. "What happens at the school is that boys are flogged," he recalled in *Boyhood*. "It happens every day. Boys are ordered to bend over and touch their toes and are flogged with a cane." Something of an outsider at school because he acted more English than Afrikaner—English was spoken in the Coetzee household—he was also picked-on by the rougher Afrikaner boys. He chose outsider positions, as well, calling himself a Roman Catholic when actually the family had no religion and choosing the Russians over the Americans in the years of the early Cold War. Coetzee found his time in Worcester both at home and school to be "a time [spent] gritting his teeth and enduring."

Some relief came with occasional visits to the family farm, now run by his father's brother. It was here that Coetzee first gained an appreciation for nature, both its beauty and its darker side. Christmases were spent among a large extended family, and there were hunting trips as well. Finally the family left the provinces to return to Cape Town, where his father once again set up a law practice. But this move ultimately turned out badly: the father went seriously in debt, only to be bailed out at the last

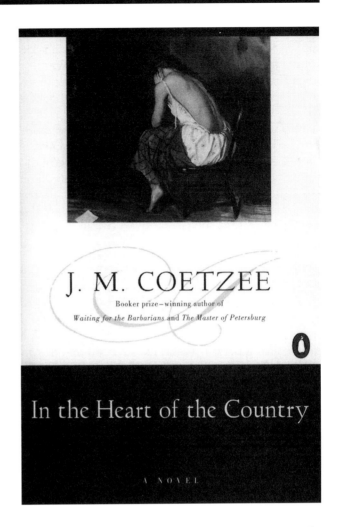

Set in the Western Cape of South Africa in the early 1800s, Coetzee's second novel tells the tale of a lonely young woman filled with vengeance.

minute by a relative. Coetzee watched this near tragedy with the clear eye of a child, recording it all and growing to dislike his father because of it. His mother subsequently went back to her teaching career to help support the family.

Meanwhile, Coetzee was finding joy in books and stories told over the radio or at the movies. *Treasure Island, The Swiss Family Robinson, Scott of Africa,* the Hardy Boys books, the Enid Blyton mystery stories, and tales of the French foreign legion by P. C. Wren all entertained him as a youngster. He was also impressed and bemused by a book his Aunt Annie had in her shelves: an autobiographical novel written by Coetzee's great grandfather and which his aunt had translated into Afrikaans and printed in a small edition. She thereafter sold these to the bookshops of Cape Town or door to door, and those she could not sell remained in her book room. Cricket was also an early passion. "Cricket is not a game," he wrote in *Boyhood*. "It is the truth of life." School in Plumstead, on the outskirts of Cape Town, was less eventful than in Worcester; there were no beatings, but, studying under Catholic brothers, Coetzee found little excitement either. With the death of Aunt Annie, Coetzee felt that an early chapter of his life had come to an end. Thinking of her and all the books she once had, especially that by his great grandfather, he wondered, "How will he keep them all in his head, all the books, all the people, all the stories? And if he does not remember them, who will?" Questions such as these set the young Coetzee on the road to becoming a writer himself.

Attending the University of Cape Town, Coetzee received degrees in mathematics and English, writing his master's thesis on Ford Madox Ford. Thereafter he moved to London for a time where he worked for IBM as a computer programmer by day, a struggling poet by night. He was also married in 1963 and ultimately had two children. Finally he decided to quit his double life and, traveling to the United States, he completed his doctorate in English at the University of Texas, writing his dissertation on Samuel Beckett. His first academic appointment was at the State University of New York at Buffalo, as an assistant professor, a post he held until 1971. Returning to South Africa in 1972, he became a lecturer in English at the University of Cape Town. While still in America, he was deeply troubled by the Vietnam War as well as by the apartheid situation in his native South Africa. Both of these situations he addressed in his first publication, *Dusklands*.

Early Fiction

Though many of his stories are set in South Africa, Coetzee's lessons are relevant to all countries, as *Books Abroad*'s Ursula A. Barnett wrote of *Dusklands*, which contains the novellas *The Vietnam Project* and *The Narrative of Jacobus Coetzee*. "By publishing the two stories side by side," Barnett remarked, "Coetzee has deliberately given a wider horizon to his South African subject. Left on its own, *The Narrative of Jacobus Coetzee* would immediately have suggested yet another tale of African black-white confrontation to the reader." *The Vietnam Project* introduces Eugene Dawn, employed to help the Americans win the Vietnam War through psychological warfare. The assignment eventually costs Dawn his sanity. The title character of *The Narrative of Jacobus Coetzee*, a fictionalized ancestor of the author, is an explorer and conqueror in the 1760s who destroys an entire South

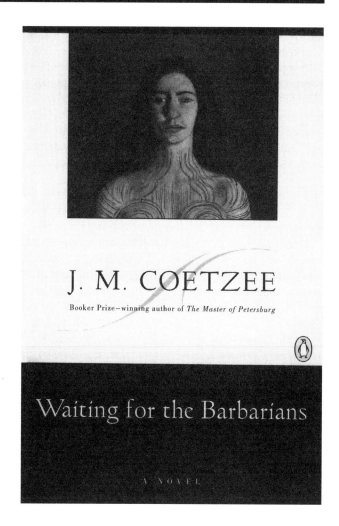

J. M. COETZEE

Booker Prize–winning author of *The Master of Petersburg*

Waiting for the Barbarians

A NOVEL

Once a loyal servant of the Empire, the Magistrate becomes a sympathizer to those he helped oppress after he witnesses their cruel and unjust treatment by the Empire.

African tribe over his perception that the people have humiliated him through their indifference and lack of fear. H. M. Tiffin, writing in *Contemporary Novelists*, found that the novellas in *Dusklands* are "juxtaposed to offer a scarifying account of the fear and paranoia of imperialists and aggressors and the horrifying ways in which dominant regimes, "empires," commit violence against "the other" through repression, torture, and genocide." Attwell, writing in *J. M. Coetzee*, called Coetzee's first novel "an agonizing encounter both with colonial violence, and with the discursive legacy it leaves to its heirs." Both Dawn and the Coetzee ancestor, Attwell noted, are "mythographers" of colonialism, and the novel therefore "juxtaposes subject-positions within twentieth-century American imperialism and eighteenth-century Dutch colonialism." With this first novel,

Coetzee laid out his own personal artistic map: an oblique method of dealing with the colonialism of his day and an appropriation of history to suit the higher needs of fiction.

Coetzee's second novel and his first to be published internationally, *In the Heart of the Country*, also explores racial conflict and mental deterioration. A spinster daughter, Magda, tells the story in diary form, recalling the consequences of her father's seduction of his African workman's wife. Both jealous of and repulsed by the relationship, Magda murders her father, then begins her own affair with the workman. Set in the wastelands of the Western Cape of South Africa in the early nineteenth century, this second novel still preserves at least a realistic setting. The integrity of Magda's story, however, eventually proves questionable. "The reader soon realizes that these are the untrustworthy ravings of a hysterical, demented individual consumed by loneliness and her love/hate relationship with her patriarchal father," Barend J. Toerien reported in *World Literature Today*. Magda's "thoughts range widely, merging reality with fantasy, composing and recomposing domestic dramas for herself to act in and, eventually introducing voices . . . to speak to her from the skies," Sheila Roberts noted in *World Literature Written in English*. "She imagines that the voices accuse her, among other things, of transforming her uneventful life into a fiction." Writing in *A Story of South Africa: J. M. Coetzee's Fiction in Context*, Susan VanZanten Gallagher noted that Magda's wild imaginings were actually a search "for a linguistic way to overcome the patterns of oppression." In other words, an appropriation of history, or 'her'-story in this case, to the higher needs of making some kind of fictional sense of the world.

World Literature Today's Charles R. Larson found *In the Heart of the Country* "a perplexing novel, to be sure, but also a fascinating novelistic exercise in the use of cinematic techniques in prose fiction," describing the book as reminiscent of an overlapping "series of stills extracted from a motion picture." Indeed, the book was written in a series of numbered paragraphs, as if from a cinematic storyboard. Writing in the 1997 critical study, *J. M. Coetzee*, Dominic Head observed, "In some ways, *In the Heart of the Country* is Coetzee's most difficult and forbidding novel." Head went on to explain: "It is a disruptive and disturbing book which offers an implicit admission of the semi-impotence of the white intellectual/writer in South Africa, and an oblique reflection of South Africa literary culture, and Afrikaner mythology." Head pointed out that the South

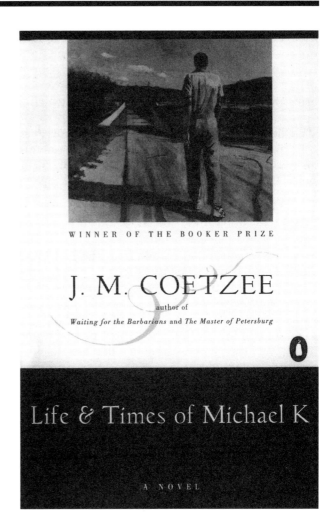

WINNER OF THE BOOKER PRIZE

J. M. COETZEE

author of
Waiting for the Barbarians and *The Master of Petersburg*

Life & Times of Michael K

A NOVEL

Michael K tries to return his ailing mother to her rural home in South Africa, even though the country is in the midst of civil war in this 1983 novel.

African edition of this "inward-looking" novel provided the dialogue in Afrikaans, while the narration was in English. Head also noted a "lyrical mode" that shows itself in bits of this second novel, a potential that "begins to be developed in important ways through Coetzee's oeuvre from this point onward."

Gains International Repute

Coetzee followed *In the Heart of the Country* with *Waiting for the Barbarians*, in which the author, "with laconic brilliance, articulates one of the basic problems of our time—how to *understand* . . . mentality behind the brutality and injustice," Anthony Burgess wrote in *New York* magazine. With this novel, winner of the James Tait Black Memorial Award and the Geoffrey Faber Award, Coetzee gained international attention and a worldwide audience. In the book, set in an unnamed colonial outpost of an unnamed Empire, a Magistrate attempting to protect the peaceful nomadic people of his district is imprisoned and tortured by the army that arrives at the frontier town to destroy the "barbarians" on behalf of the Empire. The horror of what he has seen and experienced affects the Magistrate in ways that he cannot understand. His central obsession becomes the washing of the feet of one of these "barbarians," a girl who has had her ankles broken and her eyes seared by her torturers.

"With its vague setting and loose allegorical resonances," Gallagher commented, "*Waiting for the Barbarians* is much more distant from the historical world than Coetzee's first two books." Doris Grumbach, writing in the *Los Angeles Times Book Review,* found *Waiting for the Barbarians* a book with "universal reference," an allegory which can be applied to innumerable historical and contemporary situations. "Very soon it is apparent that the story, terrifying and unforgettable, is about injustice and barbarism inflicted everywhere by "civilized" people upon those it invades, occupies, governs." "The intelligence Coetzee brings us in *Waiting for the Barbarians* comes straight from Scripture and Dostoevsky," Webster Schott asserted in the *Washington Post Book World.* "We possess the devil. We are all barbarians." Derek Wright commented in the *International Fiction Review* that *Waiting for the Barbarians* "is a timeless parable of Empire," and it is this very timelessness which makes the tale so universal in appeal. Head felt that *Waiting for the Barbarians* "crystallizes the central issue of debate concerning the ethical vision of Coetzee's fiction, and his importance as a novelist." Noting the "obvious ramifications" for the white opponent of apartheid that are allegorically delivered in the story, Head called the novel "a kind of plateau" in writing for Coetzee's early works. Gallagher felt that the novel is "Coetzee's most powerful," partly because it grew directly out of the contemporary debate in South Africa about state-sponsored torture. This debate in turn was sparked by the death of the black leader Stephen Biko in 1977 while in detention.

In *Waiting for the Barbarians,* Coetzee succeeded, according to Christopher Lehmann-Haupt in a *New York Times* review, "in creating a tragic fable of colonialism that surpassed the boundaries of his native South Africa and made universal the agony of its conscience-stricken European protagonist." With his 1983 novel, *Life and Times of Michael K,* Coetzee moved beyond such a plateau, according to Lehmann-Haupt. With this book, Coetzee "dis-

tances himself in yet another way," according to Gallagher: "although it takes place in South Africa, it is set in an unspecified future of civil war and chaos." Gallagher further noted that this novel is Coetzee's "first attempt to center his narrative in a non-white character." The Michael of the title is a disfigured and supposedly slow-witted municipal gardens laborer who plans to return his aging and ill mother to her ancestral home so that she can die among her own people. She does not, however, survive the trip, and Michael is left to carry her ashes to her homeland far from Cape Town. Unable to dig a hole in the hard soil, Michael scatters his mother's ashes with the topsoil. He decides not to return to Cape Town, but remain here, apart from history and war. Squatting in an abandoned farmhouse, he plants pumpkins and melons from seeds he finds. The earth is generous to Michael, and even when he is sick, he relies on his crop to make him well. The land heals Michael, while all about is war and chaos. "The land has exercised its power," Scrogin noted. "Michael is not a soldier, or a retarded boy or a refugee, but a gardener."

Reviewing this novel in the *New York Times Book Review,* Cynthia Ozick commented, "Mr. Coetzee's landscapes of suffering are defined by the little by little art of moral disclosure—his stories might be about anyone and anyplace." Ozick further noted, however, that such tales "defy the vice of abstraction: they are engrossed in the minute and concrete." Reviewing the novel in *Maclean's,* Mark Abley found that the *Life and Times of Michael K* "begins as a study of an apparently ordinary man; it develops into a portrait of an exceptional human being, written with unusual power and beauty." Other critics observed the debt Coetzee's art owes to earlier writers such as Kafka. Reviewing the novel in the *Chicago Tribune Book World,* Larson described the author as "writing from a tradition that might be identified as Kafkaesque," noting that Michael K. shares the same initial as the protagonist of Kafka's K in *The Trial.* "Moreover," Larson wrote, "the world in which he tries to operate is unknowable in many of the same ways as Kafka's inexplicable reality. South Africa, one concludes, has become the reality of Kafka's nightmares." Coetzee's *Life of Michael K* won both the Booker Prize and the Prix Femina Etranger and put his name solidly on the international literary map.

South African Departures and Returns

Foe, a retelling of Daniel Defoe's *Robinson Crusoe,* marked a transitional stage for Coetzee, according to Nicholson in *West Coast Review*. Nicholson found many areas in which *Foe* differs from Coetzee's previous work. "Coetzee initially appeared to me to have all but abandoned his usual concerns and literary techniques" in *Foe*, Nicholson commented. "I was mistaken. More importantly, though, I was worried about why he has chosen now to write this kind of book; I found his shift of focus and technique ominous. Could he no longer sustain the courage he had demonstrated [in *Waiting for the Barbarians* and *The Life and Times of Michael K.*], turning instead to a radically interiorized narrative?" Nicholson concluded, "Perhaps *Foe* is best viewed as a pause for recapitulation and evaluation, transitional in Coetzee's development as a writer." Nichols, however, writing in *Southern Humanities Review*, found that Coetzee had not strayed far from his usual topics. "Like all of Coetzee's earlier works, *Foe* retains a strong sense of its specifically South African origins, a sociopolitical subtext that runs along just below the surface of the narrative," Nichols remarked.

Nichols's description of Coetzee's role as "an archeologist of the imagination, an excavator of language," is nowhere more telling that in *Foe*. Central to this idea are the mute Friday, whose tongue was cut out by slavers, and Susan Barton, the castaway who struggles to communicate with him. Daniel Foe, the author who endeavors to tell Barton's story, is also affected by Friday's speechlessness. Both recognize their duty to provide a means by which Friday can relate the story of his escape from the fate of his fellow slaves who drowned, still shackled, when their ship sank, but also question their right to speak for him. "The author, whether Foe or Coetzee, . . . wonders if he has any right to speak for the one person whose story most needs to be told," Nichols noted.

"Friday is . . . the tongueless voice of millions." G. Scott Bishop, reviewing the novel in *World Literature Today*, noted firstly that all of Coetzee's novels "offer the privileged, predominantly white world an illuminating if not disconcerting picture of the political and moral entanglements in the postcolonial world." Bishop went on to note of *Foe*, in particular: "Left doubting author and genre, we are entrenched in doubt, and it is that experience which makes *Foe* so effective. It is a distinctly political novel which forces the reader into the political experience of doubting author, authorial voice, and authority." Other critics have pointed to linguistic and thematic similarities in other works by Coetzee: the silence of Michael K. and the too bountiful and fanciful recollections of Magda. As Gallagher concluded, "*Foe*

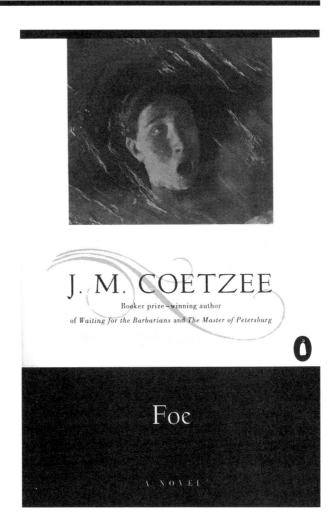

Coetzee retells the story of *Robinson Crusoe* through the eyes of Susan Barton, a former castaway involved with Crusoe, and Friday, Crusoe's former manservant.

ultimately addresses the issue of how one can write for—in support of—the Other without presuming to write for—assuming power over—the Other."

In *Age of Iron* Coetzee addresses the crisis of South Africa in direct rather than allegorical form. It is the story of Mrs. Curren, a retired professor dying of cancer and attempting to deal with the realities of apartheid in Cape Town. *Age of Iron* is "an unrelenting yet gorgeously written parable of modern South Africa, . . . a story filled with foreboding and violence about a land where even the ability of children to love is too great a luxury," Michael Dorris wrote in *Tribune Books*. As her disease and the chaos of her homeland progress, Mrs. Curren feels the effects her society has had on its black members; her realization that "now my eyes are open and I can never close them again" forms the basis for her growing rage against the system. After her housekeeper's son and his friend are murdered in her home, Mrs. Curren runs away and hides beneath an overpass, leaving her vulnerable to attack by a gang. She is rescued by Vercueil, a street person she has gradually allowed into her house and her life who returns her to her home and tends to her needs, as the cancer continues its destruction. The book takes the form of a letter from Mrs. Curren to her daughter, living in the United States because she cannot tolerate apartheid.

"Dying is traditionally a process of withdrawal from the world," Sean French commented in *New Statesman and Society*. "Coetzee tellingly reverses this and it is in her last weeks that [Mrs. Curren] first truly goes out in the baffling society she has lived in." As her life ends, Mrs. Curren's urgency to correct the wrongs she never before questioned intensifies. "J. M. Coetzee's new novel is short and simple," commented Peter Reading in the *Times Literary Supplement*. "There is no clutter and the writing seems to have been purged of "style." The allegorical element, while present, is not laboured. . . . Coetzee . . . manages to address the large issues of life, love and death, South Africa and internecine political intractability." Writing in *Critical Perspectives on J. M. Coetzee*, Graham Huggan called *Age of Iron* Coetzee's "most immediate novel to date," and one that directly deals with the problems of his homeland. Huggan also pointed out that the years during which the novel was written, 1986 to 1989, were turbulent not only in the country as a whole with thousands of black deaths in the cities and townships, but also for Coetzee personally. During this time Coetzee lost three people close to him through tragic death: his mother, father, and son, Nicholas. Huggan called *Age of Iron* "an elegy: an attempt, through narrative, to come to terms with the grief of personal loss while mourning the collective losses of a war-torn society." "In this chronicle of an aged white woman coming to understand, and of the unavoidable claims of her country's black youth, Mr. Coetzee has created a superbly realized novel whose truths cut to the bone," Lawrence Thornton declared in the *New York Times Book Review*.

Reviewers have noted that Coetzee seems to intersperse hard-hitting books with more abstract, less visceral novels. After the edginess of *Life and Times of Michael K*, came the more intellectual *Foe*. After the directness of *Age of Iron*, Coetzee similarly left South African themes behind for a more "labyrinthine" approach in *The Master of Petersburg*, according to Patrick McGrath, writing in the *New York Times Book*

Review. The central character in the book is the Russian novelist Fyodor Dostoevsky, but the plot is only loosely based on his real life. In Coetzee's story, the novelist goes to St. Petersburg upon the death of his stepson, Pavel. He is devastated by grief for the young man, and begins an inquiry into his death. He discovers that Pavel was involved with a group of nihilists and was probably murdered either by their leader or by the police. During the course of his anguished investigation, Dostoevsky's creative processes are exposed; Coetzee shows him beginning work on his novel *The Possessed*.

In real life, Dostoevsky did have a stepson named Pavel; but he was a foppish idler, a constant source of annoyance and embarrassment to the writer. The younger man outlived his stepfather by some twenty years, and when Dostoevsky died, he did not allow Pavel near his deathbed. Some reviewers were untroubled by Coetzee's manipulation of the facts. "This is not, after all, a book about the real Dostoevsky; his name, and some facts connected to it, form a mask behind which Coetzee enacts a drama of parenthood, politics and authorship," Harriett Gilbert explained in *New Statesman and Society*. She went on to praise Coetzee's depiction of "the barbed-wire coils of grief and anger, of guilt, of sexual rivalry and envy, that Fyodor Mikhailovich negotiates as he enters Pavel's hidden life. From the moment he presses his face to the lad's white suit to inhale his smell, to when he sits down, picks up his pen and commits a paternal novelist's betrayal, his pain is depicted with such harsh clarity that pity is burnt away. If the novel begins uncertainly, it ends with scorching self-confidence." McGrath called the novel "dense and difficult . . . [one] that frustrates at every turn." McGrath further commented, "But despite that difficulty, the figure who emerges from these pages, the master himself . . . will seize any imagination still susceptible to the complicated passions of the Slav soul. He will reveal himself as a profound man in the throes of a furious struggle to wring meaning and redemption from the death of a son." Joseph Frank concluded a lengthy *New Republic* review of Coetzee's seventh novel by noting that *The Master of Petersburg* "is an enigmatic and rather puzzling book whose aim is difficult to unravel. . . . One thing, though, can be stated quite unequivocally: Coetzee is an intriguing and ingenious writer."

A Second Booker: The Compleat Man of Letters

In 1999, Coetzee published his eighth novel, *Disgrace*, and returned to South African themes. Set in the post-apartheid era, the novel looks at the after-effects of empire. David Lurie is 52 and courting disaster. Twice married and twice divorced, he is a professor of modern languages at Cape Town University College and is a victim of new regimes. He has recently been named an adjunct professor of communications at his college, which has reconfigured itself as Cape Technical University. Lurie has little faith in language to communicate any of mankind's real needs; he does not take his new posting seriously. Instead he rather pressingly seduces one of his young students.

Refusing to show contrition for his misdeed, Lurie is fired and resolves to do something with his waning years. He heads to the Eastern Cape where his daughter Lucy has a small farm on which she cultivates flowers and boards dogs. There he determines to write a libretto based on Byron's last years; he settles in at the farm, also working part-time as a volunteer at an animal shelter. But soon Lucy is attacked and raped by three black men while Lurie is forced to watch. Lucy goes into a deep depression and Lurie tries to come to terms with himself, with the violence, and with his entire life as a result of this one telling incident. Increasingly, Lurie's work at the animal shelter itself takes on a new importance, as a sort of atonement.

Reviewers greeted this new novel with strong praise. A reviewer for the *New Yorker* called *Disgrace* "compulsively readable," but also "an authentically spiritual document, a lament for the soul of a disgraced century." This same reviewer went on to comment that Coetzee "writes with scalpel-like economy of effect; his sentences are coiled springs, and the energy they release would take other writers pages to summon." *Newsweek*'s Laura Shapiro described the book as a "slim novel with a bleak powerful story to tell." She further observed, "Coetzee writes with a cool, calm lucidity that fends off despair, and his characters find a kind of peace in acceptance, if not hope." A contributor for the *Wall Street Journal* called *Disgrace* "the most powerful novel this year," while a reviewer for the *Christian Science Monitor* noted, "It may be that 200 pages have never worked so hard as they do in Coetzee's hands." Michael Gorra, writing in the *New York Times Book Review,* commented, "Even though it presents an almost unrelieved series of grim moments, "Disgrace" isn't claustrophobic." Gorra noted the use of present tense in the book which, "allows for the sublime exhilaration of accident and surprise," and concluded that the book "surely deserves" the Booker Prize it was awarded, but that such an

award "may, in time, come to seem among the least of this extraordinary novel's distinctions."

Coetzee is also the author of several nonfiction works, including *White Writing: On the Culture of Letters in South Africa, Doubling the Point: Essays and Interviews,* and *Giving Offense: Essays on Censorship.* In *White Writing,* the author "collects his critical reflections on the mixed fortunes of "white writing" in South Africa, "a body of writing [not] different in nature from black writing," but "generated by the concerns of people no longer European, yet not African,"" Shaun Irlam observed in *MLN.* The seven essays included in the book discuss writings from the late seventeenth century to the present, through which Coetzee examines the foundations of modern South African writers' attitudes. Irlam described the strength of *White Writing* as its ability "to interrogate succinctly and lucidly the presuppositions inhabiting the language with which "white writers" have addressed and presumed to ventriloquize Africa." In the *Rocky Mountain Review of Language and Literature,* Barbara Temple-Thurston noted, "Coetzee's book reiterates impressively how cultural ideas and language bind and limit the way in which we interpret our world." In *Doubling the Point: Essays and Interviews,* a collection of critical essays on Samuel Beckett, Franz Kafka, D. H. Lawrence, Nadine Gordimer, and others, Coetzee presents a "literary autobiography," according to Ann Irvine in a *Library Journal* review. Discussions of issues including censorship and popular culture and interviews with the author preceding each section round out the collection.

Giving Offense: Essays on Censorship is Coetzee's first collection of essays in ten years, since *White Writing* appeared. In these more recent essays, written over a period of about six years, Coetzee, a writer quite familiar with the varying forms of censorship and the writer's response to them, attempts to complicate what he calls "the two tired images of the writer under censorship: the moral giant under attack from hordes of moral pygmies and the helpless innocent persecuted by a mighty state apparatus." Coetzee discusses three tyrannical regimes: Nazism, Communism, and apartheid. Drawing upon his training as an academic scholar, as well as his experiences as a fiction writer, he argues that the censor and the writer have often been "brother-enemies, mirror images one of the other" in their struggle to claim the truth of their position. Martha Bayles, writing in the *New York Times,* called this book "an extraordinary collection of essays. . . . Mr. Coetzee does not cast himself as the noble, freedom-

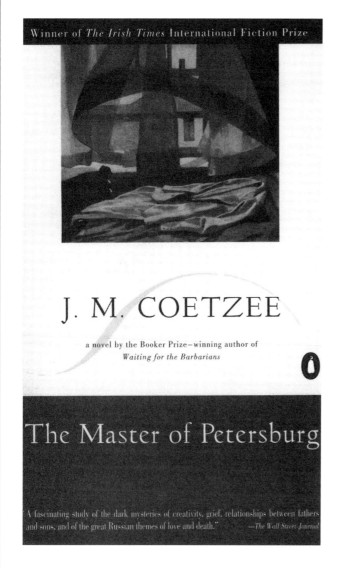

Winner of *The Irish Times* International Fiction Prize

J. M. COETZEE

a novel by the Booker Prize–winning author of
Waiting for the Barbarians

The Master of Petersburg

"A fascinating study of the dark mysteries of creativity, grief, relationships between fathers and sons, and of the great Russian themes of love and death." —*The Wall Street Journal*

In this novel, the author imagines the life of nineteenth-century Russian novelist Fyodor Dostoevsky after his stepson died in St. Petersburg in 1869.

loving artist; he finds this role almost as narrow and predictable. . . . Instead, he seeks to demonstrate the complexity and insidiousness of censorship's aims."

In *Boyhood: Scenes from Provincial Life,* Coetzee experiments with autobiography, a surprise, as Caryl Phillips in the *New Republic* noted, for a writer "whose literary output has successfully resisted an autobiographical reading." Written in the third person, *Boyhood,* claimed Denise S. Sticha in *Library Journal,* "reads more like a novella than a true autobiography. Coetzee develops his character, a young boy on the verge of adolescence, through a richly detailed interior monolog." He recounts his life growing up in Worcester, South Africa, where he moved with his family from Cape Town after his

father's latest business failure. There, he observes the contradictions of apartheid and the subtle distinctions of class and ethnicity with a precociously writerly eye. Rand Richards Cooper, writing for the *New York Times Book Review,* stated that "Coetzee's themes lie where the political, the spiritual, the psychological and the physical converge: the nightmare of bureaucratic violence; or forlorn estrangement from the land; a Shakespearean anxiety about nature put out of its order; and the insistent neediness of the body." Reviewing the book in *New York Times,* Michiko Kakutani called *Boyhood* "a fiercely revealing, bluntly unsentimental work that both creates a telling portrait of the artist as a young man and illuminates the hidden courses of his art."

Another experimental work is the hybrid fiction-nonfiction *The Lives of Animals,* which has a strong statement for animal rights. Written for the Tanner Lectures at Princeton University, such works are generally philosophical essays, but "Coetzee subverts that formula," according to a writer for *Kirkus Reviews,* "by shaping his talks into fictional lectures given by an elderly novelist, Elizabeth Costello." This fictionalized novelist holds forth on the meat packing business as an analog of the death camps in the Third Reich, further working the argument for animal rights that was examined in both *Boyhood* and *Disgrace.* "Coetzee takes no prisoners; there is always suffering on the road to salvation," according to the contributor to *Kirkus Reviews. Booklist*'s Marlene Chamberlain called *The Lives of Animals* a book for "Coetzee fans and others interested in the links between philosophy, reason, and the rights of nonhumans," while Ian Hacking, writing in the *New York Review of Books* found *The Lives of Animals* to be "a genuinely troubling book."

In addition to his writing, Coetzee produces translations of writings in Dutch, German, French, and Afrikaans, serves as editor for others' work, and teaches at the University of Cape Town. "He's a rare phenomenon, a writer-scholar," Ian Glenn, a colleague of Coetzee's, told the *Washington Post*'s Allister Sparks. "Even if he hadn't had a career as a novelist he would have had a very considerable one as an academic." Coetzee told Sparks that he finds writing burdensome. "I don't like writing so I have to push myself," he said. "It's bad if I write but it's worse if I don't."

But write he does, and in forms as diverse as the novel and essays, though it is the novel form in which he has indisputably excelled and for which he is known internationally. As Gallagher conclud-

If you enjoy the works of J. M. Coetzee, you might want to check out the following books and films:

Sheila Gordon, *Waiting for the Rain*, 1987.
Beverley Naidoo, *No Turning Back*, 1997.
Hazel Rochman, *Somehow Tenderness Survives: Stories of Southern Africa*, 1988.
Cry, the Beloved Country, a film starring James Earl Jones and Richard Harris, 1995.

ed in her study of the writer, "The novels of J. M. Coetzee . . . both arise out of history and transform history. The ethical and artistic attention he pays to the unique problems of his troubled country provide a model for other twentieth-century writers with their own historical contexts and problems. . . . He speaks to us all about ourselves because he speaks about himself and his country. . . . Coetzee's novels reveal the possibilities and dangers of fiction in the twentieth century."

■ Works Cited

Abley, Mark, review of *Life and Times of Michael K*, *Maclean's*, January 30, 1984, p. 49.

Attwell, David, *J. M. Coetzee: South Africa and the Politics of Writing*, University of California Press, 1993, pp. 1, 35.

Barnett, Ursula A., review of *Dusklands*, *Books Abroad*, Spring, 1976.

Bayles, Martha, "The Silencers," *New York Times*, September 22, 1996, p. 33.

Bishop, G. Scott, "J. M. Coetzee's *Foe*: A Culmination and a Solution to a Problem of White Identity," *World Literature Today*, Winter, 1990, pp. 54-57.

Burgess, Anthony, review of *Waiting for the Barbarians*, *New York*, April 26, 1982, pp. 88, 90.

Chamberlain, Marlene, review of *The Lives of Animals*, *Booklist*, March 15, 1999, p. 1262.

Coetzee, J. M., *Waiting for the Barbarians*, Penguin, 1982.

Coetzee, J. M., *Age of Iron*, Random House, 1990.

Coetzee, J. M., *Giving Offense: Essays on Censorship*, University of Chicago Press, 1996.

Coetzee, J. M., *Boyhood: Scenes from Provincial Life*, Viking, 1997.

Cooper, Rand Richards, review of *Boyhood*, *New York Times Book Review*, November 2, 1997, p. 7.

Review of *Disgrace, Christian Science Monitor*, November 10, 1999.

Review of *Disgrace, New Yorker*, November 15, 1999.

Review of *Disgrace, Wall Street Journal*, October 26, 1999.

Dorris, Michael, review of *Age of Iron*, *Tribune Books*, September 16, 1990, p. 3.

Frank, Joseph, review of *The Master of Petersburg*, *New Republic*, October 16, 1995, pp. 53-57.

French, Sean, review of *Age of Iron*, *New Statesman and Society*, September 21, 1990, p. 40.

Gallagher, Susan, VanZanten, *A Story of South Africa: J. M. Coetzee's Fiction in Context*, Harvard University Press, 1991.

Gilbert, Harriet, review of *The Master of Petersburg*, *New Statesman and Society*, February 25, 1994, p. 41.

Gorra, Michael, "After the Fall," *New York Times Book Review*, November 22, 1999, p. 7.

Grumbach, Doris, review of *Waiting for the Barbarians*, *Los Angeles Times Book Review*, May 23, 1982, p. 4.

Hacking, Ian, "Our Fellow Animals," *New York Review of Books*, June 29, 2000, pp. 20, 22, 24-26.

Head, Dominic, *J. M. Coetzee*, Cambridge Univesity Press, 1997, pp. 49, 71-72.

Huggan, Graham, "Evolution and Entropy in J. M. Coetzee's *Age of Iron*," *Critical Perspectives on J. M. Coetzee*, edited by Graham Huggan and Stephen Watson, St. Martins Press, 1996, p.191.

Irlam, Shaun, review of *White Writing*, *MLN*, December 1988, pp. 1147-50.

Irvine, Ann, review of *Doubling the Point*, *Library Journal*, June 1, 1992, p. 124.

Kakutani, Michiko, "Childhood Hurt and Fear As a Writer's Inspiration," *New York Times*, October 7, 1997, p. E8.

Larson, Charles L., review of *In the Heart of the Country*, *World Literature Today*, Summer, 1978, p. 510.

Larson, Charles L., review of *Life and Times of Michael K*, *Chicago Tribune Book World*, January 22, 1984, section 14, p. 27.

Lehmann-Haupt, Christopher, review of *Life and Times of Michael K.*, *New York Times*, December 6, 1983, p. C22.

Review of *The Lives of Animals*, *Kirkus Reviews*, February 15, 1999, p. 264.

McGrath, Patrick, "To Be Conscious Is to Suffer," *New York Times Book Review*, November 29, 1994, p. 9.

Nichols, Ashton, review of *Foe*, *Southern Humanities Review*, Fall, 1987, pp. 384-86.

Nicholson, Maureen, "If I Make the Air around Him Thick with Words," *West Coast Review,* Spring, 1987, pp. 52-58.

Ozick, Cynthia, review of *Life and Times of Michael K, New York Times Book Review,* December 11, 1983, pp. 1, 26.

Phillips, Caryl, review of *Boyhood, New Republic,* February 9, 1998, p. 37.

Reading, Peter, "Monstrous Growths," *Times Literary Supplement,* September 28-October 4, 1990, p. 1037.

Roberts, Sheila, review of *In the Heart of the Country, World Literature Written in English,* Spring, 1980, pp. 19-36.

Schott, Webster, review of *Waiting for the Barbarians, Washington Post Book World,* May 2, 1982, pp. 1-2, 12.

Scrogin, Michael, "Apocalypse and Beyond: The Novels of J. M. Coetzee," *Christian Century,* May 18-25, 1988, pp. 503-05.

Shapiro, Laura, "African Anger: A Booker Prize Winner," *Newsweek,* November 15, 1999, p. 90.

Sparks, Allister, *Washington Post,* October 29, 1983.

Sticha, Denise S., review of *Boyhood, Library Journal,* September 1, 1997, p. 181.

Temple-Thurston, Barbara, review of *White Writing, Rocky Mountain Review of Language and Literature,* vol. 53, nos. 1-2, 1989, pp. 85-87.

Thornton, Lawrence, "Apartheid's Last Vicious Gasp," *New York Times Book Review,* September 23, 1990, p. 7.

Tiffin, H. M., "Coetzee, J. M.," *Contemporary Novelists,* 4th edition, St, James Press, 1986, pp. 190-91.

Toerien, Barend J., review of *In the Heart of the Country, World Literature Today,* Spring, 1978, pp. 245-47.

Wright, Derek, "Fiction as Foe: The Novels of J. M. Coetzee," *International Fiction Review,* Summer, 1989, pp. 113-18.

■ For More Information See

BOOKS

Contemporary Literary Criticism, Volume 66, Gale, 1991, Volume 117, Gale, 1997.

Goddard, Kevin, *J. M. Coetzee: A Bibliography,* National English Literary Museum, 1990.

Jolly, Rosemary Jane, *Colonization, Violence, and Narration in White South African Writing: Andre Brink, Breyten Breytenbach, and J. M. Coetzee,* Ohio University Press, 1996.

Kossew, Sue, *Pen and Power: A Post-Colonial Reading of J. M. Coetzee and Andre Brink,* Rodopi, 1996.

Kossew, Sue, editor, *Critical Essays on J. M. Coetzee,* G. K. Hall, 1998.

Moses, Michael Valdez, editor, *The Writings of J. M. Coetzee,* Duke University Press, 1994.

Penner, Dick, *Countries of the Mind: The Fiction of J. M. Coetzee,* Greenwood Publishing Group, 1989.

PERIODICALS

Africa Today, third quarter, 1980.

America, September 25, 1982.

Ariel: A Review of International English Literature, April, 1985, pp. 47-56; July, 1986, pp. 3-21; October, 1988, pp. 55-72.

Booklist, November 1, 1994, p. 477; April 1, 1996, p. 1328; August, 1997, p. 1869; January 1, 1998, p. 726.

Books and Culture, March, 1997, p. 30.

Books in Canada, August/September, 1982.

Boston Globe, November 20, 1994, p. B16.

British Book News, April, 1981.

Chicago Tribune Book World, April 25, 1982; November 27, 1994, p. 3.

Christian Science Monitor, December 12, 1983; May 18, 1988, pp. 503-05.

Contemporary Literature, summer, 1988, pp. 277-85; fall, 1992, pp. 419-31.

Critique: Studies in Modern Fiction, winter, 1986, pp. 67-77; spring, 1989, pp. 143-54.

Encounter, October, 1977; January, 1984.

English Journal, March, 1994, p. 97.

Globe and Mail (Toronto), August 30, 1986.

Harper's, June 1999, p. 76.

Library Journal, September 1, 1994, p. 213; March 15, 1996, p. 70.

Listener, August 18, 1977.

London Review of Books, September 13, 1990, pp. 17-18.

Los Angeles Times Book Review, January 15, 1984; February 22, 1987; November 20, 1994, p. 3.

MLN, December 17, 1990, pp. 777-80.

Nation, March 28, 1987, pp. 402-05; February 6, 1995, p. 170; July 27, 1998, p. 30.

Natural History, June, 1999, p. 18.

New Republic, December 19, 1983; February 6, 1995, pp. 170-72; October 16, 1995, p. 53; November 18, 1996, p. 30.

New Statesman and Society, November 21, 1997, p. 50.

Newsweek, May 31, 1982; January 2, 1984; February 23, 1987.

New Yorker, July 12, 1982.

New York Review of Books, December 2, 1982; February 2, 1984; November 8, 1990, pp. 8-10; November 17, 1994, p. 35; November 20, 1997, p. 24.

New York Times, February 11, 1987; April 11, 1987; November 18, 1994, p. C35; October 7, 1997, p. B7.

New York Times Book Review, February 22, 1987; September 22, 1996, p. 33; November 2, 1997, p. 7; December 6, 1998, p. 96.

Publishers Weekly, September 5, 1994, p. 88; January 22, 1996, p. 52; July 28, 1997, p. 59; February 8, 1999, p. 193; November 22, 1999, p. 42.

Research in African Literatures, fall, 1986, pp. 370-92.

Sewanee Review, winter, 1990, pp. 152-59; April, 1995, p. R48.

South Atlantic Quarterly, winter, 1994, pp. 1-9, 33-58, 83-110.

Spectator, December 13, 1980; September 20, 1986.

Time, March 23, 1987; November 28, 1994, pp. 89-90; November 29, 1999, p. 82.

Times (London), September 29, 1983; September 11, 1986; May 28, 1988.

Times Literary Supplement, November 7, 1980, p. 1270; January 14, 1983; September 30, 1983; September 23, 1988, p. 1043; March 4, 1994, p. 19; January 9, 1998, p. 6.

Tri-Quarterly, spring-summer, 1987, pp. 454-64.

Village Voice, March 20, 1984.

Voice Literary Supplement, April, 1982.

Wall Street Journal, November 3, 1994, p. A16.

Washington Post Book World, December 11, 1983; March 8, 1987; September 23, 1990, pp. 1, 10; November 27, 1994, p. 6.

World Literature Today, autumn, 1981; autumn, 1988, pp. 718-19; winter, 1990, pp. 54-57; winter, 1995, p. 207; autumn, 1996, p. 1038.

World Literature Written in English, spring, 1986, pp. 34-45; autumn, 1987, pp. 153-61, 174-84, 207-15.*

—Sketch by J. Sydney Jones

Christopher Paul Curtis

■ Personal

Born May 10, 1954(?), in Flint, MI; son of Herman (an auto worker) and Leslie Curtis; married Kaysandra (a nurse); children: Steven, Cydney. *Education:* University of Michigan-Flint, B.A., 1996.

■ Addresses

Home—Windsor, Ontario, Canada.

■ Career

Writer. Fisher Body Plant, Flint, MI, assembly line, 1972-85; also assistant to Senator Don Riegle, Lansing, MI; warehouse clerk, Automatic Data Processing, Allen Park, MI.

■ Awards, Honors

Best Books, *Publishers Weekly* and *New York Times Books Review,* both 1995, and Golden Kite Award, Coretta Scott King Text Honor, Best Books for Young Adults, and Newbery honor, American Library Asso-

ciation, all 1996, all for *The Watsons Go to Birmingham-1963;* Newbery Medal, American Library Association, and Coretta Scott King Award, American Library Association, both 2000, both for *Bud, Not Buddy.*

■ Writings

The Watsons Go to Birmingham-1963, Delacorte, 1995.
Bud, Not Buddy, Delacorte, 1999.

■ Adaptations

The Watsons Go to Birmingham-1963 has been recorded on audiocassette, Ingram, 1996.

■ Work in Progress

Bucking the Sarge, a novel about a 15-year-old boy in Flint, Michigan, whose mother is a scam artist.

■ Sidelights

With two books to his credit, Christopher Paul Curtis has earned not only a Newbery Medal, but also a Newbery honor and two Coretta Scott King awards for his fictional narratives about African-Americans from his native Flint, Michigan. Set historically, both of Curtis's novels explore themes of racism, belonging, love, hope, and the meaning of family. His debut title, *The Watsons Go to Birmingham-1963,* incorporates the infamous Birmingham church bombing in 1963, an incident in which the Watsons—off from their home in Flint to visit a grand-mother in the South—become involved. Narrated by the ten-year-old son of the family, Kenny, the book uses the vernacular and insights of a child that age. Curtis's second novel, *Bud, Not Buddy*, again uses a ten-year-old narrator, the eponymous and motherless Bud, who sets off during the Great Depression from his home in Flint to track down the man he thinks is his father. Both books deal with serious, even tragic topics, but Curtis manages a light touch, a unique blending of "comedy and pathos," as a reviewer for *Publishers Weekly* put it. It is a mix that has served Curtis well in both literature and life.

Raised in Flint, Michigan, like the characters in his first novel, Curtis grew up in a family of five, many of whom were avid readers. He counts Toni Morrison and Kurt Vonnegut as his favorite writers. But upon graduation from high school in 1972, Curtis took a job at the Fisher Body Plant No. 1, just like his father. Intended as a summer job before he went off to college at the University of Michigan-Flint, this employment lasted thirteen years. Even during his years on the assembly line, Curtis had the desire to write. Curtis and his partner decided on a time-saving alternative: they would each do thirty in a row instead of alternating, one on and one off. Curtis then used his thirty-minute break to write. Finally, after years of putting his dreams of a college education on hold, he began attending classes at the University of Michigan part-time, while holding down another job, and finally graduated in 1996.

A Time to Write

During that time, encouraged by winning the University's Hopwood prize for a rough draft of a story inspired by a road trip Curtis and his family had taken to Florida, Curtis agreed with his wife Kaysandra's suggestion that he take a year off and see what he could do as a writer. He spent his days at a table of the children's section of his local public library writing the first draft of his novel longhand. With the strong support of his family—his wife assumed many of their financial responsibilities while son Steven typed his father's handwritten manuscript into the family's computer every night—the story was completed by the end of 1993, and Curtis entered his manuscript in a national writing contest, where it came to the attention of Delacorte editors. Although his story did not meet the content guidelines specified for contest eligibility, Delacorte editor Wendy Lamb was thrilled with

the novel and began making arrangements to publish it.

The Watsons Go to Birmingham recounts everyday events in the life of Kenny Watson, a ten-year-old African-American boy. Blessed with a quick wit and a crossed eye, Kenny lives in the industrialized city of Flint, Michigan, along with his parents, little sister, and bossy older brother, Byron. Kenny believes that everyone in his neighborhood must think his family is nuts—the "Weird Watsons." Byron, who has just turned thirteen, has made the transformation from bossy older brother to teenage juvenile delinquent almost overnight: he starts to act bad, flushing flaming tissue parachutes down the toilet, dying his hair bright red and then getting it "conked" (straightened), and generally bullying his younger siblings around—including little sister Joetta, a kindergartner trying to keep up with her older brothers.

During the summer of 1963, Kenny's parents decide to take a vacation to Birmingham, Alabama, the home of Grandma Sands, to see if she can shake some sense into the obstinate and unruly Byron. After packing everything they'll need for the trip—roadside restaurants that served blacks weren't common in the segregated South of the 1960s—everyone piles into the family car, the "Brown Bomber," to begin the long journey. In Birmingham, the mood of the novel shifts, as the lighthearted hijinx of the Watson brood suddenly become overshadowed by the racial tensions of the era. Kenny and his family experience racial violence first hand when four teens are killed after a bomb explodes in the Sunday school classroom where little Joetta has been. Although the young girl is physically unharmed, she and the rest of her family return to Michigan transformed by their experiences.

Back in Flint, Kenny falls into depression over the violence he has witnessed and hides behind the sofa. Family myth has it that the pets will go there when sick because of the restorative benefits of the couch. Finally Kenny's older brother, Byron, in an act of maturity, draws him out of his hiding place and is able to convince him that even though he cannot control outside events, he still has a family to count on.

Remarking on the shift between the lighthearted first part of Curtis's novel and its tragic ending, Betsy Hearne wrote in the *Bulletin of the Center for Children's Books*: "The contrast is startling, innovative, and effective . . . showing how—and why—the Civil Rights movement affected individual African Americans." *Horn Book* reviewer Martha V. Parravano simi-

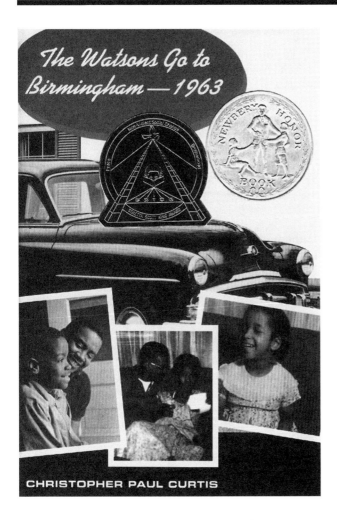

Curtis received a Newbery Honor in 1996 for this story about a Michigan family who travels to Alabama and experiences southern racism firsthand.

larly asserted that "Curtis's control of his material is superb as he unconventionally shifts tone and mood, as he depicts the changing relationship between the two brothers, and as he incorporates a factual event into his fictional story." Kermit Frazier of the *New York Times Book Review* concluded *The Watsons Go to Birmingham-1963* was "a marvelous debut, a fine novel about a solid and appealing family."

In addition to his talent for spinning an imaginative and entertaining tale, Curtis based parts of his book on memories of his own childhood, as well as on an historic event—the actual bombing of Birmingham's Sixteenth Avenue Baptist Church in September of 1963 which left four young girls dead. Although Curtis was not a witness to that event, he did a great deal of research in writing his novel. And he did not consciously prepare his tale for a certain intended audience. "Perhaps because Curtis

didn't think the novel would be for children when he started it, there's nothing heavy-handed or preachy about the Watsons' brush with the civil rights movement," noted Linnea Lannon in an article on Curtis for the *Detroit Free Press*. Curtis's debut novel has also been praised for its warmly drawn characters and its vivid settings. "When the "Weird Watsons" drive to Birmingham . . . to visit Grandma," wrote Ann Valentine Martino in the *Ann Arbor News*, "you feel like you're riding along in the back seat—with Kenny's little sister drooling in your lap." Gwen A. Tarbox, writing in *St. James Guide to Young Adult Writers*, lauded Curtis for his "detailed and poignant description of the inner life of an African-American family," and also for his tempering of such themes with "a humorous style that is unique and geared to appeal to young adults as well as to children."

Bud, Not Buddy

The success of Curtis's first novel convinced him to go for a career in writing, though he did not quit his day job. Instead he took some time off and worked on an adult novel before turning his hand—quite literally—to another juvenile book. Again written in longhand, *Bud, Not Buddy* seizes on a further crucial time in twentieth-century history, the Great Depression. It is 1936 in Flint, and Bud Calloway—Bud and definitely not Buddy as his mother has stipulated—is having a miserable time of it in his Dickensian orphanage. His mother died four years earlier; since that time he has been through two foster homes and is about to enter his third. He has had enough, and decides to set out on his own to find the man he thinks is his father. Herman E. Calloway is a bass player in a well known jazz band in Grand Rapids. Bud's mother has collected flyers from many of the musician's appearances. These clues—as well as the coincidence of the last name—lead Bud to believe that the man is his natural father.

On the road Bud gets some help from strangers who provide a surrogate for the family which he has never had. Walking through a small town at night he does not realize his life is in danger, for the citizens have a law that coloreds must be out of the city limits by sundown. Saved by a good-natured pitcher for the Negro leagues, Lefty Lewis, Bud gets a lift all the way to Grand Rapids where he hopes to find his namesake. Once there, however, it seems that the renowned jazz musician is "old, cold, and cantankerous," according to Kathleen Isaacs in *School Library Journal*. The band members prove friendlier,

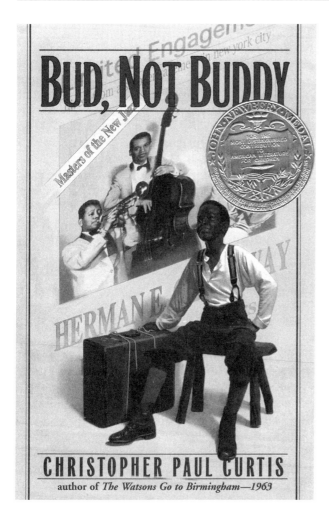

Bud Calloway is determined to find out who his father is at all costs in this Newbery Medal book published in 1999.

however. They take Bud in and teach him to play an instrument, and in the end a surprising relationship is discovered between Bud and Calloway.

"While the circumstances surrounding Bud's return to his family may gently chafe against credulity," wrote Janice M. Del Negro in the *Bulletin of the Center for Children's Books*, "Curtis' characterizations are so strong they make coincidence acceptable." Del Negro went on to comment, "The resourceful Bud is a hero readers will take immediately to heart." Isaacs felt that the "lively humor contrasts with the grim details of the Depression-era setting and the particular difficulties faced by African Americans at that time." "Bud," Isaacs concluded, "is a plucky, engaging protagonist. . . . Curtis has given a fresh, new look to a traditional orphan-finds-a-home story." A reviewer for *Publishers Weekly* also pointed out Curtis's use of comedy, commenting that, despite his

If you enjoy the works of Christopher Paul Curtis, you might want to check out the following books and films:

Joyce Hansen, *The Gift Giver*, 1980.
Mildred D. Taylor, *The Gold Cadillac*, 1987.
Walter Dean Myers, *Slam!*, 1996.
Crooklyn, a film by Spike Lee, 1994.

authentic portrayal of Bud's harsh reality, Curtis still manages to make "readers laugh." And Holly J. Robins, writing in *U.S. News and World Report*, commented, "Only Bud's sense of humor and weird slang keep the story light. He says "kiss my wrist" to sound tough—a phrase Curtis made up."

Martha Davis Beck, reviewing this second novel in *Riverbank Review*, noted that Curtis once again used bits of his own family history to enrich the details of the book: his two grandfathers provided models for the musician and the baseball player. Beck went on to remark, "Curtis writes with humor and sensitivity and makes readers care about the characters he creates. In the process, he offers up a significant slice of American history." And reviewing *Bud, Not Buddy* in the *New York Times Book Review*, Lois Metzger called the novel "funny, eloquent, deeply sad and delightful (usually all at once)." Metzger concluded, "In this powerfully felt novel, Bud opens up, unfolds and finds exactly what he's looking for."

Delacorte had high hopes for Curtis's second novel, even before the Newbery. They had gone back to press four time for a total of 65,000 hardcover copies in print; with the announcement of the Newbery Medal, they went back for a fifth printing, with 100,000 total in print. And Curtis was ecstatic with the news. Writing in *Time* magazine, Paul Gray noted that Curtis did not really look the bookish part. "Chalk it up as yet another evil of stereotyping," Gray wrote, "but the term children's-book author does not summon to most minds the image of a 6-ft. 2-in., 240-lb. man with dreadlocks." As Curtis told Gray, the Newbery Medal was already changing his life: "As soon as this award was announced, my wife went from house hunting to mansion hunting."

Curtis continues to plan books for the future. Among other possible works is a sequel to *Bud, Not Buddy*. Presumably these too will be written longhand. But whether computer generated or scratched out on a yellow legal pad, the expectation will be for the signature Curtis approach to fiction. As Tarbox put it in her entry in *St. James Guide to Young Adult Writers*, "Most importantly, Curtis treats his subject with respect, but also reaffirms the value of humor and love in the face of tragedy."

■ Works Cited

Beck, Martha Davis, review of *Bud, Not Buddy*, *Riverbank Review*, Fall, 1999, pp. 35-36.

Review of *Bud, Not Buddy*, *Publishers Weekly*, November 1, 1999, p. 57.

Del Negro, Janice M., review of *Bud, Not Buddy*, *Bulletin of the Center for Children's Books*, November, 1999, p. 89.

Frazier, Kermit, "Alabama Bound," *New York Times Book Review*, November 12, 1995, p. 23.

Gray, Paul, "Best *Buddy*," *Time*, January 31, 2000, p. 68.

Hearne, Betsy, review of *The Watsons Go to Birmingham-1963*, *Bulletin of the Center for Children's Books*, January, 1996, pp. 157-58.

Isaacs, Kathleen, review of *Bud, Not Buddy*, *School Library Journal*, September, 1999, p. 221.

Lannon, Linnea, "A Happy Ending," in *Detroit Free Press*, December 27, 1995, pp. 1C, 5C.

Martino, Anne Valentine, "Story of Civil Rights and a Family from Flint," *Ann Arbor News*, April 8, 1996, p. D1.

Metzger, Lois, "On Their Own," *New York Times Book Review*, November 21, 1999, p. 32.

Morris, Holly J., "Bud to World: "Kiss My Wrist,"" *U.S. News and World Report*, January 31, 2000, p. 61.

Parravano, Martha V., review of *The Watsons Go to Birmingham-1963*, *Horn Book*, March-April, 1996, pp. 195-96.

Tarbox, Gwen A., "Curtis, Christopher Paul," *St. James Guide to Young Adult Writers*, 2nd edition, edited by Tom Pendergast and Sara Pendergast, St. James Press, 1999, pp.208-09.

■ For More Information See

PERIODICALS

Booklist, August, 1995, p. 1946; July, 1997, p. 1830; September 1, 1999, p. 131.

Detroit Free Press, January 18, 2000, pp. 1A, 8A.

Journal of Youth Services, Summer, 2000, pp. 9-12, 16.

Kirkus Reviews, October 1, 1995, p. 1426.

Kliatt, January, 1998, p. 8.

Library Journal, February 1, 1997, p. 127.

Publishers Weekly, October 16, 1995, p. 62; December 18, 1995, pp. 28-30.

School Library Journal, October, 1995, p. 152.

Teacher Librarian, March, 1999, p. 54.

Time, October 4, 1999, p. 108.*

—Sketch by J. Sydney Jones

Daphne du Maurier

■ Personal

Born May 13, 1907, in London, England; died April 19, 1989, in Par, Cornwall, England; daughter of Gerald (an actor and manager) and Muriel (an actress; maiden name, Beaumont) du Maurier; married Frederick Arthur Montague Browning (a lieutenant-general and former treasurer to the Duke of Edinburgh), July 19, 1932 (died, 1965); children: Tessa (Mrs. David Montgomery), Flavia Browning Tower, Christian. *Education:* Attended schools in London, Paris, and Meudon, France. *Politics:* "Center." *Hobbies and other interests:* Walking, sailing, gardening, country life.

■ Career

Writer, 1931-89.

■ Member

Bronte Society, Royal Society of Literature (fellow).

■ Awards, Honors

National Book Award, 1938, for *Rebecca;* Dame Commander, Order of the British Empire, 1969.

■ Writings

NOVELS

The Loving Spirit, Doubleday (Garden City, NY), 1931.
I'll Never Be Young Again, Doubleday, 1932.
The Progress of Julius, Doubleday, 1933.
Jamaica Inn (also see below), Doubleday, 1936, abridged edition, edited by Jay E. Greene, bound with *The Thirty-Nine Steps* by John Buchan, Globe Publications, 1951.
Rebecca (also see below), Doubleday, 1938.
Frenchman's Creek (also see below), Gollancz (London), 1941, Doubleday, 1942.
Hungry Hill (also see below), Doubleday, 1943.
The King's General, Doubleday, 1946, abridged edition, edited by Lee Wyndham, Garden City Books, 1954.
The Parasites, Gollancz, 1949, Doubleday, 1950.
My Cousin Rachel (also see below), Gollancz, 1951, Doubleday, 1952.
Mary Anne (fictionalized biography of author's great-great grandmother), Doubleday, 1954.
The Scapegoat, Doubleday, 1957.
Three Romantic Novels: Rebecca, Frenchman's Creek, Jamaica Inn, Doubleday, 1961.
(With Arthur Quiller-Couch) *Castle d'Or,* Doubleday, 1962.
The Glass-Blowers, Doubleday, 1963.
The Flight of the Falcon, Doubleday, 1965.
The House on the Strand (Literary Guild selection), Doubleday, 1969.
Rule Britannia, Gollancz, 1972, Doubleday, 1973.

Four Great Cornish Novels (contains *Jamaica Inn, Rebecca, Frenchman's Creek,* and *My Cousin Rachel*), Gollancz, 1978.

SHORT STORY COLLECTIONS

Come Wind, Come Weather, Heinemann (London), 1940, Doubleday, 1941.

The Apple Tree: A Short Novel and Some Stories, Gollancz, 1952, published as *Kiss Me Again, Stranger: A Collection of Eight Stories, Long and Short,* Doubleday, 1953, published as *The Birds, and Other Stories,* Pan Books (London), 1977.

The Breaking Point, Doubleday, 1959, published as *The Blue Lenses, and Other Stories,* Penguin (London), 1970.

Early Stories, Todd, 1959.

The Treasury of du Maurier Short Stories, Gollancz, 1960.

Don't Look Now, Doubleday, 1971, published as *Not after Midnight,* Gollancz, 1971.

Echoes from the Macabre: Selected Stories, Gollancz, 1976, Doubleday, 1977.

The Rendezvous, and Other Stories, Gollancz, 1980.

PLAYS

Rebecca (three-act; based on author's novel of same title; produced on the West End at Queen's Theatre, 1940, produced on Broadway at Ethel Barrymore Theatre, 1945), Gollancz, 1940, Dramatists Play Service (New York City), 1943.

The Years Between (two-act; produced in Manchester, England, 1944, produced on the West End at Wyndham's Theatre, 1945), Gollancz, 1945, Doubleday, 1946.

September Tide (three-act; produced on the West End at Aldwych Theatre, 1948), Gollancz, 1949, Doubleday, 1950, revised edition with Mark Rayment, Samuel French (New York City), 1994.

My Cousin Rachel (adapted from author's novel of same title), edited by Diana Morgan, Dramatists Play Service, 1990.

OTHER

Gerald: A Portrait (biography of author's father), Gollancz, 1934, Doubleday, 1935.

The du Mauriers (family history and biography), Doubleday, 1937.

Happy Christmas, Doubleday, 1940.

Spring Picture, Todd, 1944.

(Co-author) *Hungry Hill* (screenplay; based on author's novel of same title), Universal Pictures, 1947.

(Editor) *The Young George du Maurier: A Selection of His Letters, 1860-1867,* P. Davies, 1951, Doubleday, 1952.

The Infernal World of Branwell Bronte (biography), Gollancz, 1960, Doubleday, 1961.

(Editor) Phyllis Bottome, *Best Stories,* Faber, 1963.

Vanishing Cornwall (history and travel), Doubleday, 1967.

Golden Lads: Sir Francis Bacon, Anthony Bacon and Their Friends, Doubleday, 1975.

The Winding Stair: Francis Bacon, His Rise and Fall, Gollancz, 1976, Doubleday, 1977.

Myself When Young: The Shaping of a Writer (autobiography), Doubleday, 1977, published as *Growing Pains: The Shaping of a Writer,* Gollancz, 1977.

The "Rebecca" Notebook, and Other Memories, Doubleday, 1980.

Daphne du Maurier Classics, Doubleday, 1987.

Enchanted Cornwall: Her Pictorial Memoir, M. Joseph (London), 1990.

Letters from Menabilly: Portrait of a Friendship, edited by Oriel Malet, M. Evans (New York City), 1994.

■ Adaptations

Alfred Hitchcock directed *Jamaica Inn* for Paramount Pictures in 1939, *Rebecca* for United Artists in 1940 (it won an Academy Award for best motion picture as well as a citation by the Film Daily Poll as one of the ten best pictures of the year), and *The Birds* for Universal Pictures in 1963. *Frenchman's Creek* was filmed by Paramount in 1944, *Hungry Hill* by I. Arthur Rank in 1947, *My Cousin Rachel* by Metro-Goldwyn-Mayer (MGM) in 1953, *The Scapegoat* by MGM in 1959, *Don't Look Now* by Paramount in 1973, and the novella "The Breakthrough" as *The Lifeforce Experiment* by Astral Film Enterprises, 1994. *Rebecca* was adapted as a television mini-series in 1979 by the British Broadcasting Corp. and adapted for the stage by Clifford Williams in 1994. *Jamaica Inn* was adapted for television in 1985 by Harlech Television. The television film *The Birds II: Land's End,* 1994, is a sequel to *The Birds.*

■ Sidelights

When Daphne du Maurier died at age 81 in 1989 at her home in her beloved Cornwall, England, obituary writers around the world sharpened their pencils. A writer in the London *Times* called her "one of the most popular novelists in the English-speaking world," with works that "became best sellers . . . almost automatically both in this country and in the United States." The same obituary writer noted that du Maurier "had a natural gift both for the evocation of atmosphere and for the maintenance of sus-

An orphan girl becomes involved with smugglers in Alfred Hitchcock's 1939 film adaptation of du Maurier's *Jamaica Inn*.

pense . . . she trafficked in dreams, dreams of a kind that seem to be inherent in the unconscious minds of many women, indeed of many men." Her best known novels, including *Jamaica Inn, Rebecca, Frenchman's Creek, The Scapegoat, My Cousin Rachel,* and *The House on the Strand*, "represent two classes into which her fiction falls, the cloak-and-dagger romance on the one hand and the Gothic novel on the other." Sarah Booth Conroy, writing in the *Washington Post*, also noted du Maurier's ability to lead "enchanted readers into a dream world, endowing them with fantastic abilities to become specters/spectators in strange lives, and for the space of her tales, to dwell in wonderfully wayward places." Conroy further commented, "Eagerly, insatiably, hundreds of thousands of us followed her down the drive to Rebecca's Manderley, *Frenchman's Creek, The House on the Strand, Jamaica Inn* and other elusive spaces in 13 bestselling novels, many short stories and seven classic movies." Writing in the

Sunday Times, Margaret Forster, who would later publish a biography of du Maurier, singled out *Rebecca* as a "seminal work for the post-war generation, just as *Jane Eyre* was for mid-Victorians." She also praised the movies made by Alfred Hitchcock of that novel and of her short story, "The Birds," which "showed how scarifying effects could be underpinned by a psychological strength in the text." Forster concluded her laudatory appraisal of du Maurier's creative life: "If all our popular bestsellers were of her excellence then there would be no need to deplore their existence, and the silly snobbery existing between "pulp" fiction and literary fiction would vanish."

Reading du Maurier was long considered less than a literary pursuit. John Raymond, writing in the *New Statesman*, once called her "a kind of poor woman's Charlotte Bronte." Kelly, writing in 1987 before du Maurier's death, declared, "The literary establishment clearly wants nothing to do with Daphne du Maurier. There are no critical essays or books about her. . . . The fact that millions of people read her novels certainly works against her approval by literary critics, who are not inclined to prize what the popular audience does." In *Daphne du Maurier: Haunted Heiress,* a critical/biographical analysis of the author by Nina Auerbach, the noted critic titled her first chapter "Reading Furtively, by Flashlight," and began her book, "All books seem better when I'm not supposed to be reading them. I never should read Daphne du Maurier, but I regularly do." Such guilty delight in the work is part of the du Maurier charm, but Templeton noted a sea change in du Maurier's critical assessment. "Du Maurier was most proficient in creating psychological or Gothic thrillers," he noted, "often having some connection to the past or set in the past, that focus on the struggle or an individual against an oppressive environment." Such books, according to Templeton, "are strong on characterization, setting, and plot." Yet despite the fact that du Maurier was able to live comfortably on the earnings from her books, and despite honors such as being made a dame of the British empire in 1969 for her literary contributions, "du Maurier did not occupy a place in the literary canon during her lifetime— much to her disappointment." However, Templeton went on to point out that a "reassessment of the canon has led in recent years to the "discovery" of several previously neglected figures in British literature, most of them women. This list includes Daphne du Maurier." Since du Maurier's death, there have been several full-scale biographies and more critical analyses in the works. Like the heroine of one of her own Gothic thrillers, du Maurier has persevered on her own terms.

Daughter of a Theatrical Family

Daphne du Maurier's life in the arts was, in many ways, determined by her parentage. Du Maurier was the granddaughter of George du Maurier, a painter/illustrator and author of the novels *Peter Ibbetson, Trilby,* and *The Martian.* She was also the great-great-granddaughter of Mary Anne Clarke, mistress of the son of King George III, "strong, courageous, and capable of dealing with a man's world on her own terms," according to Templeton, writing in *Dictionary of Literary Biography.* More importantly, she was one of three daughters of the stage actor, Gerald du Maurier, famous for such roles as the gentleman burglar, Raffles, and the detective, Bulldog Drummond. So popular and well known was Gerald du Maurier, that in 1929 he

leased his family name to a tobacco company for one of its elegant brand of cigarettes. Muriel Beaumont, her mother, was also an actress. Daphne du Maurier thus grew up in the rarified environment of the arts, but also in thrall to her theatrical father, at once a gadfly and a puritanical bully. The family lived a comfortable existence in a house in Cumberland Terrace, with a nursery at the top of the house "staid and traditional," according to Forster in her biography, *Daphne Du Maurier: The Secret Life of the Renowned Storyteller.* Forster went on to note, however, "downstairs was the ever-thrilling presence of Gerald, who would swoop and enfold [the three daughters] and draw them into his own exciting existence. He played marvelous imaginative games with them, read to them, took them with him to the theater, involved himself in their lives totally when he was with them, and they saw themselves blessed with such a father. As indeed, until adolescence, they were." Muriel Beaumont, however, was not included in such fun and games. "Poor darling M[other] was I a trial to her?" du Maurier wondered in her 1977 autobiographical sketch, *Myself When Young: The Shaping of a Writer.* "Never ill mannered, never rude, of that I am sure, but perhaps I made some unfortunate remark that caught her in an off mood. She was not an easy person to understand, both as a child and as a growing adolescent I could never feel quite sure of her, sensing some sort of disapproval in her attitude towards me. Could it be that, totally unconscious of the fact, she resented the ever growing bond and affection between [father] and myself?" Du Maurier went on to note that the child "who cannot rush to his or her mother in moments of stress, telling all, will look elsewhere for comfort, or become a loner."

In Daphne's case, the child sought comfort in her father's attention, in that of her maternal grandparents, and in the servants' hall below stairs at the sprawling Queen Anne house in fashionable Hampstead, where the family moved when Daphne was still a young girl. Also at this time and through her adolescence, Daphne began wishing she were born a boy, and as a teenager even took on a male persona, Eric Avon. Much has been made of this by some critics, such as Templeton, who posited this was the "awakening of lesbian tendencies," in the teenager. Others attribute it to a strong sense of gender inequality at the time and to her father's disappointment in not having a male heir to carry on the du Maurier name. But du Maurier seemed to have the usual schoolgirl crushes on both men and women. At fourteen she was strongly attracted to a

Joan Fontaine portrays the new bride of a country gentleman, played by Laurence Olivier, who is haunted by the memory of his first wife in Alfred Hitchcock's Oscar-winning film adaptation of du Maurier's best-selling novel *Rebecca*.

much older male cousin whom she met while on summer holiday at the seashore; at eighteen as a student at a finishing school near Paris, she was infatuated with one of the female teachers. An introspective youth, du Maurier felt that her sisters Angela and Jeanne were much more popular than she, always surrounded by friends and filled with fun. In fact, those around the young du Maurier felt that if she was alone, it was by her choice, for outwardly she was self-assured and quite attractive.

Throughout her adolescence and teenage years one other passion existed as well: writing. Du Maurier began writing light verse and short stories while still a student; her prose was strongly inspired by the work of Somerset Maugham. "All of these early works," according to Templeton, "are filled with disgust and pessimism concerning the human condition." During her time in France, from 1925 to 1926, du Maurier was influenced by the writings of

Katherine Mansfield and Guy de Maupassant, and continued her own writing in letters, journals, and short stories. Forster, writing in *Daphne du Maurier*, described three early short stories written by the nineteen-year-old as having "one striking thing in common: the male characters are thoroughly unpleasant. They are bullies, seducers and cheats. The women, in contrast, are pitifully weak creatures, who are endlessly dominated and betrayed, never capable of saving themselves and having only the energy to survive."

Returning to England in 1926, du Maurier took up writing in earnest, and when the family bought a home in the West country, in Cornwall, the young woman suddenly discovered a real sense of freedom and liberation from the endless social pressures of London. Here the women all seemed to live in pants and rubber boots, and the outdoor life suited du Maurier well. "Here was the freedom I desired, long sought-for, not yet known," du Maurier later wrote in *Myself When Young*. "Freedom to write, to walk, to wander, freedom to climb hills, to pull a boat, to be alone. . . . I remembered a line from a forgotten book, where a lover looks for the first time upon his chosen one—'I for this, and this for me.'" The house, Ferryside, in the village of Fowey on Cornwall's south coast, afforded du Maurier the opportunity to learn to live with the water, and she became proficient at handling a small boat on her own.

Increasingly, du Maurier spent more and more time in Cornwall, less and less in London. University was not, at the time, thought fashionable for a young woman of her standing, so du Maurier continued her own education, working daily on her writing and reading extensively. In addition, she was learning the ways and the lore of the people of Cornwall. In particular, she was learning about the history of Fowey and of the old Rashleigh family and their seat, Menabilly. Coming across that house one day, she immediately fell in love with it and formed an obsession that would last until she finally occupied it herself during the Second World War.

Desperate to become independent of her family's allowance, du Maurier holed herself up in Cornwall and began writing her first novel in late October, 1929. Inspired by a local family of boat builders whose history she had researched, her novel quickly took form as an historical romance. In ten weeks she had completed the manuscript titled *The Loving Spirit*, the story of Janet Coombe, a resourceful and courageous woman who fears the bonds of domesticity yet longs for the security of marriage. Once married, however, she finds that she is unable to tame her continual restlessness; she does, however, find fulfillment in her son, Joseph. He, like his mother, displays the Coombe spirit of the title. After Janet's death, the book continues to detail the lives of subsequent generations of the Coombe clan, with Joseph becoming captain of a ship built in his mother's honor, then focusing on Christopher, one of Joseph's sons, and finally, with Christopher's daughter, Jennifer.

Du Maurier had the book typed up and sent it off to an agent friend of the family who miraculously placed it with the publisher Heinemann only two months after she had finished the writing. The book did well upon publication, becoming something of a mini-best seller in England. A reviewer for the *Spectator* felt the work was "gracious," but also noted that "When Miss du Maurier gains firmer artistic control of her emotions, and ceases to write "literary" Cornish, her work will be admirable indeed." With publication in the United States, H. C. Harwood noted in the *Saturday Review* that *The Loving Spirit* "has the right stuff in it for which a better form may easily be found, by an author obviously possessing and enjoying a love of romantic fiction." "All in all, however, the reviews were favorable and predicted a bright future for the young novelist," noted Kelly in his critical study. "It would take a few more years for du Maurier to perfect her form." Kelly noted that du Maurier instinctively tapped into the need in her audience for fantasy and escape from reality, something that is supplied in overabundance in modern-day literature, but which at the time of du Maurier's first book was relatively new. Here was a new formula for novels: a romantic history for women—though not restricted to that audience alone—and written by a woman.

Even before publication of her first novel, du Maurier had completed her second, *I'll Never Be Young Again*, a novel, like many of hers, narrated by a man. Here the struggle is for Dick, who aspires to be a great writer, to break free of the control of his despised father, a famous poet. Later, in middle age, he realizes he does not have the stuff to become great and accepts his mediocrity. Published in 1932, this book was less successful mechanically, but, as Kelly remarked, it was "an important one in du Maurier's development as a writer, and it laid the groundwork for her next novel, *The Progress of Julius*," the first of her psychological thrillers.

Meanwhile du Maurier's personal life was also undergoing a revolution. Having lived something of a wild life as a young woman, in 1931 she met and three months later married Major Frederick Arthur Browning. Together the couple had three children, Tessa, Flavia, and Christian, and for the next twenty years the family followed the frequent moves of Browning, who eventually reached the rank of lieutenant general in the army. In 1934, du Maurier's father died at the relatively young age of sixty-one following an operation for cancer. Du Maurier's fourth book, *Gerald: A Portrait*, was a biography of her father.

This period of du Maurier's creative life is capped off with her fourth novel, *Jamaica Inn*, a "haunting tale," according to Kelly, set on Cornwall's Bodmin Moor in 1835 and featuring a strong, assertive heroine, Mary Yellan. This was the novel, according to Templeton in *Dictionary of Literary Biography*, that "finally persuaded the critics that [du Maurier] was a writer of talent." Templeton went on to describe the novel as a "tightly crafted Gothic horror story, much more quickly paced than her previous novels." *Jamaica Inn* was also a commercial success, selling in three months more copies than her previous three novels together.

Somewhat reminiscent of *Jane Eyre* and *Wuthering Heights,* the novel follows young Mary who, after the death of her mother, is sent to her aunt and uncle who run the isolated inn of the title. Here Mary falls under the spell of Jem, her uncle's brother, and also uncovers a Druidic cabal which includes her aunt, uncle, and the local vicar. The vicar masterminds a plot whereby passing ships are decoyed onto the rocks and then robbed. But when Mary's aunt and uncle are about to repent and go to the police, the mad vicar kills them. In turn, the vicar is murdered by the enigmatic Jem. "The novel's strength," according to Templeton, "derives not so much from this plot as from the vivid characters and the dramatic landscape." Reviewing the novel in the *Spectator,* the writer Sean O'Faolain commented, "*Jamaica Inn* [makes] one realise how high the standard of entertainment has become in the modern novel. I do not believe R. L. Stevenson would have been ashamed to have written [it]. . . ." So popular was the novel that Alfred Hitchcock turned it into a film version several years later, securing du Maurier's name and reputation.

Rebecca

As usual, du Maurier did not rest on her laurels but started a new book. Posted in Alexandria, Egypt with her husband, she started a fifth novel in 1936, one with which her name would thereafter become almost synonymous. Beginning with the famous opening sentence, "Last night I dreamt I went to Manderley again," the novel *Rebecca* plumbs fully the genre of Gothic romance. The manuscript was eventually finished once du Maurier and her husband returned to England and was published in 1938.

The novel, something of an updated Cinderella story, tells of a working-class woman who falls in love with the lonely and mysterious Maxim de Winter, whom she meets in Monte Carlo while in the service of a rather gauche old social climber. The aristocratic Maxim is recently widowed and the two fall in love and are soon married, much to the surprise and disgust of the old woman upon whom the heroine was dependent. Now the second Mrs. De Winter, the young woman returns with Maxim to his family mansion, Manderley, in the south of England. Once there, however, the nameless heroine of the novel finds that she is forever in the shadow of the first wife, Rebecca, and that the malevolent housekeeper, Mrs. Danvers, wants only to protect the memory of this dead woman. Jealousy grips the new mistress of the house, but finally the bride discovers that such jealousy is unnecessary: Maxim in fact hated his wayward first wife and indeed may have killed her. Now Rebecca's miscreant cousin, Favell, is blackmailing Maxim, who is finally charged with Rebecca's murder. At the last minute, new evidence comes up that exonerates him at trial, but there is no happy homecoming, for Mrs. Danvers burns Manderley down to avenge her beloved Rebecca. Yet for Maxim and his new wife, this is a blessing in disguise; they are now free to start their life together anew.

This tale with, its echoes of Charlotte and Emily Bronte, was an instant success throughout the English-speaking world and remains in print over sixty years after its initial publication. The novel had 45,000 copies in print just a month after publication in England and has run to forty-two printings and sold in the millions worldwide. Reviewing the novel in the *Christian Science Monitor,* the English writer V. S. Pritchett set the tone for the critical response to most of du Maurier's best work. One the one hand, the critic praised the novel: "Many a better novelist would give his eyes to be able to tell a story as Miss du Maurier does, to make it move at such a pace and to go with such mastery from surprise to surprise. . . . From the first sinister rumors to the final conflagration the melodrama is excellent." But "melodrama" is the operative word here. Pritchett went on to complain about the "very morbid side to this apparently harmless fairy tale," and also to point out the "crude unreality of the tale." Many of the other reviews at the time replicated this left-handed praise. A reviewer for the *Times Literary Supplement,* for example, also noted, "The conventions of a story of this kind are not the conventions of the so-called realistic novel, and it would be absurd to reproach Miss du Maurier for her fine, careless rapture. In its kind, *Rebecca* is extraordinarily bold and confident, eloquent and accomplished to a degree that merits genuine respect." This reviewer's insistence on the phrase "of its kind" again is operative here; the same writer further called *Rebecca* "dope literature" in comparison with Tolstoy or Proust. As Kelly pointed out, "The assumed canon of literary saints, the snobbery, and the sexism that lie behind these reviews are fairly common features of the male literati that ruled the journals and newspapers during the past hundred years and that, to this day, have denied du Maurier her proper place in modern European and American culture. . . ."

The film version of *Rebecca*, starring Joan Fontaine and Lawrence Olivier, won Academy Awards for best picture and for cinematography in 1940, further popularizing both the novel and its author. Writing in *The Rebecca Notebook and Other Memories* over forty years after publication of *Rebecca*, du Maurier was still trying to figure out why it was such a success: "Although I had then written four previous novels. . . . the story of Rebecca became an instant favourite with readers in the United Kingdom, North America, and Europe. Why, I have never understood! It is true that as I wrote it I immersed myself in the characters, especially in the narrator, but then this has happened throughout my writing career; I lose myself in the plot as it unfolds, and only when the book is finished do I lay it aside. I may add, finally and forever." Writing in *Books*, not long after publication of *Rebecca*, John Patton attributed the novel's success to the fact that it was, "first and last and always a thrilling story." Patton further commented, "Du Maurier's style in telling her story is exactly suited to her plot and her background, and creates the exact spirit and atmosphere of the novel. The rhythm quickens with the story, is always in measure with the story's beat. And the writing has an intensity, a heady beauty, which is itself the utterance of the story's mood." Whatever the reason for its tremendous success, the fact is that the book has enjoyed very robust health with both the reading public and viewers: there was a remake for a television mini-series in 1979. As Kelly concluded, "*Rebecca* is the classic gothic romance of the twentieth century and as such will be around long after the high priests and priestesses of the current literary establishment have perished."

A Quartet of Romantic Suspense Novels

Du Maurier basked in the delight of her sudden fame for a time, and then went back to what she knew best, writing. *Frenchman's Creek* was published in 1941, *My Cousin Rachel* in 1951, *The Scapegoat* in 1957, and *Flight of the Falcon* in 1965. According to Jane S. Bakerman, writing in *And Then There Were Nine . . . More Women of Mystery*, these books are, in addition to *Jamaica Inn* and *Rebecca*, the six novels on which du Maurier's "auctorial reputation rests most firmly." There were certainly a bevy of others, including *The King's General*, *Hungry Hill*, and *The House on the Strand*, but the core of her work can be seen in these six.

Schoolchildren run for their lives as thousands of birds attack them in this 1963 Hitchcock film version of du Maurier's terrifying short story "The Birds."

The war, which began in 1939, did not stop du Maurier's output. She did her part, yet still found time for her fiction. *Frenchman's Creek* is, according to Templeton, "a dark tale of Cornwall during the reign of Charles II." With the protagonist, Lady St. Columb, du Maurier presents another female caught between the twin poles of a desire for independence and a need for domestic security. The Lady leaves her husband for a French rogue who has, himself, fled domestic non-bliss and temporarily turned pirate. Though Lady St. Columb does return to her husband in the end, her relationship with the genial scoundrel, Jean-Benoit Aubrey, allows her to explore her duality—her "boy in the box" as du Maurier called the same notion in herself. It was the sense that another, male and stronger, self was buried deep within. "As with du Maurier's best works in this genre," commented Templeton, "*Frenchman's Creek* is enlivened by a dramatic landscape and the avoidance of stereotypes." Another popular novel like *Rebecca*, film rights to *Frenchman's Creek* were purchased and a movie came out during the war, in 1944.

In 1943 a dream of nearly two decades was fulfilled when du Maurier and her children moved into Menabilly, leased from the Rashleigh family for twenty years. The lease was ultimately extended and du Maurier much improved the place at her own expense, but in the late 1960s she was forced to move when one of the Rashleigh heirs chose to live there. Du Maurier was made Lady Browning in 1946 when her husband was knighted, and after the war Browning became comptroller of the treasurer to the then Princess Elizabeth, a position that kept him in London most of the time, with only infrequent trips home to Cornwall.

In 1943 du Maurier published *Hungry Hill*, a dynastic saga and one of her least successful novels, filmed for a movie in 1947 with a screenplay co-authored by du Maurier. This was followed in 1946 by *The King's General*, memorable, according to Kelly, for its female protagonist, Honor Harris, one of du Maurier's new "independent and fearless" heroines, and in 1949 by *The Parasites*, a semi-autobiographical novel that deals with a theatrical family and their art-minded children. Out of the usual du Maurier mold, *The Parasites* did not do well critically.

Du Maurier revived her plucky-heroine formula for a book that outsold even *Rebecca* at the time, *My Cousin Rachel*. Narrated by the insecure orphan, Philip Ashley, the story tells a sort of gender-switch gothic tale in which Philip's guardian and cousin, Ambrose Ashley, on vacation in Italy, falls in love with and marries their mutual cousin, Rachel, whose husband has recently died. Appraised of the wedding in Italy, Philip is at first jealous. But when cousin Ambrose urges him to come to Italy, Philip rushes to his guardian, fearful for his life at the hands of Rachel, only to find him dead of a supposed brain tumor. Cousin Rachel is nowhere to be found initially, and Philip vows revenge. When they meet, Philip falls in love with her. Playing a deadly double game, he tries to find out if he will be her next victim, but instead Rachel herself is the next to die, and the end of the novel comes with the reader not knowing if the mysterious Rachel is guilty or not of Ambrose's death. Filmed in 1952, the resulting movie version of *My Cousin Rachel* starred Richard Burton and Olivia de Haviland.

In the 1954 novel, *Mary Anne*, du Maurier wrote a fictionalized portrait of her great-great grandmother, and in 1957 she published *The Scapegoat*, a novel that dealt more directly with the doppelganger theme that crops up throughout du Maurier's fiction. In this case, two men, doubles for each other physically, trade places. John, a history teacher doing research in France, takes the place of Jean de Gue, whom he meets in Le Mans. Over drinks, it is de Gue who proposes the switch and before John can agree or disagree, he passes out. When he awakens in the morning, he finds himself in de Gue's dysfunctional home. There is a mother addicted to morphine, a suicidal daughter and wife, and himself up to his elbows in trouble for having murdered his sister's fiance. Reluctant at first, John soon takes on his new role of Jean with verve, working to save the family business and give meaning to the lives of those around him. When the real Jean de Gue writes that he is coming back, John realizes that he does not want to trade places. He waits for his double with a gun, but is thwarted in his murder attempt by a priest. John reluctantly leaves this new life, but cannot return to the old. As the novel ends, John is driving toward a monastery.

Reviewing the novel in the *New York Times Book Review*, Anthony Boucher remarked, "The concept of the impostor . . . is one of the most absorbing premises in fiction; and Miss du Maurier's John . . . joins a succession of great maskers. . . ." Boucher went on to describe the book as "a mystery novel plus," and one that gives "a subtly disturbing Pirandellian hint that truth may be simply what it seems to you." This novel was also filmed, starring Alec Guinness and Betty Davis.

With his retirement in 1959, Browning came to live full time once again with his wife at Menabilly. He died in 1965. In 1969, du Maurier was honored by being named a Dame Commander of the Order of the British Empire. That same year she was forced to move to another house, Kilmarth, only half a mile distant from her beloved Menabilly.

Du Maurier novels from the 1960s include *The Glassblowers*, a book that traces her own family line back to an eighteenth-century family of glassblowers, and *The House on the Strand*. This novel deals with time travel and the powers of hallucinogenic drugs in which a twentieth-century narrator finds himself in the fourteenth century after taking an experimental drug. There he falls in love with Isolda. *The Flight of the Falcon* was published in 1965 and is, as Templeton described it, "a nightmarish tale of the quest for power" and "one of du Maurier's most psychologically complex novels." Armino Fabbio is an Italian tour guide in this novel in which "[I]llusion and reality, fiction and fact . . . blend together," according to Kelly. In flashbacks, Armino remembers and researches his long dead brother Aldo, a mysterious blend of both good and evil, who loved to dominate both men and women. He identified himself with a fifteenth-century duke called the Falcon who threw

Nicholas Roeg directed *Don't Look Now,* a 1973 psychological thriller based on du Maurier's short story of the same name.

himself from the walls of his castle believing that he was the son of God and could therefore fly. Armino, in the present, attempts to unravel the real story of his brother, and as he does, the novel takes on "the form of a mystery," according to Kelly. But suddenly Armino is confronted with a living Aldo, returned as it were, from the dead, and now leading a small band of disaffected students. In the culminating scene, Aldo straps on a set of wings and dives to his death from a tower, just as his historical alter ego had done. Armino is left to pick up the scattered remnants of his life and find a meaning in the present.

The critics took particular glee in pillorying *The Flight of the Falcon.* Patricia MacManus, writing in *Book Week,* called the book a "little fire-sale item" in du Maurier's "brand name . . . popular fiction field," while a reviewer for the *New Yorker* called it an "extraordinarily dull book." However Kelly pointed out that it was difficult to understand the critics. They "fell for the superficial psychology of a basically conventional, sentimental novel like *The Scapegoat,*" while they "chose to ignore the complex and compelling study of a demonic mind and of an insane quest for power and sexual domination in

The Flight of the Falcon." As Kelly noted, this novel "explores the theme of lost innocence."

Du Maurier's final novel, *Rule Britannia,* published in 1972, is a story of the American invasion of England and the resistance put up by the Cornish people. Much below the par of her usual entertainments, the book was panned by most critics. Templeton, for example, dismissed it as a "jingoistic satire," while Joseph Kanon, writing in the *Saturday Review,* called it "a slight piece of writing so ephemeral that it defies categories."

The Short Stories and Beyond

As has been noted, many critics believe that du Maurier's best work is to be found in her short fiction, in such collections as *The Apple Tree, The Breaking Point,* and *Not after Midnight and Other Stories.* From the first volume is the story "The Birds," about a small town attacked by thousands of birds. This story was filmed by Hitchcock for the popular 1963 movie of the same title. Reviewing the first collection of stories, republished as *Kiss Me Again, Stranger,* John Barkham noted in the *New York Times Book Review* that du Maurier "is a firm believer in keeping her readers on tenterhooks," and that "The Birds" was a "hair-raising battle against the winged warriors that darken the sky." Other notable stories from the same collection include "The Motive" and the title story, "Kiss Me Again, Stranger." The collection "explores horror in a variety of forms," according to Sylvia Berkman, reviewing *Kiss Me Again, Stranger* in the *New York Herald Tribune Book World:* "in the macabre, in the psychologically deranged, in the supernatural, in the fantastic, [and] most painfully of all, in the sheer cruelty of human beings in interrelationship." Berkman also praised du Maurier for her "sense of shock-timing" which is "exceptionally skilled." Forster, writing in her biography, *Daphne Du Maurier,* pointed out that the novella included in the collection, "Monte Verita," was a statement by du Maurier of the belief that "there is something wrong with sex between men and women—it spoils relationships, it drains energy, it gets in the way of self-fulfillment." For Forster, this story was one more clue to what she saw as du Maurier's "secret life" of bisexuality if not lesbianism.

Du Maurier's third major collection of stories was published in the United States as *Don't Look Now,* after its title story, adapted for a successful and quite terrifying film in 1973, starring Julie Christie and Donald Sutherland. John and Laura, an English couple, are vacationing in Venice in an attempt to

If you enjoy the works of Daphne du Maurier, you might want to check out the following books and films:

Jonathan Aycliffe, *Naomi's Room,* 1992.
Robert Bloch, *American Gothic,* 1974.
Stephen King, *Rose Madder,* 1995.
The Shining, a film starring Jack Nicholson, 1980.

distract themselves from the grief at the loss of their daughter, Christine, who drowned. However, their vacation is anything but restful. John is plagued by the continual image of a small figure dressed in a red coat who he becomes convinced is his daughter. His wife Laura, meanwhile, has befriended a couple of elderly sisters who are equally convinced that they have made contact with the dead Christine who says her parents are in grave danger and must leave Venice immediately. John, however, ignores this warning and finally is able to corner the figure in red, which turns out to be a deranged dwarf on a killing spree, and who kills John by slashing his throat. Kelly noted that the "gothic setting of decaying Venice, the mad dwarf, the recurring glimpses into the future, the suspense, and the violence all go to make up an exciting story." Kelly also drew attention to "A Border-Line Case," another story in the same collection, "a curious story of romantic incest," as he described it, as well as to "The Rendezvous," from the 1980 collection of previously published short stories, *The Rendezvous and Other Stories.* In this tale, an older writer falls in love with a beautiful young woman only to be tormented by the fact of her love for a sexually attractive but vacuous young man.

Du Maurier wrote mostly nonfiction in her last years, including a work on the Brontes, a biography of Francis Bacon, and books about Cornwall, in addition to autobiographical pieces. She died at her home, Kilmarth, on April 19, 1989, and her death was met with tributes from around the world. A critical reassessment of her work followed not long thereafter. One example of such a renewed look at du Maurier comes in the introduction to Avril Horner's and Sue Zlosnik's 1998 study, *Daphne du Maurier: Writing, Identity and the Gothic Imagination.* The authors wrote: "Daphne du Maurier's public identity as a romantic novelist and a story-teller who can spin a good yarn has eclipsed for too long her versatility as a writer. In her published works,

which span the years 1931 to 1989, she experimented with several genres including the family saga, biography, women's romantic fiction, the Gothic novel, and the short story."

For too long, du Maurier was considered to be merely the precursor, if not founder of women's romantic fiction, which now burdens the racks at supermarkets. "Perhaps du Maurier wrote too much," remarked Kelly, "catered too cynically to the popular taste of her audience, but she created the classic gothic novel of the twentieth century, setting the state for hundreds of imitators." This in itself is no mean feat. Robert Louis Stevenson once noted, "The great creative writer shows us the realization and the apotheosis of the day-dreams of common men. His stories may be nourished with the realities of life, but their true mark is to satisfy the nameless longings of the reader, and to obey the ideal laws of the day-dream." By those criteria, du Maurier is a master. As Forster concluded in her biography, "[Du Maurier's] novels and stories gave pleasure to millions, and among them were at least three worthy of a place in the literary canon. . . . It was the fire of her imagination which warmed and excited her millions of readers, and still does."

■ Works Cited

Auerbach, Nina, *Daphne du Maurier: Haunted Heiress,* University of Pennsylvania Press, 2000, p. 1.

Bakerman, Jane S., "Daphne du Maurier," *And Then There Were Nine . . . More Women of Mystery,* Bowling Green State University Press, 1985, pp. 12-29.

Barkham, John, "The Macabre and the Unexpected," *New York Times Book Review,* March 8, 1953, p. 5.

Berkman, Sylvia, "A Skilled Hand Weaves a Net of Terror," *New York Tribune Book Review,* March 15, 1993, p. 4.

Boucher, Anthony, "Another Man's Life," *New York Times Book Review,* February 24, 1957, pp. 5, 26.

Conroy, Sarah Booth, "Daphne du Maurier's Legacy of Dreams," *Washington Post,* April 23, 1989, pp. F1, F8.

du Maurier, Daphne, *Rebecca,* Avon, 1971, p. 1.

du Maurier, Daphne, *Myself When Young: The Shaping of a Writer,* Doubleday, 1977.

du Maurier, Daphne, *The Rebecca Notebook and Other Memories,* Doubleday, 1980.

Review of *Flight of the Falcon, New Yorker,* July 17, 1965, p. 108.

Forster, Margaret, "Queen of Menacing Romance," *Sunday Times,* April 23, 1989, p. G8.

Forster, Margaret, *Daphne du Maurier: The Secret Life of the Renowned Storyteller,* Doubleday, 1993, pp. 7-8, 42, 207, 416.

Harwood, H. C., "New Novels," *Saturday Review,* February 28, 1931, p. 311.

Horner, Avril, and Sue Zlosnik, *Daphne du Maurier: Writing, Identity and the Gothic Imagination,* St. Martin's Press, 1998, p. 1.

Hurley, Margaret, "Behind the Curtain," *Saturday Review,* November 7, 1959, p. 23.

Kanon, Joseph, review of *Rule Britannia, Saturday Review,* January, 1973, p. 85.

Kelly, Richard, *Daphne du Maurier,* Twayne, 1987, pp. 108, 112, 133, 142-43.

Review of *The Loving Spirit, Spectator,* February 28, 1931, p. 320.

MacManus, Patricia, "Starting a Flap," *Book Week,* July 11, 1965, p. 18.

"Obituary of Daphne du Maurier," *Times,* April 20, 1989.

O'Faolain, Sean, "New Novels," *Spectator,* January 24, 1936, p. 144.

Patton, John, review of *Rebecca, Books,* September 25, 1938.

Pritchett, V. S., "Daphne du Maurier Writes a Victorian Thriller," *Christian Science Monitor,* September 14, 1938, p. 12.

Raymond, John, review of *My Cousin Rachel, New Statesman,* August 11, 1951.

Stevenson, Robert Louis, "A Gossip on Romance," *Memoirs and Portraits,* Scribner's, 1900, p. 255.

"Survival," *Times Literary Supplement,* August 6, 1938, p. 517.

Templeton, Wayne, "Daphne du Maurier," *Dictionary of Literary Biography,* Volume 191: *British Novelists Between the Wars,* Gale, 1998, pp. 84-94.

■ For More Information See

BOOKS

Contemporary Literary Criticism, Gale, Volume 6, 1976, Volume 11, 1979.

Cook, Judith, *Daphne: A Portrait of Daphne du Maurier,* Bantam, 1991.

Leng, Flavia, *Daphne du Maurier: A Daughter's Memoir,* Mainstream Publishing (Edinburgh), 1994.

Shallcross, Martyn, *The Private World of Daphne du Maurier,* Robson, 1991.

Short Story Criticism, Volume 18, Gale, 1995, pp. 124-39.

PERIODICALS

Atlantic, April 1942.
Best Sellers, May 1, 1963; October 15, 1969.

Books, August 2, 1931; February 1, 1942.
Books and Bookmen, January 1973.
Canadian Forum, October 1938.
Chicago Tribune Book World, September 21, 1980.
Christian Science Monitor, September 14, 1938; October 2, 1969; September 21, 1977.
Commonweal, April 10, 1942.
Critic, September 1978.
Detroit News, November 13, 1977.
Feminist Review, Summer, 1996, pp. 95-106.
Ladies' Home Journal, November 1956.
Life, September 11, 1944; February 6, 1970.
Listener, June 9, 1977.
Los Angeles Times, October 3, 1980.
Manchester Guardian, January 10, 1936; August 5, 1938; September 19, 1941; August 3, 1951.
Nation, November 11, 1931.
New Statesman and Nation, March 14, 1931; August 11, 1951.
Newsweek, September 26, 1938; January 9, 1950; June 24, 1954.
New Yorker, February 7, 1942; February 9, 1952; September 23, 1967.
New York Herald Tribune Book Review, February 10, 1952.
New York Times, August 2, 1931; April 26, 1936; September 25, 1938; February 1, 1942; February 10, 1952.
New York Times Book Review, October 26, 1969; October 17, 1971, pp. 56-57; November 6, 1977; September 21, 1980.
Observer (London), July 16, 1967.
Outlook, August 5, 1931.
Poetics Today, Summer, 1993, pp. 285-308.
Publishers Weekly, February 18, 1939; January 31, 1948.
Saturday Review, April 24, 1937; September 24, 1938; June 19, 1943; January 12, 1946; February 7, 1948; January 7, 1950; February 9, 1952; July 19, 1952; March 14, 1953; February 23, 1957; October 11, 1969.
Saturday Review of Literature, December 12, 1931; April 25, 1936; September 24, 1938; February 14, 1942.
Science Fiction Chronicle, February, 1988, p. 42.
Sight and Sound, May, 1996, pp. 29-31.
Spectator, August 12, 1938; September 19, 1941; August 10, 1951; May 14, 1977; November 15, 1980.
Springfield Republican, January 11, 1942.
Theatre Arts, March 1945.
Time, November 3, 1947; January 16, 1950; February 11, 1952; June 21, 1954; February 25, 1957; February 23, 1962.

Times Literary Supplement, March 5, 1931; January 11, 1936; September 13, 1941; June 3, 1977; December 26, 1980.
Washington Post Book World, December 27, 1987, p. 8.

■ Obituaries

PERIODICALS

Chicago Tribune, April 20, 1989.
Los Angeles Times, April 20, 1989, pp. 3, 24.
New York Times, April 20, 1989, p. B13.
Washington Post, April 20, 1989.*

—Sketch by J. Sydney Jones

Susan Fletcher

■ Personal

Born May 28, 1951, in Pasadena, CA; daughter of Leland (an engineer) and Reba (a teacher; maiden name, Montgomery) Clemens; married Jerry Fletcher (a marketing consultant), June 4, 1977; children: Kelly. *Education:* University of California, Santa Barbara, B.A. (with honors), 1973; University of Michigan, M.A., 1974.

■ Addresses

Home and office—17387 Canyon Dr., Lake Oswego, OR 97034. *Agent*—Emilie Jacobson, Curtis Brown Ltd., 10 Astor Place, New York, NY 10003.

■ Career

Writer. Campbell-Mithun (advertising agency), Minneapolis, MN, and Denver, CO, media buyer, 1974-77, advertising copywriter, 1977-79; Portland Community College, Portland, OR, lecturer, 1988-90.

■ Member

Society of Children's Book Writers and Illustrators-Northwest, Authors Guild, Phi Beta Kappa.

■ Awards, Honors

Oregon Book Award, 1990, Young Adults' Choice, International Reading Association (IRA), 1991, Young Readers' Choice nomination, Pacific Northwest Library Association, 1992, and South Carolina Young Adult Book Award nomination, 1992-93, all for *Dragon's Milk;* International Youth Library Selection, 1992, for *The Stuttgart Nanny Mafia;* Outstanding Book of 1993, *World Book Encyclopedia* Annual Supplement, 1994, finalist, Oregon Book Award, 1994, Best Books for Young Adults, American Library Association (ALA), 1995, Young Adults' Choice, IRA, 1995, Sequoyah Award nomination, 1995-96, and Texas Lone Star Reading List, 1996-97, all for *Flight of the Dragon Kyn;* Best Books, *School Library Journal,* 1998, Blue Ribbon award, *Bulletin of the Center for Children's Books,* 1998, Children's Literature Choice List, 1999, Pennsylvania Young Readers' Choice nomination, and Dorothy Canfield Fisher Award nomination, both 1999-2000, and Notable Books for Older Readers, ALA, Best Books for Young Adults, ALA, Notable Children's Trade Book in the Field of Social Studies, National Council on the Social Studies and Children's Book Council, and Junior Library Guild Selection, all for *Shadow Spinner;* Sequoyah Award nomination, 1998-99, for *Sign of the Dove.*

■ Writings

NOVELS

The Haunting Possibility (mystery), Crosswinds, 1988.

The Stuttgart Nanny Mafia, Atheneum, 1991.
Shadow Spinner, Atheneum, 1998.

FANTASY NOVELS

Dragon's Milk, Atheneum, 1989.
Flight of the Dragon Kyn (prequel to *Dragon's Milk*),
    Atheneum, 1993.
Sign of the Dove, Atheneum, 1996.

OTHER

Contributor to periodicals, including *Ms., Woman's
    Day, Family Circle*, and *Mademoiselle*.

■ Sidelights

Susan Fletcher is the author of a popular trilogy that
includes the books *Dragon's Milk, Flight of the Dragon
Kyn*, and *Sign of the Dove*, as well as of several other
novels for young readers. With a medieval setting
inspired by pictures of the Welsh countryside from
where Fletcher traces her roots, the trilogy features
Fletcher's imaginative, dragon-centered plots,
which have won praise from reviewers and readers
alike. Calling 1993's *Flight of the Dragon Kyn* "a joy to
read," *Booklist* contributor Deborah Abbott added:
"Fletcher pens some of the best yarns around."

Born in Pasadena, California, in 1951, Fletcher and
her family moved to Ohio when she was seven
years old. She had dreamed of being a writer ever
since she entered the third grade. "Back then my
name was Susan Clemens," she once explained.
"One day my teacher told us about a famous author
named Mark Twain, whose real name was Samuel
Clemens, whose daughter's name was Susan. It was
fate, I thought. I decided not to become the daughter of a famous author (which is impossible to
arrange), but to become a famous author myself
(which is difficult enough)."

Returning to California in sixth grade, Fletcher graduated from high school in 1969, having spent her
senior year as fiction editor of her school's literary
magazine. She enrolled at the University of California at Santa Barbara and earned her bachelor's
degree in English. She then moved to Michigan,
where she earned her master's degree in English
from the University of Michigan. Moving again to
Colorado, Fletcher got a job with a local advertising
agency and met her soon-to-be husband, Jerry; they
were married in June of 1977. Moving again, this
time to Minneapolis, Minnesota, she put her writing
talent to work creating copy for radio advertise-
ments, which she enjoyed and was good at. When

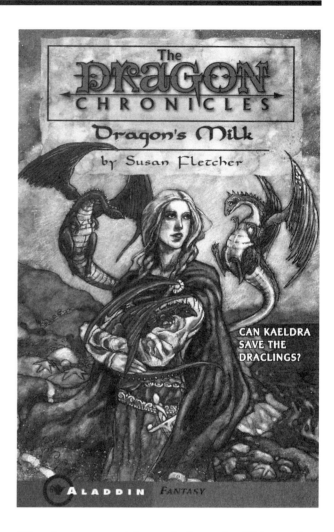

When her younger sister needs dragon's milk to cure her
illness, Kaeldra uses her special ability to communicate
with dragons to help.

her husband relocated to Portland, Oregon, Fletcher
planned to look for a similar position, but those
plans changed when she discovered that she and her
husband would soon be having a child. Magazine
writing became her new focus—it was something
Fletcher could do from home—and from there it was
a short step to becoming a children's book writer.

Fletcher's first novel for young readers, 1988's *The
Haunting Possibility*, was inspired by Oregon's Lake
Oswego area and the practice of draining the lake
each winter to allow dock repairs to be made. Learning the nuances of characterization and plotting as
she went, Fletcher completed the manuscript and sent
it to almost twenty publishers before it was accepted.
She quickly involved herself in a local group of children's writers, meeting several editors and gaining
constructive criticism of her work in the process.

The "Dragon" Books

In an essay published in *Something about the Author Autobiography Series* (*SAAS*), Fletcher recalled how the seed of her "Dragon" novels was planted: "While I was sending out *The Haunting Possibility*, an idea began to tease at the edges of my mind. . . . [The town librarian] had directed me to some really fine fantasy novels for children, and I began to be drawn to that genre." Fletcher also chose to write fantasy fiction because she was troubled by the portrayal of female protagonists in the fairy tales she had read as a child. As she put it, "the typical fairy-tale heroine would sit around being beautiful, singing nicely, and being kind to birds and animals until her boyfriend—The Prince—came along and solved all her problems for her." That type of character was not one Fletcher cared to perpetuate, and she set out to write fantasy fiction in response to the fairy-tale genre. "I decided to write a story about a girl who had the courage to solve her own problems," she explained. Thinking back to her own early teens, she discovered one task in particular that required extraordinary amounts of courage, fortitude, bravery, patience, and just plain hard work: babysitting the La Rue kids, a group of four unruly boys that lived down the street from her when she was young.

Originally intended as a feminist fairy tale, *Dragon's Milk* revolves around a baby-sitting adventure that takes place in a fantasy kingdom called Elythia. Kaeldra, the protagonist, is an adopted child whose emerald-green eyes identify her as a descendent of the dragon-sayers, humans who are able to communicate with the fire-breathers telepathically. When her younger sister, Lyf, becomes ill with a fever and can only be made well again by drinking dragon's milk, Kaeldra must search for a dragon. She finds one and agrees to babysit for its three offspring, called draclings, in exchange for the milk. The mother goes out to find food, planning to return in a short while; unfortunately, she is killed, leaving Kaeldra to protect the draclings from men who want to destroy them.

Critics found *Dragon's Milk* entertaining and imaginative. Focusing on the novel's blend of action, suspense, magic, and romance, they also noted Fletcher's clever and convincing portrayal of the young dragons. "The three draclings, each with an individual personality, are endearing in the clumsy way of young animals," noted *School Library Journal* contributor Susan M. Harding, concluding that "with its satisfying heroine, [*Dragon's Milk*] is a thoroughly enjoyable story."

After she lures several dragons out of the sky for King Orrik, fifteen-year-old Kara learns that the king intends to kill them in this 1993 fantasy.

The story of the dragons continues in *Sign of the Dove,* as the last of the dragon's eggs begins to hatch. Healed with dragons' milk as a child, Lyf's eyes have since turned green, and she is now being sought, along with other green-eyes, by those who would use her power to call dragons for evil. While taking flight with Kaeldra, Kaeldra's husband Jeorg, and three dragon hatchlings, Lyf soon finds herself alone and in charge of the draclings, who get stronger and more curious with each passing day. Although not enthusiastic about her role as protector, Lyf—now a young teen—attempts to save the dragons from enemies who would kill them for their hearts, which are rumored to have healing powers. *Booklist* contributor Sally Estes praised the book as "a rousing story filled with well-realized dragon lore."

"As [Lyf] struggles to save the . . . draclings, always hungry and always mischievous, she grows in competence and independence," according to *Horn Book* contributor Ann A. Flowers. Because of the transformation of its heroine, *Sign of the Dove* is a very personal statement for its author. In 1989 Fletcher was diagnosed with cancer, and fought the disease for a year before receiving a clean bill of health. While she found it impossible to write about her feelings as she confronted the possibility of losing the battle against cancer, those feelings found their way into her fiction in another way. "During the time when I was writing *Sign of the Dove*," she recalled in *SAAS*, "I heard a Jewish couple speaking about the people who helped the German Jews during the Holocaust. . . . Suddenly, I realized that the book I was writing was about rescuers—people who help those who are in trouble, at risk to themselves and with no expectation of gain. On some level, it was about the people who helped *me*. And so the book is dedicated to them—my rescuers."

The background to both *Dragon's Milk* and *Sign of the Dove* is laid out in *Flight of the Dragon Kyn*. In the novel, fifteen-year-old Kara, who has a natural gift for calling down birds from the sky, is called before King Orrik and asked to work her power to bring certain dragons to ground. Birds and dragons are rumored to be close relatives, and these particular dragons have been laying waste to the kingdom of Kragland and are held responsible for the deaths of both the father and brother of the king's future wife, Princess Signy. Aided by Skava, a wild gyrfalcon, Kara sets out on her quest, realizing too late that she is calling the dragons to their death at the hand of the king. Also, by helping King Orrik, Kara gets on the wrong side of the king's brother Rog, who has designs of his own on the kingdom. Fleeing to the hills, she takes refuge with a dragon "kyn," or family, and helps them find a home far from human unkindness.

Calling *Flight of the Dragon Kyn* "a solid fantasy in a medieval . . . setting," Kathryn Jennings added in a review for *Bulletin of the Center for Children's Books* that "there's plenty of drama, romance, and knavery to keep genre fans happy." Joyce W. Yen agreed in her *Voice of Youth Advocates* appraisal of the book, praising Fletcher's incorporation of "a budding romance, an inner struggle, and a power struggle" into "an intriguing novel" full of interesting characters. In fact, one of these characters required Fletcher to do her homework; in preparation for writing *Flight of the Dragon Kyn*, Fletcher volunteered at a local zoo and learned the habits of birds of prey— their sleeping patterns, what they eat, their social behaviors. Thus she was able to fully realize a character that *School Library Journal* contributor Margaret

In this final book of the "Dragon Chronicles," Lyf embarks on a dangerous and important journey in order to save three dragons from certain death.

A. Chang cites among the book's "most engaging": the gyrfalcon Skava.

Pens Suspense Novels

In addition to her fantasy novels, Fletcher has written several other suspenseful books that appeal to teen readers. In *The Stuttgart Nanny Mafia*, published in 1991, Aurora MacKenzie tries every trick under the sun to get Tanja, her nineteen-year-old au pair, fired and sent packing back to Germany, thus opening the way for Aurora and her mother to spend more quality time together, away from her mother's new husband and new baby. Praised by *Booklist* contributor Deborah Abbott for highlighting the emotions of stepchildren "pushed out by new family members and having to cope with the dynamics of a changed situation," *The Stuttgart Nanny Mafia* is similar to *Dragon's Milk* and *Sign of*

If you enjoy the works of Susan Fletcher, you might want to check out the following books and films:

Andre Norton, *Beast Master*, 1959.
Vivian Vande Velde, *Dragon's Bait*, 1992.
Patricia C. Wrede, *Dealing with Dragons*, 1990.
Dragonheart, a film starring Dennis Quaid and Sean Connery, 1996.

---

the Dove in that its roots are in Fletcher's own experience. As she would later note in *SAAS:* "Bits of [my daughter Kelly's] life sometimes make their way into my books. After reading parts of *The Stuttgart Nanny Mafia*, Kelly protested, "Mom, you plagiarized my life!""

In her 1998 book *Shadow Spinner*, Fletcher provides an explanation for the amazing wealth of tales amassed by famous Persian storyteller Shahrazad in *1001 Arabian Nights*. In Fletcher's imaginative novel, a crippled orphan named Marjan, handmaiden to the princess Shahrazad, becomes the source for many of the tales used by her mistress to postpone her death. Noting that the story is a fictional take on a traditional tale, *Horn Book* reviewer Mary M. Burns asserted that "Fletcher puts her own spin on the source material, telling a tale in which the pace is consistent, the characters interesting, and the plot impelling." *Booklist* contributor Hazel Rochman praised, in particular, Fletcher's preface to each of the book's chapters, "about how we find ourselves in our stories, how sharing stories brings strangers together." And Patricia A. Dollisch, writing in *School Library Journal*, declared that "there are no weak spots in the telling of this tale. Even the minor characters make real impressions. The voices are clear and the dialogue works beautifully . . . [but] it is the structure that really makes this book sing."

Fletcher writes her books for young readers from an office inside her Oregon home. Her books are created in several stages. First comes research, followed by a first, sometimes very rough, draft—"I allow myself to write really badly at first if I need too," she admitted in *SAAS*. Several other drafts will follow

until the words "sound right." Fletcher also benefits from her editor and critique group, but, as she once stated, "my own inner ear is the final test."

■ Works Cited

Abbott, Deborah, review of *Flight of the Dragon Kyn*, *Booklist*, January 15, 1994, p. 931.

Abbott, Deborah, review of *The Stuttgart Nanny Mafia*, *Booklist*, December 15, 1991, pp. 764-65.

Burns, Mary M., review of *Shadow Spinner*, *Horn Book*, July, 1998, p. 488.

Chang, Margaret A., review of *Flight of the Dragon Kyn*, *School Library Journal*, November, 1993, p. 108.

Dollisch, Patricia A., review of *Shadow Spinner*, *School Library Journal*, June, 1998, p. 145.

Estes, Sally, review of *Sign of the Dove*, *Booklist*, May 1, 1996, p. 1506.

Fletcher, Susan, essay in *Something about the Author Autobiography Series*, Volume 25, Gale, 1998, pp. 95-116.

Flowers, Ann A., review of *Sign of the Dove*, *Horn Book*, September-October, 1996, p. 595.

Harding, Susan M., review of *Dragon's Milk*, *School Library Journal*, November, 1989, pp. 107-08.

Jennings, Kathryn, review of *Flight of the Dragon Kyn*, *Bulletin of the Center for Children's Books*, January, 1994, p. 153.

Rochman, Hazel, review of *Shadow Spinner*, *Booklist*, June 1, 1998, p. 1746.

Yen, Joyce W., review of *Flight of the Dragon Kyn*, *Voice of Youth Advocates*, February, 1994, p. 380.

■ For More Information See

PERIODICALS

Booklist, November 1, 1989, p. 547.

Books for Keeps, May, 1999, pp. 28-29.

Bulletin of the Center for Children's Books, September, 1991, p. 10; July, 1998, p. 394.

Kirkus Reviews, October 15, 1993, p. 1239; May 1, 1998, p. 657.

Publishers Weekly, August 16, 1991, p. 58.

School Library Journal, May, 1996, p. 112.

Voice of Youth Advocates, August, 1996, p. 168.

E. M. Forster

annual Clark Lectures at Cambridge University, 1927, Rede Lecturer, 1941, W. P. Ker Lecturer, 1944; made lecture tour of United States in 1947. Member of general advisory council, British Broadcasting Corp., and writer of numerous broadcasts; was a vice-president of the London Library.

■ Personal

Born Edward Morgan Forster, January 1, 1879, in London, England; died June 7, 1970, in Coventry, England; son of Edward Morgan Llewellyn and Alice Clara (Whichelo) Forster. *Education:* King's College, Cambridge, B.A. (second-class honors in classics), 1900, B.A. (second-class honors in history), 1901, M.A., 1910. *Hobbies and other interests:* Forster was greatly interested in music and is said to have been an accomplished amateur pianist.

■ Career

Lived in Greece and Italy after leaving Cambridge in 1901, remaining abroad until 1907, except for a brief visit to England in 1902; lectured at Working Men's College, London, for a period beginning in 1907; made first trip to India in 1912; Red Cross volunteer in Alexandria, 1915-19; returned to England after the war where he was literary editor of the Labor Party's *Daily Herald* for a time, and contributed reviews to journals, including *Nation* and *New Statesman;* served as private secretary to the Maharajah of Dewas State Senior, 1921; lived in England, writing and lecturing, 1921-70. Gave

■ Member

American Academy of Arts and Letters (honorary corresponding member), Bavarian Academy of Fine Arts (honorary corresponding member), Cambridge Humanists (president), Reform Club.

■ Awards, Honors

James Tait Black Memorial Prize, and Prix Femina Vie Heureuse, both 1925, both for *A Passage to India;* LL.D., University of Aberdeen, 1931; Benson Medal, Royal Society of Literature, 1937; honorary fellow, King's College, Cambridge, 1946; Litt.D., University of Liverpool, 1947, Hamilton College, 1949, Cambridge University, 1950, University of Nottingham, 1951, University of Manchester, 1954, Leiden University, 1954, and University of Leicester, 1958; Tukojimo III Gold Medal; Companion of Honour, 1953; Companion of Royal Society of Literature; Order of Merit, 1969.

■ Writings

Where Angels Fear to Tread (novel), Blackwood, 1905, Knopf, 1920..

The Longest Journey (novel), Blackwood, 1907, Knopf, 1922, with introduction by Jeffrey Meyers, Bantam Classics, 1997.

A Room With a View (novel), Edward Arnold, 1908, Putnam, 1911.

Howards End (novel), Putnam, 1910, Random House, 1989, published with appendices and criticism, edited by Paul B. Armstrong, Norton, 1997, also with history and criticism, edited by Alistair M. Duckworth, Bedford Books, 1997.

The Celestial Omnibus, and Other Stories, Sidgwick & Jackson, 1911, Knopf, 1923.

The Story of the Siren (short story), Hogarth Press, 1920.

The Government of Egypt (history), Labour Research Department, 1921.

Alexandria: A History and a Guide, W. Morris, 1922, 3rd edition, Doubleday-Anchor, 1961.

Pharos and Pharillon (history), Knopf, 1923, 3rd edition, Hogarth Press, 1943.

A Passage to India (novel), Harcourt, 1924.

Anonymity: An Enquiry, V. Woolf, 1925.

Aspects of the Novel (Clark Lecture, 1927), Harcourt, 1927.

The Eternal Moment, and Other Stories, Harcourt, 1928, reprinted, 1970.

A Letter to Madan Blanchard (belles lettres), Hogarth Press, 1931, Harcourt, 1932.

Goldsworthy Lowes Dickinson (biography), Harcourt, 1934, new edition, Edward Arnold, 1945.

Abinger Harvest (essays), Harcourt, 1936, reprinted, 1966.

What I Believe (political), Hogarth Press, 1939.

Nordic Twilight (political), Macmillan, 1940.

England's Pleasant Land (pageant play), Hogarth Press, 1940.

Virginia Woolf (criticism; Rede Lecture, 1941) Harcourt, 1942.

The Development of English Prose Between 1918 and 1939 (criticism; W. P. Ker Lecture, 1944), Jackson & Co. (Glasgow), 1945.

The Collected Tales of E. M. Forster (previously published as *The Celestial Omnibus* and *The Eternal Moment*), Knopf, 1947 (published in England as *Collected Short Stories of E. M. Forster*, Sidgwick & Jackson, 1948).

(Author of libretto with Eric Crozier) *Billy Budd* (based on the novel by Herman Melville; music by Benjamin Britten), Boosey & Hawkes, 1951, revised edition, 1961.

Two Cheers for Democracy (essays), Edward Arnold, 1951.

Desmond MacCarthy, Mill House Press, 1952.

The Hill of Devi, Harcourt, 1953 (published in England as *The Hill of Devi: Being Letters from Dewas State Senior*, Edward Arnold, 1953; also see below).

Battersea Rise (first chapter of *Marianne Thornton* see below), Harcourt, 1955.

Marianne Thornton: A Domestic Biography, 1797-1887, Harcourt, 1956.

E. M. Forster: Selected Writings, edited by G. B. Parker, Heinemann Educational, 1968.

Albergo Empedocle and Other Writings (previously unpublished material, written 1900-15), edited by George H. Thomson, Liveright, 1971.

Maurice (novel), Norton, 1971, reprinted, 1987.

The Life to Come and Other Stories, Norton, 1973.

The Hill of Devi and Other Indian Writings (includes *The Hill of Devi*), edited by Oliver Stallybrass, Holmes & Meier, 1983.

Selected Letters of E. M. Forster, edited by Mary Lago and P. N. Furbank, Harvard University Press, Volume 1: *1879-1920*, 1983, Volume 2: *1921-1970*, 1984.

Commonplace Book, edited by Philip Gardner, Stanford University Press, 1985.

Original Letters from India, Hogarth Press, 1986.

The New Collected Short Stories by E. M. Forster, Sidgwick & Jackson, 1987.

(With Rod Mengham) *The Machine Stops: And Other Stories*, E. M. Forster Works, Volume 7, Trafalgar Square, 1998.

The Prince's Tale and Other Uncollected Writings, Abinger Edition of E. M. Forster, Volume 17, Andre Deutsch Ltd, 1998.

Also author of *Reading as Usual* (criticism), 1939. Author of unfinished novel, "Arctic Summer," published in *Tribute to Benjamin Britten on His Fiftieth Birthday*, edited by Anthony Gishford, Faber, 1963. Author of plays, *The Heart of Bosnia*, 1911, and *The Abinger Pageant*, 1934, and script for film, *Diary for Timothy*.

CONTRIBUTOR

Arnold W. Lawrence, editor, *T. E. Lawrence by His Friends*, J. Cape, 1937.

Hermon Ould, editor, *Writers in Freedom*, Hutchinson, 1942.

George Orwell, editor, *Talking to India*, Allen & Unwin, 1943.

Peter Grimes: Essays, John Lane, for the governors of Sadler's Wells Foundation, 1945.

Hermon Ould, editor, *Freedom of Expression: A Symposium*, Hutchinson, 1945.

S. Radhakrishnan, *Mahatma Gandhi: Essays and Reflections on His Life and Work,* 2nd edition, Allen & Unwin, 1949.

Hermon Ould: A Tribute, [London], 1952.

The Fearful Choice: A Debate on Nuclear Policy, conducted by Philip Toynbee, Wayne State University Press, 1959.

Also contributor to *Aspects of England,* 1935, and *Britain and the Beast,* 1937.

AUTHOR OF INTRODUCTION

(And notes) Virgil, *The Aeneid,* translated by E. Fairfax Taylor, Dent, 1906.

(And notes) Eliza Fay, *Original Letters from India, 1799-1815,* Harcourt, 1925.

Constance Sitwell, *Flowers and Elephants,* J. Cape, 1927.

George Crabbe, Jr., *The Life of George Crabbe,* Oxford University Press, 1932.

Maurice O'Sullivan, *Twenty Years A-Growing,* Chatto & Windus, 1933.

Mulk Raj Anand, *Untouchable,* Wishart, 1935.

Alec Craig, *The Banned Books of England,* Allen & Unwin, 1937.

K. R. Srinivasa Iyengar, *Literature and Authorship in India,* Allen & Unwin, 1943.

Goldsworthy Lowes Dickinson, *Letters from John Chinaman and Other Essays,* Allen & Unwin, 1946.

Huthi Singh, *Maura,* Longmans, Green, 1951.

Zeenuth Futehally, *Zohra,* Hind Kitabs (Bombay), 1951.

Peter Townsend, editor, *Cambridge Anthology,* Hogarth Press, 1952.

Forrest Reid, *Tom Barber,* Pantheon, 1955.

Dickinson, *The Greek View of Life,* University of Michigan Press, 1958.

D. Windham, *The Warm Country,* Hart-Davis, 1960.

Guiseppe Tomasi di Lampedusa, *Two Stories and a Memory,* translated by A. Colquhoun, Pantheon, 1962.

Frank Sargeson, *Collected Stories,* MacGibbon & Kee, 1965.

OTHER

Author of notes for various books, including William Golding's *Lord of the Flies,* Coward, 1955. Work is represented in collections, including *The Challenge of Our Time,* Percival Marshall, 1948, and *Fairy Tales for Computers,* Eakins Press, 1969.

Contributor to journals and periodicals, including *Listener, Independent Review, Observer, New Statesman, Nation, Albany Review, Open Window, Athenaeum, Egyptian Mail,* and *Horizon.*

■ Adaptations

A Passage to E. M. Forster, a play based on his works, was compiled by William Roerick and Thomas Coley, and produced in New York, N.Y. at Theatre de Lys in October, 1970. *A Room With a View* was adapted as a play by Stephen Tait and Kenneth Allcott, produced in Cambridge, February, 1950, and published by Edward Arnold, 1951; it was adapted for film by Merchant-Ivory Productions and released by Cinecom in 1986. *A Passage to India* was adapted for the stage by Santha Rama Rau, and published by Edward Arnold, 1960; it was produced in London in 1960 and on Broadway in 1962; the television adaptation by John Maynard was produced by the BBC, and broadcast by NET in 1968; it was adapted into a film, directed by David Lean, and released by Columbia Pictures in 1984. *Where Angels Fear to Tread* was adapted as a play by Elizabeth Hart, S. French, 1963; it was also adapted for a film by Fine Line Features in 1991. *Howards End* was adapted for stage by Lance Sieveking and Richard Cottrell and produced in London in 1967; the BBC production, adapted by Pauline Macaulay, was broadcast in 1970; a movie adaptation was produced by Merchant-Ivory Productions in 1991. *Maurice* was adapted into a film by Merchant-Ivory Productions and released by Cinecom in 1987. Sound recordings have been made of all of Forster's novels.

■ Sidelights

At first glimpse, the work of the British novelist and essayist, E. M. Forster, would hardly be thought to be the stuff of Hollywood. His finely detailed novels explore the Edwardian world of society and morality and focus on such themes as salvation through love, the deficiency of traditional Christianity and the repressiveness of English society and culture. In early novels such as *Room with a View* and *Where Angels Fear to Tread,* his protagonists, both male and female, are able to shuck off the heavy coils of civilization only by traveling outside their native country—sometimes with disastrous results. Forster's books are novels of manners, much in the same vein of Jane Austen. There is little action, much discussion. His longer and more substantive novels, such as *Howard's End* and *A Passage to India,* are considered among his finest work. In *Howard's End,* he depicts his own vision of a unified society through good will and higher beliefs, and, in *A Passage to India,* a picture of the Indian subcontinent and the differences between East and West.

Not necessarily the stuff of Hollywood dream factories, and indeed, during his lifetime, Forster rejected bids to film his novels, fearful how they would be adapted. Yet after his death in 1970, five of his six novels—including his posthumously published homosexual novel, *Maurice,* have been adapted for motion pictures. *The Longest Journey* is the only Forster novel to yet escape such cinematic adaptation. Incredibly, Forster is widely known for his works long after his death, by a movie-going generation. This is a fitting irony for a writer whose works were critically acclaimed during his lifetime, but never overly popular with the reading public.

The adjectives "great" and "important" are often used to describe Forster, but another one, "elusive," according to Philip Gardner in *E. M. Forster, The Critical Heritage,* is equally apropos. "In the profoundest sense," noted John Sayre Martin in his *E. M. Forster: The Endless Journey,* "Forster's elusiveness is a quality of his mind—a mind at once humanistic and sceptical." Martin further observed, "Unlike the nineteenth-century novelist whose assured tone derives in great measure from his subscription to a publicly acknowledged code of values, Forster, without such a code, is tentative and exploratory."

There is nothing tentative or exploratory, however, about the Forster industry that has developed to describe every nuance and utterance of this great English stylist. Beginning with Lionel Trilling's breakthrough critical study in 1943, *E. M. Forster,* there have been dozens of full-scale analyses of his fiction, and a clutch of biographies, including the 1978 work, *E. M. Forster: A Life,* by P. N. Furbank, who personally knew Forster at Cambridge. With the publication of *Maurice* in 1970 and of his short stories with homosexual themes, *The Life to Come and Other Stories,* in 1972, critical studies about the man and his works increased in number. Now, books about Forster far outnumber the books by this author who stopped writing fiction in 1924 after publication of his sixth and arguably finest novel, *A Passage to India.*

"His gifts," commented Frederick P. W. McDowell in *Dictionary of Literary Biography,* "are manifest and manifold: an ability to imagine characters and situations of surpassing aesthetic and human significance; a speculative power and a philosophical acuteness; moral seriousness, sensitivity, and catholic sympathies . . . an abundant humor, wit, and irony; and incisiveness of insight," among a catalogue of other literary virtues. McDowell concluded, "Though his canon is a slender one, it is sui

generis. No one else ever wrote quite like Forster, and in his case the style is indeed the man and the man is inseparable from the style." "How did E. M. Forster manage to elude the Nobel Prize in Literature?" wondered Joseph Epstein in *Commentary,* fifteen years after the death of the English novelist. Epstein calculated that Forster missed out on the Prize "no fewer than thirty or forty times" between the writing of his last novel and his death in 1970 at ninety-one. This non-selection "put him in a select little club," according to Epstein, "Tolstoy, Henry James, Chekhov, and Proust being among its most distinguished members."

From Melcombe Place to Cambridge

Edward Morgan Forster was born on the first day of 1879 at 6 Melcombe Place in the fashionable Marleyborne district of London. As McDowell pointed out in *Dictionary of Literary Biography,* Forster was the product of a "divided inheritance": seriousness and morality from his father's forebearers, the Thorntons, and an enjoyment of aesthetics from his maternal ancestors, the Wichelos. Forster's father, Edward Morgan Llewellyn Forster, died of tuberculosis a year and a half after his son's birth, leaving his wife and son dependent upon relatives for support. Forster and his mother, Alice Clara (Lily), left London for the leafier climes of Hertfordshire, renting Rooksnest, a house near Stevenage that later became the setting for one of Forster's most popular novels, *Howards End.*

When he was eight, Forster's great-aunt, Marianne Thornton, died, leaving the young boy a legacy of 8,000 pounds, then a small fortune; enough to secure him an education and make it possible for him to write without worrying about sales. "Those early years made a deep impression," Forster later wrote *The Hill of Devi,* "which no amount of suburbanism or travel has dispelled. When I think of England it is of the countryside, and I still think of her thus though so little of our countryside remains."

This childhood idyll came to an end when Forster attended preparatory school at Kent House in Eastbourne from 1880 to 1893. The boys at Kent House bullied him and took delight in calling him "Mousie." Forster later entered Tonbridge School as a day student, his mother changing residences to Tonbridge for this purpose. His four years at Tonbridge were by and large unhappy ones as well, for as a day student and not a lodger he was bullied even worse than he had been at Kent House.

Things improved, however, when Forster entered King's College at Cambridge University. Here he began to find a niche for himself, found friendships of like-minded youths, and was even elected to the exclusive club called the Apostles. There were powerful and inspiring dons with whom Forster studied during his Cambridge years, including G. E. Moore and Goldsworthy Lowes Dickinson. It was also at Cambridge where Forster began to write with serious intentions. "It was Cambridge that first set me off writing," Forster once recalled in an interview with David Jones in the *Listener.* "At one time my tutor suggested to me that I might write. He did it in a very informal way. He said in a sort of drawling voice, "I don't see why you should not write," and I being very diffident was delighted at this remark and thought, after all why shouldn't I write? And I did. It is really owing to . . . that start at Cambridge that I have written." Additionally, it was through a friendship with another undergraduate, H. O. Meredith, that Forster first came to a conscious understanding of his homosexuality. This relationship was "mostly platonic," according to McDowell in his critical work, *E. M. Forster,* with the "physical expression of feeling . . . limited to romping and cursory caresses." McDowell sums up these years in the same book: "Cambridge University meant for E. M. Forster a liberation of the spirit, a milieu in which the individual could thrive as an individual and develop his full capacities. . . . Cambridge, in short, showed him the way to the reconciling of extremes, the achieving of a vital middle way, the attainment of proportion as a dynamic ongoing process. . . ." Friendships secured at Cambridge were also influential later in Forster's life. Fellow Apostles such as Lytton Strachey, John Maynard Keynes, Leonard Woolf, and Desmond MacCarthy, later became members of the Bloomsbury group of artists, writers, and intellectuals who helped shape England's cultural path for over a generation.

Travels Abroad and First Publication

With Forster's graduation from Cambridge in 1901, he began a year of travel in Europe with his mother. The pair traveled to Italy, Sicily, and Austria, visiting every museum, gallery, and church they could. This trip, however, reinforced his mother's concern for her son's welfare: he sprained his ankle at one point, and then later broke his arm as he walked up the steps to St. Peter's. In Florence he overheard some gossip about an Englishwoman that started him writing on a first novel. Back in London, mother and son took rooms in the Kingsley Hotel in

Bloomsbury, and Forster began a twenty-year affiliation as a teacher at the Working Men's College in London. In 1903 Forster went alone to Greece, and returning to England, published his first fiction, the short story, "Albergo Empedocle," in *Temple Bar.* He also contributed stories and articles to the *Independent Review,* a small magazine founded by several Cambridge dons, including Dickinson, G. M. Trevelyan, and his former tutor who started him writing, Nathaniel Wedd. Stories published in this review include "The Road from Colonus" and "The Story of a Panic."

McDowell asserted in *E. M. Forster* that the "years 1902 to 1910 might be regarded as the Jane Austen and George Meredith years in Forster's development, years in which he wrote, quite spontaneously, four novels, all of them revealing elements of greatness." In 1903 Forster began writing *A Room with a View,* though it was not published until 1908. He and his mother and grandmother moved to Weybridge where they all shared a house; his one release from his writing was playing the piano. He also began work on *Where Angels Fear to Tread,* which became his first published novel in October, 1905, released just after he returned from Germany, where he tutored the children of the Countess von Arnim at Nassenheide.

Martin described the elements of this first novel: "A socially preposterous marriage between a middle-class English widow and an Italian youth ten years her junior that culminates in kidnapping, homicide, and physical torture. . . ." Lilia Herriton, a widow, is tired of her staid suburban life in Swanton. When Lilia threatens to become an embarrassment to her in-laws, they manage to pack her off to Italy in the company of Caroline Abbott, a seemingly conservative and sensible woman whom the matriarch of the family, Mrs. Herriton, trusts. But once in Italy, primal forces take over. There Lilia meets the much younger Gino Carella, who demonstrates a certain animal magnetism. Lilia, powerfully attracted to Gino, and with Caroline's collusion, marries the Italian.

Getting wind of the affair, Mrs. Herriton dispatches her son, Philip, to stop the marriage, but he arrives too late. The marriage goes badly for Lilia. She becomes almost a captive, forced to be shut in while Gino goes about his social rounds, and when she dies in childbirth, it is almost a welcome release for her. Subsequently Gino begins to tug at the Herritons, sending Lilia's first child, Irma, who has remained in Swanton, postcards from her little Italian brother. Again dispatched by his mother, Philip,

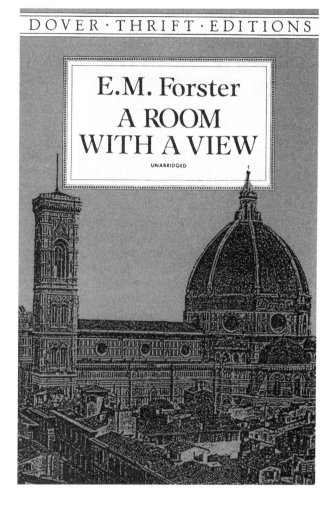

Forster pokes fun at British society in this 1908 work about Lucy Honeychurch, a young woman who struggles to break traditional Victorian attitudes.

accompanied by his even more fervent sister, Harriet, intends to bring the second child back to England. Caroline also goes back to Italy, planning to adopt the little boy herself and thus make amends for her earlier actions.

But when both Philip and Caroline see how tender Gino is with the boy, they decide against their plans. Not so Harriet, however, who kidnaps the boy. The child is subsequently killed in an accident on the way to the train. Injured in the accident, Philip decides he must break the news to Gino, who in turn tortures the Englishman by twisting his broken arm. Caroline comes to the rescue in time to stop the men, and makes them take a sort of ritual drink together, sharing the milk prepared for the dead baby. Irrevocably altered by the experiences, both Philip and Caroline must leave Italy but both also know that life in Swanton will be impossible after this bracing breath of liberation. Forster seems to be saying that the instinctual life as represented by Gino, even though it can be cruel and brutish, is preferable to the cosseted life of suburbia, represented by Mrs. Herriton and Swanton. Forster also made it known that the real point of the novel was the "improvement of Philip," as he wrote to Robert Trevelyan.

As a first novel, *Where Angels Fear to Tread* was well received critically. As P. N. Furbank noted in his biography, *E. M. Forster: A Life*, the novel "received an excellent press, almost all the reviewers recognizing a new and personal voice in the book." Furbank went on to quote a reviewer for the *Bookseller* who spoke of ""a brilliance and a unique charm"" in the writing, and the *Bookman*, even warmer, said perceptively, ""This is a book which one begins with pleased interest and gradually finds to be astonishing."" Furbank also noted a review from the influential literary editor of the *Daily News*, C. F. G. Masterman, in which the editor wrote, ""Not often has the reviewer to welcome a new writer and a new novel so directly conveying the impression of power and an easy mastery of material."" There were further positive reviews in the *Spectator* and the influential *Times Literary Supplement*. McDowell, writing in his *E. M. Forster*, found *Where Angels Fear to Tread* a "subtle, complex, and refreshing novel," and further observed that in its "total impact, it justifies the opinion that Forster from the first was an artist of maturity and power."

Forster quickly turned his hand to a new novel, *The Longest Journey*, which follows the fortunes of the artist-intellectual Rickie Elliot as he searches for truth in life. During the composition of this book Forster met Syed Ross Masood, an Indian then visiting England, whom he tutored in Latin. The two became lifelong friends, and it was Masood who later, in 1912, inspired Forster to travel in India, a journey that would lead to the writing of his most famous book, *A Passage to India*. But for now, in 1906 and 1907, the journey was one of discovery for his protagonist, Elliot.

Forster's second novel opens in Rickie's rooms at Cambridge where he and some undergraduate friends are discussing philosophy. Stewart Ansell is arguing for the philosophy of G. E. Moore, while another character, Tilliard, is a spokesman for Plato. This opening scene lets the reader know what is in store: *The Longest Journey* is most definitely a novel of ideas. Rickie himself stands apart from these arguments. Ansell, somewhat in love with Rickie, is jealous of callow Agnes Pembroke and her brother, a master at Sawston School, when they interrupt this discussion. Agnes is overprotective of Rickie, with his deformed foot and educated manner, and when he speaks of writing short stories, Agnes supports him only if he goes about it in a diligent, middle class way. Rickie and Ansell are real friends, and Rickie has even been to the other's home, above his father's drapery shop. Ansell has made it to Cambridge on merit rather than connections, and Rickie is fascinated by Ansell's father, so uneducated yet so intelligent about the world and so encouraging of his son to get whatever education he can in the world.

Yet Agnes manages to snare Rickie, and they become engaged at Rickie's own bit of idyllic Eden, a dell he has discovered near the college. Upon their marriage, Rickie settles in with Agnes at Sawston School as a Latin master, though a very junior one. In this section of the novel, Forster addresses all of his own hurts at the hands of school bullies as a day student. Such private schools come off as less than adequate in Forster's novel.

On a visit to his ancestral home in Wiltshire, his aunt, Mrs. Failing, reveals to Rickie that a boy with whom he grew up, Stephen Wonham, is actually his half brother. Stephen is the result of his mother's affair with a local farmer. Stephen is also an instinctual sort, like his father, adopted by the Failings when Rickie's mother reluctantly returned to her husband. Rickie then leaves his wife, with the prompting of Ansell, after learning of some duplicity on her part concerning Stephen. The brothers are close for a time, but when Stephen breaks a promise and resumes drinking, Rickie feels a personal betrayal. He saves his half-brother, drunk and passed out on the railroad tracks, but Rickie himself is killed in the process.

McDowell has noted that *The Longest Journey* is "the most elusive of Forster's novels and one of the most difficult to assess." It is a novel about youth and about a man who seeks a truth that seems forever to elude him. From Cambridge to Sawston and then to Wiltshire, Rickie journeys to the heart of the matter, and seemingly fails at every turn. Yet in the end, it is the journey that is important. "Rickie is the man of good intentions and inherent distinction whose occasional blindness about people and whose irresoluteness result in tragedy," McDowell remarked in *Dictionary of Literary Biography*. In this novel, Forster experimented with the use of nature as both symbol and theme, at once inspiring and destructive. The structure of the book is also complex and the writing and use of psychological insight also pushed

forward the talents of the young writer. If reviews of his first novel had been on the whole positive, the critical reception of *The Longest Journey* was even more laudatory. As Nicola Beauman noted in her book, *Morgan: A Biography of E. M. Forster,* the young author "was being discussed by critics who did not merely "approve" but applauded rapturously; and who produced over twenty, mostly lengthy, reviews almost all united in their praise. To see, nowadays, the intelligence of the comments, the references to "genius," the depth of understanding generally displayed is, from the aspect of a biography, a rather confusing exercise. How can someone of twenty-eight receive plaudits like this and still not be moved." While most found the book to have elements of greatness and inspired writing in it, some also despaired of the strong element of pessimism in the novel and the overabundance of deaths. *The Longest Journey* remains one of Forster's most enigmatic works, the only novel not adapted for a film. Yet, as McDowell concluded, "If [the novel] lacks perfection in the execution, it is nevertheless a brilliant and highly evocative work."

From Italy to Howards End

Forster's third published novel was the first he began, with an initial working title of "Lucy," and which happily reinvented itself over the course of many years of writing to *A Room with a View.* McDowell, writing in *Dictionary of Literary Biography,* described it as Forster's "most halcyon and direct" novel, and one that "celebrates the magical time of youth." McDowell also felt the novel was Forster's "purest social comedy" and his most "Jane Austen-like . . . in its observations of the minutiae of human behavior and in its dry, undercut, ironic, aphoristic style." This third novel also became one of his most popular books, not only with the critics and Bloomsbury crowd, but also with the reading public.

Set in both Italy and England, *A Room with a View* is also about a search. Lucy Honeychurch is looking for meaning in her life, and eventually finds it via a young and impassioned man who ousts her finely mannered and cold-blooded fiance in the process. On a tour of Italy with her older chaperone, cousin Charlotte Bartlett, Lucy makes the acquaintance of the Emersons, father and son, at a pension in Florence. When the men offer to give up their rooms with a view so that the ladies might enjoy their first stay in Florence, the fates of Lucy and of the young Emerson, George, become inextricably bound. Like the elder Ansell in *The Longest Journey*, the elder Mr.

Emerson is a plain-spoken type of large imagination and heart. A proponent of a free and natural life, he influences his son with such a philosophy, and George willfully kisses the young and seemingly brittle Lucy one afternoon on a hillside over Florence. Discovered in this act by her chaperone, Lucy is spirited away from Italy, back to the safety and snug security of her family at Windy Corner in Surrey. There the reader meets Lucy's loving mother and her playful brother Freddy. Also in tow in England is Cecil Vyse, a pompous, bookish man who lives on inheritance and has no ambition in the world but to possess Lucy as he might a fine painting. After his third proposal, Lucy finally accepts, but when the Emersons show up in the neighborhood and rent a local villa, Lucy is slowly drawn to the vital young George over her staid and priggish Cecil. Ultimately, after misunderstanding and reversals, Lucy rejects Cecil and marries George. They return to the pension in Italy where they first met, giving the novel a framing structure.

"Of the six novels that Forster completed," observed Oliver Stallybrass in an introduction to a 1977 edition, "*A Room with a View* has, if not the longest gestation period . . . at least the most complicated pre-natal history." Forster began making notes for the novel in 1901, and over the next seven years constructed the novel piece by piece. Forster himself felt the novel was slight, but that it contained some of the best characters that he had yet attempted. As a result, it "has always been a favourite with the general public," according to Stallybrass. "The overall movement of the novel," according to McDowell in *E. M. Forster*, "results in enlightenment for Lucy, after several divagations into falsehood." McDowell also pointed to Forster's use of music imagery in the novel, in particular Lucy's peculiar facility in interpreting Beethoven sonatas, to reveal the inner life of characters.

Though less widely reviewed than his earlier *The Longest Journey*, the new novel did enjoy some critical success. Writing in the *Nation*, Masterman praised the novel's fusion of a "satiric scrutiny of conversation" with the "hidden life of nature and the spirit." Writing in the *Times Literary Supplement*, fellow Bloomsbury-ite Virginia Woolf commented that the novel had "cleverness, much fun, occasional beauty, originality, and strength," but also noted that the characters were not adequate for the purposes of the novel. That Lucy refused to become a victim of Victorian ideals, choosing the life-affirming George over the controlling Cecil, was a confirmation of Forster's position that life must be lived outside the bounds of proscribed fashion. McDow-

ell concluded in *Dictionary of Literary Biography*, "Forster's memorable characters, his wit and stylistic control, his awareness of the nuances of manners and behavior and especially of their comic aspects, his fresh celebration of nature, his satirist's insight into social mores and values, and his open sensibility revealed in *A Room with a View* make of it a memorable novel and a delightful one as well."

With his first three novels, Forster achieved a degree of critical as well as popular success, but it was his fourth, *Howards End*, that put him on the map as not only a comic social author but as a profound and stylistically acute novelist. Shortly after publication of *A Room with a View*, Forster began work on this new novel, partly inspired by the house in Hertfordshire, Rooksnest, where he had spent his youth.

In this "epic" novel, according to McDowell, Forster explores the divisions inherent in England at the time; divisions along the lines of class and culture. To do so, he employs two families whose members and histories intertwine one another. The Schlegels are a family that cherishes the connection of relationships, and the value of art, while the Wilcoxes are more the family of action—businessmen and empire builders of the modern England. Margaret Schlegel attempts to connect the two through her marriage to Henry Wilcox, an attempt that is only partially successful. Margaret does not wholly endorse Henry's materialism or his world view. This clash of classes is underscored by Margaret's sister's love affair with Leonard Bast, a worker with intellectual aspirations who is economically ruined by poor career advice from Henry.

Both as social comedy and symbolic novel, *Howards End* is considered among Forster's greatest achievements. Critics of the day were quick to point out the high literary quality of his novel. A reviewer for the *Times Literary Supplement*, for example, noted, "Mr. E. M. Forster has now done what critical admirers of his foregoing novels have confidently looked for—he has written a book in which his highly original talent has found full and ripe expression." This same reviewer went on to call *Howards End* "a very remarkable and original book." Reviewing the novel in the *Daily News*, R. A. Scott-James commented, ""Only connect . . ." is Mr. Forster's motto. It is because he has taken this motto not only for his book but also for his method of work that he has achieved the most significant novel of the year. . . . Mr. Forster has written a connected novel. . . . [It] rises like a piece of architecture full-grown before us. It is all bricks and timber, but it is mystery, idealism, a far-reaching symbol." In a *Nation* review, Edward Garnett praised the book for its "far-sighted criticism of middle-class ideas," noting further that it "is a book that says most effectively those very things that the intelligent minority feel, but rarely arrive at formulating." "This novel," noted a reviewer for the *Athenaeum*, "taken with its three predecessors, assures its author of a place amongst the handful of living authors who count." Later reviewers and critics concurred with these early pronouncements. Woolf, writing on the novels of E. M. Forster in *The Death of the Moth and Other Essays*, noted, "None of the books before *Howards End* and *A Passage to India* altogether drew upon the full range of Mr. Forster's powers. . . . In *Howards End* the lower, the middle, the upper middle classes of English society are so built up into a complete fabric." Lionel Trilling, writing in his pioneering critical work *E. M Forster*, called *Howards End* the writer's "masterpiece" because it "develops to their full the themes and attitudes of the early books and . . . justifies these attitudes by connecting them with a more mature sense of responsibility." Modern critics have examined the novel from the point of view of the ambivalent narrator and from a feminist perspec-

tive, as an example of imperialist literature and of the metropolitan novel at its zenith. Much has also been written of the movie adaptation of the book as well, and reviewing that film in the *New Yorker*, Terrence Rafferty called *Howards End*, the novel "the most nearly perfect" of Forster's six larger works of fiction. Rafferty went on to note that Forster wanted "desperately to imagine the possibility of a consciousness that would lift the English above the petty particularities of their daily lives—so desperately that he's willing to undermine his greatest gift as a novelist, which is for realistic, precise observation." McDowell summarized the effects of the novel in *Dictionary of Literary Biography:* "*Howards End* represents a remarkable fusion of social realism and poetic symbolism, its meaning related at once to human beings as they are and to human beings as they might become. . . . The novel rates highly for its compelling characters, for its merging of character and situation with abstractions; for the interplay of the various segments of the middle class upon one another; for the fusion of the comic and the tragic visions; for the depiction of the romance quest of the truth as taking place in contemporary Edwardian England; for its juxtaposition of the realistic and the

Judy Davis and Nigel Havers appear in David Lean's 1984 film adaptation of Forster's *A Passage to India*.

archetypal; and for a poet's sensitivity to the beautiful and the ineffable."

Forster was at the height of his powers with *Howards End*, yet he would not publish another novel for fourteen years with the advent of *A Passage to India*. Meanwhile, however, he was hard at work at other novel-length works. *Arctic Summer,* a novel about a strange triangle between Venetia Vorlase, her husband, Martin, and the enigmatic Lieutenant March. Forster put this novel aside in 1912, unfinished; a fragment was published in 1980. A collection of short stories, *The Celestial Omnibus, and Other Stories,* was published in 1911. The collection included his 1904 tale, "The Story of a Panic," which Carroll Viera, writing on Forster's short fiction in *Dictionary of Literary Biography,* called "a prototype of Forster's longer fiction" which "focuses on an upper-middle-class male who is jolted out of his complacency" by a walk in the Italian woods. The young man, Eustace, thereafter becomes a devotee of nature and comes out of his middle-class isolation. This early collection, which also included "The Road from Colonus," about a British tourist revitalized by a visit to Greece, received mixed reviews, according to Viera, ranging from "wildly enthusiastic to unimpressed."

Forster began his final novel in 1913, shortly after returning from his initial travels in India, but then put it down for the completion of *Maurice*. During the war years, he served for a time in Alexandria as a "searcher" for the Red Cross, interviewing wounded soldiers for news of those missing in action. During this interval, he made the acquaintance of the Coptic poet, C. P. Cavafy, and later helped to publicize his work. He also had his first mature physical relationship while in Egypt. In 1919 he returned to England, living again with his mother in Weybridge, and wrote for several publications, including the *Nation* and the *Athenaeum*. He also became literary editor of the *Daily Herald*. A second visit to India in 1921, working as a private secretary to the Rajah, set him to work again on *A Passage to India*. Meanwhile he was also publishing books of travel, including *Alexandria: A History and Guide*, and books of essays, such as *Pharos and Pharillon*. His name was also spreading across the Atlantic with publication of much of his early work in the Untied States.

Finally, in 1924, Forster published *A Passage to India* to unanimous critical praise, winning the James Tait Black Memorial Prize and the Femina Vie Heureuse for the book. It is the book for which Forster is best known, and one that has spawned a flotilla of critical studies, exploring every nuance and symbol,

every inspiration and semicolon. Written on two levels, it explores the political situation in India as well as the spiritual. On the first level, it looks at the tension between British and native Indians as well as that between Hindus and Moslems. On the spiritual plane, it focuses on the search for the infinite and deals with the unexplained in quotidian life. The main characters of the story are a young Indian surgeon, Dr. Aziz; Mrs. Moore, an elderly visiting Englishwoman and mother of Ronald Heaslop, the City Magistrate of Chandrapore; Miss Adela Quested, visiting India with Mrs. Moore and engaged to Ronald; and Cecil Fielding, Principal of the Government College and friend to Aziz.

Aziz and Mrs. Moore meet one night at a mosque and become friends. Her young friend, Adela, is equally eager to meet the real India, not simply the bits of the Raj served up for most visiting English. A tea party held at Mr. Fielding's brings Mrs. Moore and Aziz together once more. Heaslop, however, rather priggish and suspicious of the Indians, shows up to escort the ladies home and throws a damper on things. Adela begins to have second thoughts about her pending marriage to Ronald Heaslop. Meanwhile, Dr. Aziz wants to give his new English friends a real treat, and arranges a visit to the Marabar Caves, located some miles distant. But the visit proves a disaster when Mrs. Moore becomes dislocated by the booming echo inside the mysterious caverns. Inside, Mrs. Moore has something of a darkly mystical experience, sensing a booming nothingness at the very center of life. Adela too enters a cave alone but rushes out minutes later claiming that Dr. Aziz has attacked her. Aziz is arrested.

At the subsequent trial, the Anglo and Indian communities are torn asunder. When Mrs. Moore claims to her son that she is sure Aziz is innocent, she is shipped off to a coastal port awaiting embarkation to England. The Indians at the trial chant for Mrs. Moore, their friend, to be returned to give true testimony. But unknown to any of them, Mrs. Moore has already died aboard ship. Dramatically, when Adela gives her testimony, she breaks down and withdraws her charges against Aziz. Shocked by this turn of events, Heaslop withdraws his proposal, and Adela is sent back to England. Fielding subsequently marries Mrs. Moore's daughter Stella, and his friendship with Aziz comes to a close. The gulf between the two men, as that between British and Indians, is too large to bridge.

Critical acclaim met the book upon publication. Rose MaCaulay, reviewing the novel in the *Daily*

Forster's novel *Howard's End* is brought to life in this Academy Award-winning 1992 film.

News, told readers to have no fear; this novel of India gives "full scope" to Forster's literary powers. "It is a novel that," MaCaulay concluded, "from most novelists, would be an amazing piece of work. Coming from Mr. Forster, it is not amazing, but it is, I think, the best and most interesting book he has written." Edwin Muir, the distinguished Scottish novelist, called the book "a very accomplished novel" in a review in the *Nation,* further commenting that it "is a triumph of the humanistic spirit over material difficult to humanize." Critics throughout the rest of the century echoed such praise, finding particulars to like. Glen O. Allen, for example, writing in *Perspectives on E. M. Forster's "A Passage to India,"* called attention to his meticulous "omission of extraneous detail," and also praised the novel for its philosophical insights. Other critics have pointed to Forster's borrowings from Hinduism in the novel, or to his reconciliation of Victorian thought with modernism. Malcolm Bradbury, writing in *Aspects of E. M. Forster,* noted that Forster "has served as an embodiment of the virtues he writes about; he has shown their function, and their destiny; he has left, for other writers and other men, a workable inheritance." Writing in *E. M. Forster's "A Passage to India,"* editor Harold Bloom called the book "Forster's most famous work," and one "that can sustain many readings, so intricate is its orchestration. It is one of only a few novels of this century that is written-through, in the musical sense of thorough composition." In his *E. M Forster,* Lionel Trilling called the novel Forster's "most comfortable," in which Forster is in total control of his material. "The restraint of our emotions is an important element in the book's greatness," Trilling further asserted. "Great as the problem of India is," Trilling concluded, "Forster's book is not about India alone; it is about all of human life."

A Man of Letters

A Passage to India was Forster's swan song as a novelist. It has been said of him that he spent the first part of his life building a reputation as a great novelist, and the second half living like a great novelist. Indeed this final novel falls almost exactly in the mid-point of Forster's long life. Shortly after publication, he and his mother moved to Surrey, having inherited a lease on a home there. He lived in Surrey until the death of his mother in 1945, whereupon he became an Honorary Fellow at King's College, Cambridge, and lived out his life in rooms there. In

If you enjoy the works of E. M. Forster, you might want to check out the following books and films:

John Galsworthy, *The Forsyte Saga*, 1922.
D. H. Lawrence, *The Rainbow*, 1927.
The French Lieutenant's Woman, a film starring Meryl Streep, 1981.
Sense and Sensibility, a film starring Emma Thompson, 1995.

the second half of his life he was known as the grand old man of English letters, publishing essays and criticism, some of it collected in books such as *Abinger Harvest, What I Believe, Two Cheers for Democracy*, and *The Hill of Devi*. There was also his important contribution to the art and craft of novel writing, *Aspects of the Novel*, as well as biographies: *Marianne Thornton (1797-1887): A Domestic Biography*, and *Goldsworthy Lowes Dickinson*. Reviewing such nonfiction pieces in *Dictionary of Literary Biography*, Philip Gardner wrote: "Forster's essays, with their unique blend of elusive charm, clarity of utterance, and authoritative moral concern, combine with his fiction not only to offer a lasting record of one man's "aliveness," but to reach out toward his readers and continually reinvolve them in it." A further story collection was also published, the 1928 *The Eternal Moment and Other Stories*. Forster also became a prolific radio announcer and commentator, protesting against BBC censorship during the Second World War. He made visits to the United States, as well, giving lectures and speeches on art. Forster also collaborated on the libretto for *Billy Budd* for the opera by Benjamin Britten. There were honors during his lifetime as well, including an Order of Merit, and Forster did manage to have a private life. Two long affairs with London policemen provided him a reasonable facsimile of the realities of the world that he presented so well on paper.

But in the end, it is the novels Forster is remembered for. When he died of a stroke in June of 1970, at ninety-one years of age, he had already undergone something of a literary canonization. Posthumous publication of his homosexual writings deepened such an appreciation for his work. And it is the work that portrays the life. The typical Forster hero/heroine, like himself, was a person in search of truth, of meaning, and sense in the world. These men and women take chances and look outside the narrow confines of proper societal behavior to find their own paths. Such seekers, like Lucy Honeychurch and George Emerson in *A Room with a View*, or Margaret Schlegel in *Howards End*, might meet happy fates; others like Mrs. Moore in *A Passage to India*, Lilia Herriton in *Where Angels Fear to Tread*, Rickie Elliot in *The Longest Journey*, or Leonard Bast in *Howards End*, might be destroyed by such a search. But in the end, it is the search, the journey, Forster tells us over and over, that is important in life. "The visionary element is strong in Forster," McDowell wrote in *Dictionary of Literary Biography*, "and gives his fiction a certain timelessness, as in it he reaches from this world to a kingdom that is mythic and archetypal, to one that partakes not only of the everyday but of the eternal." As Forster told Jones in his *Listener* interview eleven years before his death, "I suppose such views and beliefs that I have, have come out incidentally in my books. . . . Anyone who has cared to read my books will see what high value I attach to personal relationships and to tolerance and, I may add, to pleasure. Pleasure one is not supposed to talk about in public however much one enjoys it in private. But if I have had any influence I should be very glad that it had induced people to enjoy this wonderful world into which we are born, and of course to help others to enjoy it too."

■ Works Cited

Allen, Glen O., "Structure, Symbolism, and Theme in E. M. Forster's "A Passage to India,"" *Perspectives on E. M Forster's "A Passage to India:" A Collection of Critical Essays*, edited by V. A. Shahane, Barnes and Noble, 1968, pp. 121-41.

Beauman, Nicola, *Morgan: A Biography of E. M. Forster*, Hodder and Stoughton, 1993, p. 191.

Bloom, Harold, "Introduction," *E. M. Forster's "A Passage to India*, Chelsea House, 1987, p. 1.

Bradbury, Malcolm, "Two Passages to India: Forster as Victorian and Modern," *Aspects of E. M. Forster*, edited by Oliver Stallybrass, Edward Arnold, 1969, pp. 123-42.

Epstein, Joseph, "One Cheer for E. M. Forster," *Commentary*, September, 1985, pp. 48-57.

Forster, E. M. *The Hill of Devi*, Edward Arnold, 1983.

Forster, E. M., *Selected Letters of E. M. Forster*, Volume 1, edited by Mary Lago and P. N. Furbank, Collins, 1983, pp. 83-89.

Furbank, P. N., *E. M. Forster: A Life*, Harcourt, Brace, 1978, p. 135.

Gardner, Philip, *E. M. Forster, The Critical Heritage*, Routledge and Kegan Paul, 1973, p. 12.

Gardner, Philip, *Dictionary of Literary Biography*, Volume 98: *Modern British Essayists*, Gale, 1990, pp. 123-39.

Garnett, Edward, review of *Howards End*, *Nation*, November 12, 1910.

Review of *Howards End*, *Athenaeum*, December 3, 1910, p. 696.

Review of *Howards End*, *Times Literary Supplement*, October 27, 1910.

Jones, David, "E. M. Forster on His Life and His Books," *Listener*, January 1, 1959.

MaCaulay, Rose, review of *A Passage to India*, *Daily News*, June 4, 1924.

Martin, John Sayre, *E. M. Forster: The Endless Journey*, Cambridge University Press, 1976, pp. 2, 4, 13.

Masterman, C. F. G., review of *A Room with a View*, *Nation*, November 28, 1908.

McDowell, Frederick P. W., *E. M. Forster*, 2nd edition, Twayne, 1982, pp. 3, 7, 21, 46.

McDowell, Frederick P. W., "E. M. Forster," *Dictionary of Literary Biography*, Volume 34: *British Novelists, 1890-1929: Traditionalists*, Gale, 1984, pp. 121-51.

Muir, Edwin, review of *A Passage to India*, *Nation*, October 8, 1924, pp. 379-80.

Rafferty, Terrence, "Yes, But," *New Yorker*, May 4, 1992, pp. 74-76.

Scott-James, R. A., review of *Howards End*, *Daily News*, November 7, 1910.

Stallybrass, Oliver, "Introduction," *A Room with a View*, Edward Arnold, 1977, p. vii.

Trilling, Lionel, *E. M. Forster*, New Directions, 1943.

Viera, Carroll, "E. M. Forster," *Dictionary of Literary Biography*, Volume 162: *British Short-Fiction Writers, 1915-1945*, Gale, 1996, pp. 106-16.

Woolf, Virginia, review of *A Room with a View*, *Times Literary Supplement*, October 22, 1908.

Woolf, Virginia, "The Novels of E. M. Forster," reprinted in *The Death of the Moth and Other Essays*, Harcourt, Brace, 1967, pp. 342-50.

■ For More Information See

BOOKS

Armstrong, Paul B. (editor), *Howards End: Authoritative Text, Textual Appendix, Backgrounds and Contexts, Criticism*, Norton, 1997.

Bakshi, Parminder Kaur, *Distant Desire: Homoerotic Codes and the Subversion of the English Novel in E. M. Forster's Fiction*, P. Lang (New York City), 1995.

Bandyopaadhyaacya, Surabhi, *E. M. Forster: A Critical Linguistic Approach*, Allied (New Delhi), 1995.

Beer, J. B., *The Achievement of E. M. Forster*, Barnes & Noble, 1963.

Beer, J. B., editor, *"A Passage to India": Essays in Interpretation*, Barnes & Noble, 1985.

Borrello, Alfred, *An E. M. Forster Dictionary*, Scarecrow, 1971.

Borrello, Alfred, *An E. M. Forster Glossary*, Scarecrow, 1972.

Bradbury, Malcolm, editor, *Forster*, Prentice-Hall, 1966.

Bradbury, Malcolm, *Possibilities: Essays on the State of the Novel*, Oxford University Press, 1973, pp. 91-120.

Brander, Laurence, *E. M. Forster*, Hart-Davis, 1968.

Brower, Reuben A., *The Fields of Light: An Experiment in Critical Reading*, Oxford University Press, 1951, pp. 182-98.

Colmer, John, *E. M. Forster: The Personal Voice*, Routledge & Kegan Paul, 1975.

Contemporary Literary Criticism, Gale, Volume 1, 1973, Volume 2, 1974, Volume 3, 1975, Volume 4, 1975, Volume 9, 1978, Volume 10, 1979, Volume 13, 1980, Volume 15, 1980, Volume 22, 1982, Volume 45, 1987, Volume 77, 1993.

Cowley, Malcolm, editor, *Writers at Work: The Paris Review Interviews*, First Series, 1958.

Crews, F. C., *E. M. Forster: The Perils of Humanism*, Princeton University Press, 1962.

Das, G. K., *Forster's India*, Rowman & Littlefield, 1978.

Das, G. K. and J. B. Beer, editors, *E. M. Forster: A Human Exploration, Centenary Essays*, New York University Press, 1979.

Duckworth, Alistair M. (editor), *Howards End: Complete, Authoritative Text with Biographical and Historical Contexts, Critical History, and Essays from Five Contemporary Critical Perspectives*, Bedford Books, 1997.

Eldridge, C. C., *The Imperial Experience: From Carlyle to Forster*, St. Martin's Press (New York City), 1996.

Gardner, Philip, *E. M. Forster*, Longman, 1977.

Godfrey, Denis, *Forster's Other Kingdom*, Barnes & Noble, 1968.

Gowda, H. H. Anniah, *A Garland for E. M. Forster*, Literary Half-Yearly, 1969.

Gransden, Karl Watts, *E. M. Forster*, Grove, 1962, revised edition, Oliver & Boyd, 1970.

Herz, Judith Scherer, *The Short Narratives of E. M. Forster*, St. Martin's Press, 1988.

Herz, Judith Scherer and Robert K. Martin, editors, *E. M. Forster: Centenary Revaluations*, Macmillan, 1982.

Johnstone, J. K., *The Bloomsbury Group*, Noonday, 1954.

Kelvin, Norman, *E. M. Forster*, Southern Illinois University Press, 1967. Levine, June P., *Creation and Criticism: A Passage to India*, University of Nebraska Press, 1971.

King, Francis E., *E. M. Forster and His World*, Scribners, 1978.

Kirkpatrick, B. J., *A Bibliography of E. M. Forster*, Clarendon Press, 1985.

Lago, Mary, *E. M. Forster: A Literary Life*, St. Martin's Press (New York City), 1995.

Land, Stephen K., *Challenge and Conventionality in the Fiction of Forster*, 1990.

Lavin, Audrey A. P., *Aspects of the Novelist: E. M. Forster's Pattern and Rhythm*, P. Lang (New York City), 1995.

Levine, June Perry, *Creation and Criticism: "A Passage to India,"* University of Nebraska Press, 1971.

MaCaulay, Rose, *Writings of E. M. Forster*, Harcourt, 1938, new edition, Barnes & Noble, 1970.

Martin, Robert K., and George Piggford, editors, *Queer Forster*, University of Chicago Press, 1997.

May, Brian, *The Modernist as Pragmatist: E.M. Forster and the Fate of Liberalism*, University of Missouri Press, 1997.

McConkey, James, *The Novels of E. M. Forster*, Archon Books, 1971.

McDowell, Frederick P. W., editor, *E. M. Forster: An Annotated Bibliography of Writings about Him*, Northern Illinois University Press, 1977.

Meyers, Jeffrey, *Fiction and the Colonial Experience*, Rowman & Littlefield, pp. 29-54.

Natwar-Singh, K., editor, *E. M. Forster: A Tribute*, Harcourt, 1964.

Oliver, H. J., *The Art of E. M. Forster*, Cambridge University Press, 1960.

Rapport, Nigel, *The Prose and the Passion: Anthropology, Literature, and the Writing of E. M. Forster*, St. Martin's Press (New York City), 1994.

Rose, Martial, *E. M. Forster*, Arco, 1971.

Rosecrance, Barbara, *Forster's Narrative Vision*, Cornell University Press, 1982.

Rosenbaum, S. P., editor, *The Bloomsbury Group: A Collection of Memoirs, Commentary and Criticism*, University of Toronto Press, 1975.

Rosenbaum, S. P., *Victorian Bloomsbury: The Early Literary History of the Bloomsbury Group, volume one*, St. Martin's Press, 1987.

Rutherford, Andrew, *Twentieth Century Interpretations of A Passage to India*, Prentice-Hall, 1970.

Sahni, Chaman L., *Forster's "A Passage to India": The Religious Dimension*, Arnold Heinemann, 1981.

Schorer, Mark, editor, *Modern British Fiction*, Oxford University Press, 1961.

Shusterman, David, *The Quest for Certitude in E. M. Forster's Fiction*, Indiana University Press, 1965.

Stallybrass, Oliver, editor, *Aspects of E. M. Forster*, Harcourt, 1969.

Stape, J.H., *E. M. Forster*, Routledge, 1998.

Stone, Wilfred, *The Cave and the Mountain*, Oxford University Press, 1966.

Summers, Claude J., *E. M. Forster*, Ungar, 1983.

Swinnerton, Frank, *The Georgian Literary Scene*, Dent, 1938, revised edition, 1951.

Tambling, Jeremy, *E. M. Forster*, St. Martin's Press (New York City), 1995.

Thomson, George H., *The Fiction of E. M. Forster*, Wayne State University Press, 1967.

Warren, Austin, *Rage for Order*, University of Michigan Press, 1948.

Wilde, Alan, editor, *Critical Essays on E. M. Forster*, G. K. Hall, 1985.

Zabel, Morton Dauwen, *Craft and Character*, Viking, 1957.

PERIODICALS

Booklist, February 15, 1994, p. 100; April 15, 1994, p. 1547.

Books and Bookmen, August, 1970.

Chicago Tribune, April 9, 1986, April 1, 1987.

Christian Century, July 22, 1970.

Criterion, October, 1934.

Critical Inquiry, autumn, 1985, pp. 59-87.

Criticism, winter, 1980, pp. 40-56.

Dublin Review, 1946.

Encounter, Volume 9, 1957.

Forum, December, 1927.

Globe and Mail (Toronto), January 14, 1984, March 8, 1986.

Journal of Modern Literature, March, 1983, pp. 109-24; summer, 1988, pp. 121-40.

Kliatt, July, 1993, p. 48; January, 1994, p. 48; September, 1995, p. 55; November, 1995, p. 55; May, 1996, p. 47; July, 1996, p. 54; July, 1998, p. 51.

Library Journal, February 1, 1993, p. 132; May 1, 1993, p. 133; February 15, 1994, p. 204; November 1, 1994, p. 126; November 1, 1996, p. 121; May 15, 1999, p. 146; June 15, 1999, p. 113.

Listener, July 9, 1970.

Literary Half-Yearly, July, 1992, pp. 23-30.

Los Angeles Times, March 31, 1987, October 1, 1987, November 22, 1987.

Los Angeles Times Book Review, August 3, 1986.

Mademoiselle, June, 1964.

Modern Fiction Studies, autumn, 1961, pp. 258-70; summer, 1967, pp. 195-210.

Modern Philology, August, 1981, pp. 45-60.

Nation, June 29, 1970, November 29, 1971.

National Review, April 13, 1992, pp. 5-57.

New Republic, October 5, 1949, January 1, 1964.

New Statesman and Society, May 29, 1992, pp. 32-33.

Newsweek, June 22, 1970, September 21, 1987.

New Yorker, September, 1959.

New York Review of Books, May 14, 1992, p. 3; May 6, 1999, pp. 39-40.

New York Times, December 18, 1985, March 7, 1986, May 30, 1986, September 13, 1987, September 18, 1987, October 4, 1987; March 13, 1992, p.C3.

New York Times Book Review, December 29, 1968, January 8, 1984; October 6, 1996, p. 38.

Novel, fall, 1988, pp. 86-105.

PMLA, December, 1955, pp. 934-54; January, 1984, pp. 72-88.

Scrutiny, September, 1938.

Textual Practice, summer, 1991, pp. 195-218.

Theology, April, 1940.

Times (London), February 4, 1982, December 29, 1983, March 14, 1987.

Times Literary Supplement, June 22, 1962, April 16, 1982, April 5, 1985, May 24, 1985; August 2, 1996, p. 24; April 24, 1998, p. 36.

Twentieth Century Literature, July, 1961, pp. 51-63; (E. M. Forster issue) summer-fall, 1985; winter, 1992, pp. 365-85.

Vogue, January 1, 1965.

Washington Post, October 2, 1987.

Washington Post Book World, January 1, 1984.

Wide Angle, October, 1989, pp. 42-51.

Wilson Library Bulletin, April, 1993, p. 73.

■ Obituaries

PERIODICALS

Christian Science Monitor, June 18, 1970.

Listener, June 18, 1970.

New Statesman, June 12, 1970.

New York Review of Books, July 23, 1970.

New York Times, June 8, 1970.

Observer, June 14, 1970.

Time, June 22, 1970.

Washington Post, June 8, 1970.*

—Sketch by J. Sydney Jones

Paula Fox

Personal

Born April 22, 1923, in New York, NY; daughter of Paul Hervey (a writer) and Elsie (de Sola) Fox; married Richard Sigerson in 1948 (divorced, 1954); married Martin Greenberg, June 9, 1962; children: (first marriage) Adam, Gabriel, Linda. *Education:* Attended Columbia University, 1955-58.

Addresses

Home—Brooklyn, NY.

Career

Author. Has worked in numerous occupations, including model, saleswoman, public relations worker, machinist, staff member for the British publisher, Victor Gollancz, reader for a film studio, reporter in Paris, France, and Warsaw, Poland, for the British wire service Telepress, English-as-a-second-language instructor, and teacher at the Ethical Culture School in New York City and for emotionally disturbed children in Dobbs Ferry, New York;

University of Pennsylvania, Philadelphia, professor of English literature, beginning 1963.

Member

PEN, Authors League of America, Authors Guild.

Awards, Honors

Finalist in National Book Award children's book category, 1971, for *Blowfish Live in the Sea*; National Institute of Arts and Letters Award, 1972; Guggenheim fellowship, 1972; National Endowment for the Arts grant, 1974; Newbery Medal, American Library Association, 1974, for *The Slave Dancer*; Hans Christian Andersen Medal, 1978; National Book Award nomination, 1979, for *The Little Swineherd and Other Tales*; *A Place Apart* was selected one of *New York Times*'s Outstanding Books, 1980, and received the American Book Award, 1983; Child Study Children's Book Award from the Bank Street College of Education and one of *New York Times*'s Notable Books, both 1984, Christopher Award and Newbery Honor Book, both 1985, and International Board on Books for Young People Honor List for Writing, 1986, all for *One-Eyed Cat*; Brandeis Fiction Citation, 1984; Rockefeller Foundation grant, 1984; *The Moonlight Man* was selected one of the *New York Times*'s Notable Books, 1986, and one of the Child Study Association of America's Children's Books of the Year, 1987; Silver Medallion, University of Southern Mississippi, 1987; *Boston Globe/Horn Book* Award for fiction and Newbery Honor Book, 1989, for *The Village by the Sea*. Empire State Award for children's literature, 1994.

■ Writings

FOR JUVENILES

Maurice's Room, illustrated by Ingrid Fetz, Macmillan, 1966.

A Likely Place, illustrated by Edward Ardizzone, Macmillan, 1967.

How Many Miles to Babylon?, illustrated by Paul Giovanopoulos, David White, 1967.

The Stone-Faced Boy, illustrated by Donald A. Mackay, Bradbury, 1968.

Dear Prosper, illustrated by Steve McLachlin, David White, 1968.

Portrait of Ivan, illustrated by Saul Lambert, Bradbury, 1969.

The King's Falcon, illustrated by Eros Keith, Bradbury, 1969.

Hungry Fred, illustrated by Rosemary Wells, Bradbury, 1969.

Blowfish Live in the Sea, Bradbury, 1970.

Good Ethan, illustrated by Arnold Lobel, Bradbury, 1973.

The Slave Dancer, illustrated by Eros Keith, Bradbury, 1973.

The Little Swineherd and Other Tales, Dutton, 1978, new edition illustrated by Robert Byrd, Dutton Children's Books, 1996.

A Place Apart, Farrar, Straus, 1980.

One-Eyed Cat, Bradbury, 1984.

(Author of introduction) Marjorie Kellogg, *Tell Me That You Love Me, Junie Moon*, Farrar, Straus, 1984.

The Moonlight Man, Bradbury, 1986.

Lily and the Lost Boy, Orchard Books, 1987, published in England as *The Lost Boy*, Dent, 1988.

The Village by the Sea, Orchard Books, 1988, published in England as *In a Place of Danger*, Orchard Books, 1989.

Monkey Island, Orchard Books, 1991.

(With Floriano Vecchi) *Amzat and His Brothers: Three Italian Tales*, illustrated by Emily Arnold McCully, Orchard Books, 1993.

Western Wind, Orchard Books, 1993.

The Eagle Kite, Orchard Books, 1995.

Radiance Descending, D.K. Inc., 1997.

FOR ADULTS

Poor George, Harcourt, 1967.

Desperate Characters, Harcourt, 1970, reprinted with an afterword by Irving Howe, Nonpareil, 1980.

The Western Coast, Harcourt, 1972.

The Widow's Children, Dutton, 1976.

A Servant's Tale, North Point Press, 1984.

The God of Nightmares, North Point Press, 1990.

■ Adaptations

Desperate Characters was adapted as a motion picture by Paramount, 1970; a cassette and a film strip accompanied by cassette have been produced of *One-Eyed Cat* by Random House.

■ Sidelights

Best known for her "uncompromising integrity," according to *Horn Book*'s Alice Bach, American writer Paula Fox has crafted distinguished careers in both children's books and adult fiction. Among the former are novels such as *The Slave Dancer, One-Eyed Cat, The Village by the Sea, Monkey Island, The Eagle Kite*, and *Radiance Descending*. In such juvenile and YA novels Fox pulls no punches; she deals with subjects from abandonment to the misery of AIDS and puts her youthful protagonists in difficult situations and exotic locales, from an island off the coast of northeastern America to an island in the Aegean. "Children know about pain and fear and unhappiness and betrayal," Fox once told *Authors and Artists for Young Adults (AAYA)*. "And we do them a disservice by trying to sugarcoat dark truths. . . . We must never, ever try to pull the wool over children's eyes by "watering down" powerful stories."

"Paula Fox believes children have the right to know what to expect from life," Bach noted in her *Horn Book* overview of the author's works. "She acknowledges confusion. Nowhere in her books does she imply there are solutions to grief, abandonment, loneliness. . . . By admitting to the universality of fear, puzzlement, and foolish behavior, she invites the reader to scream, to snicker, to laugh, to admit pain." It is a formula that readers and critics alike have responded to positively, for her books prove to be popular many years after initial publication and have won numerous awards, including the prestigious Hans Christian Andersen Medal, the Newbery Medal, and the American Book Award for Children's Fiction Paperback.

In addition to her award-winning picture books, chapter books, novels for intermediate readers, and realistic fiction for young adults, Fox has also authored novels for adults, such as *Desperate Characters*, which was adapted for a motion picture. Fox has been described by *Nation* contributor Blair T. Birmelin as "one of our most intelligent (and least appreciated) contemporary novelists." Fox does not feel the need to distinguish between her adult and juvenile fiction, however. She commented in John Rowe Townsend's *A Sense of Story: Essays on Contemporary Writers for Children*, "I never think I'm writing for children, when I work. A story does not start *for* anyone, nor an idea, nor a feeling of an idea; but starts more for oneself." As *School Library Journal* contributor Linda Silver noted, "So few authors write equally well for children and adults that Paula Fox and Isaac Bashevis Singer (who do) should be noted." Silver went on to comment, "Fox's polished prose is so restrained that at times it is cryptic." And as Fox noted in her acceptance speech for the Hans Christian Andersen Medal, reprinted in *Bookbird*, she sees no general difference in the division between children's and adult literature. "The heart of the matter, I believe, is that the art of storytelling is, ultimately, the art of truth. In the imaginative effort that lies behind a good story, there is no difference between writing for children and for adults."

A Peripatetic Childhood

Fox spent her childhood moving from place to place and school to school. Her father was what Fox described to *AAYA* as "an itinerant writer." Working in New York City, he earned a living by rewriting plays by other authors, as well as writing several of his own, and later he went to Hollywood and England to work for film studios. While her parents were traveling about, Fox was sent elsewhere. As she recalled in *AAYA*, "As for me, my home for the first six years of my life was with a congregational minister who had been a newspaperman . . . before he had found his vocation in the ministry. He was an ardent historian of the Revolutionary period in American history, particularly as it unfolded in the Hudson Valley, where he spent a large part of his life. Every morning he went to his study, and over the years there issued from his Remington typewriter sermons, items he wrote for a local newspaper . . . essays . . . [and] poems." Fox lived with the minister and his invalid mother in a Victorian house overlooking the Hudson River. With his active and curious mind, the minister had a profound influence on Fox. He taught her to read and to appreciate the works of authors such as Rudyard Kipling, Eugene Field, Mark Twain, Washington Irving, and Walt Whitman; and he also told her tales of the Rev-

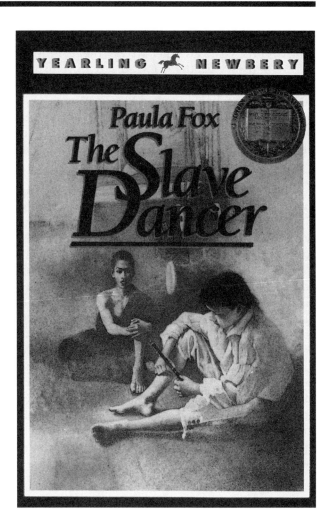

Thirteen-year-old Jessie is thrown aboard a slave ship to play his fife for slaves in Fox's Newbery Medal-winning novel.

olutionary War and other historical events. All these stories inevitably rubbed off on the young Fox. "When I was 5, I had my first experience of being a ghost writer—of sorts," Fox related to *AAYA*, recalling how the minister once accepted her suggestion to write a sermon about a waterfall. For "an instant," she later added, "I grasped consciously what had been implicit in every aspect of my life with the minister—that everything could count, that a word, spoken as meant, contained in itself an energy capable of awakening imagination, thought, emotion." It was this experience that first inspired Fox to become a writer.

When Fox was six years old, she left the minister's home to live in California for two years, and in 1931 she moved again, this time to live with her maternal grandmother on a sugar plantation in Cuba. Here, Fox quickly picked up Spanish from her fellow students while attending classes in a one-room school-house. Three years after her arrival, the revolution led by Batista y Zaldivar forced Fox to return to New York City. By this time in her life, Fox had attended nine schools and had hardly ever seen her parents; she found solace and stability by visiting public libraries. "I learned young that public libraries are places of refuge and stability amid chaos and confusion," Fox told *AAYA*.

Fox worked several different jobs after finishing high school, ranging from machinist to working for a publishing company and a newspaper. "I knew I wanted to travel and was able to find jobs that would enable me to do so," Fox recalled. Her desire to travel led her to a position with a leftist British news service that assigned her to cover Poland after World War II. Later, she returned to the United States, married, and had children, but the marriage ended in divorce. Afterwards, Fox resolved to finish her education, attending Columbia University for four years, until she could no longer afford the expense and had to leave before receiving her diploma. Despite the lack of a degree, Fox's knowledge of Spanish helped her find a job as an English teacher for Spanish-speaking children. She also found other teaching positions, including one as a teacher for the emotionally disturbed.

In 1962, Fox married an English professor and moved to Greece for six months where her husband—recipient of a Guggenheim fellowship—studied and wrote. All this time, she harbored hopes of one day becoming a writer, "but for a long time it remained a shining, but elusive, goal," she told *AAYA*. But with the trip to Greece, Fox was finally able to realize her dream, working full time as a writer.

Early Works

Fox's first publication, *Maurice's Room,* appeared in 1966, and is, as Townsend noted in *A Sounding of Storytellers,* "a blessedly funny book." The story about a boy who is such an avid collector that only he and one friend can enter his room safely, *Maurice's Room* "is a hilarious, subversive book, full of casual joys," according to Townsend. The book was well received and was followed a year later by *A Likely Place,* the story of a young boy whose parents fuss over-much about him. His salvation comes about when he is left under the care of the yogurt and yoga-loving Miss Fitchlow, who gives the boy room to maneuver. Townsend dubbed this second book "dry" and "subtle."

Victoria Finch's life changes after her father dies and she and her mother move from Boston to New Oxford.

Fox's third book, *How Many Miles to Babylon?,* is longer and more complex than the first two. James is a young black boy growing up in Brooklyn. With his father out of his life and his mother in the hospital, James is left in the care of three aunts and soon falls into the clutches of a juvenile gang of dog thieves. He travels with the gang to Coney Island, where they explore the deserted funhouse. While there, he is able to set the dogs free and escape back to his aunts where his mother, released from the hospital, is waiting for him. Townsend observed that on the surface this novel "is a straightforward story," but that there are symbolic undertones and an almost "dreamlike" quality to the book. Writing in *Horn Book,* Ruth Hill Viguers observed that the writing in *How Many Miles to Babylon?* is "subtle, making the understated story almost nightmarish in its excitement."

A similar journey of discovery comes in *The Stone-Faced Boy,* in which Gus, the middle child of five, ventures out into the snow one night to free a stray dog that has gotten caught in a trap. Once again, the youthful protagonist is able to prove himself. A dog again figures in the 1968 *Dear Prosper,* this time as the narrator of a memoir. The dog in question, it seems, is self-educated, and writes his memoir to Prosper, his next-to-last owner. Here he recounts his infancy in New Mexico, his time spent on a cattle ranch, and the course of events that led him from a life of pampered luxury in Boston to a circus and to abandonment in Paris. A contributor to *Kirkus Reviews* observed that the writing is "clipped" and "economical," and "puts people in perspective." Margaret F. O'Connell, praising the book in the *New York Times Book Review* for its "offbeat" approach, concluded the book made a dog's life seem "downright adventurous."

Overall, Fox's juvenile novels have a complexity and sincerity that make them popular with readers and critics alike. These books cover a wide range of subjects, including parental conflict, alcoholism, and death. Frequently, her young protagonists are emotionally withdrawn children who undertake a journey that is symbolic of their emotional development. In *Blowfish Live in the Sea,* for example, nineteen-year-old Ben travels from New York to Boston to see his estranged, alcoholic father after a twelve-year absence. Because of a past trauma involving a lie his father told him, Ben has withdrawn into himself to the point where he no longer speaks to anyone. His sister Carrie is the only family member who tries to reach out to Ben. The importance of Ben and Carrie's journey to Boston, explained a *Horn Book* reviewer, is that "each step . . . relays something further in their tenuous gropings towards an understanding of themselves and of others."

Novel of Slavery Leads to Newbery Medal

Of all of her books, the controversial yet highly acclaimed *The Slave Dancer,* winner the 1974 Newbery Medal, is the work for which Fox is best known. It is the story of a New Orleans boy who is kidnapped and placed on a slave ship bound for West Africa. The boy, Jessie Bollier, is chosen for his ability to play the fife; his task aboard ship is to "dance" the slaves so they can exercise their cramped limbs. Eventually, Jessie escapes when the ship's crew is drowned in a storm, but he is forever scarred by his experience. Despite the praise *The*

Ned learns the responsibility of handling a gun after he shoots his new Daisy air rifle and injures a cat.

Slave Dancer has received, a number of critics have complained that Fox's portrayal of the slaves made them appear to be merely dispirited cattle, and they accused the author of excusing the slave drivers as being victims of circumstance. Binnie Tate, for example, commented in *Interracial Books for Children:* "Through the characters' words, [Fox] excuses the captors and places the blame for the slaves' captivity on Africans themselves. The author slowly and systematically excuses almost all the whites in the story for their participation in the slave venture and by innuendo places the blame elsewhere." Albert V. Schwartz, also writing in *Interracial Books for Children,* felt that book promoted racist viewpoints because of the passive representation of the black victims. "The Black people are only pathetic sufferers," Schwartz commented. "No "fight back" qualities whatever are found in these characters. . . . For them the author provides no balance."

Presenting more of a middle ground between condemnation and praise was Julius Lester, writing in the *New York Times Book Review*. "What saves [this] book from being a failure," wrote Lester, "is the quality of [the] writing, which is consistently excellent." However Lester also found problems with *The Slave Dancer*. "With such good writing, it is too bad that the book as a whole does not succeed." Lester felt that while the novel "describes" the horrors of such slave ships, it "does not re-create them, and if history is to become reality, the reader must live that history as if it were his own life." Lester complained that readers of Fox's book were "spectators" rather than "fellow sufferers."

Other reviewers, however, regarded *The Slave Dancer* as a fair and humane treatment of a sensitive subject. In her *Horn Book* essay, Bach called the book "one of the finest examples of a writer's control over her material. . . . With an underplayed but implicit sense of rage, Paula Fox exposes the men who dealt in selling human beings." Writing in *Children's Book Review*, C.S. Hannabuss commented on Fox's "concise and carved style," and went on to note that "Fox once again gets into a child and looks out on a harsh and dangerous world. For the nightmare of the voyage is shown in the very moments of realisation, growing fear and panic and disgust gripping the reader too at deep levels of consciousness." Hannabuss concluded that *The Slave Dancer* "extends the belief that [Fox] is one of the most exciting writers practicing for children and young people today." In *Dictionary of Literary Biography*, Anita Moss wrote that *The Slave Dancer* "is historical fiction at its finest, for Fox has meticulously researched every facet of the slave trade and of the period." Comparing the book to Joseph Conrad's *Heart of Darkness*, Moss further observed that it "takes the reader on a voyage that reveals a haunting glimpse into the abyss of human evil. . . . *The Slave Dancer* is clearly Fox's masterpiece, and it is fast becoming a classic in American children's literature."

Novels of Abandonment and Hope

No other work by Fox has been quite as controversial as *The Slave Dancer*, though the author continues to deliver bittersweet messages to today's youth. Other award-winning children's novels by Fox, such as *A Place Apart*, *One-Eyed Cat*, and *The Village by the Sea*, are similarly concerned with relationships, strong characterization, and emotionally troubled protagonists. *A Place Apart* concerns Victoria Finch, a thirteen-year-old girl whose comfort and security are shaken when her father dies suddenly. Victoria's

Catherine struggles to understand her divorced father who is kind, fun, and interesting during by day, but a drunk at night in Fox's 1986 novel.

grief, writes *Washington Post Book World* contributor Katherine Paterson, "is the bass accompaniment to the story. Sometimes it swells, taking over the narrative, the rest of the time it subsides into a dark, rhythmic background against which the main story is played." Victoria must also come to terms with her infatuation with Hugh, a manipulative boy who "exerts . . . a power over her spirit," according to Paterson. "This is almost an adult novel," remarked Zena Sutherland in a *Bulletin of the Center for Children's Books* review, "subtle and percipient in its relationships, mature in its bittersweetness; the characters are firmly drawn and the style is grave and polished." Writing in the *New York Times Book Review*, novelist Anne Tyler complimented Fox on a "story without gimmicks or exaggerations." Tyler concluded, "[Fox] writes a honed prose, avoiding all traces of gee-whillikers tone, and her language is simple and direct. *A Place Apart* is a book apart—quiet-voiced, believable and often very moving."

One-Eyed Cat, declared *Dictionary of Literary Biography* contributor Moss, "is one of Fox's finest literary achievements." The title refers to a stray cat that the main character Ned accidentally injures with an air rifle. The guilt Ned feels afterwards plagues him through most of the rest of the book, even making him physically ill at one point. He finally confesses his thoughtless act to his mother, who in turn confesses that she had once deserted Ned and his father when he was younger. Recognizing these flaws leads Ned to a reconciliation with his parents and with himself. Tyler, reviewing the novel in *New York Times Book Review*, felt that the book was "full of well-drawn, complicated characters," and that there was "integrity in the plot." Tyler went on to comment, "Most important, though, is what the story can teach young readers about grown-ups' expectations of them." *Horn Book*'s Ethel L. Heins observed, "The much-honored author writes with an artlessness that conceals her art, using the nuances of language to reveal the subtleties of human experience and to push back the frontiers of a young reader's understanding."

A typical Fox device is to put a main character in an unfamiliar and hostile setting. This occurs in *Lily and the Lost Boy*, in which three youngsters are visiting a Greek island, and again, In *The Village by the Sea*. In this book, a girl, Emma, is sent to live with her uncle and neurotic, alcoholic aunt for two weeks when her father has to go to the hospital for heart surgery. Unable to cope with her hateful aunt and troubled about her father's health, Emma finds some solace in creating a make-believe village on the beach. But, as Rosellen Brown relates in the *New York Times Book Review*, "Emma's miniature haven is ultimately beyond her protection. She can only cherish the building of it, and then the memory." Reviewing the novel in *School Library Journal*, Amy Kellerman observed that the "cancerous effect of envy and the healing properties of love and self-esteem are driven home poignantly and with a gentle humor that runs throughout the book." Kellerman concluded, "Fox has given readers another treasure for reading alone or reading aloud."

Continuing her practice of placing her young protagonists in difficult circumstances, Fox, in *Monkey Island*, examines the issue of homelessness and

When her father turns very ill, Emma must stay with strict Aunt Bea and Uncle Crispin in their log home above the beach.

explores the more general childhood fear of abandonment. The story concerns an eleven-year-old middle-class boy named Clay Garrity. His father loses his job as a magazine art director and abandons his family. Because his mother is eight months pregnant and can't work, Clay fears the social services department will take him away and put him in a foster home. Clay decides to leave home and live on the streets, where he is befriended by two kindly homeless men. Finally, however, a bout of pneumonia brings Clay to the attention of the social services, and he is put in a foster home. By the end of the novel, the family is reunited, with Clay, his new baby sister, and mother moving into an apartment together after the mother has secured work. "The novel individualizes the problems of homeless people and puts faces on those whom society has made faceless," remarked Ellen Fader in a *Horn Book* review. Fader felt "readers' perceptions will be changed after reading the masterfully crafted *Monkey Island.*" Writing in the *New York Times Book Review,* Dinitia Smith called the novel "delicate and moving," and a "relentless story that succeeds in conveying the bitter facts" of homelessness.

In *Western Wind,* Fox has been praised for taking a rather well-worn premise in children's literature—a lonely young girl is sent by her parents to live with an elderly relative who proves to be quite wise—and making it original and interesting. This is achieved mainly by Fox's depiction of the young heroine's grandmother, an eccentric painter who lives on a remote island off the coast of Maine in a house without indoor plumbing. Patricia J. Wagner in the *Bloomsbury Review* lauded Fox's literary skills and concluded that both "adult and junior fiction writers should study her work with care." Ilene Cooper, on the other hand, writing in *Booklist,* offered oblique criticism of this novel and much of Fox's writing: "Fox's work can be like a piece of fine lace. You admire its beauty and the delicate craftsmanship that went into its making, but you don't always know what to do with it. And sometimes you just get tired of so much lace." Betsy Hearne, however, reviewing *Western Wind* in the *Bulletin of the Center for Children's Books*, observed that Fox "uses an isolated situation, as she has done before, to delve into a child's deepening awareness." Hearne further commented, "Fox's style especially suits this taut narrative, into which she slips similes that are frequent but consciously plain to suit the setting."

Homosexuality and AIDS are the issues that Liam Cormac and his family must come to terms with in *The Eagle Kite.* Young Liam's father is dying from the HIV virus. His immanent death and the circumstances under which he contracted the disease cause the family almost unbearable grief; they also provide the narrative struggles through which some memorable characters are defined. Though his mother tells him that his father contracted AIDS from a bad blood transfusion, Liam now remembers seeing his father embrace a young man on the beach several years earlier. Coming to terms with this memory and with the present day reality is at the heart of this novel. Writing in *Voice of Youth Advocates,* W. Keith McCoy described the book as "a brief, but intense, portion of one young boy's life," and further noted that "Fox's spare prose enhances the emotions that are buffeting the Cormacs." In *The Washington Post Book World,* Elizabeth Hand called the book "beautifully written," and reviewing the novel in *Horn Book,* Nancy Vasilakis remarked on its "painstaking honesty." Vasilakis concluded, "This

will be a hard novel for teens to absorb, but well worth the effort."

Such honesty is also displayed in Fox's 1997 novel *Radiance Descending,* the story of a boy struggling to ignore his brother who is suffering from Down's syndrome. Adolescent Paul Coleman is tired of his brother, Jacob. Having just moved to Long Island from New York City, Paul is eager to avoid the eternal laughter of his brother, and the way he messes up the table and Paul's room. Though Jacob idealizes Paul, Paul is also tired of the way his parents focus all attention on the lovable but simple younger brother. Slowly, however, Paul comes to realize that the mere fact of avoiding Jacob is still focusing on him, and that there may be a middle ground. Escorting Jacob to his Saturday morning allergy shots, Paul is forced into Jacob's world: into its slower pace and the loyal friends who inhabit it. "Older readers will find many layers of meaning in this novel," noted a reviewer for *Publishers Weekly.* "Younger readers may be put off by a few esoteric allusions . . . but will still be able to recognize the gradual blossoming of Paul's compassion." Edward Sullivan, writing in *Voice of Youth Advocates*, felt that *Radiance Descending* "is a quiet, introspective novel told with great eloquence." Sullivan went on to write, "Fox's every word is chosen with care, and every sentence masterfully crafted," and concluded that the novel is "moving and touching." A contributor for *Kirkus Reviews* remarked that the story was "worthwhile" and "poignant" if for no other reason than the "authentic delineation of a loving family's coping with one member's special needs."

Fox's career has been long and distinguished. Though she has won less notoriety for her adult fiction than for her works for children, she has continued to contribute in the latter field, as well, with her popular *Desperate Characters,* and publishing *A Servant's Tale* in 1984 and *The God of Nightmares* in 1990. Such novels are, according to Linda Simon writing in *Commonweal,* "concerned with the cataclysmic moments of private lives, and the quiet desperation of ordinary people." But it is decidedly for her contributions in children's literature that Fox is deservedly best known. As Cathryn M. Mercier noted in an essay on Fox in *St. James Guide to Young Adult Writers,* "In every novel, Fox attributes significant capabilities to her readers. She pays tribute to their emotional, intellectual, and psychological abilities with layered, probing narratives, identifiable characters who achieve genuine illumination, and lucid, striking prose." Mercier further pointed out, "Although some critics occasionally label her work

If you enjoy the works of Paula Fox, you might want to check out the following books:

Theresa Nelson, *The Beggars' Ride*, 1992.
Gary Paulsen, *Nightjohn*, 1993.
Colby Rodowsky, *What about Me?*, 1989.
Joyce Sweeney, *The Spirit Window*, 1998.
Jean Thesman, *The Rain Catchers*, 1991.

"depressing," most praise her integrity in writing honestly about relationships and emotional development. Her craft seems effortless; her vision essential and eloquent."

■ Works Cited

Bach, Alicia, "Cracking Open the Geode: The Fiction of Paula Fox," *Horn Book*, September-October, 1977, pp. 514-21.

Birmelin, Blair T., review of *A Servant's Tale*, *Nation*, November 3, 1984.

Review of *Blowfish Live in the Sea*, *Horn Book*, November-December, 1970.

Brown, Rosellen, review of *The Village by the Sea*, *New York Times Book Review*, February 5, 1989, p. 37.

Cooper, Ilene, review of *Western Wind*, *Booklist*, October 15, 1993, p. 432.

Review of *Dear Prosper*, *Kirkus Reviews*, April 1, 1968, p. 393.

Fader, Ellen, review of *Monkey Island*, *Horn Book*, September-October, 1991, pp. 596-97.

Fox, Paula, "Acceptance Speech—1978 H. C. Andersen Author's Medal," *Bookbird*, December 13, 1978, pp. 2-3.

Hand, Elizabeth, review of *The Eagle Kite*, *Washington Post Book World*, May 7, 1995, p. 14.

Hannabuss, C. S., review of *The Slave Dancer*, *Children's Book Review*, Winter, 1974-75.

Hearne, Betsy, review of *Western Wind*, *Bulletin of the Center for Children's Books*, September, 1993, pp. 9-10.

Heins, Ethel L., review of *One-Eyed Cat*, *Horn Book*, January-February, 1985, pp. 57-58.

Kellerman, Amy, review of *The Village by the Sea*, *School Library Journal*, August, 1988, p. 93.

Lester, Julius, review of *The Slave Dancer*, *New York Times Book Review*, January 20, 1974.

McCoy, W. Keith, review of *The Eagle Kite*, *Voice of Youth Advocates*, June, 1995, pp. 93-94.

Mercier, Cathryn M., "Fox, Paula," *St. James Guide to Young Adult Writers*, 2nd edition, edited by Tom Pendergast and Sara Pendergast, St. James Press, 1999, pp. 292-93.

Moss, Anita, "Paula Fox," *Dictionary of Literary Biography*, Volume 52: *American Writers for Children since 1960: Fiction*, Gale, 1986.

O'Connell, Margaret F., review of *Dear Prosper*, *New York Times Book Review*, July 21, 1968, p. 22.

Paterson, Katherine, review of *A Place Apart*, *Washington Post Book World*, February 8, 1981.

Review of *Radiance Descending*, *Kirkus Reviews*, September 1, 1997, p. 1389.

Review of *Radiance Descending*, *Publishers Weekly*, July 27, 1997, p. 202.

Schwartz, Albert V., review of *The Slave Dancer*, *Interracial Books for Children*, Volume 5, number 5, 1974.

Silver, Linda, "From Baldwin to Singer: Authors for Kids and Adults," *School Library Journal*, February, 1979, pp. 27-29.

Simon, Linda, review of *A Servant's Tale*, *Commonweal*, January 11, 1985.

Smith, Dinitia, "No Place to Call Home," *New York Times Book Review*, November 10, 1991, p. 52.

Sullivan, Edward, review of *Radiance Descending*, *Voice of Youth Advocates*, February, 1998, p. 383.

Sutherland, Zena, review of *A Place Apart*, *Bulletin of the Center for Children's Books*, November, 1980, p. 52.

Tate, Binnie, review of *The Slave Dancer*, *Interracial Books for Children*, Volume 5, number 5, 1974.

Townsend, John Rowe, *A Sense of Story: Essays on Contemporary Writers for Children*, Lippincott, 1971.

Townsend, John Rowe, "Paula Fox," *A Sounding of Storytellers: New and Revised Essays on Contemporary Writers for Children*, Lippincott, 1979, pp. 55-64.

Tyler, Anne, "Staking Out Her Own Territory," *New York Times Book Review*, November 9, 1980, p. 55.

Tyler, Anne, "Trying to Be Perfect," *New York Times Book Review*, November 11, 1984, p. 48.

Vasilakis, Nancy, review of *The Eagle Kite*, *Horn Book*, September-October, 1995, pp. 608-9.

Viguers, Ruth Hill, review of *How Many Miles to Babylon,?*, *Horn Book*, September-October, 1967.

Wagner, Patricia J., review of *Western Wind*, *Bloomsbury Review*, March-April, 1994.

■ For More Information See

BOOKS

Authors of Books for Young People, 3rd edition, edited by Martha E. Ward et al, Scarecrow Press, 1990.

Children's Books and Their Creators, edited by Anita Silvey, Houghton Mifflin, 1995.

Children's Literature Review, Volume 1, Gale, 1976, Volume 44, 1997.

Contemporary Literary Criticism, Gale, Volume 2, 1974, Volume 8, 1978.

Kingman, Lee, editor, *Newbery and Caldecott Medal Winners, 1966-1975,* Horn Book, 1975.

PERIODICALS

Booklist, March 15, 1993, p. 64; February 1, 1995, p. 1003; September 1, 1997, p. 124.

Chicago Tribune, April 9, 1995, p. 7.

Children's Book Review, December, 1972.

English Journal, November, 1996, p. 132.

Horn Book, August, 1969; December, 1970; August, 1974; October, 1978; April, 1984; July-August, 1993, p. 468; March-April, 1994, p. 198; September-October, 1997, p. 569.

Los Angeles Times Book Review, September 25, 1988; July 16, 1995, p. 27.

Ms., October, 1984.

Newsweek, March 16, 1970; September 27, 1976; December 1, 1980.

New Yorker, February 7, 1970; November 1, 1976.

New York Review of Books, June 1, 1967; October 5, 1972; October 28, 1976; June 27, 1985.

New York Times, February 10, 1970; September 22, 1972; September 16, 1976.

New York Times Book Review, February 1, 1970; October 8, 1972; October 3, 1976; July 12, 1981; November 11, 1984; November 18, 1984; July 8, 1990, p. 18; November 10, 1991, p. 52; November 10, 1993, p. 52; April 10, 1994, p. 35.

Publishers Weekly, April 6, 1990; April 12, 1993, p. 64; August 23, 1993, p. 73; April 10, 1994, p. 35; February 20, 1995, p. 207; January 13, 1997, p. 36.

School Library Journal, August, 1991, p. 164; April, 1992, p. 42; July, 1993, p. 90; December, 1993, p. 111; February, 1995, p. 63; April, 1995, p. 150; September, 1997, p. 216.

Voice of Youth Advocates, December, 1993, p. 290; June, 1995, p. 93; October, 1995, p. 210.*

—Sketch by J. Sydney Jones

Adele Griffin

■ Personal

Born July 29, 1970, in Philadelphia, PA; daughter of John Joel Berg (a business manager) and Priscilla Sands Watson (a school principal); married Erich Paul Mauff (an investment banker). *Education:* University of Pennsylvania, B.A. (English), 1993. *Politics:* Democrat.

■ Addresses

Home—154 West 18th St., #7D, New York, NY 10011. *E-mail*—erichmauff@aol.com. *Office*—215 Park Ave. So., New York, NY 10003. *Agent*—Charlotte Sheedy, c/o Sterling Lord Literistic, 65 Bleecker St., New York, NY 10012.

■ Career

Children's author. Clarion Books, New York, NY, assistant editor, 1996-98, freelance manuscript reader, 1996—.

■ Member

Society of Children's Book Writers and Illustrators, "Young Penn Alum," Friends of the New York Public Library, 92nd Street Young Men's Christian Association (YMCA) of New York.

■ Awards, Honors

National Book Award nomination, National Book Foundation, 1997, and Notable Book citation, American Library Association (ALA), 1997, both for *Sons of Liberty;* Books for the Teen Age, New York Public Library, 1997, and *Parenting Magazine* Award, 1997, both for *Split Just Right;* Blue Ribbon designation, *Bulletin of the Center for Children's Books,* Best Books, *Publishers Weekly* and *School Library Journal,* Notable Book, ALA, Best Books for Young Adults, ALA, and 100 Titles for Reading and Sharing, New York Public Library, all 1998, all for *The Other Shepards.*

■ Writings

Rainy Season, Houghton Mifflin, 1996.
Split Just Right, Hyperion, 1997.
Sons of Liberty, Hyperion, 1997.
The Other Shepards, Hyperion, 1998.
Dive, Hyperion, 1999.

■ Sidelights

The author of several highly acclaimed books for younger readers, Adele Griffin has blended a realistic style with a focus on family to fashion what she called "total escapism" in an interview with Edward T. Sullivan in *Voice of Youth Advocates.* "If a book can get you so absorbed that you don't even realize that it's gotten darker in the room and you need to turn on a light because you spent the last three hours being completely immersed in that story—that's a good story," Griffin told Sullivan. Many such good stories have come from Griffin in the course of only a few years; with her third novel, *Sons of Liberty,* she became a National Book Award finalist. Griffin is, according to Sullivan, "one of today's best writers of middle grade fiction."

Griffin did not initially intend to become a writer, but a job out of college at Macmillan's Children's Books reintroduced her to the world of such books. "One of my most treasured childhood memories is the excitement I felt going book shopping before summer vacation," Griffin once commented. "I looked forward to our family's annual visit to New York City and trip to Brentano's, where I was allowed to purchase as many books as I wanted, a joyful extravagance. I knew what I liked: stories about princesses, tough heroines who, defying all odds, would rise from a garret or cottage adjacent to the requisite bog to become a mogul—usually of a department store. I did *not* like science fiction, fantasy, or books about boys."

First Effort Meets with Success

Griffin's well-received debut novel, *Rainy Season,* was lauded in a *Publishers Weekly* review as "ambitiously conceived and sharply observed." The story follows Lane Beck, a fearful twelve-year-old girl, and her belligerently bold younger brother Charlie through a single transformative day. The Beck family is living on an army base in the Panama Canal Zone in 1977, when resentment of American imperialism is at its peak. The story's setting is key mainly for its contribution of danger and suspense, but the history and politics relevant to the Canal Zone are also discussed in an author's note. *Horn Book* reviewer Nancy Vasilakis wrote that the Panama setting "adds a faint aura of decadence to the narrative." Janice M. Del Negro of the *Bulletin of the Center for Children's Books* maintained that the story's atmosphere is "strongly evoked but never intrusive," adding that "the politics are present but always in the background" of Griffin's work. In anticipation of a battle with the children on the opposite side of the Zone, the Beck children and their friends begin building a fort.

Tensions escalating outside the family are paralleled by the strains existing within the family. Lane is prone to panic attacks, Charlie to bully-like behav-

Adele Griffin's first novel introduces readers to Lane—a twelve-year-old girl who must confront her families' past in order to help her young brother, Charlie.

ior, and both children's problems are being deliberately ignored by their parents. Lane's concern for her brother forces her to break the family's pathological silence about the grief they feel over older sister Emily's death in a car accident. *School Library Journal* contributor Lucinda Lockwood commented favorably on Griffin's "evocative" writing and the author's ability to "capture the setting and the nuances of adolescent relationships." A *Publishers Weekly* critic commended the way "Griffin unfolds the events of the day and lets the reader make sense of them," revealing the nature of the tragedy "deep into her story without resorting to melodrama or otherwise manipulating the characterizations." Del Negro concluded that "[T]he image of Lane opening a box of photographs and reclaiming the older sister she loves is one that will remain with readers long after the book is closed."

Danny searches for the true story of her life when she learns that her mother has been keeping secrets and making up stories in Griffin's 1997 novel.

Griffin's next book, *Sons of Liberty*, again adopts the more serious tone of her first novel. Through seventh-grader Rock Kindle, Griffin seriously examines the complicated issues faced by members of a dysfunctional family. Rock has always looked up to his father, and in imitation of his father's behavior, has become a bully. Rock's older brother, Cliff, has lost patience with their father's clearly warped sense of militancy, which prescribes regular doses of humiliation and such bizarre punishments as waking the boys up in the middle of the night to do chores and calisthenics. When the family shatters, no longer able to stand the strain, Rock is forced to choose between loyalty to his father and loyalty to his newly discovered sense of self. In a starred review, a *Publishers Weekly* critic praised Griffin's use of "pointedly jarring dialogue" and her "keen ear for adolescent jargon." *Horn Book* reviewer Kitty Flynn

credited the development of Rock's character with providing "the tension in what could have been a superficial treatment of the issues." A National Book Award finalist, *Sons of Liberty* also was a 1997 Notable Book from the ALA.

With *The Other Shepards*, Griffin created a supernatural teen romance about a girl named Holland and her obsessive-compulsive sister Geneva. The two are passing their adolescent years in a world that is haunted by the memory of three older siblings who died before the two sisters were even born. In the guise of Annie, a mural painter, the spirit of the older sister breathes color into the moribund Shepard family. A *Publishers Weekly* critic wrote that Griffin "spins a taut story of two girls . . . who must confront the unknown in order to liberate themselves. . . . Griffin's story offers a resounding affirmation that fears

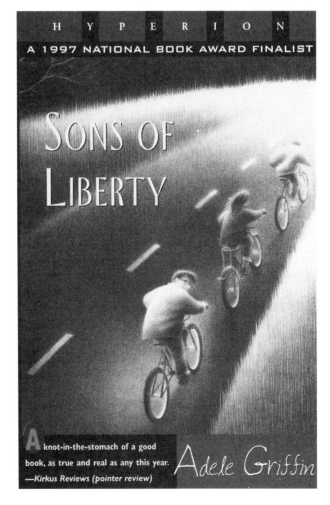

After Rock Kindle, a Revolutionary War enthusiast, helps his friend Liza run away from home, he starts to question his own family bonds.

An artist, hired to paint in the home of two sisters, helps the girls begin to heal from a tragedy that occurred twenty years prior.

are to be faced, not denied, and life is to be lived, not mourned." In a *Booklist* review, Cooper lauded the way Griffin "paints Annie so carefully she seems as real as a kiss from a first boyfriend, and what can be more real than that?" Cooper concluded her positive assessment of *The Other Shepards* by asserting: "[C]arefully crafted both in plot and language, this book shows the heights that popular literature can scale." Griffin won a 1998 Best Books for Young Adults citation for this effort.

Exploring New Territory

With her 1999 fiction offering, *Dive*, Griffin made a departure from her earlier work, creating what Sullivan, writing in *Voice of Youth Advocates*, termed her most "introspective" story to date. Eleven-year-old Ben and his stepbrother Dustin have a distant rela-

tionship; Dustin is remote, hard to reach. Ironies abound in Ben's life, for he has chosen to continue living with his stepfather Lyle when that man and Ben's biological mother split up. Dustin, on the other hand, stayed with Ben's mother, leaving his own biological dad. Ben seeks stability; Dustin is a free spirit who does not care about a dependable home. But when Dustin is injured, Lyle and Ben rush to the hospital to visit him. Ben's last-minute attempts to establish a connection with his stepbrother come to nothing, however, when Dustin dies.

In part inspired by incidents from Griffin's own life—she too had a stepbrother both distant and estranged who died tragically young—this fifth novel allowed the author to explore new territory in

In Griffin's 1999 novel, eleven-year-old Ben stays with his new stepfather after his mother and older stepbrother leave to begin a new life.

If you enjoy the works of Adele Griffin, you might want to check out the following books and films:

Judy Blume, *Deenie,* 1973.
Chris Crutcher, *Ironman,* 1995.
Barbara Park, *Mick Harte Was Here,* 1995.
Ordinary People, a film directed by Robert Redford, 1980.

a new way. Del Negro, reviewing the book for *Bulletin of the Center for Children's Books,* found it to be written in "a clean, introspective style." While noting that "Griffin has a talent for emotional imagery," Del Negro also felt "the main character is burdened by an overabundance of self-awareness without enough action in the plot to balance it." Sullivan, reviewing the title in *Voice of Youth Advocates,* also found the book "dark and introspective" and written in "stark, taut prose." Sullivan, however, went on to observe, "Ben's personal story is engrossing throughout; his struggles to define the meanings of his relationships are compelling. . . . Griffin expertly grasps the complicated dynamics of family life."

"The voices in my writing are those of the children I have listened to hear and have strained to remember, voices that speak from the secret world we too soon leave," Griffin once commented. "My goal, as I continue my career, is to write books for all young people . . . who look forward to a trip to the library or bookstore with great joy, and who are companioned by the friendship of a favorite book."

■ Works Cited

Cooper, Ilene, review of *Split Just Right, Booklist,* June 1 and 15, 1997, pp. 1702-03.

Cooper, Ilene, review of *The Other Shepards, Booklist,* August, 1998, p. 1999.

Del Negro, Janice M., review of *Rainy Season, Bulletin of the Center for Children's Books,* February, 1997, p. 207.

Del Negro, Janice M., review of *Split Just Right, Bulletin of the Center for Children's Books,* September, 1997, p. 11.

Del Negro, Janice M., review of *Dive, Bulletin of the Center for Children's Books,* December, 1999, pp. 130-31.

Devereaux, Elizabeth, interview with Griffin in "Flying Starts: Six First-Time Children's Book Authors Talk about Their Fall '96 Debuts," *Publishers Weekly,* December 16, 1996, p. 32.

Edwards, Carol A., review of *Split Just Right, School Library Journal,* June, 1997, p. 117.

Flynn, Kitty, review of *Sons of Liberty, Horn Book,* January-February, 1998, p. 72.

Lockwood, Lucinda, review of *Rainy Season, School Library Journal,* November, 1996, pp. 104-05.

Review of *The Other Shepards, Publishers Weekly,* September 21, 1998, p. 86.

Phelan, Carolyn, review of *Sons of Liberty, Booklist,* September 15, 1997, p. 235.

Review of *Rainy Season, Publishers Weekly,* October 14, 1996, p. 84.

Review of *Sons of Liberty, Publishers Weekly,* September 8, 1997, p. 77.

Sullivan, Edward T., review of *Dive, Voice of Youth Advocates,* December, 1999, p. 334.

Sullivan, Edward T., "Introducing Adele Griffin," *Voice of Youth Advocates,* December, 1999, pp. 320-21.

Vasilakis, Nancy, review of *Rainy Season, Horn Book,* March-April, 1997, p. 198.

Vasilakis, Nancy, review of *Split just Right, Horn Book,* July-August, 1997, p. 455.

■ For More Information See

PERIODICALS

Booklist, September 15, 1999, p. 256.

Kirkus Reviews, April 1, 1997, p. 555; August 15, 1997, p. 1305.

New York Times Book Review, March 14, 1999, p. 31.

Publishers Weekly, April 7, 1997, p. 93.

Rosa Guy

■ Personal

Surname rhymes with "me"; born September 1, 1925 (some sources say 1928), in Diego Martin, Trinidad, West Indies; came to the United States in 1932; daughter of Henry and Audrey (Gonzales) Cuthbert; married Warner Guy (deceased); children: Warner. *Education:* Attended New York University; studied with the American Negro Theater.

■ Addresses

Home—New York, NY.

■ Career

Writer, 1950—. Lecturer.

■ Member

Harlem Writer's Guild (co-founder; president, 1967-78).

■ Awards, Honors

American Library Association "Best Book for Young Adults" citations, 1973, for *The Friends*, 1976, for *Ruby*, 1978, for *Edith Jackson*, 1979, for *The Disappearance*, and 1981, for *Mirror of Her Own*; "Children's Book of the Year" citations from Child Study Association, 1973, for *The Friends*, and 1986, for *Paris, Pee Wee, and Big Dog*; "Outstanding Book of the Year" citation from the *New York Times*, 1973, for *The Friends*, and 1979, for *The Disappearance; The Friends* was selected one of *School Library Journal*'s "Best of the Best" Books, 1979; *The Disappearance* and *Edith Jackson* were selected among the New York Public Library's Books for the Teen Age, 1980, 1981, and 1982; Coretta Scott King Award, 1982, for *Mother Crocodile*; Parents' Choice Award for Literature from the Parents' Choice Foundation, 1983, for *New Guys around the Block*; Other Award (England), 1987, for *My Love, My Love; or, The Peasant Girl.*

■ Writings

YOUNG ADULT FICTION

The Friends, Holt, 1973.
Ruby: A Novel, Viking, 1976.
Edith Jackson, Viking, 1978.
The Disappearance, Delacorte, 1979.
Mirror of Her Own, Delacorte, 1981.
New Guys around the Block, Delacorte, 1983.
Paris, Pee Wee, and Big Dog, illustrated by Caroline Binch, Gollancz, 1984, Delacorte, 1985.
And I Heard a Bird Sing, Delacorte, 1986.
The Ups and Downs of Carl Davis III, Delacorte, 1989.
Billy the Great, illustrated by Caroline Binch, Doubleday, 1992.
The Music of Summer, Delacorte, 1992.

OTHER

Venetian Blinds (one-act play), first produced at Topical Theatre, New York, 1954.

Bird at My Window (adult novel), Lippincott, 1966.

(Editor) *Children of Longing* (anthology), Holt, 1971.

(Translator and adapter) Birago Diop, *Mother Crocodile: An Uncle Amadou Tale from Senegal*, illustrated by John Steptoe, Delacorte, 1981.

A Measure of Time (adult novel), Holt, 1983.

My Love, My Love; or, The Peasant Girl (adult novel), Holt, 1985.

The Sun, the Sea, a Touch of the Wind (adult novel), Dutton, 1995.

Also contributor to *Ten Times Black*, edited by Julian Mayfield, Bantam, 1972, and *Sixteen: Short Stories by Outstanding Writers for Young Adults*, edited by Donald R. Gallo, Delacorte, 1984.

Guy's novels have been translated into many languages, including Japanese, German, Danish, French, and Italian. Contributor to periodicals, including *Cosmopolitan, New York Times Magazine, Redbook*, and *Freedomways*.

■ Adaptations

Documentary of *The Friends*, Thames Television, 1984; *My Love, My Love; or, The Peasant Girl* was adapted in 1990 for the Broadway musical, *Once on This Island*, premiering at the Booth Theater, New York, and revived in 1999 for the Cab Calloway School of the Arts.

■ Sidelights

"In a voice full of probing and anguished sensitivity, Rosa Guy examines the intersection of race and class in twentieth-century urban America," according to Laurie Ann Eno writing in *St. James Guide to Young Adult Writers*. Eno further commented, "The lives of the forgotten ones haunt her world, taking and shaping for themselves identities which society would deny and destroy." R. Baines, writing in *The Junior Bookshelf*, put Guy's work into perspective: "Rosa Guy is a black author writing with power, authority and insight about an underprivileged and inward looking world which is strange to most of us. Her themes are distressing, disturbing and unappealing ones which she deals with honestly and sympathetically." In her ten novels for teens and four adult novels, Guy traces the fault lines of race in America, the disparities and inequalities between blacks and whites as well as between African Americans and African West Indians. Guy has experienced both, a black growing up in New York City, and an immigrant from Trinidad among Harlem blacks who were born in America.

A writer for *Books for Keeps* described Guy as "the creator of some of the most memorable adolescent characters in modern literature" and further remarked that her "stories are hard-hitting and compellingly realistic, with a powerful message for young people," and that Guy herself "demonstrates a deep understanding and sympathy for young people and the many difficulties they face growing up or purely surviving today." If the stories she tells in such award-winning novels as *Friends, Ruby, Edith Jackson, The Disappearance, New Guys around the Block, And I Heard a Bird Sing*, and *The Music of Summer* are grippingly realistic as well as controversial—she was the first to deal with lesbianism in a teen novel—Guy's ultimate message is one of hope. Her urban background "is unsparingly painted in her novels," commented Beverly Anderson in the *Times Educational Supplement*. "There is no attempt to glamorize the characters or setting, but her message to the young is an optimistic one. Many of her main characters come to feel that they can take control of their lives and climb out of the destructive environment in which they are placed."

"I am a storyteller," Guy wrote in an essay for *Horn Book*. "I write about people. I want my readers to know people, to laugh with them, to be glad with them, to be angry with, to despair with people. And I want them to have hope with people. I want a reader of my work to work a bit more and to care. . . . A novel to me is an emotional history of a people in time and place. If I have proven to be popular with young people, it is because when they have finished one of my books, they not only have a satisfying experience—they have also had an education."

Trinidad Roots, Harlem Upbringing

Guy was born on September 1, 1925 (though some sources note 1928 as her year of birth), the second daughter of Henry and Audrey Cuthbert. Her first seven years were spent in Trinidad, West Indies, at the time of her birth still a British colony. "How proud we were to be a part of that great empire on which the sun never set," she recalled for Jerrie Norris in *Presenting Rosa Guy*. "We learned from British books and rejected as nonsense our folklore—clinging rather to the books that made for great dreams, accepting everyone's myth as our reality." But Trinidad's deep cultural traditions did not go unnoticed. "My life in the West Indies, or course, had a profound influence on me," Guy told Norris. "It made me into the type of person I imagine I am today. The calypso, the carnival, the religion that permeated our life—the Catholic religion—superstitions, voodoo, the zombies, the djiuns, all of these frightening aspects of life that combine the lack of reality with the myth coming over from Africa, had a genuine effect on me." In addition, the rich tradition of storytelling "evidenced in the rhythm of everyday Trinidadian speech," according to Norris, developed in the young Guy a feeling for the imaginative use of language.

Such effects ended, however, when, at age seven, Guy and her family came to the United States, settling in Harlem. Theirs was part of a long-held custom of blacks from the West Indies to go north for the promise of a better future. Marcus Garvey, founder of the Universal Negro Improvement Association and a pivotal figure in black resurgence in America, himself came from Jamaica. The parents went first to America, joined later by Rosa and her older sister, Ameze. Life was hard for the family in the United States, settling into their new surroundings in the midst of the Great Depression. Shortly after the arrival of the daughters, Mrs. Cuthbert fell ill and the children were sent to cousins in the Bronx, who were strong Garveyites. This was a seminal experience for young Rosa, and Guy later attributed much of her love for language and her activism in the cause of human rights to the influence of Garvey and his teachings.

Guy's mother ultimately died of her illness, and the sisters returned to their father for a time, and he remarried a rather flamboyant woman from the South. The father struggled in vain to do well in business, and by the time Rosa was a teenager, he too had died and the two girls were on their own in New York. Years of institutions and foster homes followed. "The whole [experience] of always being on the outside looking in, in a way formed me," she told Norris. Ameze, the older sister, looked out for younger Rosa, until Ameze too, fell ill. Guy quit school at age fourteen and took a job in a brassiere factory to support them. These were hard years, and not only because of economic adversity. Guy also suffered for her race and religion. Victimized for being "colored" in a largely white society, she was also ostracized by other blacks for her West Indian origins and Catholicism. •

By age sixteen, Guy had already married, and in 1942 had a son. Her husband, meanwhile, was among the hundreds of thousands of other Americans to serve in the military during the Second World War. Guy soon became involved with the American Negro Theater, introduced to the group by a young actor with a day job at the garment factory. She studied acting with the troupe, among whom were such future stars as Sidney Poitier and Harry Belafonte. With the end of the war, however, Guy's husband moved the family to Connecticut. But when the marriage fell apart in 1950, Guy and her son moved back to New York and helped found the Harlem Writers Guild. Again working in the brassiere factory by day. Guy honed her writing skills at night, as did others in the collective, including the poet Maya Angelou. "All of us were workers, doing some other type of work," Guy recalled to Norris. "And every evening I had to come home to write. Mornings, I had a son to get dressed and off to school, and then I'd go to work. I did this for a period of years." Her first breakthrough was a one-act play, *Venetian Blinds,* she wrote with a part in it especially suited to her. The play was staged off-Broadway and gave Guy her first taste of public exposure, both as a writer and actor. It would, however, take another dozen years for her first novel to be published.

An Artist Emerges in the 1960s

"The 1960s, for all its traumas, was one of the most beautiful periods in American history," Guy wrote in *Top of the News.* "Only yesterday? So it seems to those of us who lived through it. Television sets were in the homes but had not yet taken over the responsibility of parents. Drugs on the streets had not yet changed youth gangs, fighting over turf, into addicts, robbing everybody's turf." These were years of promise for American blacks with the civil rights movement and sit-ins and segregation laws being struck down North and South. But these were also dark years, with the killings of Malcolm X and Martin Luther King, Jr. Guy was not personally immune from such turbulence: her ex-husband was murdered in 1962 and Guy decided to leave the U.S. for a time, settling in Haiti, where she began her first novel, *Bird at My Window.* She had earlier turned her hand to short stories, but finally focused on the longer form to tell the story of Wade Williams, a thirty-eight-year-old African American whose life has been one long spiral downward.

The reader meets him first in the prison ward of a New York hospital, secured in a straight jacket after having tried to kill his beloved sister. Through flashbacks, the reader is taken down the painful journey of Wade's life, experiencing racism and violence at almost every turn. Published in 1966, the novel won mostly positive reviews. Thomas L. Vince, reviewing *Bird at My Window* in *Best Sellers*, called it "the most significant novel about the Harlem Negro since James Baldwin's *Go Tell It on the Mountain*." Vince further noted, "This is Rosa Guy's first novel, but considering the intensity and power it evokes, we can expect more from such a promising talent." Writing in *Dictionary of Literary Biography*, Leota S. Lawrence called this adult novel "ambitious and courageous." Lawrence went on to explain, "Guy attempts not only to explore the racial forces that help to cripple the black man, but she also looks within the black family and shows how racism can destroy familial relationships with disastrous results." Brooks Johnson, writing in the *Negro Digest*, praised the book for its depiction of Harlem and the forces that lead to the "gradual amoralization of a black man in Harlem," but Johnson also criticized what he felt was "false-sounding" dialogue coming out of "very unlikely mouths."

With the assassination of Dr. King in 1968, Guy went on a voyage of discovery in America to record the voices of young black Americans and find out what they were thinking. As she noted in the preface to *Children of Longing*, the resulting nonfiction book published in 1970, "I especially wanted to know how these painful events affected their lives and their ambitions. I traveled throughout the United States from coast to coast, going into black high schools and colleges in urban and rural areas, into writers' workshops, the cotton fields and ghettos, seeking answers from young black people between the ages of thirteen and twenty-three." Guy presented the responses of these young people without corrections of spelling, grammar, or syntax, providing the actual voices of young blacks coming of age in the turbulent Sixties. The one overwhelming opinion voiced, according to Lawrence in *Dictionary of Literary Biography*, was that these youths "all want to stand up and be counted." Lawrence further noted, "*Children of Longing* can easily serve as a companion piece to Guy's later fiction, and if there were any doubt as to the authenticity of her themes and characters, a reading of *Children of Longing* would quickly dispel them." Indeed, as Norris pointed out, many of the incidents first recorded by her teenage interviewees in *Children of Longing* later found their way into both characters and incidents of her later novels. Norris concluded, "In *Children*, Guy brought her readers face to face with the devastating realities

with which so many young people must struggle. But she demonstrated through their words a new perspective that spoke of pride and hope, and of a belief in cooperative efforts for social change."

Becomes a YA Novelist

Guy spent much of the early 1970s out of the United States, travelling in the Caribbean and living for a time in both Haiti and Trinidad. Living in the West Indies, she decided to build her second novel around her own experiences as a transplanted West Indian. The result was *The Friends*, Guy's first novel for young adults and the first of what became a popular and best-selling trilogy, including *Ruby* (1976) and *Edith Jackson* (1978). These novels explore the relationships between two black families, the Cathys, originally from the West Indies, and the Jacksons, African Americans living in Harlem. Throughout these tales, Guy tackles the difficult and sensitive issues of racism in America and hostility between African Americans and African West Indians. She also focuses on themes such as the difficulties of communication between parents and children, the struggle for acceptance, and homosexuality, once a taboo topic in teen literature. The characters that people these novels, Phylissia, Edith, and Ruby, were all youngsters Guy had known when she and her sister had lived in an orphans' home in New York.

The Friends "is Guy's most critically praised work," according to Norris. Phylissia Cathy and Edith Jackson are the friends of the title, two teenagers who come to trust and understand one another after a stormy beginning. Edith is Harlem born and raised, street smart, poor, and growing up almost on her own. Phylissia, on the other hand, is educated and proud, a recent immigrant from the West Indies who is struggling with her outsider status and her oppressive father. Both girls need a friend, but culture and family play against such a relationship. Edith takes Phylissia under her protective wing at school, and the girls form an unlikely bond for a time, but a visit to the Cathys' home proves disastrous for the friendship. Shortly thereafter Phylissia's mother dies and the young girl's relationship with her father becomes even more strained. Phylissia is left to develop a sense of herself on her own.

Guy's second novel and first YA effort was lauded by critics and quickly found a home in the canon of Young Adult literature. Reviewing the novel in the *New York Times Book Review*, Alice Walker called *The Friends* a "heart-slammer," noting that the book is labeled for juveniles. "So be a juvenile while you

THE AWARD-WINNING NOVEL *THE NEW YORK TIMES* CALLS A "HEART-SLAMMER"

THE FRIENDS
BY ROSA GUY
AUTHOR OF **RUBY** AND **EDITH JACKSON**

In this 1973 novel, her first for young adults, Guy presents the relationship between two friends, Phylissia Cathy and Edith Jackson.

read it," Walker advised. "Rosa Guy will give you back a large part of the memory of those years that you've been missing." *Horn Book*'s Ethel L. Heins called it "a penetrating story of considerable emotional depth," and one that was "often tragic but ultimately hopeful—of complex, fully-realized characters and of the ambivalence and conflicts in human nature." A reviewer for the *Times Literary Supplement* felt that Guy's evocations of New York in particular "make this a vigorous and unusual book." The book did especially well in England, where it, as well as the third novel in the trilogy, became required reading in secondary schools.

Phylissia's older sister is featured in the second novel in the series, *Ruby,* in which this pretty but

rather vapid girl is desperately unhappy, being dubbed an "Uncle Tom" at her school because of her West Indian background. She finds little consolation at home with Phylissia forever reading and her father withdrawn and distant, and is slowly attracted to a strong black girl, Daphne, with whom she ultimately forges a lesbian relationship. A reviewer for *Publishers Weekly* called *Ruby* "an intensely sensitive novel talking directly to teenagers," while Walker, writing in *The Black Scholar*, remarked that the novel is at heart "a love story, and like most love stories it is about the search for someone who cares."

Guy completed her trilogy with *Edith Jackson,* in which she focuses on the life of the scruffy teenager who once befriended Phylissia. Edith, now living in a foster home, tries to take care of her three orphaned sisters, vowing to be the mother for them as soon as she reaches adulthood at age eighteen. Edith tries valiantly to create a family for her three sisters, but becomes pregnant instead herself. Finally she decides not to have the baby, but to prepare herself to make something of her life instead. By the end of the novel, she realizes that she must come to terms with herself before she can be responsible for others. As Lawrence noted, "*Edith Jackson* completes Guy's statement about the failure of the American society—the home, the school, the church, and the state—to meet the complex needs of its young people." Writing in *Horn Book*, Paul Heins noted that this final novel in the trilogy "is powerful in its depiction of character and creates scenes memorable for their psychological truth." Zena Sutherland remarked in *Bulletin of the Center for Children's Books* that Guy's "characterization is excellent, the writing style smooth, and the depiction of an adolescent . . . strong and perceptive." Reviewing the English paperback publication of *Edith Jackson*, Audrey Laski, writing in the *Times Educational Supplement*, called this concluding volume "an almost unbearably powerful and somehow entirely unmelodramatic account of the horrors that can assail an orphaned ghetto family in care."

The Streets of Harlem and Beyond

Guy has also written a second trilogy of books set largely in Harlem and Brooklyn, featuring young Imamu Jones, a teenager who has dropped out of school after his father was killed in Vietnam and his mother began drinking. The first novel, *The Disappearance*, opens with Imamu arrested for supposedly taking part in the armed robbery of a grocery store. He is found innocent at the trial when it is learned he did not know that one of his friends had a gun with him. A volunteer social worker, Ann Aimsley, persuades the judge to make her Imamu's legal guardian and the boy goes to live with them in Brooklyn. However, when the Aimsley's daughter disappears and suspicion fall on him for a time, Imamu vows to find the missing girl.

"This is a story about fear and its tragic consequences," noted Katherine Paterson in the *Washington Post Book World*. "This is a harsh book, but not a hopeless one," Paterson further commented. "For Rosa Guy, the writer, is not primarily a black or a woman, but one of that rare and wonderful breed, a storyteller." Jean Fritz, reviewing the novel in the *New York Times Book Review*, dubbed the book "both a cliff-hanger and a shrewd commentary on human nature." *Times Educational Supplement* reviewer Geoff Fox found the novel to be a "harsh, relentless and exciting tale of the streets," as did David Rees, writing in the *Times Literary Supplement*, though Rees found that the book was "marred by absurdly improbable twists in the plot."

In the second novel of the Imamu Jones trilogy, *New Guys around the Block*, Imamu, with Olivette and Pierre Larouche, investigates burglaries in a nearby white neighborhood. Again, suspicion falls for a time on Imamu as the burglar, and he vows to track down the criminal to clear his own name. Suspicion thereafter falls on a recently released convict whom the police corner but who dies to avoid capture. Yet Imamu is unconvinced. In the end he discovers the real perpetrator is the one nobody has suspected. In this second Imamu Jones tale, "Guy demonstrates . . . that she is a skillful creator of the mystery/suspense tale," according to Lawrence. "But more important is her relentless effort to focus on the realities of the urban ghettos in which black youths are trapped." Most reviewers conceded the bleakness of this background, and searched for the tiny rays of hope Guy provided in the plot. "The reader cannot resist rooting for Imamu, with his intelligence and growing self-awareness," commented Selma G. Lanes in the *New York Times Book Review*. "One hopes this novel will be read by countless other Imamus in need of encouragement."

In the third book in the series, *And I Heard a Bird Sing*, Imamu is reunited with his widowed mother, helps her to overcome her drinking habit, and finds a job that he likes, delivering food to white customers in Brooklyn. But racism rears its head when he takes a special interest in a young disabled girl and in the girl's aunt. When the young girl, Margaret, is found murdered, Imamu is on the scene to bring the perpetrator to justice. "Guy again proves her skill at creating stirring stories about real people," wrote a reviewer for *Publishers Weekly*.

Departures for Guy from her usually gritty novels, are several books written for a younger age group, picture books, and a novel featuring a non-black protagonist. In the 1981 *Mirror of Her Own*, Guy presents a far different picture than the streets of a ghetto. Set in an affluent, white suburban neighborhood, the book tells the story of shy, plain, and stuttering Mary who tries to win acceptance with the in-crowd at school. Most reviewers felt the novel was a pale comparison beside Guy's other work. Lawrence, for example, called it "anticlimactic" when placed beside her trilogies. With the 1984 *Paris, Pee Wee, and Big Dog*, Guy wrote for much younger readers for the first time, revealing an adventure-filled day in the life of three New York boys. Bruce Brooks, reviewing the title in the *New York Times Book Review*, noted, "Miss Guy gives us no heavy social lessons about our urban horrors and keeps the boys free of "turning-point experiences." Instead, they have a play day that is both tough and fun, and so do we." *Booklist*'s Hazel Rochman called the book "an upbeat inner city story" with "usually cheerful, action-packed adventures." In *The Ups and Downs of Carl Davis III*, Guy presents the trials and tribulations of young Carl when he is sent from the dangerous inner city to live with his grandmother in South Carolina. In letters home, the reader learns of his attempts to teach the kids at his new school— and his history teacher—about black history and of their resistance to listen to him. "Carl is sincere and funny," commented a reviewer for *Publishers Weekly*, "a character readers won't soon forget." *Horn Book*'s Lois F. Anderson felt that "Guy has created a unique role model for young adolescents searching for answers."

With her 1992 novel, *The Music of Summer*, Guy moved even farther afield from Harlem, to a vacation house on Cape Cod where Sarah, a dark-skinned African American, does not fit in with the light-skinned, frivolous crowd gathered around her old friend, Cathy. Sarah, an aspiring concert pianist, is about to return to New York when a new house-guest arrives, Jean Pierre, a development worker headed for Africa. Soon Sarah falls for this committed young man and she must choose between her dreams of a career and his idealism. Libby K. White, writing in *School Library Journal*, found the novel to be an "engrossing and uplifting title for readers of all backgrounds," while *Booklist*'s Candace Smith felt that "Guy vividly captures the pain of peer pres-

AN IMAMU JONES MYSTERY

THE DISAPPEARANCE

ROSA GUY

After being acquitted of armed robbery and murder, Imamu Jones becomes the primary suspect when a young girl disappears in this 1979 work.

If you enjoy the works of Rosa Guy, you might want to check out the following books:

Virginia Hamilton, *The Planet of Junior Brown*, 1971.
Walter Dean Myers, *Mouse Rap*, 1990.
Eleanora E. Tate, *A Blessing in Disguise*, 1995.
Mildred D. Taylor, *The Road to Memphis*, 1990.
Rita Williams-Garcia, *Like Sisters on the Homefront*, 1994.

sure as well as the excitement of first love," and that "Sarah's search for self rings true."

Guy is also the author of two picture books, the African tale, *Mother Crocodile*, which she adapted and translated, and *Billy the Great*, which tells of Billy's growing friendship with the boy next door, Rod. Race figures in—Billy's family is black and Rod's white—but class is even stronger: Billy's is middle class, Rod's working class. Yet in the end, the boy's find common ground in a story that demonstrates, as *Booklist*'s Janice Del Negro wrote, "while parents may think they know best, kids sometimes know better." A reviewer for *Publishers Weekly* was less laudatory: "A ponderous lesson in overcoming

prejudice overwhelms this insubstantial story about friendship and parental short-sightedness."

Guy has also written three further novels for adults, in addition to her debut *Bird at My Window*. These include *A Measure of Time, My Love, My Love; or, The Peasant Girl*, and *The Sun, the Sea, a Touch of the Wind*. In *Measure*, Guy tells the story of a self-made millionaire, Dorine Davis, who grew up poor and black in Alabama, and succeeds in Harlem through the years of the Harlem Renaissance, the Great Depression, and into the beginnings of the civil rights movement of the 1950s. Lawrence noted that there was enough material in the novel for two books, but when telling the story of Dorine, "it succeeds." *My Love* is basically a reworking of the Hans Christian Andersen tale, "The Little Mermaid," a "strange fairy tale," according to Angeline Goreau writing in the *New York Times Book Review*, that "is a moving evocation of the political realities of the Caribbean." *My Love* was adapted for a musical that opened off-Broadway in 1990. And Guy's 1995 novel, *The Sun, the Sea, a Touch of the Wind*, "tells a story of resurrection and renewal," according to a reviewer for *Publishers Weekly*. The novel relates the tale of an African American artist who flees to the supposed solitude of Haiti as a palliative to a near nervous breakdown, only to find that her emotional and mental anguish are compounded by the island's extremes: wealth juxtaposed against poverty. *Booklist*'s Donna Seaman felt that "Guy lives up to her reputation as a lyrical interpreter of human relationships, both personal and political, in her new novel," dubbing the tale "psychologically harrowing and culturally acute."

"I write for people—all people, young and old, black, white, or any others whom my book might fall into the hands of," Guy once noted in *School Library Journal*. "I write about ordinary people who do ordinary things, who want the ordinary—love, warmth, understanding, happiness. These things are universal. But no life is ordinary." It is Guy's gift to make the quotidian full of detail and uniqueness, and to find hope in the darkest corners of life. "There are no good guys," Guy wrote in her *School Library Journal* essay. "There are no bad guys. We are all good guys. We are all bad guys. And we are all responsible for each other." Lawrence concluded in *Dictionary of Literary Biography*, "Guy's reputation as a writer has long been established. Her contribution to the literature of young adults, especially that of young blacks, has been inspiring."

■ Works Cited

Anderson, Beverly, "The Orphan Factor," *Times Educational Supplement*, June 3, 1983, p. 42.

Anderson, Lois F., *The Ups and Downs of Carl Davis III*, *Horn Book*, September October, 1989, p. 629.

Review of *And I Heard a Bird Sing*, *Publishers Weekly*, June 12, 1987, p. 86.

"Authorgraph No. 30: Rosa Guy," *Books for Keeps*, January, 1985, pp. 12-13.

Baines, R., review of *Ruby*, *The Junior Bookshelf*, April, 1982, p. 76.

Review of *Billy the Great*, *Publishers Weekly*, October 5, 1992, p. 71.

Brooks, Bruce, "The Concrete Canyon Raiders," *New York Times Book Review*, November 10, 1985, p. 36.

Del Negro, Janice, review of *Billy the Great*, *Booklist*, September 1, 1992, p. 66.

Eno, Laurie Ann, "Guy, Rosa (Cuthbert)," *St. James Guide to Young Adult Writers*, 2nd edition, edited by Tom Pendergast and Sara Pendergast, St. James Press, 1999, pp. 338-39.

Fox, Geoff, "Songs of Innocence and Experience," *Times Educational Supplement*, June 6, 1980, p. 27.

Fritz, Jean, review of *The Disappearance*, *New York Times Book Review*, December 2, 1979, p. 40.

Goreau, Angeline, review of *My Love, My Love; or, The Peasant Girl*, *New York Times Book Review*, December 1, 1985, p. 24.

Guy, Rosa, "Preface," *Children of Longing*, Holt, 1970.

Guy, Rosa, "All about Caring," *Top of the News*, Winter, 1983.

Guy, Rosa, "Young Adult Books: I Am a Storyteller," *Horn Book*, March-April, 1985, pp. 220-21.

Guy, Rosa, "Innocence, Betrayal, and History," *School Library Journal*, November, 1985.

Heins, Ethel L., review of *The Friends*, *Horn Book*, March-April, 1974, p. 152.

Heins, Paul, review of *Edith Jackson*, *Horn Book*, September-October, 1978, p. 524.

Johnson, Brooks, "Books Noted," *Negro Digest*, March 1, 1966, p. 33.

Lanes, Selma G., review of *New Guys around the Block*, *New York Times Book Review*, August 28, 1983, p. 22.

Laski, Audrey, review of *Edith Jackson*, *Times Educational Supplement*, March 1, 1985, p. 29.

Lawrence, Leota S., "Rosa Guy," *Dictionary of Literary Biography*, Volume 33: *Afro-American Fiction Writers after 1955*, Gale, 1984, pp. 101-6.

"Lives against the Odds," *Times Literary Supplement*, September 20, 1974, p. 1006.

Norris, Jerrie, *Presenting Rosa Guy*, Twayne, 1988.

Paterson, Katherine, "A Family of Strangers," *Washington Post Book World*, November 11, 1979, p. 21.

Rees, David, "Approaching Adulthood," *Times Literary Supplement*, July 18, 1980, p. 807.

Rochman, Hazel, review of *Paris, Pee Wee, and Big Dog*, *Booklist*, December 1, 1985, p. 572.

Review of *Ruby*, *Publishers Weekly*, April 19, 1976, pp. 80-81.

Seaman, Donna, review of *The Sun, the Sea, a Touch of the Wind*, *Booklist*, August, 1995, p. 1929.

Smith, Candace, review of *The Music of Summer*, *Booklist*, April 15, 1992, pp. 1521-22.

Review of *The Sun, the Sea, a Touch of the Wind*, *Publishers Weekly*, July 3, 1995, p. 49.

Sutherland, Zena, review of *Edith Jackson*, *Bulletin of the Center for Children's Books*, March, 1979, pp. 116-17.

Review of *The Ups and Downs of Carl Davis III*, *Publishers Weekly*, May 19, 1989, p. 85.

Vince, Thomas L., review of *Bird at My Window*, *Best Sellers*, January 15, 1966, p. 403.

Walker, Alice, review of *The Friends*, *New York Times Book Review*, November 4, 1973, p. 26.

Walker, Alice, review of *Ruby*, *The Black Scholar*, December, 1976, pp. 51-52.

White, Libby K., review of *The Music of Summer*, *School Library Journal*, February, 1992, p. 108.

■ For More Information See

BOOKS

Black Authors and Illustrators of Children's Books, 2nd edition, Garland, 1992.

Children's Literature Review, Volume 13, Gale, 1987.

Contemporary Literary Criticism, Volume 26, Gale, 1983.

Tate, Claudia, editor, *Black Women Writers at Work*, Continuum, 1983.

PERIODICALS

Booklist, October 15, 1994, p. 413.

Bulletin of the Center for Children's Books, November, 1985, p. 47; March, 1992, p. 180; January, 1993, p. 146.

English Journal, November, 1988, p. 90.

Horn Book, March-April, 1985, pp. 220-21; March-April, 1993, pp. 195-96.

Kirkus Reviews, June 15, 1995, p. 802.

Kliatt, May, 1997, p. 6.

New York Times Book Review, June 7, 1992, p. 22.

New York Times Magazine, April 16, 1972.

Publishers Weekly, December 20, 1991, p. 83.

School Library Journal, November, 1985; January, 1986, p. 84; June, 1989, p. 124.

Times Educational Supplement, June 3, 1983, p. 42; July 11, 1986, p. 25.

Times Literary Supplement, September 20, 1974; December 14, 1979; July 18, 1980; August 3, 1984; February 14, 1992, p. 27.

Voice of Youth Advocates, June, 1992, pp. 95, 142; December, 1992, p. 268.

Washington Post, January 9, 1966; November 11, 1979; December 17, 1985.

Wilson Library Bulletin, November, 1989, p. 15.*

—Sketch by J. Sydney Jones

Libby Hathorn

■ Personal

Full name, Elizabeth Helen Hathorn; surname is pronounced "hay-thorn"; born September 26, 1943, in Newcastle, New South Wales, Australia.

■ Addresses

Agent—Tracey Adams, McIntosh and Otis, New York, NY.

■ Career

Teacher and librarian in schools in Sydney, Australia, 1965-81; worked as a deputy principal, 1977; consultant and senior education officer for government adult education programs, 1981-86; full-time writer, 1987—. Sydney University, part-time lecturer in English and children's literature, beginning in 1982; writer in residence at the University of Technology, Sydney, 1990, Woollahra Library, 1992, and at Edith Cowan University, 1992. Consultant to the Dorothea Mackellar National Poetry Competition/Festival for children, 1992-93; speaker for student, teacher, and parent groups.

■ Awards, Honors

The Tram to Bondi Beach was highly commended by the Children's Book Council of Australia, 1982; *Paolo's Secret* was shortlisted for the Children's Book of the Year Award and for the New South Wales Premier's Literary Awards, both 1986; *All About Anna* received an Honour Award from the Children's Book Council of Australia, 1987, and was shortlisted for the Kids Own Australian Literary Award (KOALA), 1988, and for the Young Australians Best Book Award (YABBA), 1989 and 1990; Literature Board of the Australia Council fellowships, 1987 and 1988; *Looking Out for Sampson* received an Honour Award from the Children's Book Council of Australia, 1988; *The Extraordinary Magics of Emma McDade* was shortlisted for the Children's Book of the Year Award, 1990; Hathorn was highly commended in 1990 by the Society of Women Writers for the body of her work during 1987-89; *Thunderwith* was named Honour Book of the Year for older readers by the Children's Book Council of Australia, 1990, an American Library Association Best Book for Young Adults, 1991, was shortlisted for the Canberra's Own Outstanding List, KOALA, and YABBA, all 1991, and the Dutch translation received an award from Stichting Collectieve Propaganda van het Nederlands Boek (Foundation for the Promotion of Dutch Books), 1992; *So Who Needs Lotto?* and *Jezza Sez* were both named Children's Book Council of Australia notable books, 1991; New South Wales Children's Week Medal for literature, 1992; Kate Greenaway Award, United Kingdom, 1995, for *Way Home;* Australian Violence Prevention

Certificate Award, 1995; Notable Book citations from the Children's Book Council of Australia, 1993, 1996, and 1997.

■ Writings

FOR CHILDREN AND YOUNG ADULTS

Stephen's Tree (storybook), illustrated by Sandra Laroche, Methuen, 1979.

Lachlan's Walk (picture book), illustrated by Laroche, Heinemann, 1980.

The Tram to Bondi Beach (picture book), illustrated by Julie Vivas, Collins, 1981.

Paolo's Secret (novella), illustrated by Lorraine Hannay, Heinemann, 1985.

All about Anna (novel), Heinemann, 1986.

Looking out for Sampson (storybook), Oxford University Press, 1987.

Freya's Fantastic Surprise (picture book), illustrated by Sharon Thompson, Ashton Scholastic, 1988.

The Extraordinary Magics of Emma McDade (storybook), illustrated by Maya, Oxford University Press, 1989.

Stuntumble Monday (picture book), illustrated by Melissa Web, Collins Dove, 1989.

The Garden of the World (picture book), illustrated by Tricia Oktober, Margaret Hamilton Books, 1989.

Thunderwith (novel), Heinemann, 1989.

Jezza Says (novel), illustrated by Donna Rawlins, Angus & Robertson, 1990.

So Who Needs Lotto? (novella), illustrated by Simon Kneebone, Penguin, 1990.

Talks with my Skateboard (poetry), Australian Broadcasting Corp., 1991.

(Editor) *The Blue Dress* (stories), Heinemann, 1991.

Help for Young Writers (nonfiction), Nelson, 1991.

Good to Read (textbook), Nelson, 1991.

Who? (stories), Heinemann, 1992.

Love Me Tender (novel), Oxford University Press, 1992.

The Lenski Kids and Dracula (novella), Penguin, 1992.

Valley under the Rock (novel), Reed Heinemann, 1993.

The Way Home (picture book), illustrated by Greg Rogers, Random House, 1993.

Feral Kid (novel), Hodder & Stoughton, 1994.

Grandma's Shoes (picture book), illustrated by Elivia Salvadier, Little, Brown, 1994, reissued, illustrated by Caroline Magerl, Hodder, 2000.

What a Star (novel), HarperCollins, 1994.

The Wonder Thing (picture book), illustrated by Peter Gouldthorpe, Penguin, 1995.

Juke-box Jive (novel), Hodder, 1996.

The Climb (novel), Penguin, 1996.

Chrysalis (novel), Reed, 1997.

Rift (novel), Hodder Headline, 1998.

Sky Sash So Blue (picture book), illustrated by Benny Andrews, Simon and Schuster, 1998.

(With Gary Crew) *Dear Venny, Dear Saffron* (novel), Lothian, 1999.

Ghostop (novel), Headline, 1999.

The Gift, illustrated by Greg Rogers, Random House, 2000.

Also author of a libretto for a children's opera, composed by Grahame Koehne, based on *Grandma's Shoes*, that was performed at the Australian Opera Workshop.

Some of Hathorn's works have been translated into Greek, Italian, Dutch, German, French, Norwegian, Danish, and Swedish.

FOR ADULTS

(With G. Bates) *Half-Time: Perspectives on Mid-life*, Fontana Collins, 1987.

Better Strangers (stories), Millennium Books, 1989.

Damascus, a Rooming House (libretto), performed by the Australian Opera at Performance Space, Sydney, 1990.

The Maroubra Cycle: A Journey around Childhood (performance poetry), University of Technology, Sydney, 1990.

(And director) *The Blue Dress Suite* (music theatre piece), produced at Melbourne International Festival, 1991.

■ Adaptations

Thunderwith was produced as a "Hallmark Hall of Fame" television movie titled *The Echo of Thunder*. Several of Hathorn's works have also been adapted for interactive online storytelling.

■ Work in Progress

A young adult novel, *The Painter*, about a young boy's meeting with Vincent Van Gogh.

■ Sidelights

A multi-talented Australian writer, Libby Hathorn produces poetry, picture books, drama, novels, short stories, and nonfiction for children, young adults, and adults. Best known in the United States for her critically acclaimed novel *Thunderwith*, Hathorn has created works ranging from serious stories of troubled youth to lighthearted, fast-paced comedies. She writes of powerful females in her novels for junior readers, such as the protagonists in *All about Anna* or *The Extraordinary Magics of Emma McDade,* or of lonely, misunderstood teenagers in novels such as *Feral Kid, Love Me Tender,* and *Valley under the Rock.* As Maurice Saxby noted in *St. James Guide to Children's Writers,* "In her novels for teenagers especially, Hathorn exposes, with compassion, sensitivity, and poetry the universal and ongoing struggle of humanity to heal hurts, establish meaningful relationships, and to learn to accept one's self—and ultimately—those who have wronged us."

"I must have been very young indeed when I decided to become a writer," Libby Hathorn once commented. "My grandmother always kept my stories in her best black handbag and read them out loud to long-suffering relatives and told me over and over that I'd be a writer when I grew up." Though Hathorn started her career as a teacher and librarian, she did eventually become a writer. "Libby Hathorn knows exactly how today's children think and feel," observed Saxby in *The Proof of the Puddin': Australian Children's Literature, 1970-1990.* "She has an uncanny ear for the speech nuances of the classroom, playground and home. . . . [She] is always able to penetrate the facade of her characters and with skill and subtlety reveal what they are really like inside."

An Australian Upbringing

Hathorn grew up near Sydney, Australia, and recalled that at the time her parents did not own a car. "In fact, not many people on the street where I lived in the early 1950s owned cars. We had no television, either. We amused ourselves with storytelling and reading out loud and lots of games." Hathorn often read and told stories to her sisters and brother; she was encouraged by her parents, who "loved books" and had bookcases crammed with them. "Books were pretty central in our lives," she stated. "My father in particular read to us at night when he could get home in time. He was a detective and had long shifts at night that often kept him late. When he read we didn't interrupt, in fact we'd never dream of it as his voice filled the room because it seemed so obviously important to him— the ebb and flow of the language. My mother—who was very proud of her Irish ancestry—told us lots of true stories about the history of our family and also about her own girlhood."

As a child, Hathorn read "adventure books set in the Australian bush, like *Seven Little Australians,* as well as classics like *Black Beauty, The Secret Garden, Little Women,* and books by Emily and Charlotte Bronte," she once explained. She also read works by Australian authors "with considerable delight at finding Australian settings and people in print." Later, Hathorn would lend her own work an Australian flavor after noticing "the need for more books that told Australian kids about themselves."

Hathorn began writing her own stories and poems when she was still a young girl. Though she was often shy and quiet, Hathorn once noted that she could keep company "entertained with strings of stories that I made up as I went along." Her family encouraged her, and Hathorn "loved being at center stage—so I couldn't have been altogether a shy little buttercup." At school, she enjoyed reading and creative writing, and was disappointed in later years when "we had to write essays and commentaries but never, never stories or poems. I was extremely bored in my final years at school." Hathorn has also acknowledged that her high school years weren't all bad: "After all, I was introduced to the works of William Shakespeare, and particularly in my later years the poetic nature of his work touched me deeply. And best of all we studied the Romantic poets and I fell in love with John Keats and Samuel Coleridge as well as Percy Bysshe Shelley, Lord Byron, and William Wordsworth."

After graduating from high school, Hathorn worked in a laboratory and studied at night for a year before attending college full-time. Despite her parents' objections, she contemplated a career in journalism, hoping that she could learn "the art and craft of novel writing." "Anyway, my parents thought it important that I have a profession where I could earn a reasonable living—writers being notoriously underpaid," Hathorn remarked. "I was drawn to teaching; so after a year of broken specimen flasks and test tubes and discovering that my science courses did not enthrall me, I left the laboratory."

Hathorn attended Balmain Teacher's College (now the University of Technology, Sydney). "I must admit that I found the regulations of the place quite hard," she recalled. "Many of the lectures of those days seemed so dull to me that I wondered whether indeed I would last as a teacher for very long." Hathorn did enjoy her literature classes and was surprised to find that "when I came out of the rather dull years at college, I not only liked classroom teaching, but I also discovered that it was the most thrilling, absorbing, rewarding, and wonderful job anyone could have!"

From Teacher to Librarian to Author

After teaching for several years in Sydney, Hathorn applied for a position as a school librarian. "Although I was sorry to leave the intimacy of family that a classroom teacher has with her own class, the library was a new and exciting chapter for me," Hathorn once commented. "I had books, books, and more books to explore and the amazingly enjoyable job of bringing stories to every child in the school!" Her job as a librarian, the author added, "had a major influence on my decision to seriously try to publish my stories."

Hathorn's first book for children was *Stephen's Tree*, which was published in 1979. She followed this with two picture books: *Lachlan's Walk* and *The Tram to Bondi Beach*. In the genre of children's picture books, Hathorn discovered, as she explained, "such a scarcity of Australian material! I wanted to talk about our place, here and now, and have pictures that Australian children would instantly recognize. *Stephen's Tree* was a breakthrough in publishing. I had to fight with my publisher to have a gumtree on the cover. They wanted an ash or elm or oak so it would sell in England and Europe! Similarly, I was told *The Tram to Bondi Beach* should not mention Bondi. I won those fights and I must say *The Tram to Bondi Beach* has made its way onto the American market and American children didn't seem to have much trouble at all."

The Tram to Bondi Beach tells the story of Keiran, a nine-year-old boy who longs for a job selling newspapers to passengers on the trams that travel through Sydney. Keiran wants to be like Saxon, an older boy, who is an experienced newspaper seller. Reviewers commented on the nostalgic quality of the story, which is set in the 1930s. Marianne Pilla assessed the picture book in *School Library Journal*, pointing out its "smooth" narrative and "vivid" passages. *Times Literary Supplement* contributor Ann Martin called *The Tram to Bondi Beach* "a simple but appealing tale," and Karen Jameyson wrote in *Horn Book* that the book "will undoubtedly hold readers' interest."

Hathorn followed *The Tram to Bondi Beach* with *Paolo's Secret*, *All about Anna*, and *Looking out for Sampson*. As Hathorn once noted, *All about Anna*, her first novel, "is based on a wild, naughty cousin I had who drove her mother's car down the road at ten years of age and other wild deeds—a perfect

subject to write about." The book details the comic adventures of Lizzie, Harriet, Christopher, and their energetic, imaginative cousin, Anna. Lizzie, the narrator, explains that "I like being with Anna because somehow things always seem fast and furious and funny when she's around—and well, she's just a very unusual person."

Like *All about Anna, Looking out for Sampson* touches on family themes. In the book Bronwyn wishes that her younger brother, Sampson, were older so that she could have a friend instead of someone to babysit. And when Cheryl and her mother come to stay with Bronwyn's family, Bronwyn's situation worsens. A disagreeable girl, Cheryl hints that Bronwyn's parents must care more about Sampson, since they give the toddler so much attention. After Sampson is lost briefly at the beach, however, Cheryl and Bronwyn reconcile and Bronwyn's parents express their appreciation of her.

Around the time *All about Anna* was published in 1986, Hathorn decided to give up her job and become a full-time writer. "I wanted to be a full-time writer secretly all my life but when I began my working life as a teacher this dream seemed to recede," the author once explained. "And once I was married and with two children I felt I had to keep up my contribution to our lifestyle. My husband is also a teacher and I thought it would be unfair if he had to work every day while I was home writing. It was as if in the eyes of the world writing was not work! And I'm to blame for allowing myself to think like that too.

"I've changed my mind now and I wish I had had the courage to do so much sooner. While I loved teaching, after some years of it I was ready for change. I was already writing short stories but I was aching to tell longer stories, to produce a novel for older readers. This was very hard when I was working full-time and had young children—so the stories I chose to write at that time were for younger children and were either picture books or junior novels like *All about Anna* and *Looking out for Sampson*."

Among Hathorn's other books for young readers is *The Extraordinary Magics of Emma McDule*. The story describes the adventures of the title character, whose superhuman powers include incredible strength, the ability to call thousands of birds by whistling and control over the weather. Another of Hathorn's books geared towards beginning readers is *Freya's Fantastic Surprise*. In it Miriam tells the class at news time that her parents bought her a tent, a surprise that Freya attempts to top by making up fantastic stories that her classmates realize are false. Freya eventually has a real surprise to share, however, when her mother announces that Freya will soon have a new sister. Published in the United States as well as Australia, *Freya's Fantastic Surprise* was praised by critics. Louise L. Sherman noted in *School Library Journal* that "Freya's concern about impressing her classmates . . . is on target." In a *Horn Book Magazine* review, Elizabeth S. Watson called the book "a winner" and commented that "the text and pictures combine to produce a tale that proves truth is best."

Moves to Young Adult Novels

Hathorn began writing her first novel for young adults, *Thunderwith*, after receiving an Australia Council grant in 1987. "At home writing for a year, I realized that this was to be my job for the rest of my life," Hathorn once remarked. "And since I have been able to give full-time attention to my writing it has certainly flowered in many new directions. I have begun writing longer novels for young adults and I have been able to take on more ambitious projects like libretti and music theatre pieces, which I enjoy tremendously."

Thunderwith, published in 1989, is the story of four-teen-year-old Lara, who begins living with the father she barely knows after her mother dies of cancer. Lara's new home is in the remote Wallingat Forest in New South Wales, Australia. Though Lara's relationship with her father develops smoothly, he is often away on business and Lara's stepmother is openly antagonistic towards her. Lonely and grief-stricken, Lara finds solace in her bond with a mysterious dog that appears during a storm. She names the dog Thunderwith and keeps his existence a secret; she only tells the aboriginal storyteller she has befriended at school. Eventually, Lara realizes that Thunderwith has filled the space that her mother's death created, enabling her to come to terms with her loss. Lara is also able to slowly win over her stepmother and to adjust to her new home and family life.

The setting of *Thunderwith* is one with which Hathorn is intimately acquainted. As a child, she had relatives who lived in the Australian bush, and she spent many holidays in the country. "This was to prove very important to me," Hathorn once stated. "The bush weaves its own magic and it's something you cannot experience from a book or television show in a suburban setting. My holidays, especially those on my grandmother's farm in the Blue Moun-

tains, created in me an enduring love for the Australian bush. As a writer, however, up until a few years ago the settings I chose to write about were in the hub of the family and quite often in suburbia."

Hathorn came upon the idea for *Thunderwith* after her brother bought land in Wallingat Forest. "During the first holiday there a huge storm blew up at about midnight and such was the noise and intensity of it we all rose from our beds to watch it," Hathorn once said. "You can imagine how vulnerable you'd feel way out in the bush with thunder booming and lightning raging and trees whipping and bending . . . and in the midst of this fury suddenly I saw a dog. A huge dark dog dashed across the place where some hours earlier we'd had a campfire and eaten our evening meal under the stars—a lovely looking half-dingo creature.

"When I lay down again I had the image of the dog in my mind, against the landscape of the bush and storm. Again and again I saw the dog and a line of a poem seemed to fall into my head from the storm clouds above. "With thunder you'll come—and with thunder you'll go." What did it mean? What could it mean? By morning I had unravelled the mystery of the lines of poetry and I had a story about a girl called Lara whose mother dies in the first chapter and who comes to live on the farm in a forest with her dad and a new family."

The dog that Hathorn had seen became Thunderwith, "Lara's friend, her escape, and her link to her mother," as Hathorn explained. Lara's mother was modeled after Hathorn's friend Cheryl, who died of cancer before the book was finished. "I feel that Cheryl's spirit leaps and bounds all through it," the author once noted. "So you see for me there are many emotions through many experiences that weave themselves into my stories and into this story in particular—happiness in being together, the joy one feels in being surrounded by natural beauty, a dark sadness at loss, and the pain in hardships that must be endured. And the way people can change and grow even through dark and mystifyingly sad experiences. But you may be pleased to know that love and hope win out in *Thunderwith*. They have to—as I believe eventually they have to in life itself."

Thunderwith garnered praise as a sensitive, realistic, and engaging young adult novel. A *Publishers Weekly* reviewer commented that "Hathorn deftly injects a sense of wonderment into this intense, very real story." According to *Horn Book* contributor Elizabeth Watson, *Thunderwith* possesses "a believable plot featuring a shattering climax and a satisfyingly realistic resolution." Robert Strang, writing in *Bulletin of the Center for Children's Books,* commended Hathorn's "especially expert weaving of story and setting." Similarly, *Magpies* contributor Jameyson noted that Hathorn's "control over her complex subject is admirable; her insight into character sure and true; her ear for dialogue keen." Jameyson added that the author's "nimble detour from the usual route will leave readers surprised, even breathless."

An Author of Many Parts

After the success of *Thunderwith,* Hathorn moved beyond novels and picture books to publish poems for children and a story collection for young adults. Her poetry book, *Talks with My Skateboard,* is divided into several sections and includes poems about outdoor activities, school, family life, cats, and nature. The poem "Skateboard" is written from a child's perspective: "My sister has a skateboard / and you should see her go . . . She can jump and twirl / Do a twist and turn, / What I want to know / Is why I can't learn?" *Who?,* published in 1992, contains stories about ghosts, love and friendship, and mysteries, some of which are based on tales that Hathorn's mother told her. The collection includes "Who?," in which a pitiful ghost awakens a family from their beds; "An Act of Kindness," in which a family mysteriously loses their ability to remember the names of objects; and "Jethro Was My Friend," where a young girl attempts to save her beloved bird from rapidly rising floodwaters.

Hathorn published more novels, with the young adult book *Love Me Tender* and a comic work for junior readers, *The Lenski Kids and Dracula.* Hathorn once commented that *"Love Me Tender* was a story I circled for a few years. It drew on my girlhood experiences although it's about a boy called Alan. It's a gentle story set in the days of rock and roll." In the novel, Alan and his sister and brothers are abandoned by their mother and sent to live with various relatives. Alan is taken in by his bossy, unsmiling Aunt Jessie, and the story chronicles his "interior journey as hope fades that he will ever see his Mum and his family again," Hathorn explained. "Alan changes but more importantly he causes people around him—including his old aunt—to change too. Self-growth is a very important message for young people today—looking inside and finding that strength to go on." *Love Me Tender* is among Hathorn's favorite creations; the book "has a place in my heart," she once commented, because it captures the atmosphere of the author's girlhood in the 1950s.

> If you enjoy the works of Libby Hathorn, you might want to check out the following books:
>
> Carolyn Coman, *Tell Me Everything,* 1993.
> Kevin Henkes, *Protecting Marie,* 1995.
> Sheila Solomon Klass, *Next Stop: Nowhere,* 1995.

A common thread in several of Hathorn's works is the author's belief in love, hope, and the resiliency of the human spirit. "With all the faults in the world, the injustices, the suffering, and the sheer violence that I am forced to acknowledge though not accept, I still have a great sense of hope," Hathorn once noted. "Human beings never cease to surprise me with their unexpectedness, their kindness, their cheerfulness, their will to go on against the odds. That's inspiring. And I feel a sense of hope should be nurtured in young people, for they are the hope of the world. My stories may sometimes have sad endings but they are never without some hope for the future."

In several books Hathorn has combined her interest in young people with her concerns about the environment, poverty, and homelessness. "My picture book *The Wonder Thing,* written after a visit to a rainforest to "sing" about the beauty of the place, is also a plea for the survival of the earth's riches—trees, forests, mountains, and rivers," the author once explained. "There are only four to five words per page and it is a prose poem; I try to make those words the most delicately beautiful and evocative that I can. Both a recent picture book, *The Way Home,* and a recent novel, *Feral Kid,* take up the theme of the homelessness of young people. I feel strongly that we should *never* accept the fact of homeless children on our streets. A society that allows this sort of thing is not a responsible and caring society to my mind; I very much want people to look closely at stories like mine and begin asking questions about something that is becoming all too common a sight in all cities of the world."

Alan, the protagonist in Hathorn's 1996 novel, *Juke-box Jive,* is another homeless child,; his mother, who has gone to live with a new boyfriend, has abandoned him. Farmed out to his strict Aunt Jessie, Alan's life greatly improves when his aunt takes over a milk bar and installs the juke-box of the title. "This could so easily have been just a collection of cliches," remarked Mary Hoffman in a *School Librar-*

ian review of the novel. "What raises it is Libby Hathorn's honesty about Alan's feelings for his mother and his aching realiszation that the family will never all live together again." Another abandoned adolescent figures in the 1998 novel, *Rift.* Vaughan Jasper Roberts is stuck with his grandmother in an isolated coastal town when his parents take off. "At times ponderous and confusing, this is a complex novel in which Hathorn explores human fragility and courage, manipulation and madness and the comfort of habit and ritual," noted Jane Connolly in a *Magpies* review.

Hathorn also teamed up with writer Gary Crew to produce an epistolary novel between two teenagers in *Dear Venny, Dear Saffron,* and has also experimented with online storytelling on her web site, adapting the novel, *Ghostop,* from that format. And with all this different activity, Hathorn has not neglected the picture books she began with. Her 1998 *Sky Sash So Blue* tells the story of young Susannah, from a slave household, who is willing to give up her one bit of ornament—her scrap of sky-blue sash, to ensure that her sister the bride has a lovely wedding dress. *Children's Book Review Service* called this picture book a "lovely story of hardship, perseverance and love," while reviewer Carol Ann Wilson pointed out in *School Library Journal* that Hathorn employed an article of clothing, as she did in *Grandma's Shoes,* "to symbolize the indomitable spirit of family." Wilson concluded, "Susannah's narrative makes human and accessible the poignant struggles of a people, a family, and one little girl."

Hathorn acknowledged that though her writings often contain messages, "I don't ever want to write didactic books that berate people, young or old, with messages. I don't think you can really write a successful book by setting out with a "do-good" or any other kind of message in mind. I can only write what moves me in some way to laugh or to cry or to wonder. I don't know what I'll be writing about a few years hence. There is a great sense of adventure in this— and a sense of mystery about what will find me."

As for advice to aspiring young writers, Hathorn has said: "The more you write the better you write. It's as simple and as difficult as that. To write well you must develop an ease with the pen and paper or the word processor or whatever—but most of all an ease with words. To do this you must be immersed in words; they should be your friends and your playthings as well as your tools. So, young writers, write a lot and love what you write so much that you work over it and shine it up to be the best you can possibly do—and then share it with someone."

■ Works Cited

Connolly, Jane, review of *Rift, Magpies,* July, 1998, p. 38.

Hathorn, Libby, *All about Anna,* Heinemann, 1986.

Hathorn, Libby, "Skateboard," *Talks with My Skateboard,* Australian Broadcasting Corp., 1991.

Hoffman, Mary, review of *Juke-box Jive, School Librarian,* August, 1996, p. 105.

Jameyson, Karen, review of *The Tram to Bondi Beach, Horn Book,* July, 1989, p. 474.

Jameyson, Karen, review of *Thunderwith, Magpies,* March, 1990, p. 4.

Martin, Ann, "Encouraging the Excellent," *Times Literary Supplement,* July 23, 1982, p. 792.

Pilla, Marianne, review of *The Tram to Bondi Beach, School Library Journal,* July, 1989, p. 66.

Saxby, Maurice, *The Proof of the Puddin': Australian Children's Literature, 1970-1990,* Ashton Scholastic, 1993, pp. 219-21.

Saxby, Maurice, "Hathorn, Libby," *St. James Guide to Children's Writers,* 5th edition, edited by Sara Pendergast and Tom Pendergast, St. James Press, 1999, pp. 482-83.

Sherman, Louise L., review of *Freya's Fantastic Surprise, School Library Journal,* August, 1989, p. 120.

Review of *Sky Sash So Blue, Children's Book Review Service,* August, 1998, pp. 164-65.

Strang, Robert, review of *Thunderwith, Bulletin of the Center for Children's Books,* April, 1991, p. 194.

Review of *Thunderwith, Publishers Weekly,* May 17, 1991, p. 65.

Watson, Elizabeth S., review of *Freya's Fantastic Surprise, The Horn Book Magazine,* March-April, 1989, p. 199.

Watson, Elizabeth S., review of *Thunderwith, The Horn Book Magazine,* July, 1991, p. 462.

Wilson, Carol Ann, review of *Sky Sash So Blue, School Library Journal,* June, 1998, p. 108.

■ For More Information See

PERIODICALS

Australian Bookseller and Publisher, March, 1992, p. 26.

Booklist, February 15, 1998, p. 1019.

Books for Keeps, November, 1996, p. 10.

Bulletin of the Center for Children's Books, May, 1998, pp. 322-23.

Horn Book, July-August, 1998, p. 472.

Junior Bookshelf, October, 1990, p. 232.

Magpies, March, 1993, p. 31 November, 1999, pp. 10-13, 38.

Publishers Weekly, August 1, 1994, p. 79; December 18, 1995, p. 53; June 22, 1998, p. 91.

School Library Journal, May, 1991, p. 111; October, 1994, p. 123; March, 1996, p. 189.
Voice of Youth Advocates, June, 1991.

OTHER

Libby Hathorn's Web site is located at http://www. libbythathorn.com.

Alice Hoffman

■ Personal

Born March 16, 1952, in New York, NY; married Tom Martin (a writer); children: Jake, Zack. *Education:* Adelphi University, B.A., 1973; Stanford University, M.A., 1975.

■ Addresses

Home—Brookline, MA. *Agent*—Elaine Markson Literary Agency, 44 Greenwich Ave., New York, NY 10011.

■ Career

Writer, 1975—.

■ Awards, Honors

Mirelles fellow, Stanford University, 1975; Bread Loaf fellowship, summer, 1976; Notable Books of 1979 list, *Library Journal*, for *The Drowning Season*.

■ Writings

NOVELS

Property Of, Farrar, Straus, 1977.

The Drowning Season, Dutton, 1979.
Angel Landing, Putnam, 1980.
White Horses, Putnam, 1982.
Fortune's Daughter, Putnam, 1985.
Illumination Night, Putnam, 1987.
At Risk, Putnam, 1988.
Seventh Heaven, Putnam, 1990.
Turtle Moon, Berkley, 1993.
Second Nature, Putnam, 1994.
Practical Magic, Putnam, 1995.
Here on Earth, Putnam, 1997.
The River King, Putnam, 2000.

SHORT STORIES

Local Girls, Putnam, 1999.

PICTURE BOOKS

Fireflies, illustrated by Wayne McLoughlin, Hyperion, 1997.
Fireflies: A Winter's Tale, illustrated by Wayne McLoughlin, Hyperion, 1999.
Horsefly, illustrated by Steve Johnson and Lou Fancher, Hyperion, 2000.

Also author of *Independence Day*, Warner Bros., 1983, and other screenplays. Contributor of stories to *Ms*, *Rebook*, *Fiction*, *American Review*, and *Playgirl*, and *Cape Cod Stories*, Chronicle Books, 1996.

■ Adaptations

Practical Magic was produced as a motion picture of the same name, by Turner Pictures, 1998, starring

Nicole Kidman and Sandra Bullock. Many of Hoffman's novels have been adapted for audiocassette.

■ Work in Progress

A screenplay adaptation of *At Risk*, for Twentieth Century-Fox.

■ Sidelights

Human loss, frailties and fears, and the routines of everyday life stood on its head with a touch of magical realism—these qualities in part delineate the boundaries of the fictional landscape created by Alice Hoffman in her novels, short stories, and screenplays. Blending folklore, symbolism, and eccentric characters with the domestic novel of manners, Hoffman has won readers of all ages with such bestsellers as *At Risk, Turtle Moon, Practical Magic,* and *Illumination Night*. "The hallmarks" of Hoffman's style, according to Alexandra Johnson writing in *Boston Review,* are "a shimmering prose style, the fusing of fantasy and realism, [and] the preoccupation with the way the mythic weaves itself into the everyday. . . . Hoffman's narrative domain is the domestic, the daily. Yet her vision—and voice—are lyrical." Johnson went on to compare Hoffman's fictional world to that of a painting by the seventeenth century Dutch master Jan Vermeer: "a beautifully crafted study of the interior life."

Part of Hoffman's appeal is her scope; she has viewed the drama of American in the late twentieth century through the eyes of adolescent and teenage narrators, as well as through those of adults of all ages and classes. The author Frederick Busch, writing in the *New York Times Book Review,* has pointed out that Hoffman "charms us into caring for her characters." He also noted that the author "writes quite wonderfully about the magic in our lives and in the battered, indifferent world." Her stories range from romance in gangland to intergenerational relationships in a Long Island family; from incest in California to coming to terms with one's desires in Martha's Vineyard; from the plight of an adolescent AIDS victim, to a family of New England women who deal in magic. Characteristic of all Hoffman's novels is the counterpoint of her lush prose and offbeat characters, the jarring mix of magical events and everyday settings.

East Coast Upbringing

Alice Hoffman was born March 6, 1952, the daughter of a real estate salesman and a social worker.

When Hoffman was eight, her parents divorced and she was raised by her mother, in Franklin Square, Long Island. Hoffman once told Stella Dong in a 1985 *Publishers Weekly* interview that her mother "wasn't like all the other mothers in the neighborhood. She read a lot and had been to university. She wasn't domestic in the way that was expected of mothers at the time." Her love of books rubbed off on her daughter, and Alice Hoffman read voraciously as a youngster: science fiction, fairy tales, and anything to do with magic. "I was crazy about Mary Poppins and the Nesbit books and Edward Eager," she told Dong. "I really loved those stories that begin with a normal family and then all of a sudden, something magical enters their lives. Those are really wonderful books—especially when you're a kid and your own family's not so wonderful . . . just the idea that you could stumble upon all sorts of magical things."

An avid reader, Hoffman also began writing at a young age, keeping a notebook that detailed alternate identities for herself, and sketching story lines. She did not enjoy high school, and upon graduation contemplated becoming a beautician. Instead, she went to college at Adelphi University in Garden City, New Jersey. There various professors encouraged her to write. The stories Hoffman created in these years earned her a prestigious Mirelles Fellowship to Stanford University's renowned M.F.A. program in creative writing. Hoffman headed west in 1973, ready to learn the writer's craft. Studying under Albert Guerard at Stanford, whom Hoffman hailed in her *Publishers Weekly* interview as "possibly the best writing teacher in the country," the apprentice writer gained new confidence in her technique. As she told Dong, "That's when I felt that maybe I really could write after all."

Hoffman was also influenced during this time by such female authors as Doris Lessing, Margaret Drabble, Grace Paley, and Anne Tyler, and by the work of Gabriel Garcia Marquez, specifically by his groundbreaking work of magical realism, *One Hundred Years of Solitude*. Writing in the *New York Times Book Review* in May 1984, Hoffman acknowledged that the Marquez novel "changed everything for her." She now saw how the writer was free to transform the mundane into the fabulous by employing magical, fantastical, mythic, and sometimes surreal elements. Hoffman earned her master's degree in 1975, and following graduation attended the Bread Loaf Writer's Conference in Vermont.

Short Stories Lead to First Novel

Hoffman published her first short stories in magazines from *Ms* to the *American Review.* One of these stories captured the attention of a New York editor who queried Hoffman about anything novel-length that she might have in the works. Assuring the editor she had a book underway, Hoffman quickly went on her first novel, *Property Of,* which was published in 1977.

The story of a year in the life of a seventeen-year-old female protagonist, *Property Of* looks at gangs, violence, and drugs. The unnamed protagonist falls for McKay, the leader of an urban gang that claims street territory in the suburbs of New York; and the young girl, from a middle-class family, becomes the "property" of McKay. Their relationship is a troubled one, punctuated by violence and use of drugs, and though the girl finally breaks with McKay, she becomes addicted to heroin. Reviewing this first novel in the *New York Times Book Review,* Michael Mewshaw felt that Hoffman "views life as through the jagged prisms of a broken whisky bottle or a haze of heroin," and that "she brings a fierce personal intensity to it." Despite what Mewshaw found to be "stylistic tics," he praised *Property Of* as an "impressive debut."

Richard R. Lingeman writing in the *New York Times* described the novel as "[A] remarkably envisioned novel, almost mythic in its cadences, hypnotic." Lingeman concluded, "Alice Hoffman imbues her juvenile delinquents with a romantic intensity that lifts them out of sociology." Writing in the *Yale Review,* Edith Milton also thought that Hoffman's writing elevated her characters: "Hoffman creates characters touched by legend. . . . In a way, *Property Of* is a novel about our sentimental myths and romances as much as it is a novel about street gangs."

Buoyed by such critical acclaim, Hoffman began a second novel, this time turning to family dynamics with *The Drowning Season.* Long Island is the setting for this "fierce and wicked fairytale of these "modern times,"" as Jerome Charyn described the novel in the *New York Times Book Review.* Esther the White is an aging witch and grandmother. She lives in a compound with her son Phillip, who likes to try to drown himself during the Drowning Season of July and August; with Phillip's keeper, Cohen, who continually saves Philip; with her daughter-in-law; and, with her grandchild, Esther the Black. "Alice Hoffman has an extraordinary sense of the fabulous," Charyn noted, while Jean Strouse wrote in *Newsweek:* "Alice Hoffman's hallucinatory novel skims along just above the surface of the real, like a finely wrought nightmare."

The highly acclaimed novel by
ALICE HOFFMAN
Bestselling author of *HERE ON EARTH*
ILLUMINATION NIGHT

"Daringly mixing comedy with tragedy....she has created a narrative that somehow makes myth out of the sticky complexities of contemporary marriage....Her characters are branded onto one's memory."
—Christopher Lehmann-Haupt
The New York Times

The needs and desires of six very different characters come together in Alice Hoffman's haunting 1987 novel set on Martha's Vineyard.

Long Island is also the setting for Hoffman's third novel, *Angel Landing,* "a good, old-fashioned love story," according to a somewhat tongue-in-cheek Suzanne Freeman in *Washington Post Book World.* Beginning with the explosion of a half-built nuclear power plant, the story unfolds through the eyes of a "sensitive and intelligent observer, alienated from her surroundings," as Miriam Sagan characterized the book's heroine in a *Ms* review. Freeman concluded that "Alice Hoffman's writing has the magic that makes us want to believe it."

Hoffman's next book was *White Horse,* a novel that reviewer Ann Tyler of the *New York Times Book Review* observed "combines the concrete and the dreamlike" within its compass. On one level, *White*

Horse is the story of a young girl's obsession with her older brother; on the other, it is a mythic tale, dealing with legendary outlaws who appear out of nowhere riding their white horses westward. Hermione Lee, reviewing *White Horse* for the London newspaper the *Observer,* called it a "pullulating tale of incest, magic and myth in a California landscape." *Newsweek's* Peter S. Prescott commented, "I found reading this novel to be like eating my way through a pan of fudge; it's probably fattening and certainly not the kind of fare you can live on, but once in a while the sheer sensual delinquency is fun."

While pregnant with her first child, Hoffman came up with the idea for her fifth novel, *Fortune's Daughter.* In this tale the "sense of magic and elemental force arises from the central mystery of childbirth," according to Perri Klass, writing in the *New York Times Book Review.* Rae, deserted by her boyfriend after she has given up everything for him, is about to give birth to her first child and consults Lila, a fortune-teller, for some good words. Years earlier, Lila gave up for adoption her own child, a daughter. In Rae's tea leaves, Lila sees a child's death, and assumes it will be Rae's baby. However, what she has actually seen is her own baby, who has died in childhood, as Lila learns after looking up the girl's adoptive parents. Perri Klass pointed to the "confident" writing in *Fortune's Daughter,* which is "powerfully and essentially laconic, but . . . also lush"; to the "rich, vivid and sharp" description," and the "offbeat humor" that "keeps the narrative from drifting into melodrama." Susan Lardner, writing in the *New Yorker,* felt there were no "lasting surprises" in *Fortune's Daughter,* and that the "euphoria" of Hoffman's ending wears off, "leaving the reader with a gullible feeling and certain questions." Reviewer Patricia Meyer Spacks complained of "Soap opera sentimentalities of plot and characterization" which produce a novel that "almost—but not quite—transcends its sentimentalities and its often arbitrary handling of character and event." Other critics, such as Susan Dooley of *Washington Post Book World,* were more positive about Hoffman's fifth novel. Dooley wrote that "Hoffman is a marvelous writer with a painter's eye who takes the landscape of ordinary people experiencing ordinary emotions and colors them in unexpected ways."

For her sixth novel, *Illumination Night,* Hoffman turned to a Massachusetts setting, using Martha's Vineyard as the backdrop for what *Newsweek's* Laura Shapiro termed a "splendid, witchy account of faith and seduction." Hoffman presents readers with six intersecting and sometimes colliding lives.

"From a technical as well as emotional standpoint, this is an impressive, stirring performance," Jack Sullivan of the *Washington Post Book World* commented. Meanwhile, Christopher Lehmann-Haupt of the *New York Times* noted, "Ms. Hoffman writes so simply about human passions that her characters are branded onto one's memory." Gwyneth Cravens remarked in the *New York Times Book Review,* "Subtle touches here and there make this intelligent novel shine." Meanwhile, Alexandra Johnson wrote in the *Boston Review,* "*Illumination Night* is a powerful if often disturbing look at the interior lives, domestic and emotional, of a young family and the teenage girl set on destroying them all."

Critical Acclaim

Although her literary novels had won critical praise, Hoffman still had scored a real commercial success. Publication of her seventh book, *At Risk,* changed all that. Hoffman earned a one-hundred-and-fifty-thousand-dollar advance, and the initial print run was one hundred thousand copies. This story of an adolescent stricken with AIDS took off after publication, showing up on the national best seller lists and being optioned for six figures to Twentieth-Century Fox movie studios. A result of Hoffman's own musings about how she would feel if her son were at school with another child who had AIDS, *At Risk* tells the story of eleven-year-old Amanda Farrell, daughter of a comfortable middle-class family and a gifted gymnast, who contracts the virus from a blood transfusion. The novel chronicles Amanda's losing battle with AIDS and her final acceptance of the inevitable diagnosis. She is aided in this effort by a local psychic, while her family comes asunder, and relationships with the community and those around her fall apart.

"There is no easy emotional catharsis here," wrote *Newsweek's* Shapiro, "just an abundance of life that becomes, in the course of the novel, more buoyant and powerful than death and ultimately more convincing." Writing in the *Chicago Tribune Books,* Michele Souda lauded Hoffman's "flawless prose." Souda went on to note that Hoffman did not "capitulate" to the political side of the AIDS issue, but rather took "the nightmare of our time, stripped it of statistics and social rhetoric, and placed it in the raw center of family life."

However, some critics questioned Hoffman's use of such a hot-button issue. For example, *Wall Street Journal* reviewer Donna Rifkind commented on what she found to be "flat caricatures" and what she felt was exploitation of the AIDS subject "for its sen-

Sandra Bullock stars in this 1998 film adaptation of Alice Hoffman's *Practical Magic*.

timental appeal." Rifkind added, "One can only conclude that one of Alice Hoffman's particular hopes regarding this book was that the subject of AIDS would sell." However, such criticism was the exception. More typical were the comments of a *School Library Journal* reviewer who wrote, "The characterization is sensitive, realistic, and intense. This is a book of deep and honest emotions."

Hoffman moved away from contemporary topics with her next novel, *Seventh Heaven,* set in the Long Island suburbs in 1959. A divorced woman named Nora Silk disturbs some of the peace of a quiet and idyllic community with her unconventional ways, including witchcraft. Although it takes time, finally the community accepts the newcomer. Writing in the *New York Times Book Review,* Alida Becker commented, "Hoffman is out to remind us that all those suburban stereotypes, creaky facades though they may often be, are propped up by some very real, and very basic, hopes and fears."

Turtle Moon, Hoffman's ninth novel, is set in a sleepy Florida town. The book deals with a murder

and with the disappearances of a local boy named Keith and the baby of the murdered woman. Keith's mother, Lucy, sets out to unravel this mystery. As usual, Hoffman blends magical elements into the realistic story, in this case a ghost who wanders about the small town. A contributor for *Kirkus Reviews* described the novel as a "mix of murder and magic in the Florida sunshine," while a writer for *Publishers Weekly* commented, "Hoffman's new novel has commercial success written all over it." Writing in the *New York Times Book Review,* Frederick Bush concluded, "Alice Hoffman has written a magnificent examination of a troubled child about whom her readers will care enormously."

Second Nature is a story of a wild man who has been raised by wolves, and who provides a lonely suburban woman with a new lease on life. *Booklist's* Donna Seaman commented on Hoffman's "penchant for tossing bits of magic, romance, and murder into otherwise ordinary domestic dramas of divorce and parenthood." Seaman added that whereas such a mix had been "salad-like" in other novels, with *Second Nature* "the ingredients blend into a rich and satisfying concoction." A contributor for *Kirkus Reviews* concluded, "Once again, Hoffman stirs up the unlikely with the ordinary and seasons it, expertly, deliciously, with our darkest desires—her fans should wolf it down." And Howard Frank Mosher, writing in the *New York Times Book Review*, called Hoffman's tale "magical and daring. . . . [Hoffman's] richest and wisest, as well as her boldest, novel to date."

Prestidigitation as Technique and Message

Practical Magic, published in 1995, is Hoffman's eleventh novel. Once again, the author mixes magic with the mundane in telling the story of a New England dynasty of matriarchs, the Owens. The novel focuses on two of these women: the sisters Sally and Gillian, who are raised by aunts, and who have followed very different paths in life from the days when as young girls they would sneak downstairs to hear their aunts prescribing love potions for all the women of the town. But Sally and Gillian determine never to be afflicted with such sickness brought on by love. Gillian moves from man to man; while Sally follows a more settled lifestyle, she still manages to harness her emotions to her family. Writing in the Chicago *Tribune Books*, Penelope Mesic observed that "the book's deepest appeal is perhaps the sex-specific," and that *Practical Magic* is "fundamentally a novel about women whose lives are given value by their relations to other women." Michiko Kakutani, reviewing the novel in the *New York Times*, had doubts about Hoffman's use of magical realism in the novel: "None of the surreal events in Practical Magic is remotely organic to the main characters' lives or the larger public world they inhabit." Kakutani observed. He also found Hoffman's use of such techniques created "cloying cutesiness and willful contrivance." But Lorna Sage, reviewing the novel in *Times Literary Supplement*, described Hoffman's approach as "Erica Jong meets Garrison Keillor," adding that "The magic in Hoffman's plots is pervasive, but at the same time no big deal. . . . Forget the magic, this is fiction as an alternative therapy."

In *Here on Earth*, Hoffman's twelfth novel, she creates what Karen Karbo in the *New York Times Book Review* hailed as "a *Wuthering Heights* for the 90s." The novel is the story of a middle-aged mother who falls in love with the bad-boy crush of her youth and who takes her teenage daughter with her when she leaves her husband for this former love. The story "is by turns inspired, profound and dreadful," according to Karen Karbo. *Kirkus Reviews* termed it "A chilly, hopeless

If you enjoy the works of Alice Hoffman, you might want to check out the following books:

Kaye Gibbons, *Sights Unseen*, 1995.
Alice McDermott, *Charming Billy*, 1999.
Jane Smiley, *The Age of Grief*, 1987.
Anne Tyler, *The Accidental Tourist*, 1985.

love story with an unhappy conclusion. Hard to see what readers will find to like in such a tale." But Rita M. Fontinha, reviewing the novel in *Kliatt*, felt differently. "Hoffman's new book may also be her best," she commented. [It is] a lyrical and dramatic love story, set in a bleak and wintry landscape."

Hoffman's next novel, published in 2000, is *The River King*, a book that once again uses a murder to throw a town and its citizens in stark relief. Hoffman is also the author of two picture books for young readers, *Fireflies* and *Horseflies*, and of a 1999 collection of linked stories called *Local Girls*. Like several of her novels, Hoffman sets the short story collection in a sleepy Long Island suburb. Spanning the course of a decade, the inter-related tales are often narrated by and focus on the activities of Gretel Samuelson and her family, and cover the period from Gretel's adolescence to her adulthood. "Odd mystical moments crop up now and then as Gretel, starved for miracles, seesaws between wonder and sorrow," commented Sarah Ferguson in the *New York Times Book Review*. However, Ferguson ultimately felt that the stories, many of which were originally published in magazines, "suffer from a debilitating overlap when they're read as a collection." A reviewer for *Publishers Weekly*, on the other hand, commented that although "dysfunctional family fiction seems standard fare these days, Hoffman's knack for creating a sense of specific atmosphere is uncanny and unique." *School Library Journal's* Jackie Gropman praised Hoffman's narrative voice, writing that "the language is wisecracking, scintillating, descriptive, and honest."

Hoffman continues to entertain and to ask probing question about love and loss in contemporary America. With her own unique spin on magical realism, she has looked at subjects from AIDS to gangs, and taken the reader from the suburbs to small-town America. As Frederick Bush noted in the *New York Times Book Review*, "the soul is part of the action of the novel, but Ms. Hoffman's writing about it doesn't make an adult reader feel as if he's sneaking a quick half-hour of cutesy cartoons on television." Hoffman's use of magic is integral to her art in Bush's opinion. "[She] grounds her attention to magic and things of the spirit with a particularity and an insistence of the everyday," he noted.

■ **Works Cited**

Review of *At Risk, School Library Journal,* May, 1993, p. 24.

Becker, Alida, review of *Seventh Heaven, New York Times Book Review,* August 5, 1990, p. 2.

Bush, Frederick, review of *Turtle Moon, New York Times Book Review,* April, 26, 1992, p. 1.

Charyn, Jerome, "The Witches' Tale" *New York Times Book Review,* July 15, 1979, p. 13.

Cravens, Gwyneth, "Flying from the Windows, Biking down the Stairs," *New York Times Book Review,* August 9, 1987, pp. 7, 9.

Dong, Stella, "Alice Hoffman," *Publishers Weekly,* April 12, 1985, pp. 102-03.

Dooley, Susan, "Mothers and Daughters," *Washington Post Book World,* May 11, 1985, p. 19.

Ferguson, Sarah, "Islanders," *New York Times Book Review,* June 13, 1999, p. 31

Fontinha, Rita M., review of *Here on Earth, Kliatt,* May, 1998, p. 13.

Freeman, Suzanne, "Love at the Crisis Center," *Washington Post Book World,* December 21, 1980, p. 4.

Gropman, Alice, review of *Local Girls, School Library Journal,* October, 1999, p. 178.

Review of *Here on Earth, Kirkus Reviews,* June 1, 1997, p. 824.

Hoffman, Alice, "The Hum Inside the Skull—A Symposium," *New York Times Book Review,* May 13, 1984, pp. 1, 5.

Johnson, Alexandra, review of *Illumination Night, Boston Review,* October, 1987, p. 31.

Kakutani, Michiko, "Magical Realism from 2 Cultures," *New York Times,* June 2, 1995, p. C30.

Karbo, Karen, "Heathcliff Redux," *New York Times Book Review,* September 14, 1997, p. 25.

Klass, Perri, "Childbirth, with Fire and Ice," *New York Times Book Review,* March 24, 1985, p. 7.

Lardner, Susan, "Complications," *New Yorker,* July 15, 1985, pp. 83-85.

Lee, Hermione, "Frantic Obsessions," *Observer (London),* May 29, 1983, p. 30.

Lehmann-Haupt, Christopher, "Lights in the Vineyard," *New York Times,* June 25, 1987, p. A19.

Lingeman, Richard R., review of *Property Of, New York Times,* July 14, 1977, p. 25.

Review of *Local Girls, Publishers Weekly,* July 5, 1999, p. 35.

Mesic, Penelope, "Illusory Allure," *Chicago Tribune Books,* August 6, 1995, p. 5.

Mewshaw, Michael, review of *Property Of, New York Times Book Review,* July 10, 1977, p. 10.

Milton, Edith, review of *Property Of, Yale Review,* Winter, 1978, pp. 267-68.

Mosher, Howard Frank, review of *Second Nature, New York Times Book Review,* February 6, 1994, p. 13.

Prescott, Peter S., "Night Moves," *Newsweek,* April 12, 1982, p. 82.

Rifkind, Donna, review of *At Risk, Wall Street Journal,* June 9, 1988.

Sagan, Miriam, review of *Angel Landing, Ms,* February, 1981, p. 37.

Sage, Lorna, "Some Alternative Arts," *Times Literary Supplement,* July 5, 1996, p. 23.

Seaman, Donna, review of *Second Nature, Booklist,* December 15, 1993, p. 723.

Review of *Second Nature, Kirkus Reviews,* December 1, 1993, p. 1480.

Shapiro, Laura, review of *At Risk, Newsweek,* August 1, 1988, p. 52.

Souda, Michele, review of *At Risk, Chicago Tribune,* June 26, 1988.

Spacks, Patricia Meyer, review of *Fortune's Daughter, Boston Review,* September, 1985, pp. 25-26.

Strouse, Jean, "Esther the White, Esther the Black," *Newsweek,* August 20, 1979, p. 72.

Sullivan, Jack, "Better to Have Loved," *Washington Post Book World,* August 2, 1987, pp. 8, 13.

Review of *Turtle Moon, Kirkus Reviews,* February 1, 1992.

Review of *Turtle Moon, Publishers Weekly,* February 3, 1992, p. 61.

Tyler, Anne, "Ordinary Family, with a Difference," *New York Times Book Review,* March 28, 1982, pp. 11, 38.

■ **For More Information See**

BOOKS

Contemporary Literary Criticism, Volume 51, Gale, 1989.

Contemporary Popular Writers, edited by Susan Windisch Brown, St. James Press, 1996.

PERIODICALS

Booklist, March 15, 1995, p. 1283; July, 1997, p. 1774; June 1, 1998, p. 1793; March 15, 1999, p. 1259.

Belles Lettres, summer, 1992, p. 20.

Cosmopolitan, February, 1994.

Detroit News, September 5, 1990.

Globe and Mail (Toronto), August 25, 1990.

Library Journal, April, 15, 1994, p. 130; May 15, 1995, p. 95; January, 1996, p. 166; December, 1996, p. 150; July, 1997, p. 125; May 15, 1999, p. 130.

London Review of Books, August 6, 1992, p. 19.

Los Angeles Times, December 5, 1980; May 28, 1982; May 9, 1985; August 24, 1987; June 30, 1988.

Los Angeles Times Book Review, August 19, 1979; July 10, 1988; August 5, 1990; May 28, 1995, p. 1.

Magazine of Fantasy and Science Fiction, April, 1994; December, 1995, p. 46.

Ms., August, 1979; May, 1982; June, 1985.

Nation, November 26, 1990.

Newsweek, May 23, 1977; August 20, 1990.

New Yorker, May 3, 1982; July 27, 1992; April 11, 1994.

New York Times, July 25, 1987; July 4, 1988; August 10, 1990; February 24, 1994, p. C19.

New York Times Book Review, November 9, 1980; March 24, 1985; July 17, 1988; June 25, 1995, p. 25; July 16, 2000, p. 12.

People, September 3, 1990; September 5, 1994, p. 34; July 3, 1995, p. 31; September 22, 1997, p. 35.

Publishers Weekly, June 1, 1990; November 29, 1993; January 2, 1995, p. 30; March 20, 1995, p. 40; April 22, 1996, p. 67; June 16, 1997, p. 44; September 15, 1997, p. 76; May 3, 1999, p. 67.

Redbook, July, 1999, p. G1.

School Library Journal, November, 1995, p. 138; November 1997, p. 83.

Time, July 18, 1988; August 6, 1990.

Times (London), November 28, 1985; October 1, 1987; October 1, 1988.

Times Literary Supplement, April 21, 1978; March 11, 1988; March 25, 1994, p. 21; October 19, 1997, p. 24.

Village Voice, July 19, 1988.

Vogue, July, 1992.*

—Sketch by J. Sydney Jones

Francess Lantz

■ Personal

Born August 27, 1952, in Trenton, NJ; daughter of Frederick W. (an architect) and Dorthea (a secretary/treasurer; maiden name, Lingrell) Lantz; married John M. Landsberg (a physician/filmmaker), 1983; children: Preston. *Education:* Dickinson College, B.A., 1974; Simmons College, M.L.S., 1975. *Hobbies and other interests:* "I like to ride horses, kayak, hike, boogie board, and visit schools to talk to kids about my books."

■ Addresses

Office—P.O. Box 23234, Santa Barbara, CA 93121. *E-mail*—writer@silcom.com. *Agent*—Ashley Grayson, 1342 18th St., San Pedro, CA 90732.

■ Career

Children's book writer. Dedham Public Library, Dedham, MA, children's librarian, 1976-79. Speaker at schools and conferences; teacher of writing courses for adults and children at Santa Barbara City College and Montecito Union School, 1989—.

■ Member

Society of Children's Book Writers and Illustrators, California School Librarian Association, California Reading Association.

■ Awards, Honors

Best Books for Reluctant Readers, American Library Association (ALA), for *Double Play;* Pick of the List, *Booklist,* for *Dear Celeste, My Life Is a Mess;* Best Books for Young Adults, ALA, Books for the Teen Age, New York Public Library, and Young Adult Choice, International Reading Association, all for *Someone to Love;* recommended books, *Children's Book Insider,* 1998, for *Fade Far Away* and *Stepsister from the Planet Weird.*

■ Writings

YOUNG ADULT NOVELS

(As Francess Lin Lantz) *Good Rockin' Tonight,* Addison-Wesley, 1982.
A Love Song for Becky, Berkley, 1983.
Surfer Girl, Berkley, 1983.
Rock "n" Roll Romance, Berkley, 1984.
Senior Blues, Berkley, 1984.
(As Fran Lantz) *Making It on Our Own,* Dell, 1986.
(As Fran Lantz) *Can't Stop Us Now,* Dell, 1986.
Someone to Love, Avon, 1997.
Fade Far Away, Avon, 1998.

MIDDLE-GRADE NOVELS

Woodstock Magic, Avon, 1986.

Star Struck, Avon, 1986.

All Shook Up, Avon, 1987.

The Truth about Making Out, Bantam, 1990.

Mom, There's a Pig in My Bed!, Avon, 1991.

Dear Celeste, My Life Is a Mess (sequel to *The Truth about Making Out*), Bantam, 1991.

Randy's Raiders, Troll, 1994.

Neighbors from Outer Space, Troll, 1996.

Spinach with Chocolate Sauce, Troll, 1997.

Stepsister from the Planet Weird, Random House, 1997.

The Case of the Missing Mummy ("New Adventures of Mary-Kate and Ashley" series), Scholastic, 1998.

"VARSITY COACH" SERIES; UNDER PSEUDONYM LANCE FRANKLIN

Take Down, Bantam, 1987.

Double Play, Bantam, 1987.

"SWEET VALLEY TWINS" SERIES; UNDER HOUSE PSEUDONYM JAMIE SUZANNE

Center of Attention, Bantam, 1988.

Jessica's Bad Idea, Bantam, 1989.

"HARDY BOYS" SERIES; UNDER HOUSE PSEUDONYM FRANKLIN W. DIXON

Danger Unlimited, Pocket Books, 1993.

Mystery with a Dangerous Beat, Pocket Books, 1994.

OTHER

(With husband, John Landsberg, and April Rhodes) *The One and Only, No-Holds-Barred, Tell-It-Like-It-Is Santa Barbara Restaurant Guide*, Elan Press, 1988.

Rock, Rap, and Rad: How to Be a Rock or Rap Star, photographs by John Landsberg, Avon, 1992.

Be a Star!, photographs by John Landsberg, Rainbow Bridge, 1996.

Contributor to books, including *Children's Writer's & Illustrator's Market*, edited by Alice Pope, Writers Digest Books, 1999, and *The Graceful Lie: A Method for Making Fiction*, edited by Michael Petracca, Prentice Hall, 1999. Contributor to periodicals, including *Kliatt*; contributor of film and restaurant reviews to *Santa Barbara Independent*.

■ Work in Progress

You're the One, for Aladdin Paperbacks; a young adult novel; a middle-grade series.

■ Sidelights

After working as a children's librarian for several years, Francess Lantz decided that she too wanted to contribute to the wealth of literature for young people that made its way to her library's shelves. Beginning her writing efforts in the early 1980s, Lantz has developed a reputation as a respected author of fiction for both preteen and young adult readers. Among her most highly praised works are the novels *Fade Far Away, Someone to Love*, and *Dear Celeste, My Life Is a Mess*. Lantz has also contributed to the "Sweet Valley Twins," "Hardy Boys," "Varsity Coach," and "Adventures of Mary-Kate and Ashley" series under a variety of pseudonyms.

Born in 1952 in Trenton, New Jersey, Lantz displayed a passion for writing at a young age. "I loved to write stories and illustrate them," she once stated. "My father was an architect, and we spent long hours drawing together, including creating "tattoos" on each other's hands and arms with ballpoint pens."

Lantz grew up in Bucks County, Pennsylvania, where she gained a reputation as a tomboy among her friends. "My stories were usually about war, or spies, and they were always violent," she recalled. "Despite this, my fifth-grade teacher encouraged my talent and allowed me to stay inside during recess to tape record my stories with my friends."

While her early dreams involved growing up to become a famous writer, the Beatles' coming to the United States in 1964 changed everything for the twelve-year-old budding author. "I chucked literature in favor of rock "n" roll," Lantz remembered. "I took guitar lessons, wrote songs, and soon began performing. After college, I moved to Boston to become a rock star. It never happened, but I had fun trying," and, as Lantz explained on her Web site, "starvation sent me back to school to become a children's librarian."

The Librarian Begins Writing

After completing her graduate degree in 1975, Lantz got a job as a children's librarian in Dedham, Massachusetts. "I used to put on a graveyard story-hour every year (yes, I took the kids to a nearby graveyard and scared the pants off them)," the author once remarked. After a couple of years I was having trouble finding new stories that were short, easy to read aloud, and really scary. In desperation, I wrote some myself. They were a big hit with the kids and that was when I first thought, "hey, maybe I could write children's books.""

In this novel, twelve-year-old Megan is in for a surprise when she learns that her mom's new boyfriend and his daughter are really aliens from another planet.

Lantz's first manuscripts were picture-book texts, followed by a scary fantasy novel, and then two mysteries. Although none of those sold, she remained determined. That determination paid off: Lantz's next effort, a young adult novel she titled *Good Rockin' Tonight*, was picked up by a publisher, and Lantz's childhood dream of one day becoming a published author was realized.

While Lantz began her career by writing young adult novels loosely based on her own life, she eventually switched to middle-grade books, where she could add more humorous elements to her stories. In 1991's *Mom, There's a Pig in My Bed!*, Lantz captures readers with her title and doesn't let go. The story finds Dwight Ewing hoping that the earth will swallow him up, so he wouldn't have to endure his embarrassing family. After moving them to a small town, Dwight's father draws all sorts of atten-

tion to the family through his determination to raise seeing-eye pigs for blind people who have allergies to the dogs traditionally assigned to this sort of task. As a way of saving face, Dwight convinces everyone that his father is really wealthy and is engaged in his present porcine pursuits in an attempt to educate his children as to the ways of regular folks. Along with the predicted backfire to Dwight's misrepresentation, *Mom, There's a Pig in My Bed!* contains "some very funny scenes" involving swine, as well as insight into the problems that can spring from even an innocent lie, according to *School Library Journal* contributor Nancy P. Reeder. In *Stepsister from the Planet Weird*, Lantz introduces readers to Megan, who is in despair over her mother's upcoming marriage because it will mean having a "perfect" stepsister. Lantz tells her tale in the form of diary entries, and the book's "zany humor" combines with the author's "wit . . . [and] character

When Puck attempts to solve a kidnapping case that occurred at his parents' restaurant, he finds himself up to his ears in danger in this tale.

development" to result in a novel that appeals to even reluctant readers, in the opinion of *School Library Journal* reviewer Cheryl Cufari.

Recalling the Teen Years

Perhaps one of the reasons Lantz's books have proven so popular with preteen readers is that she can remember the details of her own adolescence. "I can vividly recall my feelings when I first heard the [Beatles'] *Sergeant Pepper* album, when the cute older boy I had a crush on turned to me in the hall and patted me on the head, when I learned that my father had died. At the same time," she added, "I can now view the events from an adult perspective. Both views, I feel, are required to write young children's novels. If the author can see the world through a child's eyes and nothing more, the book will be one-dimensional and claustrophobic. If the author can only view children from an adult perspective, the story will be manipulative and didactic. So far I think I've been able to integrate both perspectives. If I ever lose that ability, it will be time to stop writing children's novels and move on to something else."

While Lantz concentrated on writing for preteens during the 1980s and much of the 1990s, she has returned to her focus on young adults with her more recent novels, including *Someone to Love* and *Fade Far Away*. In *Someone to Love*, published in 1997, fifteen-year-old Sara finds that her liberal ideals conflict with her parent's self-serving, materialistic lifestyle. Sara is drawn to Iris, who represents the independence, romance, and adulthood Sara dreams of. When her parents decide to adopt the soon-to-be-born child of the free-spirited Iris, Sara finds herself withdrawing emotionally from both her father and mother during what should have been an exciting time. Again focusing on a fifteen-year-old protagonist, *Fade Far Away* is narrated by Sienna, the artistic daughter of a famous sculptor and his wife, a woman obsessed with her husband's advancement in the arts community to the exclusion of all else, including her daughter. In a novel that *Kliatt* reviewer Claire Rosser called "intense and challenging," Sienna must contradict her mother and support her father's efforts to reevaluate his priorities after he is diagnosed with a brain tumor. "This emotionally charged coming-of-age story borrows the glamorous trappings of the art world," showing Sienna coming to terms with her father's failings and her own growing sense of self, according to a *Publishers Weekly* critic.

In writing for older teens, Lantz enjoys what she sees as "more challenging stories that stretch my abilities

If you enjoy the works of Francess Lantz, you might want to check out the following books and films:

Brock Cole, *Celine*, 1989.
Berlie Doherty, *Dear Nobody*, 1992.
Leslie Howarth, *Maphead*, 1994.
What's Eating Gilbert Grape, a film starring Johnny Depp, 1993.

as a writer and, I hope, stretch my readers' abilities too. In the future," she once remarked, "I want to write more and better YA novels, and maybe some middle-grade books that are both funny and poignant." In addition to continuing to write fiction, Lantz contributes articles to magazines and newspapers, and has dabbled in nonfiction with *Rock, Rap, and Rad: How to Be a Rock or Rap Star*, which *Voice of Youth Advocates* contributor Patrick Jones praised as "an interesting book aimed at all the teens who ever wanted to see their faces on MTV." She and her family live in Santa Barbara, California, where she enjoys visiting local schools to talk to budding authors.

■ Works Cited

Cufari, Cheryl, review of *Stepsister from the Planet Weird*, *School Library Journal*, February, 1998, p. 109.
Review of *Fade Far Away*, *Publishers Weekly*, June 29, 1998, p. 60.
Jones, Patrick, review of *Rock, Rap, and Rad: How to Be a Rock or Rap Star*, *Voice of Youth Advocates*, April, 1993, p. 55.
"Planet Fran," http://silcom.com/~writer (February 18, 1999).
Reeder, Nancy P., review of *Mom, There's a Pig in My Bed!*, *School Library Journal*, January, 1993, pp. 100-01.
Rosser, Claire, review of *Fade Far Away*, *Kliatt*, May, 1998, p. 7.

■ For More Information See

PERIODICALS

Booklist, July, 1993, p. 1955; March 15, 1998, p. 1216.
Kirkus Reviews, February 1, 1997, p. 224.

ON-LINE

Francess Lantz's Web site is located at http://www.silcom.com/~writer.

Gail Carson Levine

■ Personal

Born September 17, 1947, in New York, NY; daughter of David (an owner of a commercial art studio) and Sylvia (a teacher; maiden name, Jacobson) Carson; married David Levine (a software developer), September 2, 1967. *Education:* City College of the City University of New York, B.A., 1969.

■ Addresses

Agent—Ginger Knowlton, Curtis Brown Ltd., 10 Astor Pl., New York, NY 10003.

■ Career

Children's book author. New York State Department of Labor, New York City, employment interviewer, 1970-82; New York State Department of Commerce, New York City, administrative assistant, 1982-86; New York State Department of Social Services, New York City, welfare administrator, 1986-97.

■ Awards, Honors

Best Books for Young Adults and Quick Picks for Young Adults citations, American Library Association (ALA), and Newbery Honor Book, American Library Association, all 1998, Dorothy Canfield Fisher Award, 1999, and several other state children's reading awards. all for *Ella Enchanted;* ALA Notable Book and Best Books for Young Adults, 100 Books for Reading and Sharing and Books for the Teen Age lists, New York Public Library, and *Publishers Weekly* Best Books of 1999, all 1999, and all for *Dave at Night.*

■ Writings

Ella Enchanted, HarperCollins, 1997.
Dave at Night, HarperCollins, 1999.
The Wish, HarperCollins, 2000.

THE "PRINCESS TALES" SERIES

The Fairy's Mistake, illustrated by Mark Elliot, HarperCollins, 1999.
The Princess Test, illustrated by Mark Elliot, HarperCollins, 1999.
Princess Sonora and the Long Sleep, illustrated by Mark Elliot, HarperCollins, 1999.
Cinderellis and the Glass Hill, illustrated by Mark Elliot, HarperCollins, 2000.

Also author of the script for the children's musical *Spacenapped,* produced in Brooklyn, NY. Levine's works have been translated into German, French, Italian, and Danish.

■ Adaptations

Ella Enchanted has been optioned for an original movie, produced by Miramax and has also been adapted for audiocassette by BDD; *Dave at Night* has been optioned for a movie and has also been adapted for audiocassette by Recorded Books and Listening Library; *The Wish* is being adapted for audiocassette by BDD.

■ Work in Progress

A picture based on "The Boy Who Cried Wolf," with a gender switch; an original fairy tale, *The Two Princesses of Bamar*.

■ Sidelights

Fairy tales are real. Just ask Gail Carson Levine, author of *Ella Enchanted* and *Dave at Night*. Levine was fifty when she published her first novel. A welfare administrator for much of her adult life, she spent nine long years gathering rejections for her picture book submissions. Then, turning a writing project for a class at the New School into a manuscript retelling of the Cinderella story, she hit gold. Published by HarperCollins, *Ella Enchanted* earned starred reviews from major publications and was gaining word-of-mouth popularity among middle grade readers and even adult readers before the American Library Association waved its Newbery wand, conferring on this first novel the Newbery Honor status. And poof. The world changed for Levine.

"I had already quit my day job by the time I got the award," Levine told *Authors and Artists for Young Adults (AAYA)* in an interview. "But the Newbery Honor certainly changed my life. I don't think you could find an eleven-year-old girl now who has not heard of Ella." Foreign rights were sold and a film option followed as well as speaking engagements with schools and adults. New book contracts also were in the works. Suddenly Levine, who had spent the better part of a decade trying to get the ear and eye of editors, was in control of her career. But success has not gone to Levine's head. She still takes writing classes at the New School, still confers with her writing group that helped her during the lean years of rejections, still finds time to volunteer at the local middle school in her home in New York's Hudson Valley teaching kids the skills of creative writing. Unlike the protagonist of a fairy tale, Levine knows her good luck is not simply the matter of fortune, but of years of hard work.

Growing Up in the Big Apple

Born and raised in New York City, Levine has only fond memories of her urban youth. "Manhattan was a great place to grow up," Levine told *AAYA*. "You could have independence from parents at a much younger age than kids in the suburbs who have to be driven everywhere they go. By the sixth grade I was allowed to go on the subway alone. My friends and I would have outings to the museums, to the beach. It was a wonderfully cultural place to grow up. New York City was our oyster."

The second of two daughters born to David and Sylvia Carson, Levine learned important lessons at home. Lesson one: books are good. "I devoured books as a kid," Levine recalled in her interview. "And I was omnivorous. I would read everything from *Heidi* and *Bambi,* to the "Anne of Green Gables" books and the novels of Louisa May Alcott. I also loved biographies." She was also a fan of fairy tales. "As a child I loved fairy tales because the story, the what-comes-next, is paramount." Lesson two: the arts are the most important thing in the world. "I don't think my parents intentionally meant to give me and my sister this message. My dad was a businessman who ran a commercial art studio and loved to write. My mom was a teacher who would write full-length verse plays for her students to perform. They both loved creativity and creative people. And that reverence was passed on to me and my older sister, Rani, who is a painter of Jamaican subjects as well as a professor of fine arts."

Like her older sister, Levine wanted badly to become a painter. This was a dream that followed her throughout school and much of her adult life. "I didn't plan to be a writer, even though I started writing early." In elementary school she helped found a writing club, and in high school she published some very "self-conscious" poems in a student poetry anthology, but if there was any competition at this time to her dreams of painting, it was acting, not writing. "I had the lead in a Shaw play in high school, and with other like-minded friends started an acting troupe that performed in homes for senior citizens and for orphans." The summer of her junior year, she also worked as an extra in summer stock.

Graduating from high school, Levine went to Antioch in Ohio for several years before transferring to City College in New York to graduate. "I majored in philosophy, but that was more because of the influence of one charismatic professor than for a love of the subject. And philosophy prepares one to write in

TROPHY NEWBERY

GAIL CARSON LEVINE

Ella Enchanted

Can she undo a foolish fairy's spell—and live happily ever after?

Levine's first published work, a retelling of *Cinderella*, enchanted its large reading audience and earned a Newbery Honor.

a very didactic, stiff style. There was no way I ever thought I would be a professional writer."

Welfare Administrator by Day

Levine married in 1967, and after college she began working for the New York State Department of Labor and Department of Social Services. "Most of my life has had to do with welfare, first helping people find work and finally as an administrator. The earlier experience was more direct and satisfying, and I enjoy thinking that a bunch of people somewhere are doing better today than they might have done if not for me." Levine worked this job for nearly three decades, but all the while she was continuing a rich and creative life after work hours. Her first experience in writing was the book she wrote for a children's musical, *Spacenapped*, in collabora-

tion with her husband, a musician and computer software developer.

She also continued painting, taking classes and working in oils and watercolors. "I felt most comfortable in watercolors," Levine told *AAYA*, "and worked both in figurative and abstract. But I was not a happy painter. I was very self-critical. I took a lot of adult classes through the years, but the voice in my head kept telling me I was no good. I always thought of myself as a visual artist in these years and had some shows at smaller venues."

By the late 1980s, however, Levine had found a new interest. At about the time of her parents' deaths, she began to write. "I told myself I always love to read stories, so why shouldn't I create them as well?" Early work on an art appreciation book for kids which employed an element of fantasy convinced her to take an illustration and writing class for children's books. Levine initially thought that such a class would provide the perfect mix for her talents; in the event, she quickly found out that it was the writing that attracted her, not the illustrating. "It was like a light bulb going on," Levine explained to *AAYA*. "Suddenly I knew I wanted to write. That I wasn't a painter at all."

Levine set to work on what she saw as her new career, writing children's books. Over the course of the next nine years she wrote a dozen picture books, none of which were published. "But I learned from those rejections, even though it was hard. I learned how to revise and how to stick with an idea." Her writing classes helped, as did her participation in writer's and critique groups. The writer Joan Abelove, author of the hard-hitting teen books *Go and Come Back* and *Saying It out Loud,* was a constant support in these years, as was Lucy Frank, author of humorous YA novels such as *I Am an Artichoke* and *Oy, Joy,* a later member of the writing group. Moving out of New York City also meant that Levine had a two-hour commute by train to her day job, four hours a day that she could spend working on her writing.

Then Levine had to come up with a plot for a project for a writing class she was taking. Stuck for story, she turned to one the staples of her own childhood, a fairy tale. "I decided to write a Cinderella story because it already had a plot," Levine told *AAYA*. "But looking at the original story again, I discovered I just did not care for the main character. She was such a goody-two-shoes. So obedient. For two weeks I struggled with this dilemma. Then I discovered that she was only good because she had to be, that she'd had a curse put on her when young. And I was liberated to write the story."

Ella Enchanted

Two years later, Levine had a manuscript, but not before she had had to toss almost two hundred pages away. "I got a little side-tracked in the story," she explained. "But it was so hard throwing those pages away and going back to about page twenty where I had left the real story." With a completed manuscript in hand, she sent it off to Ginger Knowlton, an agent she had met at a conference, and HarperCollins subsequently bought the manuscript.

Ella Enchanted tells the story of Ella of Frell who was, at birth, the recipient of an inadvertent curse. The fairy Lucinda, trying to be helpful, granted the "gift" of obedience on the baby, crying its head off. "That fool of a fairy Lucinda did not intend to lay a curse on me," Ella remembers in the opening of her novel. "She meant to bestow a gift. When I cried inconsolably through the first hour of life, my tears were her inspiration. Shaking her head sympathetically at Mother, the fairy touched my nose. "My gift is obedience. Ella will always be obedient. Now stop crying, child." I stopped."

But Ella, as she grows older, wants desperately to be rid of Lucinda's curse. She knows that she can never be her own person if she is always at the whim of others—she must obey whatever anyone else commands, otherwise she becomes terribly ill. As a young girl she becomes rebellious, figuring out all sorts of ways to subvert such obedience. She meets Prince Charmont at her mother's funeral, and it is there the future evil stepmother, Dame Olga, and the stepsisters, Hattie and Olive, also come into the picture. Soon Ella is sent off to finishing school with the two other girls.

Yet Ella is dissatisfied at school; she knows she must undo her curse. Escaping the school, she sets off on adventures involving centaurs, gnomes, and ogres, sometimes enjoying the help of Prince Charmont, who finds her wit and resourcefulness quite beguiling. Yet she cannot convince the fairy Lucinda to undo her spell. Falling in love with the Prince, Ella breaks the relationship off, fearful of the consequence for the Prince were he to marry someone who had to obey anybody's orders. But wanting to see him one last time, she attends a masked ball—and at this point Levine's tale and the traditional Cinderella story dovetail, the pumpkin and the glass slipper. Finally entreated by the Prince to

Young Dave Caros, an orphan, sneaks out of the strict Hebrew Home for Boys nightly to stay with his new friend, Irma, whose family is part of the Harlem Renaissance.

marry him, Ella flat out refuses, and this, lo and behold, breaks the curse on her. She has refused an order finally and is free to marry her Prince.

Critical response to Levine's debut novel was overwhelmingly positive. *Booklist*'s Ilene Cooper noted in a starred review that though others, including Robin McKinley and Donna J. Napoli had written alternate versions of fairy tales, "room must be made for Levine's superbly plotted and thoroughly enjoyable retelling of the Cinderella story." Cooper further commented that the novel was as "finely designed as a tapestry," with "a heroine so spirited that she wins readers' hearts." A writer for *Kirkus Reviews* remarked on the comic aspects of Levine's novel: "This refreshing take on one of the world's most popular fairy tales preserves the spirit of the original but adds plenty of humorous twists and a spunky, intelligent female lead." *Horn Book*'s Ann Deifende-ifer also commented on the spirit of Levine's protagonist, calling young Ella "an admirable heroine who discovers her inner strength by combating her greatest weakness." Deifendeifer further observed the "[e]xpert characterization and original ideas" which "enliven this novelization of Cinderella." A contributor for the *New York Times Book Review* dubbed the book a "high-spirited, comic first novel," while Bruce Ann Shook, writing in *School Library Journal*, felt "Ella is a delightful young woman, bright, witty, and resourceful," and the book overall was a "thoroughly enchanting novel that deepens and enriches the original tale." And a reviewer for *Voice of Youth Advocates* noted, "It is always a joyful romp to see an old friend like Cinderella in a new guise." The same writer concluded, "Everyone who has ever been in a situation where they felt forced to do something that they didn't want to do will certainly identify with Ella's predicament."

Award committees were not far behind the reviewers. First came an ALA Best Book for Young Adults listing, and the Newbery Honor. "I think the popularity of Ella stems in part from the power of fairy tales," Levine told *AAYA*. "They were always incredibly powerful in my life. They talk about very elemental things. And if you write about universal themes, you are going to have more appeal to your work. Fairy tales touch very fundamental issues. What I add to them is a new perspective, a twist. I fill in the details. What does it really feel like to have a curse put on you? What's it really like to wear seven-league boots? Those questions never bothered me as a kid, but as an adult I have begin to ponder them. Writing Ella gave me the chance to explore those missing details in fairy tales. The unexplored details are so intriguing in fairy tales, so fun to play with." Levine also pointed out what some critics saw as a feminist theme. "There is no doubt that Ella is empowered in this tale. She decides to stop being so obedient. But that was not an overt message on my part. I mean I did not write the book as a feminist tract. Rather—and I see this only with the distance of time—I was writing the book for myself. I was trying to tell myself not to be so obedient. That was my moral. But that others receive the same moral from the story is very nice."

Fairy Tales as Theme

"I don't want to box myself in with my writing. I don't want to define myself one way or the other," Levine explained to *AAYA*. "But the fact is that most of my published writing has had fairy tale elements to it, even a book which is outwardly very realistic."

Such elements are no mistake in the series of four middle grade novels written in the "Princess Tales" series: *The Fairy's Mistake, The Princess Test, Princess Sonora and the Long Sleep,* and *Cinderellis and the Glass Hill.* The series grew out of a picture book idea which Levine's editor felt would be better suited to the chapter book format. *The Fairy' Mistake* is a take-off on "Toads and Diamonds," while *The Princes Test* is a reworking of Hans Christian Andersen's "The Princess and the Pea." Both novellas are set in the mythical kingdom of Biddle. A contributor for *Publishers Weekly* felt that "Levine's talent for hilarious subversion of fairy tale motifs . . . is honed to perfection in this pair of stories." "This is grand entertainment," concluded the same contributor, "likely to appeal to anyone who appreciates deadpan delivery, reluctant royalty, and a touch of romance." Carol A. Edwards, writing in *School Library Journal*, commented, "both retellings are delightfully light-hearted, with little doubt that good will ultimately triumph over evil." Edwards further noted the "rich use of language and spirited characters, especially the female."

Princess Sonora and the Long Sleep is a retelling of "Sleeping Beauty," while *Cinderellis and the Glass Hill* is based on a little known male Cinderella fairy tale called "The Princess and the Glass Hill, "adding a gender switch for spice," according to a writer for *Booklist*. In the former title, Princess Sonora is given too many gifts by the fairies at her naming ceremony, making her hyper-smart. No sleep for the baby, for she wants to spend the evenings reading and generally improving her mind; she takes it on herself to remind the royal nursemaids to wash behind her ears. So smart is she, that she would rather prick herself on the spindle than marry the boring prince. Robin L. Gibson, reviewing the title in *School Library Journal*, concluded, "This amusing, light read will stir children's imaginations and encourage them to explore further the richness of fairy tales." "The story unfolds with fine wit and comes to a satisfying conclusion," commented *Booklist*'s Susan Dove Lempke.

A more substantial and seemingly realistic novel is Levine's 1999 *Dave at Night*. Inspired by her own father's experiences in a Jewish orphanage as a young boy, this novel traces the fortunes and misfortunes of Dave Caros, growing up in New York in the 1920s. When their woodcarving father dies, Dave's older brother goes to live with relatives, but no one can save Dave when his stepmother places

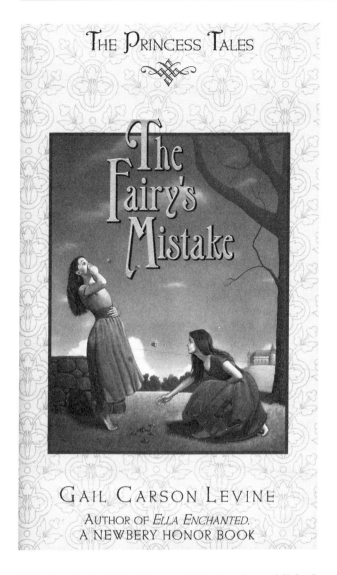

THE PRINCESS TALES

The Fairy's Mistake

GAIL CARSON LEVINE
AUTHOR OF *ELLA ENCHANTED.*
A NEWBERY HONOR BOOK

This first book of the "Princess Tales" series, published in 1999, is a lighthearted retelling of "Toads and Diamonds."

If you enjoy the works of Gail Carson Levine, you might want to check out the following books and films:

Robin McKinley, *Rose Daughter*, 1997.
Donna Jo Napoli, *Zel*, 1996.
Jane Yolen, *Briar Rose*, 1992.
Beauty and the Beast, the animated Disney film, 1991.

him in the Hebrew Home for Boys, which the boisterous eleven-year-old delights in calling the Hell Hole for Brats. Miserable in the home under the tyrannical rule of Mr. Bloom, Dave takes solace in climbing over the orphanage wall at night and wandering the streets of New York. He is befriended by the elderly Jewish fortune teller Solly who takes him along to a rent party where he meets an African American girl, Irma, about his own age. This new friend in turn introduces Dave to the delights of the Harlem Renaissance, the members of which, such as Langston Hughes, often meet at the home of Irma's mother. Finally the two parts of Dave's life—his nights of adventure and days of regimentation at the orphanage—coalesce when he manages to

reclaim his father's carving of Noah's ark which Bloom has appropriated and to come to terms with himself and his place in the world.

"Levine shows considerable writing skills here," noted *Booklist*'s Cooper, "especially when she describes the orphanage and the almost Dickensian characters who inhabit it. . . .. The hero-as-orphan story is one that has timeless appeal, and Levine plays this beautifully." A writer for *Publishers Weekly* remarked on the "chiaroscuro effect" of this novel and concluded, "This poignant and energetic novel. . .comes with an all's-well-that-ends-well conclusion that brings a sense of belonging to Dave and his orphan friends, yet delivers a surprise as well." This happy ending, as well as other elements, inspired some critics to point to the fairy tale quality of this seemingly realistic tale. Alice Case Smith, writing in *School Library Journal*, called "this charming story" a "cross between *Oliver Twist* and a fairy tale," further noting that as in all fairy tales, "characters are clearly good or evil and Dave's story ends almost happily ever after." "The magic comes from Levine's language and characterization," Smith went on to remark. And Lois Metzger also noted the "fairy tale touches" to the novel in an article for the *New York Times Book Review*. Metzger called the book "touchingly" and "beautifully" told.

Further fairy tale aspects appear in Levine's novel *The Wish*, published in 2000. Inspired by Levine's own childhood—a year she felt terribly lonely as a new student at Bronx High School of Science—this novel tells what happens when eighth-grade Wilma is granted a wish by an old woman on the subway. Wilma instantly becomes the most popular girl in school, but to her dismay she realizes this will only last a matter of weeks, as graduation is coming soon. And in Levine's original fairy tale, *The Two Princesses of Bamar*, this magical element is front and center in a book that Levine says is "darker" than most of her other works. Renee Steinberg, writing in *School Library Journal*, called *The Wish* "an enjoyable, thought-provoking, and absorbing selection."

Whether fairy tale or realistic drama, other common elements unite Levine's works. "I want my books to be exciting and hard to put down," Levine concluded to *AAYA*. "And I especially want them to be fun. I don't worry about my readers' understanding, I just write a story. Self-discovery is one of the most wonderful things about writing, and you can't do that if you are too hard on yourself. Too critical. I always tell young writers that the most important thing they can do to improve their writing is to stick with it. And have fun doing it!"

■ **Works Cited**

Review of *Cinderellis and the Glass Hill, Booklist,* January 1, 2000.

Cooper, Ilene, review of *Ella Enchanted, Booklist,* April 15, 1997, p. 1423.

Cooper, Ilene, review of *Dave at Midnight, Booklist,* June 1, 1999, p. 1829.

Review of *Dave at Night, Publishers Weekly,* August 30, 1999, p. 84.

Deifendeifer, Anne, review of *Ella Enchanted, Horn Book,* May-June, 1997, p. 325.

Edwards, Carol A., review of *The Fairy's Mistake* and *The Princess test, School Library Journal,* May, 1999, p. 92.

Review of *Ella Enchanted, Kirkus Reviews,* February 1, 1997, p. 225.

Review of *Ella Enchanted, New York Times Book Review,* July 6, 1997, p. 16.

Review of *Ella Enchanted, Voice of Youth Advocates,* February, 1998, p. 365.

Review of *The Fairy's Mistake* and *The Princess Test, Publishers Weekly,* February 15, 1999, p. 108.

Gibson, Robin L., review of *Princess Sonora and the Long Sleep, School Library Journal,* October, 1999, pp. 171-72.

Lempke, Susan Dove, review of *Princess Sonora and the Long Sleep, Booklist,* November 15, 1999, p. 627.

Levine, Gail Carson, *Ella Enchanted,* HarperCollins, 1997.

Levine, Gail Carson, interview with J. Sydney Jones for *Authors and Artists for Young Adults,* conducted March 17, 2000.

Metzger, Lois, "On Their Own," *New York Times Book Review,* November 21, 1999, p. 32.

Shook, Bruce Ann, review of *Ella Enchanted, School Library Journal,* April, 1997, p. 138.

Smith, Alice Casey, review of *Dave at Night, School Library Journal,* September, 1999, p. 226.

Steinberg, Renee, review of *The Wish, School Library Journal,* May, 2000, p. 173.

■ **For More Information See**

PERIODICALS

ALAN Review, Fall, 1997.

Bulletin of the Center for Children's Books, May, 1999, p. 104.

Horn Book, May-June, 1999, p. 332.

Kliatt, November, 1998, p. 20.

Publishers Weekly, September 13, 1999, p. 85; November 1, 1999, p. 58; April 24, 2000, p. 91.

School Library Journal, September, 1999, p. 165.

Voice of Youth Advocates, August, 1997, p. 194.

—Sketch by J. Sydney Jones

Ben Mikaelsen

Personal

Born Benjamin John Mikaelsen, November 24, 1952, in La Paz, Bolivia; son of John (a radio engineer) and Luverne (Wold) Mikaelsen; married Melanie Troftgruben (a critical care nurse), June, 1980. *Education:* Attended Concordia College, Moorhead, MN, 1971-72, and Bemidji State University, Bemidji, MN, 1975-79. *Hobbies and other interests:* Horseback riding, parachute jumping, motorcycle travel, sled dog racing, flying airplanes, scuba diving, camping, music, and study and raising of bears.

Addresses

Home and office—233 Quinn Creek Rd., Bozeman, MT 59715. *E-mail*—ben@benmikaelsen.com. *Agent*—Sandra Choron, 4 Myrtle St., Haworth, NJ 07641.

Career

Owner of awards and office supplies business, Bozeman, MT, 1980-84; owner of woodworking business, Bozeman, MT, 1984-85; writer, 1985-1992. *Military service:* U.S. Army, 1973-75, Arlington, VA; corporal; received Joint Service Commendation Medal.

Member

Society of Children's Book Writers and Illustrators, Hellgate Writers, Montana Authors' Coalition.

Awards, Honors

Spur Award, Western Writers of America, 1992, Children's Book Award, International Reading Association, 1992, Golden Sower Award, Nebraska Library Association, 1995, California Young Reader Medal, California Reading Association, 1995, Indian Paintbrush Award, Wyoming Library Association, 1995, Flicker Tale Book Award, North Dakota Library Association, 1998, all for *Rescue Josh McGuire;* California Young Reader Medal, California Reading Association, 1997, for *Sparrow Hawk Red;* Maryland Children's Choice Book Award, Maryland International Reading Association Council, 1998, for *Stranded;* Notable Books for Children, American Library Association, 1999, and Golden Spur Award for Best Western Juvenile Fiction, Western Writers of America, 1999, both for *Petey.*

Writings

Rescue Josh McGuire, Hyperion, 1991.
Sparrow Hawk Red, Hyperion, 1993.
Stranded, Hyperion, 1995.

Countdown, Hyperion, 1996.
Petey, Hyperion, 1998.

Rescue Josh McGuire has been translated into Danish and French.

■ **Work in Progress**

In September of 1998, Mikaelsen completed a research trip to Alaska for his next book, called *Touching Spirit Bear*. Mikaelsen returned from a four-month trip to do general research and photo work in February of 1999. On that trip, he and his wife drove 15,000 miles, from Bozeman, Montana, to the southern tip of South America, the Terra Del Fuego.

■ **Sidelights**

Ben Mikaelsen's award-winning first novel, *Rescue Josh McGuire*, was widely praised for its fast-paced adventure, its detailed depictions of the Montana wilderness, and its engaging portrait of a wild bear cub. Mikaelsen, who says he draws the "soul" of each of his novels from real experience, is no stranger to bears, the wilderness, or adventure. The author has had the unique experience of raising a six-hundred-pound black bear named Buffy at his home in the mountains of Bozeman, Montana. Additionally, Mikaelsen once stated that over the years he has been involved in many adventures, including "a sixteen-hundred-mile cross-country horseback trip from Minnesota to Oregon, numerous parachute jumps, racing sled dogs, playing horse polo, building a log house, private and commercial pilot training, extensive scuba diving, and worldwide travel." Although his personal adventures have entailed courage and endurance, and his fiction is engaging for its action and suspense, Mikaelsen's adventure stories are not of the rugged "man versus nature" variety. Rather, they make an appeal for peaceful coexistence between the natural and social worlds. In *Rescue Josh McGuire*, to be kind and gentle in a sometimes inhumanely bureaucratic society is the greatest act of courage.

Mikaelsen recalls his childhood from the viewpoint of a social outsider. In his early youth he lived in Bolivia, where "being raised as a minority helped me understand the self-doubt and desperate lack of self-worth many children face while growing up." Because his parents worked too far from the schools for their six children to commute, Mikaelsen and a younger brother were placed in a boarding school apart from their older siblings, permanently weak-

ening the family bonds, according to the author. Mikaelsen once explained that his boarding school was a rigid place, where "English matrons held a solid seat of law, all the way down to strappings if you didn't do things right." When Mikaelsen returned to the United States at the age of twelve, he found that schoolmates could be equally harsh and demanding. "In Bolivia," he said, "we wore uniforms—saddle shoes with high bobby socks and leather knickers with a kind of blouse-type shirt. So the first day of school in the United States, I dressed up in my best go-to-school clothes. I learned early how cruel kids can be."

Turning a Negative into a Positive

Although he felt like an outsider throughout high school, Mikaelsen now recognizes that the ways he coped with his childhood trials resulted in some positive outcomes. "Being ostracized," he said, "contributed to writing in the sense that a piece of paper became my friend. I was one of those kids that laid awake at night dreaming *before* I went to sleep. By the next morning, I would always forget the things I had been dreaming about, so I realized that if I was to capture them, I would have to put them on paper. I never thought of myself as a writer, but I enjoyed writing poetry. Back then if you were a male writing poetry you were a sissy, so I never showed anybody. That was just my own secret. A lot of my writings for many, many years came that way."

Despite his feelings of self-doubt within the social world, Mikaelsen was an adventurer, even as a child. "I was always the kid that took the dare, always the one that would climb up the telephone pole or the flag pole. I remember once when my group of friends was cliff-diving, rather than take the chance of failing in front of other kids, I swam across the lake and, all by myself, I got up the courage and dived off this cliff. Somebody heard that Ben dove off that twenty-foot rock, and that just led from one thing to another. Pretty soon it was twenty-five feet, then thirty feet, then thirty-five feet, and then it was heights no other kid would even jump off of. All of a sudden it struck me that this was the very, very first time in my life when somebody said, "gosh, that's neat." My whole body had a hunger for that attention, so I started doing other things. . . ."

By the time he was in college, Mikaelsen was skydiving. "I was able to parachute into the homecoming game and bring in the game football and things like that. Kids would say, "wow, that's pretty neat," and I felt like a hero, with more positive attention

Josh's plan to save an orphaned bear from laboratory testing backfires when he and the bear are caught in a snowstorm in the mountains of Montana.

than I'd ever received in my life." In college Mikaelsen also received encouragement about his writing for the first time. "My preferred language was Spanish," Mikaelsen said. "At five years old I could not speak English very well. I always had trouble with grammar, with spelling, with word mechanics. I was always told that that was what writing was, and because I was so poor at these things, I thought I could not be a writer." Mikaelsen recalled that in his first year of college his English professor called him to the front of the room to comment on a paper he had written, telling him immediately that his grammar skills were those of a seventh or eighth grader. With much fear, Mikaelsen asked his professor if he should drop the class. Mikaelsen remembers the professor's words: ""Oh no, no, no. I just finished reading two hundred and fifty essays, and out of them only one made me

laugh and cry, and that was yours. You're a writer."" Mikaelsen said: "That was the first time that somebody let me know that this was something special. Then I was anxious to sit down with the tutor and work on grammar and word mechanics, although I'm still terrible with that."

Being a writer, Mikaelsen soon discovered, required just as much courage as being an adventurer. "There is so much more to writing than I ever dreamed," he said. "I know when I first sat over the cliff at twenty feet above the water with nobody around, I looked down, and this monster was facing me, saying "you can't do it." I said "I can" and I jumped into the monster's face. It's the same monster that looked at me when I wanted to make my first parachute jump, and the same one I saw later when we made a cross-country horseback trip from Minnesota to Oregon in 1976. Now, when I'm writing at two o'clock in the morning, halfway through a book, I'm doubting my premise for the book, I'm doubting my story line, I'm doubting myself. It's that same identical monster that I have to jump in the face of. I began, finally, to realize that being a successful writer isn't just putting the good words down, it's facing that monster."

Raising Bears

Mikaelsen, whose childhood home in Bolivia had been high upon a fourteen-thousand-foot plateau in the Andes mountain range between Bolivia and Peru, grew up with a deeply ingrained love of mountains. Consequently, in 1980, he and his wife moved to the mountains of Bozeman, Montana. In 1984, the couple adopted Buffy, a declawed black bear cub, from a wild game farm. The adoption entailed a huge commitment. Mikaelsen once remarked: "We have probably twenty-thousand dollars invested in Buffy's facility with its pond, playground and eating area, denning area, and waste area. I spend about three to four hours a day with him when he's out of hibernation, and a half hour or forty-five minutes a day when he's in hibernation, and that's still not enough time. Buffy gets better care than most children—that's what an animal needs, and that's the only reason Buffy and I have the relationship we do, because of that tremendous amount of time."

Mikaelsen learned quickly that keeping a wild animal in captivity is not like raising a household pet. Buffy had been used in laboratory research before Mikaelsen adopted him. "I don't know what had been done with him in research," Mikaelsen said, "but it hadn't been good. He was very, very distrusting and insecure. One minute he would cuddle

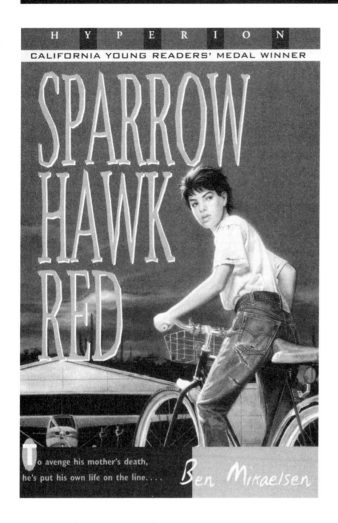

HYPERION

CALIFORNIA YOUNG READERS' MEDAL WINNER

SPARROW HAWK RED

To avenge his mother's death, he's put his own life on the line. . . .

Ben Mikaelsen

When Ricky Diaz's mother is murdered by drug smugglers, the thirteen-year-old travels to Mexico to avenge her death in this novel.

with me and hug my side as if I was the only thing he had in life, and the next minute a car horn or something would scare him and he would turn around and bite me as hard as he could. The first couple of months I had started raising him like you would a dog, and I wasn't having any luck. He was getting more independent and more angry. So then I started raising him like a child. I would give him his food in a bottle instead of a dish, and cuddle him in my arms as he drank it. I would go out and put him to bed every night and let him fall asleep in my lap. If I heard him crying then I would go out and sleep with him the rest of the night. When I started doing that I immediately had luck.

"I learned a real important lesson with Buffy, and that's that you never tame a wild animal. Buffy is not a tame animal. If something threatens him, he is a six-hundred-and-some pound very, very dangerous animal. My wife and I are the only two people that can come into his facility. If a stranger were to come into his facility without me along, he would most likely attack him. But when Buffy comes into the house (and he comes into the house a lot), he's visiting. A stranger could come in the house, and Buffy would just be as friendly as all get out. But even after a half hour of playing with him in the house, if the stranger went into Buffy's facility, he'd lay his ears back. You're dealing with really deep instincts.

"I used to think I owned Buff, that I was his master, and he should do what I said. Having that attitude almost got me killed. He would get violent when I tried to rule him. Then I finally said, "Hold it, I'm not his master, neither is he mine, but we're friends, we're going to coexist." According to Mikaelsen, learning to understand and respond to Buffy's needs rather than to try to control him was a big lesson in life. A former bear hunter himself, Mikaelsen realized while raising Buffy that he had previously been enjoying wildlife from a very limited perspective. "Any appreciation I had of a wild animal ceased at the moment I killed it. Now I feel like I've come to appreciate and understand and be amazed by the complexity of Buffy's existence." Among Mikaelsen's dedications in *Rescue Josh McGuire,* is one to ""Buffy," a 500-pound black bear who taught me to have respect and be gentle."

When it became known that Mikaelsen was successfully raising Buffy, the Fish and Game Department in Bozeman brought him other orphaned black bear cubs. Mikaelsen took care of some of these orphans while the department decided what to do with them. Since there were few viable alternatives, the orphaned cubs sometimes had to be destroyed. Although Montana has laws against shooting a mother bear with a cub, the laws are unenforceable. Mikaelsen blames spring bear hunting for the hundreds of cubs orphaned in Montana every season, and he has become an activist for more sportsman-like hunting laws in his state. The strength of his feelings about this issue triggered his first published novel. "There was one pair of cubs," he explained. "I spent probably a week trying to save their lives, staying up all night to bottle feed them. They ended up being destroyed because they couldn't find a good home. I think that was the point when I said, "Hold it, let's make it the premise of a book.""

Of Boys and Bears

Rescue Josh McGuire begins with the senseless killing of a mother bear by thirteen-year-old Josh's alcoholic father, Sam. Although Sam will not admit that

H Y P E R I O N

STRANDED

N o matter what—she's staying!

Ben Mikaelsen

After losing her foot in an accident, twelve-year-old Koby tries to prove her self-reliance by rescuing two stranded pilot whales in Ben Mikaelsen's 1995 work.

the bear he shot was a mother, Josh, who witnesses the killing, goes back to the scene during the night and finds the orphaned cub. Bringing the cub, whom he names Pokey, back home with him, Josh sets up a room for him in the barn and, despite Pokey's unpredictable biting, the two develop a very close and affectionate relationship. Relations in Josh's home, on the other hand, are severely strained. The previous year, Josh's brother, Tye, was killed in a car accident. Sam, devastated by the loss, has taken to heavy drinking and, while drunk, is abusive to his wife and his surviving son. Pokey, who is a reminder to Sam of his unacknowledged error in killing the mother bear, is doomed to almost certain death when Sam notifies the game warden of his existence. Sam tells Josh that there is no alternative but for Pokey to be delivered into the hands of medical researchers.

After thinking it over, Josh decides he cannot accept the fate that adults have devised for Pokey. Borrowing his brother's motocross cycle, he rides off in the night—with Pokey in a box on the cycle rack and his dog, Mud Flap, on the cycle's gas tank—to the mountains north of Yellowstone Park, seventy miles from his home. Josh leaves behind a note: "I can't let Pokey die so I'm running away. I'll come home when I can keep Pokey and when nobody can hunt bears anymore." After they arrive on the mountain trail, a ferocious summer blizzard breaks out, severely testing the boy's survival skills. In the days that follow, the three experience extremes of cold, deprivation, loneliness, and danger, as well as some triumphs and happy times together.

Much of the novel is divided between Josh's adventures in the mountains and the initially unsuccessful efforts of the search and rescue team to find him. When Mud Flap is badly wounded in a bear attack, Josh must overcome his distrust of the adult world in order to contact his friend Otis for help. Otis is a gruff ex-wildlife biologist who had become so frustrated with the bureaucracies intended to protect wildlife that he became a recluse, spending most of his time tending to wounded wild animals. Otis agrees to help Mud Flap, but when he drives out to pick her up, he is unknowingly followed by the police, leading to Josh's eventual rescue.

After getting into a serious motorcycle accident in the night, Josh stands in need of rescue, but, thinking that he has been deceived by his friend, he continues to try to elude the search and rescue party. Unbeknownst to Josh, his disappearance has raised the interest of the media, bringing national coverage to his call for more stringent wildlife laws. By the end of the story, Josh, a fairly naive boy who only wants to do what is right, has effectively countered the injustices of hypocritical bureaucracies, a complacent social world, and even his father's alcoholism.

Josh's point of view is limited, as any child's would be, and at the same time, clear and optimistic. Mikaelsen once remarked that he had written half of *Rescue Josh McGuire* before he could find a way to save Pokey's life. "It was a problem I was not able to solve as an adult. . . . I needed a child's point of view. From Josh's point of view, Pokey is just this precious little life that's going to end if I don't do something—it's just that simple. An adult character would have had to let the cub go and let it get killed." Josh's youthful naivete actually tempers the character Otis's adult cynicism. Otis had fought city hall for many years and had finally given up. Seeing the integrity with which young Josh takes on powerful forces, however, spurs Otis back into action.

Josh, Pokey, Mud Flap, and Otis all encounter some extremely harsh and unfair experiences. Although the outcome of the novel is highly positive, Mikaelsen does not paint a particularly rosy picture of the American way. "I am one of those people who believes that if you don't reveal the world's shortcomings, you slam the door on learning. If we try to teach kids that all bureaucracy is right and not questionable, then we eliminate any chance of improving upon the deficiencies that bureaucracies have. Likewise with parents. If a child can never look at a parent and say, "Maybe my parent is wrong, maybe what they're doing isn't right," then the parents' ways can never be improved upon."

Mikaelsen did a great deal of research for *Rescue Josh McGuire*. "When I write about issues, I get an overwhelming sense of responsibility. If I write about an issue wrongly, I do as much harm as I do good. So when I decided that I was going to take on spring bear hunting and alcoholism—gosh! I spent time with people who were in rehab; I went up to the part of the country where much of the novel takes place and, with my wife, spent the whole week camping there, laying it all out for authenticity. I also went down to the Bozeman Search and Rescue Department. I knew some of the members, and they actually sat down with me and drew a format and helped me choreograph Josh's rescue."

Drawing from Life's Experiences

For Mikaelsen, writing takes place in life and experience as well as in an author's mind. Living his books by actively entering into the adventures he writes about is, according to the author, "a fun way to keep from getting to be a mole. I think writers tend to get reclusive. I don't find the actual writing of a book healthy. I have to spend too many hours by myself. Whenever I finish a rough draft, I just clear out and head down to some waterfall somewhere and sit, trying to get away from the computer terminal, away from being a human mole."

Mikaelsen continued: "My next book, *Sparrow Hawk Red*, is an adventure story about a young boy who lives among the homeless in Mexico. Now, how in the world was I going to know what it's like to be homeless in Mexico living up here in Montana? So I actually went down and spent several weeks in a variety of places all the way from Tucson to Tijuana to Ensenada to Nogales to Mexicali. There was one

Elliot, the first teenager selected to fly in space, finds he can only communicate by shortwave radio after his space shuttle experiences problems.

point where I was standing around looking at the homeless children, thinking, "this is really good for me to stand around and look at the homeless and feel guilty." And then I thought, "Baloney, I have no more idea of what it's like to be hungry and cold than the man on the moon." One afternoon I was getting a taco; I pulled my billfold out and thought, "those homeless children don't have a billfold." So I put it away, and the next day I came back with no billfold, just a T-shirt and jeans. For the next three days I just lived among the homeless, and I got very hungry. At first, I wasn't willing to eat out of a garbage can the way I saw a lot of them do, but I did eat some pretty wretched food. Finally, I did resort to eating from a garbage can, and I did get sick. I also slept on gravel in the alleys at night with a piece of cardboard over me. I was fortunate that three days later I could just walk back across the border to a motel and my clean clothes and a hot shower. I had a feeling at that point what it was like to be homeless—at least I've seen that look in their eyes and I can write about it."

The realistic way in which Mikaelsen was able to portray Mexican street life won him unanimous appreciation from reviewers of *Sparrow Hawk Red*. In the novel, Ricky Diaz, a thirteen-year-old flying ace, discovers that his mother's death was not just an accident, but an act of retribution taken by drug smugglers against his father, who used to work for the Drug Enforcement Agency. Avenging her death requires that Ricky take on the drug cartel in a mission that has been turned down by even the most seasoned of Drug Enforcement Agents—his father. Across the border in Mexico, Ricky goes undercover as a *ratero* (a homeless street kid), and luckily receives some tips from a street-smart *ratera* named Soledad. *School Library Journal* contributor Pat Katka offered a favorable assessment of the novel, asserting that "the characterization is strong, the depiction of street life realistic, and the theme timely." A reviewer for *Quill and Quire* commented: "Soledad changes his [Ricky's] views of street kids, whom he will never again dismiss or despise." *Booklist's* Chris Sherman also noted Ricky's growth as a result of his relationship with Soledad, which taught him "the importance of his heritage and the dignity inherent in all people." Appreciative of "the pace and the chase," Roger Sutton of the *Bulletin of the Center for Children's Books* deemed the book "tremendously exciting." *Sparrow Hawk Red* is, according to Sherman, "a dynamite story, certain to appeal to even hard-core nonreaders."

Commenting further about his hands-on approach to research, Mikaelsen once said: "I can go to libraries and get a lot of my research, but I've never found the soul of my story in a library not until I was awake at four o'clock in the morning trying to bottle-feed a cub that was almost starved to death. In that struggle—the little critter struggling for life—I discovered the soul of my novel. Or when I was among the homeless, and I saw that look of hopelessness in some little kid who hadn't had a decent meal in three years and was almost naked except for his dirty underpants. When I actually felt the hunger and cold and looked into his eyes, that's where I found the soul for that story. For my next book, I worked for a month at a dolphin facility. I went out and helped find a dolphin who was caught in a shrimp net, and I also got involved in a whale stranding. That was when I found the soul of my story."

A Tale of Independence

Mikaelsen's experience at the dolphin facility led him to write *Stranded*, a book that draws parallels between a twelve-year-old girl's search for independence and a pair of beached dolphins' quest for freedom. The novel's heroine, Koby, lives with her feuding parents on a sailboat in the Florida Keys. Having lost her right foot in a bicycling accident four years earlier, Koby feels exasperated by her parents' smothering attitude at home, and self-conscious among her peers at school. When swimming in the ocean or motoring her dinghy through the Keys, though, Koby is at her free-feeling best. One day, while enjoying the water, Koby comes to the aid of a birthing dolphin caught in a net. She later encounters the dolphin and its calf in dangerously shallow water and makes a heroic effort to rescue them. Hearing of Koby's special talents, peers and parents alike begin sensing and reinforcing in Koby a new feeling of competence.

Roger Sutton of the *Bulletin of the Center for Children's Books* thought Koby a "seaworthy heroine who makes things happen. . . . Girls don't often feature in such fast-paced fare," Sutton continued, "so this is definitely welcome." *Voice of Youth Advocates* contributor Ann C. Sparanese credited Mikaelsen with creating "another winning young character willing to take on adult-size adventure and triumph over impossible odds." With nothing but praise for the book, she called *Stranded* "a heartwarming story, believable and at the same time grist for fantasies of heroism and wonderful deeds." *Kliatt* contributor Cecilia Swanson recommended the story to "animal lovers and readers who are dealing with their own struggle to be independent."

While issues and settings are important to Mikaelsen, he also sees merit in interacting with his child protagonists. "I try to imagine a child walking through the real world beside me. Then that character comes alive for me. What's wonderful then, is that it's just like having a best friend—you can never predict what your best friend will do next. In *Rescue Josh McGuire,* for instance, the part of the book where Josh had his motorcycle accident was not in my plans. While I was writing, Josh did just what Josh would do in the circumstances: he rode his cycle too fast in the dark. I put my cursor back and erased two paragraphs and I tried to write him continuing up the hill. But again, he went into the ditch, this time getting hurt even worse, and I realized that my character had come alive, and I had to let him do what he wanted to do. And it made a much better end."

For all of his talents in children's literature, Mikaelsen did not set out to become a children's writer. *Rescue Josh McGuire* was written as an adult novel; it was his publisher who suggested it be targeted to young adults. Mikaelsen said that this "taught me a real good lesson, that there is no difference in an adult book and a children's book except that the main character is a child. I realized that I can write what I want, as complexly and to whatever issues I wish. In fact, I can do anything I want, looking through a child's point of view."

Mikaelsen, who has not forgotten the challenges he faced as an insecure teenage boy, seeks to empower the children with whom he has contact. "Now I go into a school system as an author-in-residence, and I realize that every kid gets teased for something. Sometimes it's just that they live on a farm and still have the smell of manure on their shoes, or sometimes their parents cut their hair funny. When I talk to the kids I say, "Okay, the differences aren't a weakness, the differences are what make you special. That's what has made me an author; that's what has made me able to write a book. So what you do is take your differences and highlight them.""

"Children Are the Future"

Mikaelsen's books also aim at offering children new possibilities. In the novel *Countdown*, the two four-teen-year-old heroes, Vincent and Elliot, are raised by fathers who expect them to follow in their own career paths. Vincent, living in an outlying village of Kenya, is supposed to become a traditional Masai warrior, while Elliot is expected to work on the family ranch in Montana. Despite their fathers' wishes, Vincent longs to learn of the world beyond his village by going to school, and Elliot dreams of becoming an astronaut. Both boys have the chance to widen one another's horizons through their experiences as well as their unlikely relationship via short-wave radio. *Voice of Youth Advocates* contributor Brenda Moses-Allen wrote that "Mikaelsen provides a fascinating scenario of Elliot's nine months' training to become a payload specialist (one-mission astronaut)," citing the author's use of "vivid and exciting detail." *School Library Journal* reviewer Joel Shoemaker also appreciated Mikaelsen's "careful research [which] allows integration of details that lend authenticity to the tale." In another favorable assessment of *Countdown*, Chris Sherman of *Booklist* stated, "Mikaelsen weaves a provocative message through his novel and blends two fast-paced stories into a single, powerful whole."

Sixty years after being institutionalized for cerebral palsy, Petey meets Trevor—an eighth-grader who becomes his close friend.

In his novel *Petey* Mikaelsen explores attitudes toward people with disabilities and the ways those attitudes have evolved in the last century. Petey, the title character, was born in 1920 with cerebral palsy, but he was misdiagnosed as mentally retarded and sent to a mental institution. For the next fifty years, Petey experiences one loss after another, as the caretakers he has befriended move on without him. "Step by institutional step," wrote *School Library Journal* contributor Joel Shoemaker, "readers see how this tragedy could happen. More importantly, readers feel Petey's pain, boredom, hope, fear, and occasional joy." In 1977, Petey finally receives an accurate diagnosis, only to be taken away from everything and everyone familiar, and transferred to a nursing home. While at the home, Petey is defended from a group of teenage bullies by Trevor, a lonely eighth-grader facing his own personal challenges. Petey

If you enjoy the works of Ben Mikaelsen, you might want to check out the following books and films:

Rachel Anderson, *The Bus People*, 1992.
Lynn Hall, *The Soul of the Silver Dog*, 1992.
Jean Ure, *The Other Side of the Fence*, 1988.
Fly Away Home, a film starring Anna Paquin and Jeff Daniels, 1996.

and Trevor become friends, and Trevor's transformative experiences with Petey comprise the second half of the novel. "[T]his book is much more than a tearjerker," proclaimed Shoemaker, "its messages—that all people deserve respect; that one person can make a difference; that changing times require new attitudes—transcend simplistic labels." GraceAnne A. DeCandido of *Booklist* also applauded *Petey's* message, noting, "there's a real strength here in the depiction of the person inside a disability and the dignity that is a divine right."

Mikaelsen once stated: "In all my writing I try to help children discover that they count. I want to take a child on a journey that changes their emotions, attitudes, and perspective. Children are the future. Children's literature offers a sobering but exciting chance to effect that future, environmental or social. For this reason I enjoy writing to issues."

Concluding his remarks, Mikaelsen revealed: "The secret to happiness has been described to me as doing whatever you do with a passion, to the best of your ability, and for others. Writing has given me this happiness."

■ Works Cited

DeCandido, GraceAnne A., review of *Petey, Booklist*, November 1, 1998, pp. 484-85.

Katka, Pat, review of *Sparrow Hawk Red, School Library Journal*, May, 1993, p. 127.

Moses-Allen, Brenda, review of *Countdown, Voice of Youth Advocates*, June, 1997, p. 112.

Sherman, Chris, review of *Sparrow Hawk Red, Booklist*, August, 1993, p. 206.

Sherman, Chris, review of *Countdown, Booklist*, January 1, 1997, p. 856.

Shoemaker, Joel, review of *Countdown, School Library Journal*, March, 1997, p. 188.

Shoemaker, Joel, review of *Petey, School Library Journal*, November 1, 1998, p. 124.

Sparanese, Ann C., review of *Stranded, Voice of Youth Advocates*, December, 1995, p. 306.

Review of *Sparrow Hawk Red, Quill and Quire*, May, 1993, p. 37.

Sutton, Roger, review of *Sparrow Hawk Red, Bulletin of the Center for Children's Books*, June, 1993, p. 324.

Sutton, Roger, review of *Stranded, Bulletin of the Center for Children's Books*, May, 1995, p. 317.

Swanson, Cecilia, review of *Stranded, Kliatt*, January, 1997, p. 9.

■ For More Information See

PERIODICALS

Booklist, December 15, 1991, p. 758; August, 1995, p. 1949.
Bulletin of the Center for Children's Books, December, 1991, p. 100; November, 1996, p. 107.
Junior Bookshelf, December, 1992, pp. 258-59.
Kirkus Reviews, March 15, 1993, p. 377.
Publishers Weekly, October 5, 1998, p. 91.
School Librarian, February, 1993, p. 30.
School Library Journal, February, 1992, p. 108; June, 1995, p. 112.

ON-LINE

Ben Mikaelsen's Web site is located at http://www.benmikaelsen.com.

Hayao Miyazaki

■ Personal

Born January, 1941, in Tokyo, Japan; son of Katsuji (director of Miyazaki Airplane) Miyazaki; married Akemi Ota. *Education:* Graduated from Gakushuin University, 1963.

■ Career

Animator, writer, director, and illustrator. Toei-Cine, animator, 1963-71; A-Pro, animator, 1971-73; Zuiyo Pictures, animator and writer, beginning in 1973; directed his first animated television series, *Future Boy Conan*, Nippon Animation, 1978; directed his first animated film, *Castle of Cagliostro*, Tokyo Movie Shinsha, 1979; wrote and illustrated *Nausicaa of the Valley of the Winds* (comic) for *Animage*, 1984; directed *Sherlock Hound, the Detective*, 1984; cofounder of Studio Ghibli, Kichijoji, Japan, 1985—.

■ Writings

ANIMATED FILMS

(And animator) *Panda and Child* (produced in Japan as *Panda Kopanda*), Tokyo Movie Shinsha, 1972.

(And animator) *Panda and Child: Rainy Day Circus* (produced in Japan as *Pandakopanda Amefuri Saakasu No Maki*), Tokyo Movie Shinsha, 1973.

(And director) *Lupin III: Castle of Cagliostro* (produced in Japan as *Lupin III: Cagliostro no Shiro*) Tokyo Movie Shinsha, 1979.

(And director) *Nausicaa of the Valley of the Winds* (produced in Japan as *Kaze no Tani no Nausicaa*), Nibariki, Tokuma Shoten, 1984.

(And director) *Laputa: Castle in the Sky* (produced in Japan as *Tenku no Shiro Laputa*), Nibariki, Tokuma Shoten, 1986.

(And director) *My Neighbor Totoro* (produced in Japan as *Tonari No Totoro*), Nibariki, Tokuma, 1988.

(And director and producer) *Kiki's Delivery Service* (produced in Japan as *Majo no Takkyubin*), Kadono, Nibariki, Tokuma Shoten, 1989.

(And director) *Porco Rosso* (produced in Japan as *Kurenai no Buta*), Nibariki, Tokuma Shoten, 1992.

(And producer) *Whisper of the Heart* (produced in Japan as *Mimi o Sumaseba*), Nibariki, Tokuma Shoten, 1995.

(And director) *On Your Mark* (music video), Nibariki, Tokuma Shoten, 1995.

(And director) *Princess Mononoke* (produced in Japan as *Mononoke Hime*), Nibariki, Tokuma Shoten, 1997.

COMICS

(Under pseudonym Saburo Akitsu; and illustrator) *People of the Desert* (published in Japan as *Sabaku no Tami*), serialized in *Shonen Shojo Shinbun* (newspaper), 1969.

Nausicaa of the Valley of the Winds (manga comic), serialized in *Animage*, 1982.

The Journey of Shuna (published in Japan as *Shuna no Ryoko*), AM JUJU, 1983.

Tiger in the Mire (published in Japan as *Doromamire no Tora*), *Model Graphix* (magazine), 1998.

■ Adaptations

Several of Miyazaki's movies, including *Kiki's Delivery Service, My Neighbor Totoro*, and *Laputa: The Castle in the Sky*, have been adapted for full color books in the Tokuma Magical Adventure Series.

■ Work in Progress

An animated film about Chieko, a ten-year-old girl, from a real story.

■ Sidelights

"The Japanese eco-fantasist Hayao Miyazaki is an animation magician, a crowd-pleasing storyteller who is also a builder of worlds," David Chute wrote in *Film Content*. In animated movies such as *Princess Mononoke, Porco Rosso, Kiki's Delivery Service, Laputa: Castle in the Sky, My Neighbor Totoro, Nausicaa of the Valley of the Wind, The Castle of Cagliostro*, and *Panda, Little Panda*, Miyazaki displays his verve and style. Rarely resorting to computer animation, the Japanese animator and director himself hand colors individual frames in the grand old tradition of Disney movies of yore. In his 1999 import, *Princess Mononoke*, Miyazaki personally drew or oversaw the drawing of seventy per cent of the frames, over 80,000 of the 140,000 total. Though some of his films had already been distributed in the United States in the 1980s and 1990s, the Disney corporation in 1998 contracted to release many of Miyazaki's films in the United States.

Miyazaki does not simply replicate the cutesy cartoon antics of critters as in the golden age of cartooning. Instead, he ponders timeless themes from Asian folklore and mythology, delves into the psyche of his characters, and occasionally inserts blood-spattered samurai action scenes and realistic depictions of everyday life in medieval Japan. Such was the case in *Princess Mononoke*, an animated film aimed "at older kids and adults rather than tykes," according to Holly J. Morris writing in a *U.S. New and World Report* review of the movie. While other

films by Miyazaki are "far kid friendlier," as Morris put it, "complex plot and thoughtful dialogue" are "likely to bore" the young viewer, Morris felt. This, however, was far from a complaint, for Morris concluded, "serious filmgoers will see why Miyazaki is revered in Japan."

An aeronautics buff, Miyazaki also manages to throw in ample drawings of "meticulously engineered imaginary aircraft" in his movies and comics, according to Chute, propelling them "over moss-green rolling landscapes, zipping between the sprung columns of ruined castles." Such visual antics are at their best in *Castle in the Sky* and *Porco Rosso*, about a porcine flying ace. Overall, Miyazaki displays a love of mechanized stuff: of gears and finely detailed workings of engines. Chute referred to the depiction of technology overcome by nature as presented in *Nausicaa*, as the ""Flintstones" reimagined by a Zen gardener."

In her study of the animator, writer, and director, *Hayao Miyazaki, Master of Japanese Animation*, Helen McCarthy noted that many in the West like to refer to him as "the Disney of Japan." McCarthy felt that such labels may "give us a quick frame of reference, but they also prevent us from having to think too deeply about the content of the work or the individual views of the artist." McCarthy's preferred label, if labels are necessary, is "the Kurosawa of animation," referring to one of the modern master's of cinematic epic form. "Not only does [Miyazaki's] work have the same rare combination of epic sweep and human sensitivity that the great live-action director possessed," McCarthy wrote in her introduction, "but it also fails to fit into any of the neat, child-sized boxes into which the West still tends to stuff the animated art form." Morris called Miyazaki simply "one of the world's finest animators."

Coming of Age in Postwar Japan

Miyazaki was born on the outskirts of Tokyo in 1941, and thus spent his early years in a country at total war with much of the rest of the world. The war had a personal dimension in the Miyazaki household, for his father, Katsuji, worked in the family industry, Miyazaki Airplane, manufacturing parts for the fighter airplane, the Zero. Such an early acquaintanceship with flight and airplanes goes a long way to determining Miyazaki's later fascination with all aspects of aviation.

Evacuated from the Tokyo region in 1944 to avoid Allied air raids, Miyazaki and his family returned to their home in 1947. That same year his mother contracted spinal tuberculosis, an illness that kept her bedridden for the next eight years. His mother was a woman of wide interests and strong character, and had a strong influence on the young Miyazaki. Attending school in one of Japan's new elementary schools patterned after America's schools, Miyazaki also grew up influenced by Western culture. By the time he was in high school, Miyazaki was already making plans to become a cartoonist or comic book artist when he grew up.

These were the years of the inception of manga, or Japanese comics, an art form influenced by Western comics, but peculiar to Japan. Geared for readers of all ages, manga stories focus on characterization as much as on action and are often as not drawn in black and white. The good guys don't always stay good guys in manga, and sometimes they even die in the end. Manga flourished in postwar Japan and many Japanese adolescents wanted to become part of this new media. Miyazaki was influenced initially by the style of Osamu Tezuka, who helped to pioneer manga with his 1947 *New Treasure Island*. By the time he was eighteen, Miyazaki felt he had gone beyond the early master of the form and destroyed much of his early work that copied Tezuka. However, as McCarthy explained, "Tezuka's influence on the comics industry was so powerful that despite his best efforts, it was not until he started work as an animator at Toei-Cine in his early twenties that Miyazaki was able to feel he had shaken it off, through studying the creation of movement and expression."

Animation, like comics, was undergoing something of a renaissance in postwar Japan. Dubbed anime, such animated films differed from Western equivalents, as did manga from Western comics. Anime films were intended for viewers of all ages, not just kids. And they dealt with weighty themes, stories from mythology and folktale, as well as contemporary topics such as nuclear war and ecological disaster. As a teenager, Miyazaki "fell in love with the heroine of a cartoon movie," as he noted in *Course on Japanese Movies 7*. "My soul was moved," he went on, explaining his reaction to the lead character in the 1958 animated movie, *Legend of the White Serpent*. Interestingly, most of Miyazaki's protagonists are female, "young girls," wrote Chute, "extraordinarily gifted but plausibly awkward kids, testing their powers in tentative interactions with the world."

Meanwhile, though, Miyazaki was being pragmatic about an education. Entering prestigious Gakushuin Univesity, he studied political science and economics, writing his graduate thesis on the theory of Japanese industry. Miyazaki was training to play his part in Japan's postwar economic resurgence, but was also finding his own path. At the university, in addition to studying applied economics, he took part in a children's literature research society where he was exposed to storytellers from around the world employing myth and fable in their creations for juvenile readers. Graduating from university in 1963 he did not go into industry or academics, but took a job with the animation studio of Toei-Cine.

Toward Anime

Starting at the bottom of the animation food chain, Miyazaki first worked as an in-betweener: the cartoonist who fills in the gaps between initial action and final action in a sequence. One of his first projects at Toei was work on *Wolf Boy Ken*. While at Toei, he met Isao Takahata, another talented animator who would later form a production company with Miyazaki. In 1965, Miyazaki worked on the animation team for the feature *The Great Adventure of Hols*, a movie three years in the making and remarkable for its attention to detail and finely tuned animation, as well as for its unorthodox team approach to creation.

By 1969, Miyazaki was also branching out to manga, creating his own serial under a pseudonym. Finally in 1971, he left Toei, following his friend Takahata to A-Pro studio, and then two years later to Zuiyo Pictures. During this time, Miyazaki was perfecting his clean and simple style, and also traveling a great deal in Europe for backgrounds for such productions as *Alpine Girl Heidi*. In 1972, Miyazaki made his debut as a writer and animator in the short film *Panda, Little Panda*, and followed this up the next year with *Panda and Child: Rainy Day Circus*, both of which McCarthy called "charming." In 1978, he directed his first television series, *Future Boy Conan*, where a love of aeronautics and for plucky heroines, as well as plots fueled by ecological disasters were first displayed. McCarthy pointed out that though these were the years when *Star Wars* was popular in Japan, Miyazaki made little reference to such intergalactic enterprises in his series. "Miyazaki's literary and cultural influences are at work, and Fritz Lang's *Metropolis* is more significant than George Lucas's Empire." Then, in 1979, Miyazaki's first big break came: he was hired by Tokyo Movie Shinsha to direct the adaptation of a popular manga, *Lupin III*, into an action-adventure-romance animated feature, *The Castle of Cagliostro*.

Miyazaki's 1997 animated film *Princess Mononoke* follows the adventures of a girl raised by wolf gods in medieval Japan.

Early Miyazaki Features

The characters from *Lupin III* were created by the manga artist, Monkey Punch, and are among the best loved in that form and in anime. The charming rogue protagonist of the series is in turn based on a character from the French novelist Maurice Le Blanc, Arsene Lupin. Before the time of his feature film debut, Miyazaki had already directed several episodes of the television variant of the Lupin stories. With his movie, Miyazaki moved beyond the standard recipe for the stories, including historical detail into the story mix, which ultimately provided a new title: Count Alessandro of Cagliostro, who was an actual con man from the eighteenth century. McCarthy noted influences on the film from Grace Kelly to James Bond. "This range of influences and the careful tying-in of his original story to the Lupin canon attests to Miyazaki's breadth of cultural awareness and enriches a film that is very much his own," McCarthy wrote in her study of the director.

"As directed by Hayao Miyazaki, "The Castle of Cagliostro" has a vibrant look and a lot of noise variety in its settings," noted Janet Maslin in a *New York Times* review of the feature. Maslin went on to comment that as earlier versions of the Lupin stories had been made for TV, the animation for the feature presentation was still "weak when it comes to fluid body movements, but outstanding in its attention to detail." Maslin drew particular attention to the "still-life glimpses of flowers, birds and landscapes that are unusually intricate and precise." She also remarked on dialogue and action that gave the film, despite its European setting, a distinct "martial-arts ring." Already with his first feature, Miyazaki showed that he was not simply making a cartoon: the hundred plus minutes of footage demanded attention from his audience. McCarthy wrote that despite the fact that Miyazaki was working with another writer's characters and setting, he "produced a film full of charm, energy, [and] warmth." *The Castle of Cagliostro* was, she concluded, "an astonishingly assured debut feature."

Miyazaki continued to work for other film companies, moving to Telecom where he directed two episodes of the second *Lupin III* television series. In 1981 he collaborated with an Italian animator on a Sherlock Holmes spin-off for Italian TV, and with an American team on the adaptation of Windsor McCay's *Little Nemo* for the screen, a project he soon bowed out of. Instead, he took up pen for a manga series that became an epic story about a beautiful and brave girl who battles to help her people, and indeed her world, to survive in a brutal time of war. *Nausicaa of the Valley of the Winds* was immediately popular as a manga; it went through a dozen years of serialization, reaching completion only in 1994, but in 1983 Miyazaki already began adapting his story for a feature film.

Nausicaa is a beautiful young princess growing up in the distant future after a cataclysmic war has destroyed both technology and the environment. Such a scenario owes less to science fiction doomsayers than to history: Miyazaki and others of his generation themselves lived through the atomic bombings of both Hiroshima and Nagasaki. Nausicaa's is a near feudal world, but Nausicaa is at once the most sensitive of women, inquisitive and seeking, yet also brave and pure-hearted. She wants desperately to understand the world around her, especially nature. Such wonderings about nature lead Nausicaa into danger more than once, for nature, in her world, has been poisoned. "*Nausicaa* comes from the new worldviews regarding nature which came about in the 1970s," Miyazaki told Takashi Oshiguchi of the magazine *Animerica* in an interview.

Young Nausicaa lives with her father, King Jhil, in the Valley of the Winds. Her mother has been dead for many years, but still Nausicaa remembers her. In her secret room, Nausicaa studies the wonders of nature and evolution of her polluted land. Physically tough, she is equally adept with a sword and with her jet-powered glider. She grows into adulthood understanding and accepting the world around her. The Ohmu, a giant insect allowed to flourish as a result of the destruction, threatens humankind, as do poisonous plants that have likewise overtaken the earth. Poisoned fungus also threatens the humans, and finally Nausicaa must do battle to save her people. McCarthy commented in her book on Miyazaki that many fans consider *Nausicaa of the Valley of the Winds* to be his "most significant work," and a favorite with audiences since its release. Reviewing the manga version of the tale, Katherine Kan, writing in *Voice of Youth Advocates*, called it a "complicated story, but full of action which holds the attention." McCarthy concluded, "It is a beautiful and moving film, but more, it is a film without which the rest of Miyazaki's work could not be fully understood." However, with release in the West under the title *Warriors of the Wind*, major cuts were made in the original, creating a product that so incensed Miyazaki that for the next decade he and his partner Takahata refused to release their movies in Western theaters.

Studio Ghibli

Miyazaki soon saw that having his own production company would enable him to gather a production crew to create the highly detailed movies he envisioned. The same thoughts were going through his friend Takahata's mind. In 1985 they founded Studio Ghibli in a western suburb of Tokyo. A stringent work schedule with Miyazaki doing both original storyboards as well as cleaning up those of his staff, led to the release of his next feature, *Castle in the Sky*, in 1987. A visit to Wales amid a miner's strike was one of the inspirations for this boy's adventure story. Set in an alternate nineteenth century with steam still the driving power of industry, the movie features the young boy Pazu who has the adventure of his life. Sheeta, a lost princess with a mysterious blue amulet that gives its owner special powers— who quite literally falls out of the sky and into his life—aids Pazu in his mission to fight the destructive powers of an ancient civilization whose castles in the sky threaten the world. Caryn James, reviewing the movie in the *New York Times*, remarked that *Castle in the Sky* "illustrates the extraordinary quality of [Japan's] animation," and also demonstrated the difference between Japan and America in appreciation of such animated films. "[T]he film is the product of a culture where cartoons and comic books have a huge appeal for adults as well as children," James added. "Drawn in a dazzling range of jeweled and subtle colors, the film is always a joy to watch," James felt, but at two hours, it "may have a hard time finding its ideal audience." Chute called *The Castle in the Sky* "a departure for Miyazaki, at least to the extent that it's a classic "boy's movie," a high-altitude lost continent adventure story."

Next came a trio of magical movies, quieter in theme and texture than Miyazaki's earlier features. *My Neighbor Totoro* features a strange hybrid beast—part lump of dough, part seal, part feline, part bear, which became Miyazaki's most popular spin-off product line. When two little girls, Mei and her big sister Satsuki, move to a house in the country with their father while their mother recuperates in a hospital, they encounter a bevy of magical beasts who inhabit their surroundings. Of these, the cuddly beast known as Totoro is the most impressive. This familiar figure in Japanese children's literature makes his appearances to kids in time of emergency, such as when a child is lost. Seen only by children, he can make tiny seeds sprout into giant trees and travels around the countryside on his magic bus that looks not a little like a cat on wheels. Mei and Satsuki come to depend mightily in their Totoro. As McCarthy noted, "Nature and imagination work their magic for Mei and Satsuki when they most need help and comfort, showing them how powerful and precious the beautiful world around us is. . . . Its apparent simplicity masks a depth of wisdom and grace found in few works for any medium." Writing in the *New York Times,* Stephen Holden felt that while the film is "visually handsome" with its landscapes that recall "a paradisiacal garden of earthly delights," and while it can be "very charming," its tone was "so relentlessly goody-goody that it crosses the line from sweet into saccharine." Holden noted that Miyazaki's vision of family life "is even more unreal than the perkiest 1950's television sit-com." If critics disputed the qualities of the movies, fans all over the world fell in love with Totoro itself, and products from Totoro dolls to backpacks and clocks have helped to keep Studio Ghibli financially afloat over the years.

Kiki's Delivery Service, based on a popular children's book by Eiko Kadono, was Miyazaki's next project, the story of a young girl who must set out on her own, discovering her own talents and thus becoming an adult. That the young girl in question, Kiki, is a witch who can fly adds a bit of spice to this coming of age tale. She has never been away from her home in the country or from her loving parents, so when she heads off for the bright lights and big city, she is bound to have adventures. But in her efforts to forge a new life, Kiki loses sight of the magic in her life for a time—she forgets how to fly. Yet when she rescues a friend in an accident involving a dirigible, her mysterious flight ability returns—Kiki rediscovers the magic in her life. McCarthy concluded that *Kiki's Delivery Service* "is Miyazaki's affirmation of the value of ordinary humanity and everyday life," a movie with almost no external conflict; "a warm, gentle, and very beautiful film."

Miyazaki again indulges his love of flight in, *Porco Rosso,* a movie about a World War One flying ace with the head of a pig and a brave heart. Disillusioned with mankind, the hero of *Porco Rosso* has transformed himself into this porcine shape to show he has nothing more to do with the petty affairs of mankind. In the movie, set between the wars along the Adriatic, the protagonist, Marco Pagott searches for some meaning in life with his trusty airplane and finds solace in two women who love him. Planes buzz overhead as fascism grips the land below; Marco must soon face his past to help fight the inequities all around him. The highest grossing film in Japan the year of its release, *Porco Rosso* addresses adult themes more than in other films by Miyazaki: the relations between the sexes, the effects of war, and the importance of political and ethical leadership.

Princess Mononoke

The 1999 release in the U.S. of his feature, *Princess Mononoke,* put Miyazaki's name in the cinematic lexicon here. Up to that time, his movies had attracted a niche audience made up mostly of anime fans. *Princess Mononoke* got the full-scale Disney treatment, though it was released through its more artsy division, Miramax, as a result of its PG-13 rating for mature themes. With its 1997 release in Japan, the movie became the highest grossing film of all time in that country (surpassed later by *Titanic*). The historical setting is the Muromochi era (1392 to 1573) of medieval Japan. During this time, the country was just on the cusp of the Iron Age when new technologies replaced the old.

The story in this case is pure Miyazaki: in the far distant past a young girl, San, is raised by wolf gods in a pristine and primeval forest. She encounters a young man, Ashitaka, who has set out on a quest to rid himself of a curse he has sustained killing a boar god. San and her half-wild people are battling the forces of the new world, in this case their iron-making neighbors who are creating weapons that will change the world forever. As Morris wrote in *U.S. News and World Report,* when the two meet, Ashitaka "is smitten; for [San] it's hate at first sight." Nonetheless, the young man must help San in order to lift his own curse. A reviewer for *Variety* called Miyazaki's film an "exceedingly imaginative, beautifully realized animated epic," further describing the feature as "a savage and beautiful episode in the ongoing battle between man and nature." Comparing the Japanese feature with the latest episode of *Star Wars,* the same reviewer noted, "George Lucas has something to learn from Miyazaki about the graceful and organic use of myths and legends." Writing in *Entertainment Weekly,* Ty Burr commented, "There's a hard, hard beauty to animation master Hayao Miyazaki's hugely ambitious . . . epic." Noting that the story was not necessarily one for the kids, Burr concluded, "A windswept pinnacle of its art, *Princess Mononoke* has the effect of making the average Disney film look like just another toy story." And Terry Lawson, in an extended article in the *Detroit Free Press* called the movie "amazing," and one that tackles the primal power of nature as well as the themes of love, folklore, and nationalism. "It was an ambitious order for a genre some still dismiss as cartoons," Lawson noted."

But then, Miyazaki has always been ambitious in his artistic pursuits, though low-key in his self-evaluation. Miyazaki told Lawson that his primary task

If you enjoy the works of Hiyao Miyazaki, you might want to check out the following films:

Project A-ko, an anime directed by Katshuhiko Nishijima, 1986.

Grave of the Fireflies, an anime directed by Isao Takahata, 1988.

Urusei Yatsura 2: Beautiful Dreamer, an anime directed by Mamoru Oshii, 1984.

Watership Down, an animated film based on the novel by Richard Adams, 1978.

Yellow Submarine, an animated film featuring the music of the Beatles, 1968.

was to "tell truths in an emotional, involving way." However, he also noted, "It is not my job to make people think differently about animated movies. My work is in making us aware of subconscious worlds. It is always there. I'm just drawing it." In his anime films and manga creations, Miyazaki has done just that, creating an alternate vision of the world that resonates deeply on the mythic level, touching an unconscious strand in viewers both East and West.

■ Works Cited

Burr, Ty, review of *Princess Mononoke, Entertainment Weekly,* November 5, 1999, p. 50.

Chute, David, "Organic Machine: The World of Hayao Miyazaki," *Film Content,* November 1998, p. 62.

Holden, Stephen, "Even a Beast Is Sweet As Can Be," *New York Times,* May 14, 1991, p. C14.

James, Caryn, "Animated Adventure Fantasy from Japan," *New York Times,* August 18, 1989, p. C18.

Kan, Katherine, "Manga Mania," *Voice of Youth Advocates,* June 1996, pp. 83-84.

Lawson, Terry, "Japanese Animation Poised for Breakout in U.S.," *Detroit Free Press,* October 31, 1999, pp. 1G, 8G.

Maslin, Janet, "A Wolf, a Princess, a Castle in the Alps," *New York Times,* July 3, 1992, p. C10.

McCarthy, Helen, *Hayao Miyazaki: Master of Japanese Animation,* Stone Bridge Press, 1999, pp. 10, 39, 40, 53, 72, 92, 113, 116, 138, 157.

Miyazaki, Hayao, "The Current Situation of Japanese Movies," *Course on Japanese Movies 7,* Iwasami Shoten, January, 1988.

Morris, Holly J., "Beyond Mickey," *U.S. News and World Report,* October 25, 1999, p. 70.

Oshiguchi, Takashi, "The Whimsy and Wonder of Hayao Miyazaki," *Animerica 1,* July-August, 1993.

Review of *Princess Mononoke, Variety,* November 1, 1999, p. 88.

■ For More Information See

BOOKS

Bendazzi, Gianalberto, *Cartoons: One Hundred Years of Animation,* Indiana University Press, 1996.

Ledoux, Trish, and Doug Ranney, *The Complete Anime Guide: Japanese Directory and Resource Guide,* 2nd edition, Tiger Mountain Press, 1997.

PERIODICALS

Entertainment Weekly, September 4, 1998.

Hollywood Reporter, September 2, 1997; September 30, 1997; October 31, 1997.

New York Times, July 24, 1996, p. C3; September 12, 1999, p. AR46; October 21, 1999, p. B1.

People, November 8, 1999, p. 41.

U.S. News and World Report, October 6, 1997.

ON-LINE

Miyazaki's Web site is located at http://www.nausicaa.net.*

—Sketch by J. Sydney Jones

Michael Morpurgo

■ Personal

Born 1943, in St. Albans, England; married Clare Allen, 1963; three children. *Education:* King's College, London.

■ Addresses

Home—Langlands, Iddesleigh, Winkleigh, Devon EX19 8SN, England. *Agent*—Jacqueline Korn, David Higham Associates Ltd., 5-8 Lower John Street, Golden Square, London W1R 4HA, England.

■ Career

Writer, teacher, and farmer. Founder and director of Farms for City Children (educational charity). *Military service:* Royal Military Academy, Sandhurst.

■ Awards, Honors

Runner-up, Whitbread Award, 1982, for *War Horse;* Runner-up, Carnegie Medal, 1988, for *King of the Cloud Forests;* Runner-up, *Guardian* Award, 1991, for *Waiting for Anya;* Silver Pencil award, Holland; Circle d'Or prize, France; Best Books selection, *School Library Journal,* and Top of the List selection for Youth Fiction, *Booklist,* both 1995, and both for *The War of Jenkins' Ear;* Whitbread Award, 1995, for *The Wreck of the Zanzibar;* Smarties Gold Medal Award, 1997, for *The Butterfly Lion.*

■ Writings

JUVENILE FICTION

It Never Rained: Five Stories, illustrated by Isabelle Hutchins, Macmillan, 1974.

Thatcher Jones, illustrated by Trevor Ridley, Macmillan, 1975.

Long Way Home, Macmillan, 1975, Heinemann, 1996.

(Compiler with Graham Barrett) *The Story-Teller,* Ward Lock (London), 1976.

Friend or Foe, illustrated by Trevor Stubley, Macmillan, 1977.

What Shall We Do with It?, illustrated by Priscilla Lamont, Ward Lock, 1978.

Do All You Dare, photographs by Bob Cathmoir, Ward Lock, 1978.

(Editor) *All around the Year,* photographs by James Ravilious, drawings by Robin Ravilious, new poems by Ted Hughes, J. Murray, 1979.

The Day I Took the Bull By the Horn, Ward Lock, 1979.

The Ghost-Fish, Ward Lock, 1979.

Love at First Sight, Ward Lock, 1979.

That's How, Ward Lock, 1979.

The Marble Crusher and Other Stories (see also below), illustrated by Trevor Stubley, Macmillan, 1980.

The Nine Lives of Montezuma, illustrated by Margery Gill, Kaye and Ward (Kingswood, UK), 1980.

Miss Wirtles' Revenge, illustrated by Graham Clarke, Kaye and Ward, 1981.

The White Horse of Zennor: And Other Stories from below the Eagle's Nest, Kaye and Ward, 1982.

The War Horse, Kaye and Ward, 1982, Greenwillow, 1983.

Twist of Gold, Kaye and Ward, 1983, Viking, 1993.

Little Foxes, illustrated by Gareth Floyd, Kaye and Ward, 1984.

Why the Whales Came, Heinemann (London), 1985, Scholastic, 1985.

Tom's Sausage Lion, illustrated by Robina Green, A. & C. Black (London), 1986.

Jo-Jo, the Melon Donkey, illustrated by Chris Molan, Deutsch (London), 1987, Simon & Schuster, 1987, illustrated by Tony Kerins, Heinemann, 1995.

King of the Cloud Forests, Heinemann, 1988, Viking, 1988.

My Friend Walter, Heinemann, 1988.

(With Shoo Rayner) *Mossop's Last Chance,* A. & C. Black, 1988.

Mr. Nobody's Eyes, Heinemann, 1989, Viking, 1990, Viking Penguin, 1999.

Conker (see also below), Heinemann, 1989.

(With Shoo Rayner) *Albertine, Goose Queen,* A. & C. Black, 1989.

(With Shoo Rayner) *Jigger's Day Off,* A. & C. Black, 1990.

Waiting for Anya, Heinemann, 1990, Viking, 1991.

Colly's Barn (see also below), Heinemann, 1991.

(With Shoo Rayner) *And Pigs Might Fly!,* A. & C. Black, 1991.

The Sandman and the Turtles, Heinemann, 1991, Philomel, 1994.

(With Shoo Rayner) *Martians at Mudpuddle Farm,* A. & C. Black, 1992.

The War of Jenkins' Ear, Heinemann, 1993, Philomel, 1995.

Snakes and Ladders, Heinemann, 1994.

(Editor) *Ghostly Haunts,* illustrated by Nilesh Mistry, Pavilion, 1994.

Arthur, High King of Britain, illustrated by Michael Foreman, Pavilion, 1994, Harcourt, 1995.

The Dancing Bear, illustrated by Christian Birmingham, Young Lion (London), 1994, Houghton, 1996.

(With Shoo Rayner) *Stories from Mudpuddle Farm* (including the previously published *And Pigs Might Fly!, Martians at Mudpuddle Farm,* and *Jigger's Day Off*), A. & C. Black, 1995.

(With Shoo Rayner) *Mum's the Word,* A. & C. Black, 1995.

(Editor) *Muck and Magic: Tales from the Countryside,* foreword by HRH The Princess Royal, Heinemann, 1995.

The Wreck of the Zanzibar, illustrated by Birmingham, Heinemann, 1995, Viking, 1995.

Blodin the Beast, illustrated by Christina Balit, Francis Lincoln (London), 1995, Fulcrum (Golden, CO), 1995.

Long Way Home, Heinemann, 1996.

Sam's Duck, illustrated by Keith Bowen, Collins, 1996.

The King in the Forest, illustrated by T. Kerins, Simon & Schuster, 1996.

The Butterfly Lion, illustrated by Birmingham, Collins (London), 1996.

The Ghost of Grania O'Malley, Heinemann (London), 1996, Viking, 1996.

Robin of Sherwood, illustrated by Michael Foreman, Pavilion, 1996, Harcourt, 1996.

(Editor) *Beyond the Rainbow Warrior,* Pavilion, 1996.

Sam's Duck, illustrated by Keith Bowen, Collins, 1996.

The Marble Crusher (includes *The Marble Crusher, Colly's Barn,* and *Conker*), Mammoth, 1997.

Farm Boy, illustrated by Foreman, Pavilion, 1997.

Red Eyes at Night, illustrated by Tony Ross, Hodder, 1997.

Escape from Shangri-La, Philomel, 1998.

(Reteller) *Joan of Arc of Domremy,* illustrated by Foreman, Pavilion, 1998, Harcourt, 1999.

(Editor) *Animal Stories,* illustrated by Andrew Davidson, Kingfisher, 1999, HarperCollins, 1999.

Wombat Goes Walkabout, illustrated by Birmingham, Collins, 1999, HarperCollins, 1999.

Kensuke's Kingdom, illustrated by Foreman, Mammoth, Heinemann, 1999, Galaxy, 2000.

Billy the Kid, illustrated by Foreman, Pavilion, 2000.

Black Queen, Corgi, 2000.

From Hereabout Hill, Mammoth, 2000.

The Silver Swan, illustrated by Birmingham, Phyllis Fogelman Books, 2000.

Who's a Big Bully Then?, illustrated by Joanna Carey, Barrington Stoke, 2000.

OTHER

(Compiler with Clifford Simmons) *Living Poets,* J. Murray (London), 1974.

(Librettist) *Words of Songs,* music by Phyllis Tate, Oxford University Press, 1985.

Morpurgo's books have been translated into Irish, Welsh, German, Dutch, French, and several other languages.

■ **Adaptations**

Why the Whales Came was adapted for a movie titled *When the Whales Came,* 1989, by Golden Swan Films; *Sam's Duck* was adapted for television, 1992; *My Friend Walter* was adapted for a television movie, 1993, by Portobello Films for Thames Television and WonderWorks.

■ Sidelights

"A writer is a prospector," noted Michael Morpurgo in an article for *Children's Literature in Education*. "A prospector may find gold by accident or on purpose, by a mere glance at a glinting river bed or by years of laborious back-aching planning. He may never find gold at all. Of course, what a prospector does with his gold is another matter, He could drink it, invest it, pawn it, or bury it." Morpurgo, a prolific British writer of novels and picture books for children and young adults, a reteller of yarns and fables and an editor of anthologies, shares his gold with his readers. His award-winning novels include *War Horse, Why the Whales Came, King of the Cloud Forests, Waiting for Anya, The War of Jenkins' Ear, The Wreck of the Zanzibar, The Butterfly Lion,* and *Escape from Shangri-La.*

"Undoubtedly a leading figure in the field of children's books," according to a writer in *Children's Fiction Sourcebook,* Morpurgo blends adventure, fantasy and moral drama in his lyrical yet always understated prose. Consistent themes for Morpurgo are the conquest of evil by good and the vindication of virtues such as loyalty, hard work and determination, things that might seem somewhat old-fashioned in the relativistic age of cyberspace. His books are generally uplifting and teach ethical lessons, but Morpurgo is never preachy; the story is primary in his well-loved novels and picture books, although each propounds a moral dilemma. Much of Morpurgo's fiction is historical, set in the recent past, and in such exotic locales as the Scilly Islands, Renaissance Venice, and the Pyrenees, as well as in his native Devon. His subjects range from the need for tolerance to the wonders of rural life, his settings from the sea to the boarding school, and his writing combines stark realism with touches of fancy and magic. Morpurgo often uses animals in his tales, and also demonstrates an environmental concern in many of them. Additionally stories dealing with the hardships of war, either set contemporaneously, as in *Waiting for Anya* and *War Horse,* or retrospectively, as in *Mr. Nobody's Eyes* or *Escape from Shangri-La,* inform much of Morpurgo's work, himself once an army officer. Writing in *School Librarian,* Ann Jenkin called Morpurgo "a master storyteller," and Ilene Cooper, interviewing him after the U.S. publication of *The War of Jenkins' Ear,* noted the care he takes with "the small details" of writing, creating atmospheric and believable backdrops.

"I write stories, not books," Morpurgo told a prep school class in an interview with *Young Writer.* "And I write stories for me—for both the child and the adult in me. . . . My stories are about children, not for them, because I know children—they interest me, children of all ages, even adult ones." The author of over sixty books, Morpurgo is also deeply involved in working with children. A teacher for a decade, a father of three and now a grandfather, he founded with his wife Farms for City Children, a venture that brings urban kids to the country to live and work, getting closer to nature and, it is hoped, to their real selves.

"Good at Rugby and a Bit Stupid"

Morpurgo was born on October 5, 1943, in St. Albans, England, into a country that had been at war for over four years. At the age of seven he went away to a grammar school in Sussex where he was introduced to "class war," as he told *Booklist*'s Cooper. "The schoolboys and the village boys had fights and difficulties; walking along cow paths, we'd hurl insults at each other. It was an indication that there were people out there who didn't like you because of the way you spoke, and we didn't like them either. And while things have changed since the 1950s, class still seems to me to be a cancer that riddles our society." As a young schoolboy Morpurgo was thought of "as good at rugby and a bit stupid," he remarked in *Young Writer.* "As a child I think I lived up to that expectation . . . I never liked writing as a child." It was not until much later that Morpurgo began to love reading, especially the novels of Robert Louis Stevenson, Paul Gallico, and Ernest Hemingway, and the poetry of Ted Hughes, a poet laureate of England and a close friend of Morpurgo's.

At age fourteen Morpurgo entered Kings School in Canterbury, graduating in 1962. The following year he married Clare Allen, daughter of a well-known publisher. They ultimately had three children together, two sons and one daughter. Graduating from King's College in London in 1967, Morpurgo became a teacher for a time after graduation, and also served as an army officer. It was during his teaching career that he determined to become a writer. "I had a notion I could tell a tale when the children I was teaching really seemed to want to listen to the tales I told them," Morpurgo noted in *Young Writer.* "An acid test." Reading Ted Hughes's *Poetry in the Making* influenced Morpurgo to think that he too, could string words together rhythmically; it literally got him writing. "No better invitation to write was ever written and I accepted," Morpurgo remarked in *Young Writer.* "I love the sound of words, the rhythm of a sentence."

Living in the countryside, Morpurgo also wanted to introduce city-born and bred kids to the wonders of nature. To that end, he and his wife started Farms for City Children in the 1970s. Under this program, kids come to stay at the farm, work and take care of animals for several weeks. So popular has the program become, that the Morpurgo's operate three farms where more than two thousand children per year have the opportunity to get in touch with nature and themselves.

Early Works

Much of Morpurgo's early work has not been published in the United States. This includes both short novels for ten- to twelve-year-olds, and picture books for younger readers. One of his early books, *Friend or Foe*, already contains many of the elements of the Morpurgo oeuvre. Two young boys are evacuated during the London Blitz and go to live for a time with a farmer in Devon. Their peaceful idyll is destroyed, however, when a German airplane goes down nearby and the boys join in the search for the airmen. But when one of the Germans saves the boy, David, from drowning, it is unclear who is the enemy and who the friend. With this book, then, the reader deals with war and hard moral decisions foisted upon young kids, typical Morpurgo themes. Margery Fisher, reviewing the novel in *Growing Point*, felt that the "story works well" in its purpose to "serve the cause of peace by suggesting that all men are brothers."

With his early work, Morpurgo was already making a name for himself in England as a writer "successfully outside the mainstream," as Josephine Karavasil described his work in a *Times Literary Supplement* review of *Miss Wirtle's Revenge*. It is a tale about a little girl who competes successfully against a class full of boys. His 1980 *Nine Lives of Montezuma* is a short novel detailing nine narrow-escape adventures of a farmyard cat named Montezuma, one of Morpurgo's earliest animal stories. Told from the cat's point of view, the book also details the farming year as a background story, with "continuity" being the theme of the book, according to Margery Fisher of *Growing Point*. When Montezuma dies, the cat knows that there is a descendant to take its place in the scheme of things on the farm. *Junior Bookshelf* critic D. A. Young noted that the story "is told without sentimentality, though not without sentiment," and concluded that the book could be "recommended with confidence to cat-lovers of any age."

Morpurgo blended two of his favorite topics—the horrors of war, and a view of the world from the animal perspective—in his first book to be published in the United States, *War Horse*. Inspired by a painting of a horse in the village hall near Morpurgo's home, the book is the story of the First World War, seen through the eyes of Joey, a farm horse commandeered in 1914. Cavalry stood little chance against the mechanized horrors of modern war; Joey endures bombardment and capture by the Germans. He is set to work pulling ambulances and guns, worked by different masters but never forgetting young Albert, the kind son of his original owner back in England. In the end, persistence and courage pay off—Joey is reunited with Albert in Devon. Kate M. Flanagan, writing in *Horn Book*, noted that "the courage of the horse and his undying devotion to the boy" permeate this book, which she maintained was written with "elegant, old-fashioned grace." *Voice of Youth Advocates* contributor Diane G. Yates, noting that *War Horse* is based on a true story, commented: "The message about the futility and carnage of war comes across loud and clear. The characters, both human and animal, that die in the war are all the best and brightest of their generation." Fisher of *Growing Point* highlighted similarities between *War Horse* and the classic, *Black Beauty*, and concluded her review by stating that Morpurgo's book "is a most accomplished piece of story-telling, full of sympathy for an animal manipulated by man but preserving its dignity." Warmly received on both sides of the Atlantic, *War Horse* helped win an international audience for Morpurgo.

Morpurgo's next book was *Twist of Gold*, set in both Ireland and the United States. When famine hits Ireland in the 1840s, Sean and Annie O'Brien set off for America to find their father, an adventurous journey that takes them first across the ocean, and then across a continent by wagon train and river boat. A story of a childhood test, *Twist of Gold* is a "touching and inventive adventure story," according to Fisher in *Growing Point*. A *Publishers Weekly* critic called this historical fiction "Sentimental in the best sense of the word," and a novel that "remains a colorful, engaging, Dickensian read to its happy and affecting conclusion."

Gains a Wider Audience

Morpurgo's name became more widely recognized in the United States with the 1983 publication of *Why the Whales Came* and the book's subsequent adaptation for film. Set in 1914 on Bryher in the Scilly Islands off England's southwest coast, this is "a story full of compassion," according to *Children's*

Why the Whales Came
Michael Morpurgo

Two British children and a hermit form a friendship as they help save a group of beached whales in Morpurgo's 1985 story.

Fiction Sourcebook. Gracie and Daniel have been forbidden to associate with the strange old man on the far side of the island who is known as the Birdman to the locals. But soon the two youngsters learn that the old man is not some evil magician, but simply a person made lonely because of his deafness, and one who had to flee another of the islands as a youth because of a curse put on it. The three become fast friends with the war always hovering ominously in the background. Yet on Bryher there is a parallel war between the islanders and the sea and weather. When a whale washes ashore, the islanders must be convinced to help return it to the sea rather than butcher it, for it was the destruction of sea life that brought the curse to the Birdman's original island. "The success of Morpurgo's novel comes . . . from its portrait of the two children and from its exploration of the blend of superstition and communal spirit existing in an isolated settlement," noted

reviewer Marcus Crouch in *The Junior Bookshelf.* Cindy Darling Codell, writing in *School Library Journal,* commented that Morpurgo's language "is lean, yet lyrical," and that his descriptive paragraphs "let readers taste the salt of the sea and feel the grit of the islander's lives." Fisher, writing in *Growing Point,* concluded her review by dubbing the book "a forceful and exciting narrative."

Morpurgo is also noted for his picture books, and he returned to an animal-centered story with *Jo-Jo, the Melon Donkey,* a picture book for older children set in sixteenth-century Venice. When Jo-Jo helps to save the city from a flood, he becomes a hero. Amy Spaulding in *School Library Journal* noted that the "writing style follows that of the literary fairy tale, being at once simple and elegant," and *Kirkus Reviews* commented: "With a nice blend of humor and sadness, Morpurgo brings to life the vibrancy of 16th-century Venice." Other Morpurgo picture books include the "Mudpuddle Farm" series with Shoo Rayner, and for older children, *Blodin the Beast* and *The Dancing Bear,* the latter being the story of young singer Roxanne and the orphaned bear cub she has raised. When a film crew comes to her remote village to make a video, Roxanne is lured by bright lights, and decides ultimately to leave with the group, pursuing fame and fortune as an entertainer. Her bear dies the following day. As the narrator of the story, Roxanne's former teacher, says, "There's a lesson to be learned, if one just listens to my tale." *School Library Journal* contributor Kathy East, however, felt Morpurgo's lesson "likely to appeal more to adults, who will relate to the elderly narrator and his style, than to children." In a picture book published in 2000, *Wombat Goes Walkabout,* Morpurgo presents another plucky animal, a wombat searching for its mother in the Australian outback.

Morpurgo's love of animals finds its way into many of his novels for young adult readers, as well. The mythic Yeti save a lost boy in *King of the Cloud Forests;* Ocky the chimpanzee becomes a companion for Harry Hawkins in *Mr. Nobody's Eyes;* and giant turtles populate the dreams of Mike in *The Sandman and the Turtles.* In *King of the Cloud Forests,* young Ashley Anderson must make his way with a Tibetan Buddhist across China to India and safety, one step ahead of the invading Japanese. Crossing the Himalayas, he and his guide are separated. Lost and near starvation, Ashley is rescued by a band of the legendary Yeti, red-furred, ape-like creatures who revere the boy as a god. Ashley stays in their idyllic community for a time, but is finally reunited with his guide and ultimately makes it safely to England.

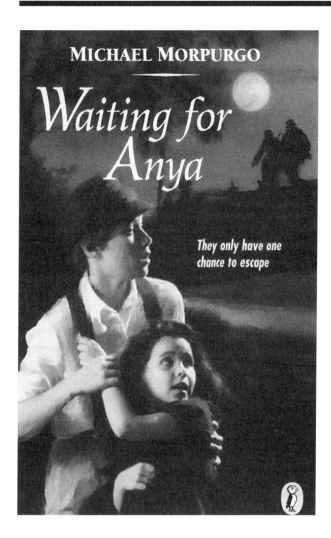

MICHAEL MORPURGO

Waiting for Anya

They only have one chance to escape

Set during World War II, Morpurgo's 1990 tale takes readers to the Pyrenees Mountains, where villagers attempt to smuggle Jewish children to Spain.

Jacqueline Simms, writing in *Times Literary Supplement,* noted that "this marvelous adventure story . . . will surely become a perennial favourite," while Roger Sutton of the *Bulletin of the Center for Children's Books* thought that this "brief and dramatic novel . . . may woo reluctant readers back to the fold." *Booklist*'s Cooper concluded, "A spellbinding read-aloud and a top-notch offering—especially to boys who think books are boring."

In *Mr. Nobody's Eyes,* the Second World War has just ended in England and young Harry Hawkins is odd-man out at home: his new stepfather thinks the boy is useless and his mother has eyes only for the recently arrived baby. Harry's lonely world is brightened when he meets Signor Blondini from a circus and his performing chimp, Ocky. When Ocky escapes from the circus, Harry at first hides the animal and then

the two run away together, living with gypsies and undergoing a terrifying adventure. Finally Harry gains his stepfather's respect and the reader is presented with a happy ending to this "compelling novel," as a writer for *Publishers Weekly* described the book. The same reviewer called special attention to Morpurgo's "[p]erceptive writing, strong characters and scenes of breathless suspense. . . ."

Award-winning Novels

Two of Morpurgo's most compelling novels with child protagonists are *Waiting for Anya* and *The War of Jenkins' Ear. Waiting for Anya* relates the story of the plight of Jewish children in World War II France. The novel is set in the Pyrenees just after the surrender of the French forces, and its protagonist, Jo, a young shepherd, becomes involved in a scheme to save the children when he discovers that a man named Benjamin is hiding them at a farm near the village of Lescun. Benjamin is smuggling the children across the border into Spain; he is also waiting for his own daughter to make her way to this safe house from Paris. Jo begins delivering supplies to the farm, a job made much riskier when the Nazis occupy Lescun and threaten to kill anyone aiding fugitives. Soon, however, the entire town of Lescun is helping to get the children across the border. Though Benjamin is captured and sent to die at Auschwitz, Anya does finally turn up at the farm and is saved at the end of this "gripping, clearly written story," as Ellen Fader described it in *Horn Book.* Betsy Hearne, reviewing the novel in *Bulletin of the Center for Children's Books,* noted that Morpurgo "injected the basic conventions of heroism and villainy with some complexities of character," and went on to remark, "[I]ndependent readers will appreciate the simple, clear style and fast-paced plot . . . commanding attention to ethics as well as action." A critic for *Kirkus Reviews* commented that Morpurgo "builds a sort of magic-amidst-the-war oasis in his descriptions of region, seasons, village, and people." "Well paced and evenly written, this WWII/Holocaust story has adventure, drama, and pathos," according to Kathryn L. Havris writing in *Voice of Youth Advocates.* Marcus Crouch, in a laudatory review for *The Junior Bookshelf,* commented that *Waiting for Anya* "is an intensely exciting story guaranteed to keep a sensitive reader on the edge of his chair." Crouch added that Morpurgo's story is "rich in the qualities which make for critical approval," concluding: "There have been many Second World War stories for the young, none which deals more convincingly with its perils and dilemmas." *Waiting for Anya* was a runner-up for the 1991 *Guardian* Award.

The War of Jenkins' Ear is an English boarding school tale, a holdover from Morpurgo's own time at school as a youth, when he and some friends gathered in a clique around a charismatic young boy, whom the others felt had special powers. In the novel, young Toby Jenkins meets a remarkable boy named Simon Christopher, who claims to be the reincarnation of Jesus. After performing miracles for Toby, Christopher begins to develop a following. The youth also tries to make peace between the townies and the boys at Redlands Preparatory School. But when someone tells the headmaster what is going on, Christopher is expelled from the school for blasphemy. *Quill and Quire* contributor Joanne Schott commented: "A strict school of 40 years ago makes a credible setting and gives scope for the complex relationships Morpurgo uses to examine questions of belief and credulity, deception and self-deception, loyalty and the pressure of doubt, and much more." Tim Rausch of *School Library Journal* commented that Morpurgo "tackles provocative themes, dealing with the issues of hate, revenge, prejudice, and especially faith in an intelligent and fresh manner." Rausch concluded, "While the novel is likely to be controversial, it will interest YAs and will assuredly provide them with numerous discussion possibilities." *School Library Journal* also put *The War of Jenkins' Ear* on its annotated list of the year's "Best Books," and other critics have compared the book to *Lord of the Flies* and *The Chocolate War*. D. A. Young, reviewing the novel in *The Junior Bookshelf*, commented, "The author may have set himself an almost impossible task but he has succeeded most wonderfully." A writer for *Kirkus Reviews* concluded, "Morpurgo is unhindered by the undeniably British locale and characters: He has written a rare novel that has the capacity to teach its potent lessons of altruism to many readers." *The War of Jenkins' Ear* was *Booklist*'s 1995 Top of the List winner for youth fiction.

The Scilly Islands, used for Morpurgo's 1985 tale, *Why the Whales Came*, also provide a setting for his 1995 *Wreck of the Zanzibar*, the story of a childhood on Bryher Island as told through the diary of Laura, and of her secret treasure—Zanzibar, a wooden tortoise. Laura's narrative is the record of a harsh life, of adversity and the will to overcome. *Junior Bookshelf* reviewer Marcus Crouch commented that *The Wreck of the Zanzibar*, while a short book, is "by no means a slight one," and praised the "beautiful timing throughout." *Horn Book*'s Elizabeth S. Watson noted that "The slight book makes a solid impact on the reader, who will finish [it] with a satisfied smile." A writer for *Publishers* Weekly remarked, "Morpurgo spins a tale as compelling as it is unusual in its setting and plot. . . . A hearty, old-fashioned survival tale that should appeal equally to both sexes." *The Wreck of the Zanzibar* won the Whitbread Award in 1995.

A further tale with an island setting is Morpurgo's *Ghost of Grania O'Malley*, a 1996 work set off the coast of Ireland. It involves young Jessie, her American cousin Jack, and the ghost of the sixteenth-century female Irish pirate, Grania O'Malley, as they battle to prevent the ecological destruction of the island. Jessie, inspired by one of the young girls who visited Morpurgo's Farms for City Children, suffers from cerebral palsy, but overcomes this disability to fight for the island she loves. Deborah Stevenson, writing in *Bulletin of the Center for Children's Books*, felt that though the novel's "many plot elements cause it to sprawl," still "readers who enjoy a good island drama will appreciate Jessie's fight for her home." Jane Gardner Connor called the book an "appealing, well-told story," in *School Library Journal*. Another ghost figures in *My Friend Walter*, in which the spirit of Sir Walter Raleigh attaches itself to young Bess Throckmorton, on a visit to London from her Devon farm. Sir Walter follows Bess back to the farm with humorous results when he tries to drive a tractor; ultimately he helps the Throckmorton's raise the money to buy the farm that was his birthplace, in this "pleasantly instructive" tale, according to Fisher in *Growing Point*. *My Friend Walter* was filmed for a television movie.

Morpurgo's 1996 novel *The Butterfly Lion* is a blend of fantasy and fiction. It is a story within a story about a ten-year-old boy who runs away from his miserable school and ends up in a dusty house where an old widow shows him the figure of a giant lion cut into the chalk hillside. This woman tells the boy about her dead husband, Bertie, who, as a youth growing up in South Africa, had as his pet and only friend, a white lion. When his father sold the lion, Bertie vowed to find him again. This he did during World War One, and then brought the animal with him to England, where it ultimately died. Bertie thereafter, spent forty years carving its likeness in the hillside, a figure visited by thousands of butterflies after the rains. Returning to school, the young boy learns that both Bertie and his widow died many years before. "The story sounds hokey," noted *Booklist*'s Kathleen Squires, "but Morpurgo evocatively captures the South African landscape and presents young, lonely Bertie's heartbreak and blossoming friendship and love . . . with genuine emotion and tender passion." Reviewing the novel in *School Library Journal,* Gebregeorgis Yohannes concluded, "In addition to being a successful adventure story, the book demonstrates the value of character—of keeping promises, standing up for one's beliefs, and courage under fire." *The Butterfly Lion,* "at once marvelous and matter-of-fact," according to a writer for *Kirkus Reviews,* won England's prestigious Smarties Gold Medal Award in 1997. "This dreamlike story is suffused with a man's lifelong love for a rare, gentle animal friend," the critic for *Kirkus Reviews* concluded.

From Myths and Legends to Tales of the Quotidian

Morpurgo has also breathed new life into old legends. His retelling of the Arthurian tales in *Arthur, High King of Britain* is "the real thing—darkness and all," according to Heather McCammond-Watts in *Bulletin of the Center for Children's Books.* McCammond-Watts explains that the Arthur of Morpurgo's book, who rescues a young time-traveler from the modern era, "is a complex character: an impetuous youth, an august yet sometimes rash ruler, a jealous lover, and a tortured man trying to live up to his epic persona." *School Library Journal* contributor Helen Gregory concluded that Morpurgo's Arthur "stands with the best." With *Robin of Sherwood,* Morpurgo added twists to the old tale—an albino Marion for example—that creates an "outstanding new version of the Robin Hood legend," according to Nancy Zachary in *Voice of Youth Advocates.* "Shelve this treasure alongside Howard Pyle's and Ian Serrailler's classic folktales," concluded Zachary. A writer for *Kirkus Reviews* called *Robin of Sherwood* "compelling" and "heartwarming," while a reviewer for *Publishers Weekly* called attention to Morpurgo's "well-paced narrative and lively characterization." *Booklist's* Carolyn Phelan called the book a "fine, original piece of storytelling, faithful to the legend of Robin Hood."

Morpurgo has also tackled the legend of the Maid of Orleans in his 1999 *Joan of Arc of Domremy,* a tale that begins in the modern day when young Eloise Hardy moves with her family to Orleans, France and begins studying legends of Joan. Steeping herself in such lore, Eloise one day hears Joan's voice telling her the story of her life. "Morpurgo is an accomplished writer and storyteller," wrote Shirley Wilton in a *School Library Journal* review. "Facts and popular beliefs, history and legend are drawn upon to create an exciting tale." A reviewer for *Publishers Weekly*

felt that Morpurgo's storytelling "is premised on faith," and concluded that the book's "polish and panoramic scope will lure and hold readers."

With *Farm Boy,* Morpurgo returned to the here and now to detail the memories of four generations of an English farming family. Set once again in Morpurgo's beloved Devon, the book tells the story of a young boy who goes to visit his grandfather on the farm. His grandfather in turn enchants the boy with tales of how farming was done before mechanization, capturing the spirit of rural life before the internal combustion engine and agribusiness. "Morpurgo's storytelling style is unhurried," noted *School Library Journal's* Lee Bock, "reflecting great skill at giving unique voices to his characters." Bock continued, "The memories of [Grandpa's] horse are particularly poignant, and readers will learn many details about life during the early part of this century and World War I." A critic for *Kirkus Reviews* called the book "a small gem" and an "expertly crafted reminder that stories can link generations."

Memories of World War II figure in *Escape from Shangri-La,* in which an old tramp, Popsicle, watching Cessie's house, turns out to be her long lost grandfather. When the old man has a stroke, he is put in the Shangri-La nursing home, but he is withering away there. Finally Cessie finds her grandfather's real home, an old lifeboat once used to evacuate the British forces from Dunkirk during the Second World War. From a photograph and news clippings, Cessie learns her grandfather took part in this heroic effort, and the sight of a faded photo of the Frenchwoman who hid him from the Germans when he fell off the boat rescuing others makes Popsicle recall the past. Cessie helps her grandfather and other residents of the home make a break for it; they head to France to track down this woman, only to discover she never returned from German arrest in 1940. Going back to England, the entire family is again happily reunited. "Readers will enjoy the climactic adventure and respond on a deeper level to the friendship between a spirited child and a lifelong loner," wrote John Peters in a *Booklist* review.

Morpurgo has timely advice for authors in the making, shared with readers in *Young Writer.* His three most important tips are: "1. Drink in the world around you. 2. Dream your dream until it becomes so involving you can't stop dreaming it. 3. Tell it from the heart, as you feel your story, as you see it." These elements can be seen in all of Morpurgo's work. As Jennifer Taylor put it in *St. James Guide to Young Adult Writers,* "Heartwarming and sensitive, Morpurgo's

If you enjoy the works of Michael Morpurgo, you might want to check out the following books:

Aidan Chambers, *Nik: Now I Know*, 1988.
Erik Christian Haugaard, *Under the Black Flag*, 1994.
Michelle Magorian, *Good Night, Mr. Tom*, 1982.
Donna Jo Napoli, *Stones in Water*, 1997.
Jill Paton Walsh, *Grace*, 1992.

imaginative empathy, whether writing about animals or people, makes for pure gold. His novels certainly open up horizons for young readers."

■ Works Cited

Bock, Lee, review of *Farm Boy, School Library Journal*, March, 1999, p. 212.

Review of *The Butterfly Lion, Kirkus Reviews*, April 15, 1997, p. 645.

Codell, Cindy Darling, review of *Why the Whales Came, School Library Journal*, February, 1987, p. 82.

Connor, Jane Gardner, review of *The Ghost of Grania O'Malley, School Library Journal*, July, 1996, p. 85.

Cooper, Ilene, review of *King of the Cloud Forests, Booklist*, July, 1988, p. 1840.

Cooper, Ilene, "The Booklist Interview," *Booklist*, January 1 & 15, 1996, p. 816.

Crouch, Marcus, review of *Why the Whales Came, The Junior Bookshelf*, December, 1985, p. 279.

Crouch, Marcus, review of *Waiting for Anya, The Junior Bookshelf*, February, 1991, pp. 35-36.

Crouch, Marcus, review of *The Wreck of the Zanzibar, Junior Bookshelf*, August, 1995, p. 148.

East, Kathy, review of *The Dancing Bear, School Library Journal*, May, 1996, p. 114.

Fader, Ellen, review of *Waiting for Anya, Horn Book*, July-August, 1991, p. 458.

Review of *Farm Boy, Kirkus Reviews*, December 15, 1998.

Fisher, Margery, review of *The Nine Lives of Montezuma, Growing Point*, November, 1980, p. 3776.

Fisher, Margery, review of *War Horse, Growing Point*, November, 1982, p. 3989.

Fisher, Margery, review of *Twist of Gold, Growing Point*, January, 1984, pp. 4183-84.

Fisher, Margery, review of *Friend or Foe, Growing Point*, January, 1985, p. 4369.

Fisher, Margery, review of *Why the Whales Came, Growing Point*, January, 1987, p. 4749.

Fisher, Margery, review of *My Friend Walter, Growing Point*, January, 1989, p. 5117.

Flanagan, Kate M., review of *War Horse, Horn Book*, December, 1983, pp. 711-12.

Gregory, Helen, review of *Arthur, High King of Britain, School Library Journal*, July, 1995, p. 89.

Havris, Kathryn L., review of *Waiting for Anya, Voice of Youth Advocates*, June, 1991, pp. 98-99.

Hearne, Betsy, review of *Waiting for Anya, Bulletin of the Center for Children's Books*, March, 1991, p. 172.

Hobson, Margaret, Jennifer Madden and Ray Pryterch, *Children's Fiction Sourcebook: A Survey of Children's Books for 6-13 Year Olds*, Ashgate Publishing, 1992, pp. 154-55.

Jenkin, Ann, review of *The Dancing Bear, School Librarian*, November, 1994, p. 153.

Review of *Joan of Arc of Domremy, Publishers Weekly*, February 22, 1999, p. 95.

Review of *Jo-Jo, the Melon Donkey, Kirkus Reviews*, December 1, 1987, p. 1677.

Karavasil, Josephine, "Matters of Rhythm and Register," *Times Literary Supplement*, March 26, 1982, p. 347.

McCammond-Watts, Heather, review of *Arthur, High King of Britain, Bulletin of the Center for Children's Books*, May, 1995, p. 317.

Morpurgo, Michael, "The Making of "Anya," or a Tale of Two Villages," *Children's Literature in Education*, December, 1993, pp. 235-39.

Morpurgo, Michael, *The Dancing Bear*, Houghton, 1996.

Morpurgo, Michael, interview with *Young Writer*, April, 1999.

Review of *Mr. Nobody's Eyes, Publishers Weekly*, January, 1990, p. 110.

Peters, John, review of *Escape from Shangri-La, Booklist*, September 15, 1998, p. 231.

Phelan, Carolyn, review of *Robin of Sherwood, Booklist*, October 1, 1996, p. 350.

Rausch, Tim, review of *The War of Jenkins' Ear, School Library Journal*, September, 1995, p. 219.

Review of *Robin of Sherwood, Kirkus Reviews*, August 1, 1996, p. 1155.

Review of *Robin of Sherwood, Publishers Weekly*, August 12, 1996, p. 84.

Schott, Joanne, review of *The War of Jenkins' Ear, Quill and Quire*, July, 1993, p. 59.

Simms, Jacqueline, "Magic Man," *Times Literary Supplement*, February 19, 1988, p. 200.

"SLJ's Best Books, 1995," *School Library Journal*, December, 1995, p. 22.

Spaulding, Amy, review of *Jo-Jo, the Melon Donkey, School Library Journal,* April, 1988, p. 87.

Squires, Kathleen, review of *The Butterfly Lion, Booklist,* June 1 & 15, 1997, p. 1704.

Stevenson, Deborah, review of *The Ghost of Grania O'Malley, Bulletin of the Center for Children's Books,* May, 1996, pp. 309-10.

Sutton, Roger, review of *King of the Cloud Forests, Bulletin of the Center for Children's Books,* July-August, 1988, pp. 234-35.

Taylor, Jennifer, "Morpurgo, Michael," *St. James Guide to Young Adult Writers,* 2nd edition, edited by Tom Pendergast and Sara Pendergast, St. James Press, 1999, pp. 603-05.

Review of *Twist of Gold, Publishers Weekly,* January 18, 1993, pp. 469-70.

Review of *Waiting for Anya, Kirkus Reviews,* March 1, 1991, p. 320.

Review of *The War of Jenkins' Ear, Kirkus Reviews,* September 1, 1995, p. 1285.

Watson, Elizabeth S., review of *The Wreck of the Zanzibar, Horn Book,* March-April, 1996, p. 198.

Wilton, Shirley, review of *Joan of Arc of Domremy, School Library Journal,* May, 1999, p. 128.

Review of *The Wreck of the Zanzibar, Publishers Weekly,* October 30, 1995, p. 62.

Yates, Diane G., review of *War Horse, Voice of Youth Advocates,* April, 1984, p. 32.

Yohannes, Gebregeorgis, review of *The Butterfly Lion, School Library Journal,* August, 1997, p. 158.

Young, D. A., review of *The Nine Lives of Montezuma, The Junior Bookshelf,* December, 1980, p. 294.

Young, D. A., review of *The War of Jenkins' Ear, The Junior Bookshelf,* August, 1993, pp. 155-56.

Zachary, Nancy, review of *Robin of Sherwood, Voice of Youth Advocates,* February, 1997, p. 330.

■ For More Information See

BOOKS

Children's Literature Review, Volume 51, Gale, 1999.

PERIODICALS

Booklist, February 1, 1984, p. 814; September 15, 1985, p. 137; July, 1988, p. 1814; November 1, 1989, p. 564; May 1, 1990, p. 1708; August, 1990, p. 2178; March 15, 1992, p. 1364; April 1, 1993, p. 1425; September 1, 1994, p. 44; September 1, 1995, p. 53; November 15, 1995, p. 560; January 1, 1996, p. 740; March 15, 1996, p. 1282; August, 1998, p. 2029.

Bulletin of the Center for Children's Books March, 1993, p. 221; December, 1995, p. 135; January, 1997, p. 181.

Carousel, Spring, 1997, p. 17; December, 1998, p. 139.

Junior Bookshelf, August, 1988, pp. 179-80; December, 1989, pp. 298-99; June, 1992, pp. 113-14; August, 1995, p. 147.

School Librarian, February, 1997, p. 33; Autumn, 2000, p. 158.

School Library Journal, September, 1987, p. 181; September, 1988, p. 200; November, 1990, p. 117; April, 1991, p. 122; December, 1991, p. 31; February, 1993, p. 94; November, 1993, p. 156; September, 1995, p. 219; December, 1995, p. 22; November 1, 1998, p. 126.

Times Educational Supplement, January 14, 1983, p. 30; January 13, 1984, p. 42; June 6, 1986, p. 54; November 27, 1987, p. 48; February 5, 1988, pp. 54, 60; March 10, 1989, p. B16; November 24, 1989, p. 27; February 15, 1991, p. 32; May 24, 1991, p. 24; July 2, 1993, p. 11; November 4, 1994, p. 89; May 31, 1995, p. 15; October 2, 1998, p. 12.*

—Sketch by J. Sydney Jones

Thylias Moss

■ Personal

Born February 27, 1954, in Cleveland, OH; daughter of a recapper for the Cardinal Tire Company and a maid; married John Lewis Moss (a business manager), July 6, 1973; children: Dennis, Ansted. *Education:* Attended Syracuse University, 1971-73; Oberlin College, B.A., 1981; University of New Hampshire, M.A., 1983.

■ Addresses

Office—P.O. Box 2686, Ann Arbor, MI 48106. *E-mail*—thyliasm@umich.edu. *Agent*—Faith Hamlin, Sanford J. Greenburger Associates, 55 Fifth Ave., New York, NY 10003.

■ Career

Poet and educator. The May Company, Cleveland, OH, order checker, 1973-74, data entry supervisor, 1974-75, junior executive auditor, 1975-79; Phillips Academy, Andover, MA, instructor, 1984-92; University of Michigan, Ann Arbor, assistant professor, 1993-94, associate professor, 1994-98, professor, 1998—. University of New Hampshire, Durham, visiting professor, 1991-92; Brandeis University, Waltham, MA, Fannie Hurst Poet, 1992.

■ Member

Academy of American Poets.

■ Awards, Honors

Award from Cleveland Public Library Poetry Contest, 1978, for "Coming of Age in Sandusky"; four grants, Kenan Charitable Trust, 1984-87; artist's fellowship, Artist's Foundation of Massachusetts, 1987; grant, National Endowment for the Arts, 1989; Pushcart Prize, 1990; Dewar's Profiles Performance Artist Award in Poetry, 1991; Witter Bynner Prize, American Academy and Institute of Arts and Letters, 1991; Whiting Writer's award, 1991; Guggenheim fellowship, 1995; MacArthur fellowship, 1996; Best Book, *Village Voice*, 1998, and nomination, National Book Critics Circle Award, both for *Last Chance for the Tarzan Holler: Poems.*

■ Writings

POETRY

Hosiery Seams on a Bowlegged Woman, Cleveland State University Press (Cleveland, OH), 1983.
Pyramid of Bone, University of Virginia Press (Charlottesville, VA), 1989.
At Redbones, Cleveland State University Press, 1990.

Rainbow Remnants in Rock Bottom Ghetto Sky, Persea (New York City), 1991.
Small Congregations: New and Selected Poems, Ecco Press (Hopewell, NJ), 1993.
Last Chance for the Tarzan Holler: Poems, Persea, 1998.

OTHER

The Dolls in the Basement (play), produced by New England Theatre Conference, 1984.
Talking to Myself (play), produced in Durham, NH, 1984.
I Want to Be (for children), illustrated by Jerry Pinkney, Dial, 1993.
Tale of a Sky-Blue Dress (memoir), Avon, 1998.

■ Adaptations

A selection of Moss's poems, read by the author, were recorded on an audiocassette titled *Larry Levis and Thylias Moss Reading Their Poems,* 1991.

■ Sidelights

Thylias Moss grew up the only child of doting parents in Cleveland, Ohio, met her future husband at age sixteen, and—though she grew up in working-class surroundings—has spent most of her adult life in the world of college English departments. Her later poetry collections have displayed a more relaxed state of mind, but Moss's early work is characterized by almost unremitting portraits of bitterness, anger, and despair.

Moss first won a poetry prize in 1978 for "Coming of Age in Sandusky." Her poems were collected for publication in 1983 as *Hosiery Seams on a Bowlegged Woman,* which was commissioned by Alberta Turner and Leonard Trawick of the Cleveland State University Poetry Center. Six years later came *Pyramid of Bone,* a volume written at the request of the University of Virginia's Charles Rowell. The book was a first runner-up in the National Book Critics Circle Award for 1989, and earned Moss praise from a reviewer in *Publishers Weekly* for her "rage and unyielding honesty." Reflecting on the difference between the author's life and her work, a critic in *Virginia Quarterly Review* observed: "If Thylias Moss's resume is sedate . . . her poetry is anything but." The poems in *Pyramid* are full of disturbing images ("the vinegar she's become cannot sterilize the needle") and agonized statements ("The miracle was not birth but that I lived despite my crimes"), the critic noted.

Moss's third book, *At Redbones,* has a marginally less negative tone, and is also more faithful in its premise to the poet's upbringing. That premise is a mythical place called Redbones; part church and part bar, it serves as a refuge of sorts. Describing her own early influences, Moss cited the "explosions on Sundays" in church, when the preacher "made [the congregation] shout, made them experience glory that perhaps was not actually there. . . . I wanted to make what the preacher called "text."" Her other strong influence, she said, was akin to a bar, though she describes it as more of a schoolroom: the family kitchen on Saturday nights, where her father would sip whiskey and speak "mostly on the dialectics of the soul, asking the forbidden questions, giving words power over any taboo."

Examines Difficult Topics

With the place called Redbones holding together the poems in her third book, Moss unites two salient influences from her childhood, but the effect is not necessarily—or even usually—comforting. Her images are of racism and brutality, a world in which the Ku Klux Klan is as ever-present as the laundry, and Christian faith offers no refuge: "Bottled Jesus is the / Clorox that whitens old sheets, makes the Klan / a brotherhood of saints." It is the world of sit-ins of the 1960s, when African Americans were denied service at the "whites-only" counters of Southern U.S. eating establishments, and sometimes beaten if they refused to give up their seats: "When knocked from the stool," she writes in "Lunchcounter Freedom," "my body takes its shape from what it falls into." This is a world rife with the old-fashioned racist imagery of Mammy in *Gone with the Wind,* of Buckwheat from *The Little Rascals* movies, of the Aunt Jemima logo on syrup bottles, her smiling face holding "Teeth white as the shock of lynching, thirty-two / tombstones," Moss writes.

Turning from race to religion, Moss describes a physical revulsion at the sacrament of Communion. In "Weighing the Sins of the World," receiving wine—Christ's symbolic blood—at the Eucharist, becomes a blood transfusion, and it turns out to be the wrong blood type, which is fatal. In "Fullness" she takes on, with similarly strong imagery, the literal substance (Christ's body) for which the bread of Communion is a symbol: "One day / the father will place shavings of his own blessed fingers / on your tongue and you will get back in line for / more. You will not find yourself out of line again. / The bread will rise inside you. A loaf of tongue."

Thylias Moss's 1991 collection of free-verse poems deals with race images, grandmothers, and history.

The pun on "out of line" in the preceding quote illustrates Moss's facility with language, one of the elements of her poetry that earned her critical praise for *At Redbones.* Sue Standing of *Boston Review,* for instance, wrote enthusiastically that "if *At Redbones* were a light bulb, it would be 300 watt; if it were whiskey, it would be 200 proof; if it were a mule, it would have an awfully big kick." Gloria T. Hull in *Belles Lettres,* also reviewing *At Redbones* along with several other works by female African-American poets (including Maya Angelou), commented that "Thylias Moss is the youngest of this group . . . and the one with whom I was most intrigued. She possesses absolutely stunning poetic skill. . . . [that] she unites with one of the bleakest, most sardonic visions I have ever encountered by an African-American woman writer." Marilyn Nelson Waniek in *Kenyon Review* was slightly more limited in her praise, but still found "a fine rage . . . at play in these pages."

With *Rainbow Remnants in Rock Bottom Ghetto Sky,* Moss continues to explore race images, and also looks at menstruation, grandmothers, and history. With this volume, however, critics were less effusive in their praise. *Choice* reviewer H. Jaskoski said that the poems offer "predictable sentiments in unexceptional free verse," and that Moss "brings up the topics young black female poets seem expected to interpret." Mark Jarman in *Hudson Review* referred to poet Charles Simic's praise of Moss as a "visionary storyteller" but added, "but she tells no stories." Jarman also assailed Moss's use of strained metaphor: though he confessed to admire the "ambition" of her poems, he wrote that she showed "a kind of complacence in assuming that putting one thing on one side of an equals sign and one on another is imagination." In some cases, critics have seemed unwilling to allow Moss sufficient freedom as a poet, as when Jarman criticized her use of a colloquialism: "This is the first poet I have encountered who . . . actually has used the word *hopefully* as it is currently employed, which is to say incorrectly."

Though *Rainbow Remnants in Rock Bottom Ghetto Sky* was met with some negative reviews, many other critics found much in the collection to praise. "Using intricately woven, well-crafted sentences, [Moss] writes accessible, sensual, feminist poems about pregnancy, bonding between women, and racial and ethnic identity," wrote Judy Clarence in *Library Journal.* Clarence added that "there's a sense of hopefulness, of the poet's and our individual ability to survive, even to rejoice, in a very imperfect world." A *Publishers Weekly* reviewer also praised the collection, declaring: "Moss refuses to accept things as they are. . . . [Her] writing expertly simulates the processes of her fecund mind, with thoughts overlapping and veering off on tangents that bring us back, with fuller knowledge, to a poem's central concern."

Prairie Schooner reviewer Tim Martin, who also praised *Rainbow Remnants in Rock Bottom Ghetto Sky,* commented that "readers who delight in originality of image, language, and the striking metaphor might be urged to read Moss. Several poems are tours de force of sheer description." Martin continued that the poet transforms everyday objects and chores into "startling new ways of seeing reality. . . . one gladly accepts as a good trade the occasional excess or lapse in exchange for the times she hits the mark and wakes us up with her use of language."

Small Congregations is a compilation drawn from the three preceding volumes and arranged into three sections. The collection's themes, according to Elizabeth Frost in *Women's Review of Books,* can be identified respectively as religious symbolism, the mythology of African-American life, and racist images. The familiar viewpoints on race and religion are combined in "The Adversary," wherein Moss expresses metaphorical sympathy for the devil as a sort of cosmic black man: "Poor Satan. His authority denied him / by a nose, a longer, pointier Caucasian nose. / Where's the gratitude for Satan who is there / for God no matter what; Satan / who is the original Uncle Tom." In her "Interpretation of a Poem by Frost," Moss both pays tribute to and parodies the poet Robert Frost's famous "Stopping by Woods on a Snowy Evening," which in her treatment becomes another instance of white racism: "A young black girl stopped by the woods, / so young she knew only one man: Jim Crow." But when Moss turns her vision away from God and whites, and inward toward the African-American home and hearth, the vision often becomes tender, as in "Remembering Kitchens": ". . .and I remove Mama's sweet potato pie, one made /—as are her best—in her sleep when she can't / interfere, when she's dreaming at the countertop / that turns silk beside her elegant leaning, I slice it / and put the whipped cream on quick, while the pie / is so hot the peaks of cream will froth; these / are the Sundays my family suckles grace."

With *I Want to Be,* a book for children illustrated by Jerry Pinkney, Moss took a new and refreshing direction. As a little African-American girl walks home, thinking about the question often asked by adults—"What do you want to be when you grow up?"—she finds in herself some intriguing answers: "I want to be quiet but not so quiet that nobody can hear me. I also want to be sound, a whole orchestra with two bassoons and an army of cellos. Sometimes I want to be just the triangle, a tinkle that sounds like an itch." Though reviewers worried that these metaphors might be a bit challenging for young readers, for adults they are much more comprehensible than those found in Moss's earlier work. The book, which suggests a different and fascinating side of Moss, found praise with critics. "The untrammeled exuberance of a free-spirited youngster, eager to explore everything, sings through a poetic story," wrote a critic for *Kirkus Reviews,* later calling the work "exhilarating, verbally and visually: the very essence of youthful energy and summertime freedom."

Moss continued her success as a poet with *Last Chance for the Tarzan Holler,* which reviewer Fred

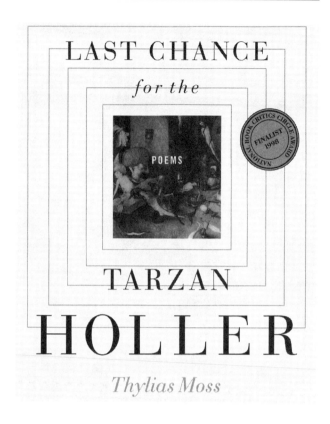

The poet received numerous accolades for her sixth collection of poetry, published in 1998.

Muratori, in *Library Journal,* called "a massive, acid-edged tribute to mortality in all of its contradictions and wrenching ironies." In this collection, which was nominated for the National Book Critics Circle Award and named a "Best Book of 1998" by the *Village Voice,* Moss seeks to "finish knowing herself / in time to begin to know something else," touching such topics as sexuality, religion, and motherhood. In his *Library Journal* review, Muratori called the work "loquacious and impassioned, precise and ragged, willing to risk even boredom in its drive to get at the heart of humanity's conflicted, necessary obsessions." A *Publishers Weekly* reviewer commented, "Moss meditates, starkly and unsentimentally, on death and motherhood, on God, and, beneath them all, on sex and power." Calling the collection's poems "unflinching" and "brilliant," reviewer Donna Seaman, in a piece for *Booklist,* called it "a book of extraordinary range."

A New Direction

Moss's second book to appear in 1998, *Tale of a Sky-Blue Dress,* marked a departure from her previous works. This book, a memoir of the author's child-

If you enjoy the works of Thylias Moss, you might want to check out the following books:

The poetry of Maya Angelou, including *The Complete Collected Poems of Maya Angelou*, 1994.
The poetry of Gwendolyn Brooks, including *Annie Allen*, 1949.
Toni Morrison, *Beloved*, 1987.
Jacqueline Woodson, *The Dear One*, 1991.

hood, recounts the physical, emotional, and sexual abuse Moss endured as a child at the hands of her babysitter, a teenage girl living in the same apartment building. The book opens with descriptions of a comfortable childhood, adoring parents, and domestic and familial rituals. The warmth of such scenes diminishes, however, when Moss's new babysitter introduces the child to humanity's dark side. The sitter, Lytta Dorsey, frequently wears a blue dress that is several sizes too small and displays an emotionally disturbed mind to her small charge. Moss, seeking to protect her loving parents from distress, endured the abuse for four years, and never told them of the tortures she was forced to submit to. She also relates in the book that she was "fascinated with the pull of darkness," according to a reviewer for *Booklist*. Moss writes that Lytta gave her "the gift of darkness" in her life, a life in which her parents had kept her wrapped in a blanket of wonder, protection, and comfort. According to *Detroit Free Press* writer Barbara Holliday, "she thinks perhaps the novelty of cruelty made it exciting." "Is it true," writes Moss in *Tale of a Sky-Blue Dress*, "that I would not be a writer, if not for Lytta?" adding however, "I am not ready to admit to her necessity in my life."

Eventually raped by her tormentor's brother with his sister's encouragement, Moss entered adolescence troubled by the abuses she had suffered. She was drawn into relationships with men that mimicked her abusive relationship with Lytta and undermined her self-esteem. Finally, at the age of sixteen, Moss met a young air force sergeant whose patient understanding and love helped her move beyond the pain of her childhood.

Tale of a Sky-Blue Dress received positive recognition from reviewers. A *Kirkus Reviews* critic called the book "an elegant, forthright exploration of the effects of evil on a fragile life" and "a stylish, well-

wrought memoir that forgoes self-pity for redemption." "This is a story that reads like poetry, even when the memories are the bleakest," declared *Tribune Books* writer Sharman Stein. *New York Times Book Review* critic Paula Friedman commented that "her analysis of her own surrender is impressive in its depth and unwillingness to settle for the simple role of victim."

■ Works Cited

Clarence, Judy, review of *Rainbow Remnants in Rock Bottom Ghetto Sky*, *Library Journal*, May 15, 1991, p. 86.

Friedman, Paula, review of *Tale of a Sky-Blue Dress*, *New York Times Book Review*, September 13, 1998, p. 26.

Frost, Elizabeth, review of *Small Congregations: New and Selected Poems*, *Women's Review of Books*, March, 1994, pp. 11-12.

Holliday, Barbara, "From Childhood Horror, a Writer Emerges," *Detroit Free Press*, 1998.

Hull, Gloria T., review of *At Redbones*, *Belles Lettres*, spring, 1991, p. 2.

Review of *I Want to Be*, *Kirkus Reviews*, August 1, 1993, p. 1006.

Jarman, Mark, review of *Rainbow Remnants in Rock Bottom Ghetto Sky*, *Hudson Review*, spring, 1992, pp. 163-64.

Jaskoski, H., review of *Rainbow Remnants in Rock Bottom Ghetto Sky*, *Choice*, February, 1992, p. 896.

Review of *Last Chance for the Tarzan Holler: Poems*, *Publishers Weekly*, February 23, 1998, p. 69.

Martin, Tim, review of *Rainbow Remnants in Rock Bottom Ghetto Sky*, *Prairie Schooner*, summer, 1994, p. 156.

Moss, Thylias, *I Want to Be*, Dial, 1993.

Muratori, Fred, review of *Last Chance for the Tarzan Holler: Poems*, *Library Journal*, February 15, 1998, p. 146.

Review of *Pyramid of Bone*, *Publishers Weekly*, January 20, 1989, p. 143.

Review of *Pyramid of Bone*, *Virginia Quarterly Review*, summer, 1989, p. 100.

Review of *Rainbow Remnants in Rock Bottom Ghetto Sky*, *Publishers Weekly*, April 15, 1991, p. 141.

Seaman, Donna, review of *Last Chance for the Tarzan Holler: Poems*, *Booklist*, February 15, 1998, p. 970.

Standing, Sue, review of *At Redbones*, *Boston Review*, February, 1991, p. 28.

Stein, Sharman, "For One Memorist, Self-pity, For Another, Self-Respect," *Tribune Books*, August 2, 1998, section 14, p. 11.

Review of *Tale of a Sky-Blue Dress, Booklist*, June 1, 1998, p. 1708.

Review of *Tale of a Sky-Blue Dress, Kirkus Reviews*, June 1, 1998, p. 799.

Waniek, Marilyn Nelson, review of *At Redbones*, *Kenyon Review*, fall, 1991, pp. 214-26.

■ For More Information See

BOOKS

Bloom, Harold, *The American Religion*, Simon & Schuster (New York City), 1992.

Contemporary Women Poets, St. James Press, 1998.

Dictionary of Literary Biography, Volume 120: *American Poets since World War II*, Gale, 1992, p. 220-22.

PERIODICALS

Booklist, October 1, 1993, pp. 353-54.

Georgia Review, winter, 1998, pp. 755-72.

Kirkus Reviews, March 15, 1998, p. 368.

Kliatt, July, 1995, p. 19.

Publishers Weekly, July 5, 1993, p. 7.

School Library Journal, September 1993, p. 216.

Melissa Scott

writer of the year; Lambda awards for Best Science Fiction/Fantasy Novel, Lambda Book Report, 1994, for *Trouble and Her Friends*, and 1995, for *Shadow Man*.

■ Personal

Born August 7, 1960, in Little Rock, AR; partner of Lisa A. Barnett (a writer) since 1979. *Education:* Harvard/Radcliffe College, B.A. (magna cum laude), 1981; Brandeis University, Ph.D., 1992.

■ Addresses

Agent—Richard Curtis, Richard Curtis Agency, 171 East 74th St., New York, NY 10021.

■ Career

Writer. Has worked as an usher, teller, answering service operator, teaching assistant, stock person, secretary, and receptionist. Founder and contributing editor of *Wavelengths*, a review of science fiction of interest to a gay/lesbian/bisexual readership.

■ Awards, Honors

John W. Campbell Memorial Award, World Science Fiction Society, 1986, for the best new science fiction

■ Writings

NOVELS

The Game Beyond, Baen (New York City), 1984.
Five-Twelfths of Heaven (part of the "Silence Leigh" trilogy), Baen, 1985.
A Choice of Destinies, Baen, 1986.
Silence in Solitude (part of the "Silence Leigh" trilogy), Baen, 1986.
The Empress of Earth (part of the "Silence Leigh" trilogy), Baen, 1987.
The Kindly Ones, Baen, 1987.
(With Lisa A. Barnett) *The Armor of Light*, Baen, 1988.
The Roads of Heaven (the "Silence Leigh" trilogy; contains *Five-Twelfths of Heaven, Silence in Solitude,* and *The Empress of Earth*), Doubleday, 1988.
Mighty Good Road, Baen, 1990.
Dreamships, Tor, 1992.
Burning Bright, Tor, 1993.
Trouble and Her Friends, Tor, 1994.
(With Barnett) *Point of Hopes*, Tor, 1995.
Proud Helios (part of the "Star Trek: Deep Space Nine" series), Pocket Books, 1995.
Shadow Man, Tor, 1995.
Night Sky Mine, Tor, 1996.
Dreaming Metal, Tor, 1997.
The Shapes of Their Hearts, Tor, 1998.
The Jazz, Tor, 2000.
(With Barnett) *Point of Dreams*, Tor, in press.

OTHER

Conceiving the Heavens: Creating the Science-Fiction Novel (nonfiction), Heinemann (Portsmouth, NH), 1997.

■ Sidelights

Melissa Scott writes science fiction and fantasy that is informed by her educational background in history and by her identity as a lesbian. She uses her stories to contemplate such issues as the impact of technology on society, the role of gender in the formation of identity, and the consequences of creating boundaries among societies with different ideologies. Reviewers have consistently praised Scott's ability to create comprehensive, believable worlds.

After her initial foray into the genre with *The Game Beyond,* in which people compete in a gaming tournament to decide who will rule a planetary community, Scott wrote *Five-Twelfths of Heaven.* The story became the first in a trilogy featuring spaceship pilot Silence Leigh, a woman who struggles against the male-dominated society of which she is a part. In the first story, financial hardship causes her to lose ownership of a spaceship left to her by her grandfather. Denis Balthasar, her guardian on her home planet, asks her to be a pilot on a voyage to Earth in his craft Sun-Treader. The novel focuses on the relationships among Leigh, Balthasar, and spaceship engineer Chase Mago as they try to reach their destination.

Silence in Solitude, the second book of the trilogy, focuses on Leigh's struggle to facilitate communication between the Earth and the rest of the interstellar community in order to prove herself as a pilot. *The Empress of Earth* concludes the trilogy as Silence and two husbands endeavor to save the Earth from rule by the villainous Rose Worlders. The novel details an entire technology inspired by the sciences of the Middle Ages and the beliefs of Aristotle. When Silence displays her magical abilities, the people of Earth regard her as a savior. Complimenting the use of the invented science, Don Sakers noted in the *Wilson Library Bulletin,* "The mystical technology is so well conceived and exhaustively thought-out that by the end one finds oneself convinced that it is real."

In 1987's *The Kindly Ones* Scott depicts lunar communities on the moons Orestes and Electra. In the novel, survivors of a space disaster form a society in which the inhabitants are expected to follow a code of honor. People who disobey are relegated to the community of "ghosts" and are forbidden to speak

to the "living." The plot revolves around the development of the Necropolis, a den of hedonism formed by the outcasts; on attempts by the living and the ghosts to communicate through Trey Maturin, a medium with the ability to convey messages between the two groups; and on the weakening of the society when the rulers of the communities begin to quarrel.

Novels Rework History

In 1988, Scott collaborated with partner Lisa A. Barnett on *The Armor of Light,* which is set in England in the 1590s. *The Armor of Light* was not the first of Scott's novels to benefit from her background in history. *A Choice of Destinies,* published in 1986, reveals

When a number of children disappear from a summer street fair, Nick Rathe is called upon to solve the mystery in this 1995 novel set during the Middle Ages.

how history could have been altered if Alexander the Great had chosen to conquer the Roman Empire instead of India. In *The Armor of Light*, Scott and Barnett employ such historical figures as playwright Christopher Marlowe and explorer Sir Walter Raleigh as they tell the story of England at a critical time in its history. In the novel, a royal astronomer predicts the ruin of England unless King James of Scotland inherits the throne. Sir Philip Sidney is dispatched by Queen Elizabeth to ensure that evil forces do not preclude James from ruling England. Don Sakers in *Wilson Library Bulletin* called *The Armor of Light* "a beautifully written, artfully crafted fantasy."

In *Mighty Good Road*, Scott develops a planetary system connected by a transportation system that allows for rapid travel from one station stop to another. The novel focuses on a mission to salvage some important cargo from an airwreck over one of the planets. When the leader of the effort to retrieve the equipment begins to ponder the circumstances of the crash, the company that commissioned the rescue mission turns against the contractors.

Dreamships, published in 1992, also focuses on a rescue mission. In this novel, pilot Reverdy Jian and partner Imre Vaughn are charged with the task of tracking down their employer's brother. They are guided by Manfred, an on-board set of systems nearly capable of displaying artificial intelligence. The programmed overseer, in fact, is so able to approximate humanity that it raises the possibility of whether it deserves rights to the same degree that humans do. Although Tom Easton of *Analog* felt that Scott occasionally provided too many details of the subterranean community from which the protagonists hail, he called *Dreamships* "thoughtful and ingenious."

Creating Fantastic Worlds

Burning Bright features Quinn Lioe, a pilot who lands on a planet where virtual-reality gaming is a serious preoccupation of the inhabitants and visitors. When Quinn involves herself in directing the Game with her own imagined scenarios, she alters the political climate of the Burning Bright community by making participants of people involved in power struggles outside of the gaming environment. As the novel progresses, Lioe threatens the fabric of Burning Bright by daring to construct a scenario that will conclude the Game. In *Voice of Youth Advocates*, Katharine L. "Kat" Kan encouraged young adult readers to make an effort to read the novel, stating that "readers will have to pay close attention to what they read, but they will be reward-

"William Gibson meets Samuel R. Delany! Melissa Scott's *Night Sky Mine* is her best book yet, with first-rate world-building and first-rate storytelling."

— Robert J. Sawyer

Ista Kelly, an orphan and the only survivor of a pirate raid on an asteroid, searches for her true identity in Scott's futuristic novel.

ed with a highly satisfying adventure with lots to think about after."

In *Trouble and Her Friends* lesbian lovers Cerise and Trouble are expert computer hackers who use their abilities to steal corporate secrets and sell them. Both Cerise and Trouble are equipped with the "brainworm," a technological enhancement that allows them to receive sensations when connected to computer networks. When Congress threatens to put a stop to the use of the brainworm, Trouble ends her life as a criminal. But she is pulled back into the criminal underworld when another hacker begins using "Trouble" as an alias. Because the new Trouble has invaded the company for which Cerise now works, both of the stable lives that the former hackers have created for themselves are threatened. The two join forces to undermine the scheme of the imposter.

Scott collaborated again with Barnett on *Point of Hopes,* a novel that is set in a fantastic city at the time of an annual celebration. The inhabitants of the city are anticipating a major astronomical event that will mark the ascendancy of a new monarch to the throne. Coincidentally, the children of the city are vanishing. The protagonist, Nico Rathe, is called upon to solve the mystery.

After writing *Proud Helios,* a novel for the "Star Trek: Deep Six Nine" series, Scott explored issues concerning gender in science fiction with *Shadow Man.* In the novel, Scott develops a galaxy that identifies five distinct genders. The use of drugs to ease the effects of faster-than-light travel has contributed to the development of the new genders. A planet in the system whose inhabitants are conservative and self-righteous, has outlawed all but two genders—male and female. When Warreven Stiller is identified as androgynous, however, the ideologies held by the people of the planet are threatened.

In *Night Sky Mine,* published in 1996, galactic police are called upon to investigate the mysterious abandonment of an asteroid owned by the Night Sky Mine company. Central to the plot are the contributions of an orphan found in a separate mining shaft years before the incident under investigation. Scott's fictional universe is also populated with computer-programs that compete with one another, reproduce, and mutate, just like organisms.

Scott returned to cyber-thrillers with a 2000 novel titled *The Jazz.* The work concerns street-smart hacker Tin Lizzy, whose first love is the "jazz," a new Internet art form that involves the manipulation of information. Lizzy teams with Keyz, a teenage hacker who has stolen an experimental "jazz" program from Gardner Garretty, a media mogul who will kill to retrieve the information. Gerald Jonas, writing in the *New York Times Book Review,* stated that the novel deals with a serious theme: "In a world awash in information of dubious provenance, whom can you trust to tell you the truth?" A *Publishers Weekly* critic praised Scott's work, concluding that the author "maintains her position . . . as one of the best writers around in portraying what life online may really be like in the future."

Throughout her career Scott has featured strong female protagonists in stories that explore—among other issues—situations brought about by the introduction of technology to communities. Her stories have earned recognition for the attention that Scott pays to developing intricate and believable universes. In addition to earning the praise of reviewers,

Scott dabbles with artificial intelligence in this critically acclaimed science fiction novel, published in 1997.

Scott has proven herself a favorite to readers; in 1986, she received a John W. Campbell Award, which is a reader's choice award given to the best new science fiction writer of the year.

Imagining "Plausible Change"

Scott commented: "I have always been most interested in the intersection of technology and society—of the hard and soft sciences—and I think that is reflected in my science fiction. I am fascinated by technology and its developments—and I enjoy the challenge of playing by the rules of the genre, getting the science as "right" as possible—but I'm more interested in the effects of that technology on characters and imagined societies than in the development of some new machine or program. In other words, I tend to set my novels fifty years after a great breakthrough, and consider its aftereffects, rather than write the story of the discovery itself. My academic training (as a historian specializing in early modern Europe) meant that I was exposed to the work of social and cultural historians, from Michel Foucault to Natalie Zemon-Davis and Simon Schama, and the tools I learned for analyzing past cultures have proved invaluable for creating future ones. (In fact, my dissertation ended up being oddly similar to my science fiction, in that it was concerned with the effects of a technological change—the development of gunpowder weapons—and the unintended consequences of the model created to make use of it.)

"Of course, since I'm a novelist rather than a futurist, all of this has to be expressed through plot and character. It's very hard to talk about the creative process without making it sound either stilted ('this developed from my interest in . . .') or mystical ('this character/place appeared . . .'), especially when both statements are always at least partially true. I tend to spend a great deal of time on the settings of my novels, cultural and social as well as physical, and to let both the plot and the characters grow organically from that process. I find that as I work out the details, particularly the ways that technology influences or upsets social norms (and vice versa), the inevitable contradictions that emerge are the most fruitful sources for the characters and their stories. I enjoy the complexity and messiness of the real world, and believe that one of the real challenges of any fiction is to model that complexity without losing sight of the structure that makes a good novel.

"It's also fairly obvious that I'm one of the few lesbians writing about queer characters whose science fiction is published by the so-called mainstream science fiction houses. I began writing about queer women first out of the usual impulse: I wanted to read about people who were "like me," and almost no one else was doing it. As I've gotten older, however, I've begun to realize that behind that superficially naive statement is something actually quite useful. Even in science fiction, there is a limited budget for novelty, both for the writer and for the reader; if one is creating something new in one part of the novel, other parts must of necessity be drawn from that which is familiar. In most of my novels, the technological and social changes are the new things, and, as a result, I draw on the people and culture in which I live to make up the balance. It's that culture, my own culture, people like me, that provides the emotional background of my novels. Certainly my fascination with masks, identity, and roles, comes from

"This is the stuff of which sense of wonder is made"—*Locus*

MELISSA SCOTT
DREAMSHIPS

"Intellectually neat, emotionally satisfying."
—*The New York Times*

A wealthy businesswoman hires a space pilot to find her brother who may have created the first artificial intelligence.

living in a culture that is deeply concerned, seriously and in play, with just these issues.

"I was drawn to science fiction largely because of the radical (in a nonpolitical sense) nature of the genre: here is a form of writing that starts from the premise that change is inevitable. Good or bad, it will happen, and the writer's job is to imagine plausible change and depict its possible consequences for people and their worlds. I've been lucky in being able to blend my own various interests into stories that catch readers' imaginations. Because, of course, science fiction, like any other fiction, is ultimately about the story, about the communication between writer and reader, the moment in which the reader is, fully, deeply, and willingly, part of the writer's world.

If you enjoy the works of Melissa Scott, you might want to check out the following books:

Octavia E. Butler, *Imago*, 1989.
Orson Scott Card, *Xenocide*, 1991.
C. J. Cherryh, *Serpent's Reach*, 1980.
Dan Simmons, *Hyperion*, 1989.
Joan D. Vinge, *Psion*, 1982.

Without the story, characters, plot, and setting, the writer has no right to ask for that participation; with it, the writer can take the reader into worlds s/he would never otherwise have considered."

■ Works Cited

Easton, Tom, review of *Dreamships*, *Analog*, October, 1992, pp. 164-65.

Review of *Jazz*, *Publishers Weekly*, May 15, 2000, p. 93.

Jonas, Gerald, review of *Jazz*, *New York Times Book Review*, June 18, 2000, p. 22.

Kan, Katharine L., review of *Burning Bright*, *Voice of Youth Advocates*, October, 1993, p. 234.

Sakers, Don, review of *The Empress of Earth*, *Wilson Library Bulletin*, May, 1988, pp. 86-87.

Sakers, Don, review of *The Armor of Light*, *Wilson Library Bulletin*, February, 1989, p. 94.

■ For More Information See

PERIODICALS

Analog Science Fiction and Fact, October, 1993, pp. 162-63.

Booklist, June 1, 1985, pp. 1373-74; October 15, 1986, p. 327; November 1, 1987, p. 437; September 1, 1987, p. 31; October 15, 1988, p. 368; November 1, 1995, p. 458; June 1, 1995, p. 1737; May 15, 1998, p. 1607.

Kirkus Reviews, May 1, 1992, p. 577; March 1, 1993, p. 266; March 15, 1994, p. 350; October 1, 1995, pp. 1387-88; June 15, 1996, p. 865; May 15, 1998, p. 701.

Library Journal, March 15, 1985, pp. 74-75; October 15, 1995, p. 91; June 15, 1995, pp. 97-98; August, 1996, p. 119; June 15, 1998, p. 111.

Publishers Weekly, May 9, 1986, p. 250; July 31, 1987, p. 73; May 4, 1992, p. 45; April 4, 1994, p. 61; June 26, 1995, p. 91; July 22, 1996, p. 230; April 27, 1998, p. 50.

Voice of Youth Advocates, June, 1985, p. 140; October, 1985, pp. 269-70; April, 1988, p. 42; April, 1989, p. 46; December, 1990, p. 302.

Wilson Library Bulletin, November, 1994, p. 103.

Kevin Smith

Personal

Born August 2, 1970, in Highlands, NJ; son of Donald (a postal employee) and Grace Smith; married Jennifer Schwalbach (a journalist), 1999; children: Harley Quinn (daughter). *Education:* Attended Vancouver Film School.

Addresses

Home—c/o 69 Monmouth St., Red Bank, NJ 07701. *Office*—View Askew Productions.

Career

Screenwriter, producer, editor, and director. Founder of View Askew, a production company, in New Jersey. Director of films, including *Clerks*, View Askew/Miramax, 1994, *Mallrats*, View Askew/Universal, 1995, *Chasing Amy*, View Askew, 1997, and *Dogma*, View Askew, 1999. Producer of films, including *Clerks*, 1994, *Mallrats*, 1995, *Good Will Hunting* (co-executive), 1997, *Chasing Amy*, 1997, *A Better Place*, 1997, *Big Helium Dog*, 1999, and *Dogma*, 1999. Editor of films, including *Mae Day: The Crum-*

bling of a Documentary, 1992, *Clerks*, 1994, *Chasing Amy*, 1997, and *Dogma*, 1999. Smith has also acted or appeared in the television series of *Clerks*, produced in 2000, and in *Independent's Day*, *Vulgar*, *Drawing Flies*, and *Mae Day: The Crumbling of a Documentary*. Owner of comic book store, Jay and Silent Bob's Secret Stash, in Red Bank, NJ. Worked variously as clerk in convenience store and in a deli, and also held a job at a community center.

Awards, Honors

Filmmakers Trophy, Sundance Film Festival, and Young Cinema Award, Cannes Film Festival, both 1994, both for *Clerks*; Independent Spirit Award, 1997, best screenplay, for *Chasing Amy*.

Writings

SCREENPLAYS

(And producer, editor, and director) *Clerks*, View Askew/Miramax, 1994.
(And producer and director) *Mallrats*, View Askew/Universal, 1995.
Overnight Delivery (uncredited), MPCA, 1996.
(And producer, editor, and director) *Chasing Amy*, View Askew, 1997.
(And producer, editor, and director) *Dogma*, View Askew, 1999.

Also wrote the script treatment for *Superman Lives*, author of screenplay for *Mae Day: The Crumbling of a Documentary*, 1992.

OTHER

(With John Pierson) *Spike, Mike, Slackers and Dykes: A Guided Tour across a Decade of American Independent Cinema*, Hyperion (New York City), 1996.

Clerks and Chasing Amy: Two Screenplays, Talk Miramax, 1997.

Dogma: A Screenplay, Grove Press, 1999.

Jay and Silent Bob: Chasing Dogma, introduction by Alanis Morrisette, illustrated by Duncan Fregredo, Oni Press, 1999.

Marvel's Finest: Daredevil Visionaries, Marvel Books, 1999.

Clerks: The Comic Books, illustrated by Jim Mahfoud and Ande Parks, Oni Press, 2000.

■ Sidelights

Writer-director Kevin Smith is "an original," according to Richard Schickel writing in *Time* magazine, "a deadpan, dead-on observer of the whole Generation X mess." With four movies to his credit he has blended profanity and raunchy humor in his witty scripts to tell tales of a couple of convenience store philosophers in *Clerks*, to show scenes from a mall in the disastrous *Mallrats*, to portray an improbable romance between a comic book creator and a lesbian in *Chasing Amy*, and to poke fun at organized religion in the controversial *Dogma*. Smith is a chronicler of America's urban twenty-somethings, an irreverent and pudgy teller of tall tales from the point of view of dazed and confused young adults. More dialogue-than plot-driven, Smith's films are mainly hermetic time capsules of life in late twentieth-century America as witnessed and lived by Generation X slackers. As Stephan Talty noted in a *Playboy* profile of the filmmaker, Smith "became one of the godfathers of Nineties indie film and helped shape its priorities: low budgets, sharp wit, personal revelation."

Smith was born on August 2, 1970, the youngest of three children, to Donald and Grace Smith, in Highlands, New Jersey. Brought up Catholic, Smith was an altar boy for much of his youth and attended religious schools. But religion was not the only influence on his youth; Smith was an inveterate fan of comic books—especially Batman—and of the *Star Wars* movies. "What other young men found in Dostoyevsky or Burroughs, Smith found in the story of Bruce Wayne," Talty reported. Smith told *Playboy* that for him Batman is "just flat-out literature with pictures. It deals thematically with literary terms and devices and characters that are so exciting. I

had no edge as far as culture goes until I got into dark, literary comics."

Uses Humor as an Outlet

Being a mediocre student and overweight as an adolescent, Smith became more of an observer than a doer. He also found humor—especially self-deprecating humor—a great protector. He was the kid who videotaped the school games; he put on schools skits with a *Saturday Night Live* edge. His father, who grew to hate his job at the post office, proved a negative role model for his son. "Early on," Talty noted, "[Smith] vowed never to work at something he didn't enjoy."

But once out of high school, it seemed that was exactly the sort of life awaiting Smith. He did not go on to college, but took a series of menial jobs, ultimately working several years as a clerk in a convenience store selling lottery tickets, junk food, and the perfect dozen eggs to finicky shoppers. He tried a writing program at the New School for Social Research in New York, but dropped out. Then, on his twenty-first birthday, he had something of a revelation. Attending a screening of *Slackers* by the Austin-based filmmaker, Richard Linklater, he "came away a changed man," according to Talty. "That was the first movie I saw that was set in the director's hometown," Smith recalled to Talty in *Playboy*. He began to think that if Linklater could do that for Austin, then he could do the same for his New Jersey hometown.

Attending the Vancouver Film School in British Columbia, Smith met Scott Mosier, with whom he has continued to work. While at school, the two would-be filmmakers began shooting a short documentary about a transsexual, but the project fell apart when their subject disappeared. They turned the project then into a discussion of *why* their film had failed, *Mae Day: The Crumbling of a Documentary*. But with less than four months under his belt at film school, Smith dropped out and returned to New Jersey where he started working again as a convenience store clerk.

Clerks

Smith worked for another year as a clerk, but all the while he was putting together a script for a movie he planned to shoot at the store. He was taking Linklater's lesson to heart: not only would he shoot on location in his town, but also in the very store where he had been working. His friend Mosier graduated

Smith wrote and directed the 1994 film, *Clerks*, on the incredibly low budget of $27,575.

from film school and came to New Jersey to help him with the film, which began shooting in early 1993. The owner of the store and of the video shop next door allowed Smith and his crew of amateur actors to shoot at night; Smith financed the shooting by taking his credit cards to the maximum, and finally even sold off his prized comic book collection to gather the $27,000 necessary for filming.

Clerks tells the story of Dante Hicks who works at a convenience store and whose life is made more difficult by a troublesome girlfriend, annoying customers, and a cast of goofy, and very profane, friends. His buddy Randal works at the neighboring video shop. Where Dante is wishy-washy and allows himself to by pushed around by his boss and customers, Randal takes every opportunity to do as little as possible and be as unaccommodating as he can to the clientele. The plot line comes from a romantic crisis: Dante's girlfriend reveals a sexual history that shakes the couple's relationship. He must now determine whether to stay with her or go back with an old girlfriend. But plot is used loosely here: the story unfolds through realistic and humorous conversations between Dante and friends who rejoice in bad language. "I like to write stuff that you don't usually see on the screen," Smith told Benjamin Svetkey in an interview for *Entertainment Weekly.* "The conversations you have with your friends—the frank sexual discussions— you never see that." The movie is a paean to working-class life, a story that draws very much from Smith's own experiences behind the counter at the Quick Stop.

An initial New York screening was attended by a small audience, among whom was a reviewer for the *Village Voice* who gave *Clerks* a good notice. Also, a scout for Robert Redford's Sundance Film Festival saw this screening, and promoted the movie for that film festival. In the event *Clerks* made a splash at Sundance, winning an award, and was purchased by Miramax co-chairman Harvey Weinstein for distribution. Shown at Cannes, *Clerks* won two more awards. Weinstein had made a wise purchase: this low-budget movie made $2.8 million dollars for the studio, and established Smith as a promising new filmmaker.

Ben Affleck and Joey Lauren Adams star in Smith's 1997 romantic comedy *Chasing Amy.*

Not only the viewing public, but also reviewers, found much to like in Smith's debut writing-directing credit. "*Clerks* looks as if it were recorded by a security camera," wrote Chris Smith in *New York Magazine.* "But like punk rock in the seventies, *Clerks* is crude, amateurish, and a totally welcome blast of stale air, compared with the warm and fuzzy *Forrest Gump* and the suffocatingly tidy *Quiz Show.* And beneath the cursing and the dirty jokes, Smith intends Dante and Randal to be strip-mall existentialists, debating the nature of free will. Grunge *Godot.*" Smith's dialogue, in fact, almost earned the movie an NC-17 rating, despite the fact that there is no nudity or violence in the film. Finally an R was bestowed upon it instead. Smith told Svetkey, "Actually, if you scrape away the [raunchy] jokes, the cynicism, the vulgar language, you're left with really sweet movies about guys who just want to fall in love."

Reviewing the film in *People Weekly,* Tom Gliatto noted, "Smith has a knack for unexpected, mildly grotesque jokes, and the movie's extraordinarily explicit dialogue is often funny and authentic-sounding." However, Gliatto went to comment that just as often, the dialogue has the "annoyingly snug rhythm of sitcom writing." A *Rolling Stone* reviewer called Smith "an astute social chronicler," and observed that "in the course of this day in the life of two clerks, Smith nails the obsessive verbal wrangling of smart, stalled twentysomethings who can't figure out how to get their ideas into motion. . .. *Clerks* supplies its own subversively witty take on Generation Next." And reviewing this movie in *Newsweek,* David Ansen wrote, "Smith's chatty, affectionate salute to brainy guys in brainless jobs exhibits a deadpan mastery of verbal comedy timing any veteran director might envy." Ansen further noted that Smith has "a fine ear for his characters' needling small talk, lovers' snits, smutty harangues and whiny obsessions."

From Peaks to Pits and Back Again

Smith had arrived. All the fanfare with *Clerks* made him a golden boy at the Hollywood studios, ever on the lookout for a spokesperson for the new generation of movie goers. These same studio heads threw millions of dollars his way for his next production, a tip of the hat to filmmakers such as John Hughes and John Landis titled *Mallrats.* But titles alone would not help Smith out with this movie about two slacker types, Brodie and T.S., and their day at the mall and attempts to win back their girlfriends on a game show. Along the way, they encounter Jay and Silent Bob (the latter played by Smith), a duo that winds its way through all of Smith's movies. "For all its shambly, incidental pleasures," wrote Richard Corliss in a *Time* magazine review, "*Mallrats* gives on the impression that as Smith ages, he isn't going to get better—just more so—and that he will find it easy to crank out low-rent, easy-on-the-ears comedies."

These were among the kindest words *Mallrats* received from the critics. More typical of the pasting it took were the comments of Michael Wilmington, writing in the *Chicago Tribune.* "*Mallrats* serves up horrendous lead acting," Wilmington commented, "murky cinematography, bland atmosphere, unengaging romance, mug-crazy cameo performances, bash-on-the-head satire, and ill-timed slapstick gags that look like outtakes from a 'Bozo the clown' show gone berserk." Worse yet, the movie was a box office failure, grossing less than his first feature. A much chastened Smith even apologized publicly at the next year's Sundance Festival for this bomb of a movie.

But Smith was not put off film-making by the experience. He developed his third feature on a tight budget of around two-hundred-and-fifty-thousand dollars and told a story with more emotional charge to it. *Chasing Amy* is a romantic comedy about the

Shannon Doherty stars in Smith's *Mallrats*, a 1995 film about two slackers and their day at the mall.

adventures of Holden, played by Ben Affleck, a creator of comic books, who falls for Alyssa, a lesbian artist, played by Smith's then girlfriend, Joey Lauren Adams. "Holden was definitely the character closest to myself I'd ever written," Smith told Talty in his *Playboy* interview. Talty called *Chasing Amy* "one of the most emotionally challenging movies of the year." A reviewer for *Rolling Stone* felt the movie was a "rude blast of gleeful provocation, a farce about emotional pain, a drama about sexual slapstick." Writing in *Harper's Bazaar*, Richard Rayner felt that *Chasing Amy* "is long, and it occasionally comes off as self-conscious and even self-indulgent." Rayner concluded, however, that in the end "you're won over by the extent to which Smith enjoys his characters and gives them space to breathe." Terry Teachout, writing in the *New York Times*, also had praise for *Chasing Amy*, noting that it is "less a sex comedy than a parable of grace and redemption." Schickel summed up the movie in *Time* as a "sad and fiercely told story" and "a brutally honest romance." *Entertainment Weekly*'s Mike D'Angelo found the movie "dramatically audacious," but he also found it "cine-

matically inept." "Smith has now made three films without yet demonstrating that he has the slightest idea of how to wield a movie camera," D'Angelo added. With his next film, Smith vowed to lay that criticism to rest.

Dogma Stirred Controversy

Smith's next film, *Dogma*, filmed in almost surreal color, caused a miniature scandal even while in production. To poke some fun at the trappings of the Catholic church, Smith tells the story of a pair of fallen angels who plan to make it back into heaven and thus negate all of existence. Learning of this, a team of heavenly superheroes come together to try to stop the two ex-angels. The film was big budget and featured big-name stars Matt Damon and Affleck as the fallen angels, Loki and Bartleby, Chris Rock as the thirteenth apostle, left out of the Bible because he was black, and the rock singer Alanis Morissette, as a female version of God. The pressure was on early in production from groups such as the Catholic League for Disney Films and its subsidiary

Smith (center) poses with (l to r) Ben Affleck, Jason Lee, Salma Hayek, and Alanis Morissette—some of the cast from the director's 1999 film *Dogma*.

Miramax to drop production. The movie was ultimately released through Lions Gate, which distanced it from Disney. Smith told Michael Atkinson in *Interview* magazine that this movie "was my own celebration of faith." "There's a lot of gray in the movie," Smith went on. ""I'm proud of the fact that the film's not very Good-versus-Evil." Also writing in the introduction to the published screenplay, Smith commented, "I'm usually an annoyingly modest or self-deprecating person, but I have to admit that I exempt *Dogma* from the usual self-derision I afford my other flicks, comics, etc. A lot of thought went into crafting it, a lot of heart, a lot of wit, and lot of myself. And because of that, I feel it's my finest hour professionally."

While it was a box-office hit, the movie received mixed reviews. Leah Rozen, reviewing *Dogma* in *People Weekly*, felt that the movie was the "gleeful—though self-indulgent and sometimes scatological—result of Smith's putting his faith to the test." Rozen concluded the movie was "[w]orth seeing, just maybe not on Sunday." *Newsweek*'s Jeff Giles also

had mixed opinions about *Dogma*, noting that "ultimately [it] makes pedestrian points. Faith is good. The rigidity of the church is bad, etc." But Giles also went on to comment, "For some reason, though, you never stop rooting for *Dogma*." Writing in *Entertainment Weekly*, Owen Gleiberman called the movie "a wild and intricate theological debate, a Sunday-school catechism session turned into a snap-crackle-and-pop thrill sermon for the mind." Gleiberman further observed, "[Smith] turns adolescent naughtiness into a style, a worldview, and *Dogma*, in its very form, is a manic act of transubstantiation." "It is not every day," concluded Gleiberman, "you get to see a movie that begins in satire, and ends in reverence, but then for Kevin Smith, they may ultimately be the same thing." And writing in *Time* magazine, Jeffrey Ressner felt that Smith raised "profound issues in a pop context" with *Dogma*, "bringing God to the mallrats, making a good movie."

The praise was sweet for Smith, but sweeter still was the serendipity of personal events. His first daughter, whom he named Harley Quinn (after the

If you enjoy the works of Kevin Smith, you might want to check out the following films:

Monty Python's Life of Brian, featuring the Monty Python comic troupe, 1979.
Slacker, written and directed by Richard Linklater, 1991.
The Truth about Cats and Dogs, starring Janeane Garofolo, 1996.

character in *Batman: The Animated Series*), was born on the weekend when *Dogma* opened. Noting that he was planning to bring her up Catholic, Smith told *Time* that he was planning to take a year off from filmmaking to help raise his child—to "do something noble," he said.

■ Works Cited

Ansen, David, review of *Clerks, Newsweek,* October 21, 1994, p. 68.
Atkinson, Michael, "Kevin Smith Stirs It Up," *Interview,* October, 1999, p. 180.
Review of *Chasing Amy, Rolling Stone,* April 17, 1997, p. 86.
Review of *Clerks, Rolling Stone,* November 3, 1994, p. 104.
Corliss, Richard, "Elegies for Degeneration X," *Time,* November 6, 1995, pp. 77-79.
D'Angelo, Mike, "Say Everything," *Entertainment Weekly,* November 38, 1997, pp. 86-87.
Giles, Jeff, "Knocking on Heaven's Door," *Newsweek,* November 15, 1999, p. 88.
Gliatto, Tom, review of *Clerks, People Weekly,* November 7, 1994, p. 28.
Gleiberman, Owen, "Loose Canon," *Entertainment Weekly,* November 12, 1999, pp. 47-48, 50.
Rayner, Richard, "Gotta Dance," *Harper's Bazaar,* May, 1997, p. 108.
Ressner, Jeffrey, "Can God Take a Joke?," *Time,* November 15, 1999, p. 103.
Rozen, Leah, "Screen," *People Weekly,* November 22, 1999, p. 39.
Schickel, Richard, "Young and Restless," *Time,* April 7, 1997, p. 76.
Smith, Chris, "Register Dog," *New York Magazine,* October 24, 1994, pp. 51-53.
Smith, Kevin, "Introduction," *Dogma: A Screenplay,* Grove Press, 1999.
Svetkey, Benjamin, "Getting the Girl," *Entertainment Weekly,* April 11, 1997, p. 25.
Talty, Stephan, "The Clerk, the Girl and the Hand Job," *Playboy,* December 1, 1998, p. 150.
Teachout, Terry, review of *Chasing Amy, New York Times,* May 25, 1997.
Wilmington, Michael, review of *Mallrats, Chicago Tribune,* October 20, 1995.

■ For More Information See

BOOKS

Pierson, John, and Kevin Smith, *Spike, Mike, Slackers and Dykes: A Guided Tour across a Decade of American Independent Cinema,* Hyperion (New York City), 1996.

PERIODICALS

America, December 4, 1999, p. 20.
American Spectator, April, 1997, p. 68.
Commonweal, December 17, 1999, p. 17.
Cosmopolitan, November, 1994, p. 24.
Entertainment Weekly, November 18, 1994, p. 79; May 19, 1995, pp. 68-71; June 23, 1995, pp. 26-29; September 29, 1995, p. 72; November 3, 1995, pp. 44-46; April 4, 1997, p. 64; November 26, 1999, p. 37.
Esquire, March, 2000, p. 217.
Film Comment, May-June, 1994, pp. 9-10.
Interview, June, 1994, p. 41; April, 1997, pp. 42-44.
Library Journal, December, 1995, p. 112.
Maclean's, November 15, 1999, pp. 16-17.
National Review, May 19, 1997, pp. 56-57.
New Republic, May 5, 1997, p. 24.
Newsweek, April 7, 1997, p. 73.
New Yorker, April 7, 1997, p. 97.
New York Times, August 1, 1999, p. AR7; September 17, 1999, p. B14; October 4, 1999, p. E1; November 12, 1999, p. B20.
New York Times Book Review, February 4, 1996, p. 8.
Playboy, June, 1997, p. 17.
Saturday Night, September, 1996, p. 110.
USA Today, March 30, 1998, p. 2D.
Variety, January 31, 1994, p. 4; October 16, 1995, p. 94; February 3, 1997, p. 46.
Wall Street Journal, November 12, 1999, p. W1.*

—Sketch by J. Sydney Jones

Gary Soto

■ Personal

Born April 12, 1952, in Fresno, CA; son of Manuel and Angie (Trevino) Soto; married Carolyn Sadako Oda, May 24, 1975; children: Mariko Heidi. *Education:* California State University, Fresno, B.A., 1974; University of California, Irvine, M.F.A., 1976. *Hobbies and other interests:* Travel.

■ Addresses

Home—43 The Crescent, Berkeley, CA 94708.

■ Career

University of California, Berkeley, assistant professor 1979-85; associate professor of English and ethnic studies, 1985-92, part-time senior lecturer in English department, 1992-93; University of Cincinnati, Elliston Poet, 1988; Wayne State University, Martin Luther King/Cesar Chavez/Rosa Parks Visiting Professor of English, 1990; Distinguished Professor, University of California at Riverside; full-time writer, 1993—.

■ Member

Royal Chicano Navy.

■ Awards, Honors

Discovery/The Nation prize, 1975; United States Award, International Poetry Forum, 1976, for *The Elements of San Joaquin;* Bess Hokin Prize from *Poetry,* 1978; Guggenheim fellowship, 1979-80; National Endowment for the Arts fellowships, 1981 and 1991; Levinson Award, *Poetry,* 1984; American Book Award, Before Columbus Foundation, 1985, for *Living up the Street;* California Arts Council fellowship, 1989; Best Book for Young Adults citation, American Library Association, 1990, and John and Patricia Beatty Award, California Library Association, 1991, both for *Baseball in April and Other Stories;* George G. Stone Center Recognition of Merit, Claremont Graduate School, 1993; Andrew Carnegie Medal, 1993; National Book Award and *Los Angeles Times* Book Prize finalist, both 1995, both for *New and Selected Poems;* American Library Association Notable Book selection, and *Parents' Choice* Award, both for *Chato's Kitchen;* Literature Award, Hispanic Heritage Foundation, 1999; Author-Illustrator Civil Rights Award, National Education Association, 1999; PEN Center West Book Award, 1999, for *Petty Crimes.*

■ Writings

POETRY FOR ADULTS

The Elements of San Joaquin, University of Pittsburgh Press, 1977.

The Tale of Sunlight, University of Pittsburgh Press, 1978.

Where Sparrows Work Hard, University of Pittsburgh Press, 1981.

Black Hair, University of Pittsburgh Press, 1985.
Who Will Know Us?, Chronicle Books, 1990.
Home Course in Religion, Chronicle Books, 1991.
New and Selected Poems, Chronicle Books, 1995.
Junior College: Poems, Chronicle Books, 1997.
A Natural Man, Chronicle Books, 1999.

PROSE FOR ADULTS

Living up the Street: Narrative Recollections (memoirs), Strawberry Hill, 1985.
Small Faces (memoirs), Arte Publico, 1986.
Lesser Evils: Ten Quartets (memoirs and essays), Arte Publico, 1988.
(Editor) *California Childhood: Recollections and Stories of the Golden State*, Creative Arts Book Company, 1988.
A Summer Life (autobiography), University Press of New England, 1990.
(Editor) *Pieces of the Heart: New Chicano Fiction*, Chronicle Books, 1993.
Nickel and Dime (novel), University of New Mexico Press, 2000.
The Effects of Knut Hamsun on a Fresno Boy (essays), Persea Books, 2001.
Poetry Lover (novel), University of New Mexico Press, 2001.

POETRY FOR YOUNG READERS

A Fire in My Hands, Scholastic, 1991.
Neighborhood Odes, Harcourt, 1992.
Canto Familiar/Familiar Song, Harcourt, 1995.

PROSE FOR YOUNG READERS

The Cat's Meow, illustrated by Carolyn Soto, Strawberry Hill, 1987, revised edition illustrated by Joe Cepeda, Scholastic, 1995.
Baseball in April and Other Stories (short stories), Harcourt, 1990.
Taking Sides, Harcourt, 1991.
Pacific Crossing, Harcourt, 1992.
The Skirt, Delacorte, 1992.
Too Many Tamales (picture book), Putnam, 1992.
Local News (short stories), Harcourt, 1993.
The Pool Party, (also see below), Delacorte, 1993.
Crazy Weekend, Scholastic, 1994.
Jesse, Harcourt, 1994.
Boys at Work, Delacorte, 1995.
Chato's Kitchen (picture book), Putnam, 1995.
Summer on Wheels, Scholastic, 1995.
The Old Man and His Door (picture book), Putnam, 1996.
Snapshots from the Wedding (picture book), Putnam, 1996.

Off and Running, illustrated by Eric Velasquez, Delacorte, 1996.
Buried Onions, Harcourt, 1997.
Novio Boy (play), Harcourt, 1997.
Petty Crimes (short stories), Harcourt, 1998.
Big Bushy Mustache (picture book), Knopf, 1998.
Nerdlandia: A Play, PaperStar, 1999.
Chato and the Party Animals (picture book), Putnam, 2000.
Jessie De La Cruz: A Profile of a United Farm Worker, Persea Books, 2000.

Soto's books have also been published in Spanish, Italian, French, and Japanese.

SHORT FILMS

The Bike, Gary Soto Productions, 1991.
The Pool Party, Gary Soto Productions, 1993.

■ Sidelights

Gary Soto is at heart a poet; everything he writes is overflowing with the vivid details of everyday life. Soto takes joy in the little things—remembered smells, voices in the distance, the pull of muscle when working. Growing up in a working class Mexican-American background in Fresno, California, in the agricultural San Joaquin Valley, he has taken that milieu and that geographical region for the subject of much of his writing. Soto, in his twenty books of poetry and prose for adults, and his nearly thirty books for young readers, has demonstrated a "seemingly total recall of his youth," as Suzanne Curley remarked in the *Los Angeles Times Book Review*. Writing in the *Bloomsbury Review*, Alicia Fields commented, "Soto's remembrances are as sharply defined and appealing as bright new coins," further adding, "[h]is language is spare and simple yet vivid." Soto has garnered such prestigious honors as an American Book Award and the Andrew Carnegie Medal, and has sold over a million copies of his books.

In award-winning poetry collections for adults, such as *The Elements of the San Joaquin, The Tale of Sunlight*, and *New and Collected Poems*, and in his autobiographical writings, including *Living up the Street, Small Faces, Lesser Evils*, and *A Summer Life*, Soto often presents a picture of hard-working laborers of California's Central Valley that is both hopeful and bleak. Soto, who worked as a laborer during his young adulthood, knows this literary territory firsthand. In his writing, as Raymund Paredes noted in the *Rocky Mountain Review*, "Soto establishes his acute sense of ethnicity and, simultaneously, his belief that certain emotions, values, and experiences transcend ethnic boundaries and allegiances." Writing in the *New York Times Book Review,* the critic Alan Cheuse called Soto "one of the finest natural talents to emerge" from among today's Chicano writers.

However, Soto is a writer first, a Chicano writer second. His characters and settings are often, as many critics have pointed out, Mexican-American, but his themes are large. As a reviewer for *Publishers Weekly* noted, Soto has an ability to make "the personal universal, and readers will feel privileged to share the vision of this man who finds life perplexing but a joy." With his children's fiction, which be began producing in 1990, with the short story collection, *Baseball in April and Other Stories,* Soto has created a world in which he tracks the sometimes perilous, sometimes hilarious journey to adulthood, as his characters struggle to gain maturity and self-awareness. Soto's books for younger readers present a cornucopia of styles: there are poetry collections, such as *A Fire in My Hands, Neighborhood Odes,* and *Canto Familiar;* short stories, including *Local News* and *Petty Crimes;* middle grade novels, such as *The Pool Party, Boys at Work, The Skirt,* and *Off and Running;* picture books, from the celebrated *Too Many Tamales* to his tales of Chato the cat; and YA novels both serious—*Taking Sides, Pacific Crossing, Jesse, Buried Onions*—and silly—*Crazy Weekend* and *Summer on Wheels.* In addition, Soto has written two plays for younger readers/performers, *Novio Boy* and *Nerdlandia,* and has filmed three short films for Spanish-speaking children. As Susan Marie Swanson noted in a *Riverbank Review* profile of the prolific author, "A child could grow up on Soto's books," starting with the picture books and graduating slowly through all the varieties he produces, coming to the adult works that he first created. "How many American authors have mapped such a journey for us to follow?" Swanson wondered. "Soto's is an extraordinary achievement."

A Barrio Youth

Soto was born on April 12, 1952, in Fresno, California, the industrial center of California's fertile San Joaquin Valley. Soto's parents were American-born, but Mexican culture was strong in the home. Field work and jobs in the packing house at the local Sunmaid Raisin plant provided economic sustenance for the family. Soto, the second of three children, later also worked in the fields and as a gardener. The death of his father when Soto was five sent the fami-

Lincoln Mendoza learns about friendship, loyalty, and competition when he must play basketball against his old schoolmates in Soto's first novel for young adults.

ly reeling, both emotionally and economically; his mother, along with the grandparents, brought up the family. Later there was a stepfather, but life was still a struggle. "I don't think I had any literary aspirations when I was a kid," Soto once told *Contemporary Authors.* "In fact we were pretty much an illiterate family. We didn't have books, and no one encouraged us to read. So my wanting to write poetry was pretty much a fluke." At various times in his youth Soto wanted to be a priest or a paleontologist—anything but a field worker picking grapes or cotton, as he did much of his youth to help out at home.

Graduating from high school in 1970, Soto first attended Fresno City College, hoping to major in geography. Quickly, however, such a dream was replaced with another: writing poetry. As Soto explained in *Contemporary Authors:* "I know the day the change began, because it was when I discovered in the library a collection of poems edited by Donald Allen called *The New American Poetry*." In particular, Soto focused on a poem by Edward Field, "Unwanted," that seemed to describe his own sense of alienation. "I discovered this poetry and thought, This is terrific: I'd like to do something like this. So I proceeded to write my own poetry, first alone, and then moving on to take classes." Transferring to California State University, Fresno, Soto studied with noted poet Philip Levine in 1972 and 1973. Under this man's tutelage, Soto learned the nuts and bolts not only of analyzing and critiquing a poem, but also of putting one together himself. Graduating magna cum laude from California State in 1974, he married Carolyn Oda the following year while working toward a master's degree in creative writing at the University of California, Irvine. Then in 1977 took a lecturer position at the University of California, Berkeley, in Chicano studies. That same year, his first book of poems was published.

A Published Poet

In his first volume of poetry, *The Elements of San Joaquin*, Soto offers a grim portrait of Mexican-American life. His poems depict the violence of urban life, the exhausting labor of rural life, and the futility of trying to recapture the innocence of childhood. In the book *Chicano Poetry*, Juan Bruce-Novoa likened Soto's poetic vision to T. S. Eliot's bleak portrait of the modern world, *The Waste Land*. Soto uses wind-swept dust as a dominant image, and he also introduces such elements as rape, unflushed toilets, a drowned baby, and men "Whose arms / Were bracelets / Of burns." Soto's skill with the figurative language of poetry has been noted by reviewers throughout his career, and in *Western American Literature*, Jerry Bradley praised the metaphors in *San Joaquin* as "evocative, enlightening, and haunting." Though unsettled by the negativism of the collection, Bruce-Novoa felt the work "convinces because of its well-wrought structure, the craft, the coherence of its totality." Moreover, he thought, because it brings such a vivid portrait of poverty to the reading public, *San Joaquin* is "a social as well as a literary achievement." This first book of poems won the United States Award from the International Poetry Forum.

Many critics have also observed that Soto's writing transcends social commentary. Bruce-Novoa said that one reason why the author's work has "great significance within Chicano literature" is because it represents "a definite shift toward a more personal, less politically motivated poetry." As Alan

Williamson suggested in *Poetry*, Soto avoids either idealizing the poor for their oppression or encouraging their violent defiance. Instead, he focuses on the human suffering that poverty engenders. Reviewing Soto's second volume of poetry, *The Tale of Sunlight*, in *Parnassus*, Peter Cooley praised the author's ability to temper the bleakness of *San Joaquin* with "imaginative expansiveness." The poems in *Sunlight*, many of which focus on a child named Molina or on the owner of a Hispanic bar, display both the frustrations of poverty and what Williamson called "a vein of consolatory fantasy which passes beyond escapism into a pure imaginative generosity toward life." Williamson cited as an example "the poem in which an uncle's gray hair is seen as a visitation of magical butterflies."

Other collections followed. *Where Sparrows Work Hard* and *Black Hair* both increased Soto's reputation as a poet to watch. Then in 1985, Soto's career took a change of direction. With publication of *Living up the Street*, he turned his hand to prose, writing vignette-like memoirs of growing up in Fresno.

Memoirs of a Barrio Youth

Soto mined the experiences of his early life in Fresno in several volumes of prose memoirs, books full of compassion, humor, and controlled anger. When Soto discusses American racial tensions in the prose collections *Living up the Street: Narrative Recollections*, and its sequel, *Small Faces*, he uses vignettes drawn from his own childhood. One vignette shows the anger the author felt upon realizing that his brown-skinned brother would never be considered an attractive child by conventional American standards. Another shows Soto's surprise at discovering that, contrary to his family's advice to marry a Mexican, he was falling in love with a woman of Japanese ancestry. In these deliberately small-scale recollections, as Paredes noted, "it is a measure of Soto's skill that he so effectively invigorates and sharpens our understanding of the commonplace." With these volumes Soto acquired a solid reputation as a prose writer as well as a poet; *Living up the Street* earned him an American Book Award. Reviewing *Living up the Street* in the *San Francisco Review of Books*, Geoffrey Dunn noted that "Soto has changed literary forms, though he returns once again to the dusty fields and industrial alleyways of his Fresno childhood" in twenty-one autobiographical short stories or vignettes. Dunne concluded that the book "is certainly a formidable work by one of America's more gifted and sensitive writers." Writing of *Small*

POINT · SIGNATURE

GARY SOTO

LOCAL NEWS

■SCHOLASTIC   A COLLECTION OF STORIES

Soto offers a mix of stories—some humorous, some sad, some frightening, some warmhearted—-in this 1993 collection.

Faces, Fields noted that the "emotional weather ranges from sunny with blue skies to dark and stormy," and the author "darts back and forth in time to form meaningful connections between past and present."

Soto's autobiographical prose continued with *Lesser Evils: Ten Quartets* and *A Summer Life.* The first of these, as Soto once explained, reflects the author's experience with Catholicism, and Soto has since declared himself a reconciled Catholic. Reviewing that collection of prose in *Western American Literature,* Gerald Haslam commented, "Gary Soto remains one of the brightest talents of his generation," and further noted that his prose sketches, written with a "universal" voice, "are adding a

dimension to his reputation." *A Summer Life,* Soto's fourth collection of reminiscences, consists of thirty-nine short essays. According to Ernesto Trejo in the *Los Angeles Times Book Review,* these pieces "make up a compelling biography" of Soto's youth. As he had done in previous works, Soto here "holds the past up to memory's probing flashlight, turns it around ever so carefully, and finds in the smallest of incidents the occasion for literature." Writing in the *Americas Review,* Hector Torres compared *A Summer Life* with Soto's earlier autobiographical texts and asserted that the later book "moves with greater stylistic elegance and richer thematic coherence."

Writing for a Younger Audience

During the early 1990s Soto turned his attentions in a new direction: children's literature. A first volume of short stories for young readers, *Baseball in April and Other Stories,* was published in 1990. The eleven tales depict Mexican-American boys and girls as they enter adolescence in Hispanic California neighborhoods. In the *New York Times Book Review,* Roberto Gonzalez Echevarria called the stories "sensitive and economical." Echevarria praised Soto: "Because he stays within the teenagers' universe . . . he manages to convey all the social change and stress without bathos or didacticism. In fact, his stories are moving, yet humorous and entertaining." In the *Americas Review,* Torres suggested that *Baseball in April* was "the kind of work that could be used to teach high school and junior high school English classes." Roger Sutton, reviewing this debut juvenile collection in *Bulletin of the Center for Children's Books,* noted that the stories are "told with tenderness, optimism, and wry humor." Sutton further commented that while Chicano children and their parents "will be pleased to find a book that admits larger possibilities than the stereotypes of the noble-but-destitute farmworker," kids from all cultures "will feel like part of this neighborhood."

Other short story collections by Soto include *Local News* and *Petty Crimes.* The former title consists of thirteen short stories, once again set in a Mexican-American barrio, offering insights into the Hispanic community and culture. There are tales of first jobs that end in disaster, of teenage blackmail, and of botched thespian attempts in a school play. "As always," noted a writer for *Kirkus Reviews,* "Soto shows that the concerns and triumphs of Latino children are no different from anyone's. . . ." A reviewer for *Publishers Weekly* called the collection a "vibrant tapestry of Chicano American neighborhoods." Soto's 1998 collection, *Petty Crimes*, gathers ten "affecting short stories," according to *Booklist*'s Hazel Rochman, portraying teenagers "both swaggering and lost." Rochman concluded, "Soto is a fine writer, and in the casual talk and schoolyard confrontations, the simple words flash with poetry." A writer for *Kirkus Reviews* described the stories in *Petty Crimes* as "a kaleidoscope of Mexican-American adolescents and the bullies they confront—bullies ranging from tough, menacing teens to life's unavoidable truths."

In 1991, Soto followed up the success of his first juvenile story collection with two new juvenile publications, a young adult novel and a book of poems for younger readers. *A Fire in My Hands* consists of twenty-three poems, some of which came from his adult collection, *Black Hair*. Each poem is prefaced with a comment about how Soto came to write it, and all of them—as so much of Soto's work does—reflect his own experiences growing up Mexican American or his experiences as a father. Reviewing the collection in *School Library Journal*, Barbara Chatton felt that "Soto's poems and thoughts provide gentle encouragement to young people who are seeking to express themselves through the use of language." *Booklist*'s Rochman remarked that the collection "will attract poetry readers and writers . . . for its candid, personal, undogmatic "advice to young poets."" Soto has since produced two more volumes of poetry for young readers, *Neighborhood Odes* (1992) and *Canto Familiar* (1995). Reviewing *Odes*, a writer for *Publishers Weekly* commented that the "Hispanic neighborhood in Soto's 21 poems is brought sharply into focus by the care with which he records images of everyday life. . . ." Renee Steinberg, reviewing the collection in *School Library Journal*, noted, "The rewards of well-chosen words that create vivid, sensitive images await readers of this collection of poems. . . . Each section is an expression of joy and wonder at life's daily pleasures and mysteries." And of Soto's 1995 collection, *Canto Familiar*, Rochman commented in *Booklist*, "this collection of simple free verse captures common childhood moments at home, at school, and in the street. . . . This is a collection to read aloud and get kids writing about themselves."

Taking Sides, Soto's first juvenile novel, was also published in 1991. The protagonist of that book, a boy named Lincoln Mendoza, appears in both *Taking Sides* and *Pacific Crossing*. As a Mexican-American eighth-grader in *Taking Sides*, Lincoln is confronted with challenges and insecurities when he and his mother move from San Francisco's Mission District to a predominantly Anglo suburb. He

works to keep his heritage intact in his new environment. Though he plays basketball for his new school, Lincoln still feels loyalty for his old team at Franklin Junior High, and when the two teams face off on the court, Lincoln learns something about friendship, loyalty, and winning. A writer for *Kirkus Reviews* felt that with this novel, Soto "creates a believable, compelling picture of the stress that racial prejudice places on minority children." Bruce Anne Shook called it a "light but appealing story" that "deals with cultural differences, moving, and basketball," in a *School Library Journal* review.

Pacific Crossing finds Lincoln and one of his friends, Tony, facing cultural challenges in another context: they embark on a voyage to Japan as exchange students. Both of them have been studying the martial art of kempo and leap at the chance to go to Japan. Once there, Lincoln comes to understand that beneath the outward differences, life with his host family in Japan is not much different than at home. Writing in the *Multicultural Review*, Osbelia Juarez Rocha called *Pacific Crossing* "cleverly crafted" and "entertaining." *Horn Book*'s Ellen Fader concluded that the novel "highlights the truisms that people are the same all over the world and that friends can be found anywhere, if one makes the effort."

With *The Skirt*, Soto turned his hand to writing novels for middle grade readers. Miata Ramirez is heartsick because she has lost her folklorico skirt on the school bus and is desperate to get it back before the dance performance. A reviewer for *Publishers Weekly* concluded that this "short novel should find its most appreciative audience at the lower end of the intended age range." *School Library Journal*'s Ann Welton felt the book was a "fine read-aloud and discussion starter," while *Horn Book*'s Nancy Vasilakis called the book an "unpretentious story for readers new to chapter books," and "a cheery snapshot of a Mexican-American family. . . ." Miata makes another appearance in the 1996 *Off and Running*, in which she and friend Anna become running mates for class office, competing against the dreaded boys. As time runs out on the election, the two girls must figure out how to change their image and win votes. *Booklist*'s Rochman felt that this "fifth-grade comedy is as lighthearted and affectionate as ever," and that some of the chapters "will make uproarious read-alouds." A reviewer for *Publishers Weekly* called Miata a "spunky and imaginative heroine."

Miata's competitor for class president in *Off and Running* is none other than Rudy Herrera, a character who made his first appearances in *The Pool Party*

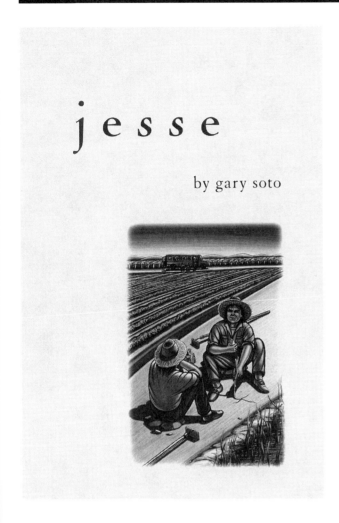

jesse

by gary soto

Filled with detailed images, Soto's 1994 novel depicts a young Mexican American, Jesse, who leaves home in search of a better future.

and *Boys at Work*, two other middle-grade novels from Soto. In *The Pool Party*, Rudy is invited to a rich girl's party and tries to figure out what he should take as an appropriate present. Soon his whole family is offering advice, and he and friend Alex pass the time in the days before the party getting into and out of scrapes. Finally they opt for a pool toy that becomes the hit of the party. Susan Marcus, reviewing the book in *School Library Journal*, called attention to "the poetic perfection Soto exhibits both in description and in authentic dialogue," as well as to the "immersion of readers into the bosom of a loving, hard-working Mexican-American family." A writer for *Kirkus Reviews* called the novel "Engaging" and "gently humorous." Rudy and friend Alex make return appearances in *Boys at Work*. When Rudy breaks an older boy's Discman at a baseball game, he is desperate to make some money to buy a new one. Crazy money-making schemes ensue in

this "easy, entertaining read," as a *Booklist* reviewer described the book. Rosie Peasley, writing in *School Library Journal*, remarked that Soto's strength "lies in the depth, warmth, and humor of his characters," and concluded that the book's "universal growing-up themes of bully-fear, friendship, and family relationships" make the novel "a reader-friendly addition." *Boys at Work* won a Newbery Honor award.

More humor is served up in *Crazy Weekend* and *Summer on Wheels*. These comic novels for young readers both feature the blood brothers Hector and Mando, two youngsters from East Los Angeles. In *Crazy Weekend*, a "winning combination of a thriller and a comedy," according to a writer for *Publishers Weekly*, Hector and Mando, witness a robbery while visiting Hector's uncle in Fresno. Karen Williams, writing in the *Christian Science Monitor* felt "Soto creates a rollicking adventurer of wise-cracking good-guys and accident-prone bad guys." Hector and Mando get together again in *Summer on Wheels*, in which they bike from East Los Angeles to the beach at Santa Monica, staying with relatives along the way. "Readers will quickly become caught up in the boys' many schemes and escapades which occur with humorous regularity," remarked Maura Bresnahan in a *Voice of Youth Advocates* review of the novel. Bresnahan further noted that "Soto has created two wonderfully believable friends in Hector and Mando. They are typical boys on the cusp of adolescence."

From Picture Books to Hard-Hitting YA Novels

Soto has ventured as well into the arena of children's picture books. *Too Many Tamales* depicts the story of Maria, a young girl who misplaces her mother's wedding ring in tamale dough while helping to prepare a Christmastime feast. Maria—with her cousins' help—embarks on a futile effort to recover the ring by consuming vast quantities of tamales. *Booklist*'s Rochman called this first venture into picture books "a joyful success," while a writer for *Kirkus Reviews* concluded, "this one should become a staple on the holiday menu." *Chato's Kitchen* introduces a cat whose efforts to entice the local "ratoncitos"—little mice—lead him to prepare abundant portions of fajitas, frijoles, enchiladas, and other foods. In a starred review, a critic for *School Library Journal* dubbed this picture book "really cool," further noting that "Soto adeptly captures the flavor of life in el barrio in this amusing tale." A writer for *Publishers Weekly* called the book "wickedly funny." Chato makes a return appearance in the

2000 work *Chato and the Party Animals.* Further picture books from Soto include *The Old Man and His Door, Big Bushy Moustache,* and *Snapshots from the Wedding,* in which the festivities are seen through the camera lens of the young flower girl, Maria. "Readers will be enthralled," observed a *Publishers Weekly* reviewer.

Soto has stated that his 1994 YA novel, *Jesse,* is a personal favorite and one in which the protagonist comes close to being autobiographical. Set in the late 1960s with the Vietnam War protests, United Farm Workers movement, and promise of a better world, the novel tells the story of sixteen-year-old Jesse who has left, both home and school, escaping boredom and the abuse of his drunken stepfather. He goes to live with his older brother, struggles with poverty, and learns firsthand about discrimination. "In this vivid, muscular portrait, the title character emerges as a complex, winning young man," commented Cathryn M. Mercier in a review of the novel in *Five Owls.* In the book, Jesse finally discovers himself as an artist. "Like Soto," Mercier noted, "Jesse has the voice of a poet." *Horn Book*'s Ellen Fader called the novel "moving" and "engrossing," and concluded that it "contains strands of both humor and despair."

In Soto's 1997 *Buried Onions,* Eddie is trying to escape the poverty and gang violence of the Fresno barrio by taking vocational classes. When his cousin is killed, he is urged by his aunt to find the killer and avenge the death of his relative, but Eddie just wants to find a way out of this claustrophobic world. A job in an affluent suburb goes awry when his boss's truck is stolen while in his care. Finally, with a gang member looking for him and with his money gone, Eddie opts to join the military in hopes that he can find a better life. "In bleak sentences of whispered beauty, Eddie tells how he dropped out of vocational college and is attempting to get by with odd jobs," remarked a critic for *Kirkus Reviews.* The same reviewer noted that this "unrelenting portrait is unsparing in squalid details," concluding that the book is a "valuable tale" and "one that makes no concessions."

Meanwhile, Soto has continued with his output for adult readers, including poetry collections such as *Junior College* and *A Natural Man,* as well as his *New and Selected Poems,* a volume selected as a finalist for the National Book Award. He has also written his first adult novels, *Nickel and Dime* and *Poetry Lover.* Yet amazingly, this writer who first won over readers for his adult volumes of poetry, increasingly is

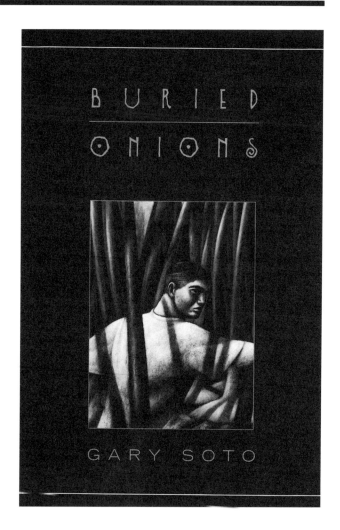

Nineteen-year-old Eddie seems destined to live his entire life in the barrio in Soto's acclaimed 1999 novel.

becoming known as a author of books for younger readers. He has left his teaching career at Berkeley to become a full-time writer.

"This poet has gassed up his car and gone forth to meet his readers," Soto remarked in an essay posted on his internet home page, by way of explaining his success. "Over a nine-year period I have spoken to three hundred thousand teachers and students, possibly more. . . . In my garage sit boxes of fan letters and hand-drawn banners proclaiming me the best writer in the world. And why such a reception? Unlike most other contemporary poets and writers, I've taken the show on the road and built a name among la gente, the people. I have ventured into schools where I have played baseball and basketball with young people, sung songs, acted in skits, delivered commencement speeches, learned three chords on a Mexican guitar to serenade teachers. . . . I have gone to prisons and mingle with people who have

If you enjoy the works of Gary Soto, you might want to check out the following books:

T. Ernesto Bethancourt, *The Me Inside of Me*, 1985.

Irene Beltran Hernandez, *The Secret of Two Brothers*, 1995.

Tiffany Ana Lopez, *Growing Up Chicano*, 1993.

Victor Martinez, *Parrot in the Oven: Mi Vida*, 1996.

Jess Mowry, *Way Past Cool*, 1992.

done time. . . . My readership is strung from large cities, such as Los Angeles, to dinky Del Rey where peach trees outnumber the population by many thousands. . . . My business is to make readers from non-readers."

■ Works Cited

Review of *Boys at Work, Booklist*, June 1, 1995, p. 1773.

Bradley, Jerry, review of *The Elements of San Joaquin, Western American Literature*, Spring, 1979.

Bresnahan, Maura, review of *Summer on Wheels, Voice of Youth Advocates*, April, 1995, pp. 27-28.

Bruce-Novoa, Juan, *Chicano Poetry: A Response to Chaos*, University of Texas Press, 1982.

Review of *Buried Onions, Kirkus Reviews*, August 1, 1997, p. 1229.

Review of *Chato's Kitchen, Publishers Weekly*, February 6, 1995, p. 84.

Review of *Chato's Kitchen, School Library Journal*, July, 1995, p. 69.

Chatton, Barbara, review of *A Fire in My Hands, School Library Journal*, March, 1992, p. 264.

Cheuse, Alan, "The Voices of Chicano," *New York Times Book Review*, October 11, 1981, pp. 15, 36-37.

Cooley, Peter, review of *The Tale of Sunlight, Parnassus*, Fall-Winter, 1979.

Review of *Crazy Weekend, Publishers Weekly*, January 31, 1994, p. 90.

Curley, Suzanne, "A Better Place to Live," *Los Angeles Times Book Review*, August 15, 1993, p. 8.

Dunn, Geoffrey, review of *Living up the Street, San Francisco Review of Books*, Summer, 1986, p. 11.

Echevarria, Roberto Gonzalez, "Growing Up North of the Border," *New York Times Book Review*, August 20, 1990, p. 45.

Fader, Ellen, review of *Pacific Crossing, Horn Book*, November-December, 1992, pp. 725-26.

Fader, Ellen, review of *Jesse Horn Book*, March-April, 1995, pp. 201-02.

Fields, Alicia, "Small But Telling Moments," *Bloomsbury Review*, January-February, 1987, p. 10.

Haslam, Gerald, review of *Lesser Evils, Western American Literature*, May, 1989, pp. 92-93.

Review of *Lesser Evils, Publishers Weekly*, March 4, 1988, p. 102.

Review of *Local News, Kirkus Reviews*, April 1, 1993, p. 464.

Review of *Local News, Publishers Weekly*, April 12,. 1993, p. 64.

Marcus, Susan F., review of *The Pool Party, School Library Journal*, p. 112.

Mercier, Cathryn M., review of *Jesse, Five Owls*, January-February, 1995, p. 64.

Review of *Neighborhood Odes, Publishers Weekly*, March 23, 1992, p. 74.

Review of *Off and Running, Publishers Weekly*, December 8, 1997, p. 74.

Paredes, Raymund, "Recent Chicano Fiction," *Rocky Mountain Review of Language and Literature*, Volume 41, numbers 1-2, 1987, pp. 126-28.

Peasley, Rosie, review of *Boys at Work, School Library Journal*, June, 1995, p. 113.

Review of *Petty Crimes, Kirkus Reviews*, March 1, 1998, p. 345.

Review of *The Pool Party, Kirkus Reviews*, June 15, 1993, p. 792.

Rocha, Osbelia Juarez, review of *Pacific Crossing, Multicultural Review*, June, 1993, pp. 76, 78.

Rochman, Hazel, review of *A Fire in My Hands, Booklist*, April 1, 1992, pp. 1437-38.

Rochman, Hazel, review of *Too Many Tamales, Booklist*, September 15, 1993, p. 151.

Rochman, Hazel, review of *Canto Familiar, Booklist*, October 1, 1995, p. 312.

Rochman, Hazel, review of *Off and Running, Booklist*, October 1, 1996, p. 362.

Rochman, Hazel, review of *Petty Crimes, Booklist*, March 15, 1998, p. 1245.

Shook, Bruce Anne, review of *Taking Sides, School Library Journal*, November, 1991, p. 124.

Review of *The Skirt, Publishers Weekly*, August 24, 1992, p. 80.

Review of *Snapshots from the Wedding, Publishers Weekly*, January 20, 1997, p. 401.

Soto, Gary, *Elements of San Joaquin*, University of Pittsburgh Press, 1977.

Soto, Gary, "Who Are Your Readers?," located on Web site, http://garysoto.com/whatsup/html.

Steinberg, Renee, review of *Neighborhood Odes, School Library Journal*, May, 1992, p. 128.

Sutton, Roger, review of *Baseball in April, Bulletin of the Center for Children's Books*, April, 1990, p. 199.

Swanson, Susan Marie, "Gary Soto," *Riverbank Review,* Fall, 1999, pp. 16-18.

Review of *Taking Sides, Kirkus Reviews*, September 15, 1991, p. 1228.

Review of *Too Many Tamales, Kirkus Reviews*, September 1, 1993, p. 1152.

Torres, Hector, review of *Baseball in April* and *A Summer Life, Americas Review,* Spring, 1991, pp. 111-15.

Trejo, Ernesto, "Memories of a Fresno Boyhood," *Los Angeles Times Book Review,* August 5, 1990, pp. 1, 9.

Vasilakis, Nancy, review of *The Skirt, Horn Book,* November-December, 1992, pp. 720-21.

Welton, Ann, review of *The Skirt, School Library Journal*, September, 1992, p. 255.

Williams, Karen, "Lands Real and Imagined," *Christian Science Monitor,* May 6, 1994, pp. 12-13.

Williamson, Alan, "In a Middle Style," *Poetry,* March, 1980, pp. 348-54.

■ For More Information See

BOOKS

Children's Literature Review, Volume 38, Gale, 1996

Contemporary Literary Criticism, Gale, Volume 32, 1985; Volume 80, 1994.

Cooper-Alarcon, Daniel Francis, *The Aztec Palimpsest: Discursive Appropriations of Mexican Culture,* UMI, 1993.

Dictionary of Literary Biography, Volume 82: *Chicano Writers*, Gale, 1989, pp. 246-52.

Hispanic Literature Criticism, Gale, 1994.

Modern American Literature, Volume 6, Continuum Publishers, 1997.

St. James Guide to Young Adult Writers, 2nd edition, St. James Press, 1999.

PERIODICALS

Booklist, November 15, 1997, p. 554; June 1, 1998, p. 1784; November 1, 1998, p. 483; February 15, 2000.

Bulletin of the Center for Children's Books, November, 1999, pp. 108-09.

Christian Science Monitor, March 6, 1985; May 6, 1994, p. 13; September 28, 1995, p. B1.

English Journal, January, 1999, pp. 122-23.

Los Angeles Times Book Review, April 16, 1995, p. 6; September 1, 1996, p. 11.

Nation, June 7, 1993, pp. 772-74.

New York Times Book Review, May 20, 1990, p. 45; December 19, 1993, p. 16.

Poetry, March, 1998, p. 339.

Publishers Weekly, March 23, 1992, p. 74; August 16, 1993, p. 103; February 6, 1995, pp. 84-85; May 25, 1998, p. 91; April, 26, 1999, p. 85; February 14, 2000, p. 175.

School Library Journal, June, 1997, p. 146; May, 1998, pp. 89, 148; September, 1998, p. 183; July, 1999, p. 55; February, 2000, p. 146.

Voice of Youth Advocates, December, 1999, p. 339.

ON-LINE

Gary Soto's official Web site is located at http://www.garysoto.com.

—Sketch by J. Sydney Jones

Paul Zindel

■ Personal

Born May 15, 1936, in Staten Island, NY; son of Paul (a policeman) and Beatrice (a practical nurse; maiden name, Frank) Zindel; married Bonnie Hildebrand (a novelist), October 25, 1973; children: David Jack, Elizabeth Claire. *Education:* Wagner College, B.S., 1958, M.Sc.Ed., 1959.

■ Addresses

Office—c/o Harper & Row, 10 East 53rd St., New York, NY 10022. *Agent*—Curtis Brown, Ltd., 10 Astor Pl., New York, NY 10003.

■ Career

Allied Chemical, New York City, technical writer, 1958-59; Tottenville High School, Staten Island, NY, chemistry teacher, 1959-69; author of books for children and young adults, playwright, and screenwriter, 1969—. Playwright-in-residence, Alley Theatre, Houston, TX, 1967.

■ Member

Actors Studio.

■ Awards, Honors

Ford Foundation grant, 1967, for drama; Children's Book of the Year, Child Study Association of America, 1968, Award for Text, *Boston Globe-Horn Book*, 1969, both for *The Pigman*; Outstanding Children's Book of the Year citations, *New York Times*, 1969, for *My Darling, My Hamburger*, 1970, for *I Never Loved Your Mind*, 1976, for *Pardon Me, You're Stepping on My Eyeball!*, 1978, for *The Undertaker's Gone Bananas*, and 1980, for *The Pigman's Legacy*; Obie Award for the Best American Play from the *Village Voice*, Vernon Rice Drama Desk Award from the New York Drama Critics for the Most Promising Playwright, and New York Drama Critics Circle Award for Best American Play of the Year, all 1970, Pulitzer Prize in Drama and New York Critics Award, both 1971, all for *The Effect of Gamma Rays on Man-in-the-Moon Marigolds*; Honorary Doctorate of Humanities from Wagner College, 1971; Best Young Adult Books citations, American Library Association, 1971, for *The Effect of Gamma Rays on Man-in-the-Moon Marigolds*, 1975, for *The Pigman*, 1976, for *Pardon Me, You're Stepping on My Eyeball!*, 1977, for *Confessions of a Teenage Baboon*, 1980, for *The Pigman's Legacy*, and 1982, for *To Take a Dare*; Maxi Award, *Media & Methods* 1973, for *The Pigman*; "Books for the Teen Age" citations, New York Public Library, 1980, for *Confessions of a Teenage*

Baboon, 1980, 1981, and 1982, for *The Effect of Gamma Rays on Man-in-the-Moon Marigolds,* 1981, for *A Star for the Latecomer,* and 1981 and 1982, for *The Pigman's Legacy.* Several of Zindel's works for young people have been named Outstanding Books by the *New York Times* and Notable Books by the American Library Association.

■ **Writings**

FOR YOUNG ADULTS; FICTION, EXCEPT AS NOTED

The Pigman, Harper, 1968.

My Darling, My Hamburger, Harper, 1969.

I Never Loved Your Mind, Harper, 1970.

The Effect of Gamma Rays on Man-in-the-Moon Marigolds, illustrated by Dong Kingman, Harper, 1971.

I Love My Mother (picture book), illustrated by John Melo, Harper, 1975.

Pardon Me, You're Stepping on My Eyeball!, Harper, 1976.

Confessions of a Teenage Baboon, Harper, 1977.

The Undertaker's Gone Bananas, Harper, 1978.

(With wife, Bonnie Zindel) *A Star for the Latecomer,* Harper, 1980.

The Pigman's Legacy, Harper, 1980.

The Girl Who Wanted a Boy, Harper, 1981.

(With Crescent Dragonwagon) *To Take a Dare,* Harper, 1982.

Harry and Hortense at Hormone High, Harper, 1984.

The Amazing and Death-Defying Diary of Eugene Dingman, Harper, 1987.

A Begonia for Miss Applebaum, Harper, 1989.

The Pigman and Me (autobiography), HarperCollins, 1992.

David and Della, HarperCollins, 1993.

Loch, HarperCollins, 1994.

The Doom Stone, HarperCollins, 1995.

Reef of Death, HarperCollins, 1998.

Raptor, Hyperion, 1998.

Rats, Hyperion, 1999.

"THE WACKY FACTS LUNCH BUNCH" SERIES; MIDDLE GRADE FICTION

Fright Party, illustrated by Jeff Mangiat, Bantam, 1993.

Attack of the Killer Fishsticks, illustrated by Jeff Mangiat, Bantam, 1993.

Fifth Grade Safari, illustrated by Jeff Mangiat, Bantam, 1993.

The 100 Laugh Riot, illustrated by Jeff Mangiat, Bantam, 1994.

OTHER FICTION

When a Darkness Falls, Bantam, 1984.

PLAYS

Dimensions of Peacocks, first produced in New York, 1959.

Euthanasia and the Endless Hearts, first produced in New York at Take 3, 1960.

A Dream of Swallows, first produced Off-Broadway, April, 1962.

The Effect of Gamma Rays on Man-in-the-Moon Marigolds (first produced in Houston, TX, at Alley Theatre, May, 1964, produced Off-Broadway at Mercer-O'Casey Theatre, April 7, 1970), Dramatists Play Service (New York), 1971.

And Miss Reardon Drinks a Little (first produced in Los Angeles at Mark Taper Forum, Los Angeles, 1967, produced on Broadway at Morosco Theatre, February 25, 1971), Dramatists Play Service, 1971, Random House, 1972.

The Secret Affairs of Mildred Wild (first produced in New York City at Ambassador Theatre, November 14, 1972), Dramatists Play Service, 1973.

Let Me Hear You Whisper [and] *The Ladies Should Be in Bed* (*Let Me Hear You Whisper* was televised on National Educational Television (NET), 1966; *The Ladies Should Be in Bed* was first produced in New York, 1978), Dramatists Play Service, 1973, *Let Me Hear You Whisper* published separately, illustrated by Stephen Gammell, Harper, 1974.

Ladies at the Alamo (first produced at Actors Studio and directed by Zindel, May 29, 1975, produced on Broadway at Martin Beck Theatre, April 7, 1977, produced as *Ladies on the Midnight Planet* in Hollywood at Marilyn Monroe Theatre, 1982), Dramatists Play Service, 1977.

A Destiny on Half Moon Street, first produced in Florida at Coconut Grove, 1985.

Amulets against the Dragon Forces, Circle Repertory Company (New York), 1989, Dramatists Play Service, 1989.

SCREENPLAYS AND TELEVISION PLAYS

The Effect of Gamma Rays on Man-in-the-Moon Marigolds, National Educational Television (NET), 1966.

Let Me Hear You Whisper, NET, 1966.

Up the Sandbox (based on Anne Roiphe's novel), National, 1972.

Mame (based on Patrick Dennis's novel *Auntie Mame*), Warner Bros., 1974.

Maria's Lovers, Cannon Films, 1984.

Alice in Wonderland, Columbia Broadcasting System (CBS), 1985.

(With Djordje Milicevic and Edward Bunker) *Runaway Train* (based on a screenplay by Akira Kurosawa), Cannon Films, 1985.

(With Leslie Briscusse) *Babes in Toyland*, National Broadcasting Co. (NBC), 1986.

A Connecticut Yankee in King Arthur's Court (based on Mark Twain's novel), NBC, 1989.

Also author of screenplay for *The Pigman* (adapted from his novel).

OTHER

Contributor of articles to newspapers and periodicals.

■ **Adaptations**

The Effects of Gamma Rays on Man-in-the-Moon Marigolds was made into a film by Twentieth Century-Fox, 1973; *The Pigman* was released as a filmstrip with cassette by Miller-Brody/Random House, 1977; *My Darling, My Hamburger* was released as a filmstrip with cassette by Current Affairs and Mark Twain Media, 1978; a filmstrip about Zindel, *Paul Zindel—Marigolds, Hamburgers, Eyeballs, and Baboons*, was released by Perfection Form Company, 1979; *The Pigman and Me* was made into a sound recording in 1995.

■ **Sidelights**

Considered a groundbreaking author of young adult literature as well as one of its most controversial contributors, Paul Zindel is well known as the creator of realistic novels that depict the teenage milieu with authenticity, humor, and panache. In addition to his books for young adults, he is the writer of several well-received plays for adults—*The Effect of Gamma Rays on Man-in-the-Moon Marigolds* received the Pulitzer Prize in 1971—as well as screenplays, an erotic mystery novel, a picture book, and mysteries and supernatural fiction for middle graders and young people. Zindel is best known for writing *The Pigman*, a novel published in 1968 that is recognized as one of the first works for adolescents to deepen the content of young adult literature. The story of two teenagers who become friends with an elderly widower and end up betraying his trust, *The Pigman* established a pattern that Zindel uses in many of his subsequent novels for young people: troubled adolescents, usually a boy and a girl,

become involved with a senior adult in situations that end tragically but lead to self-awareness.

Throughout his works, Zindel engages his characters in behaviors that were new to young adult literature when he first included them, such as smoking, drinking, swearing, having sex, enduring abortion, and showing obvious dislike of school; the author also writes about serious topics, including death by illness, suicide, divorce, and desertion. Perhaps Zindel's most provocative trademark is his treatment of his adult characters. Described by Joan McGrath of *Twentieth Century Children's Writers* as "drunkards; bullies; slatterns; dolts and drearies," the adults in Zindel's books are often parents or authority figures who treat the young adults at the center of the stories with cruelty, dishonesty, irresponsibility, or indifference. Consequently, the teens have developed personal problems and low self-esteem as well as sardonic views of life. Through their experiences, the protagonists learn lessons about coping with both life and death; although they lose some of their innocence, they begin to see the world more clearly and attain a greater sense of place within it. Zindel's young narrators, who often alternate chapters, communicate by using what the author calls "transitional pictures," letters written in cursive, lists, graffiti, and doodles. Zindel, whose literary style is considered both intimate and energetic, often includes word humor such as riddles, puns, and one-liners in his books for young people.

In assessing Zindel as a writer of young adult literature, reviewers consistently praise the author's understanding of his audience and his recreation of adolescent life. Zindel is also highly regarded for his strong characterizations, incisive dialogue, and accurate treatment of teenage concerns as well as for the candor of his subjects and themes. Zindel's themes—the search for identity, the meaning of life and death, the questioning of authority and values—are often considered universal and archetypal. Despite their essential seriousness, the author's works are filled with humor and irony. Characteristically, Zindel uses an exaggerated, mocking tone that reflects the cynical viewpoints of his teen protagonists; in addition, he employs a broadly slapstick style along with nonsensical book titles and bizarre character names, elements that are disliked by some observers.

Zindel has been criticized for vulgarity, for negative characterizations of adults, for producing an uneven literary output, and for presenting a pessimistic, satiric attitude toward society. However,

Zindel's groundbreaking 1968 novel follows two high school students, John Conlan and Lorraine Jensen, who befriend a lonely widower but eventually betray his trust.

the author has been consistently popular with young readers, who appreciate the depth and authenticity of his works as well as their exaggeration, caricature, and humor. Many adult critics recognize Zindel's contributions to young adult literature and passionate belief in the young as well as the intrinsic hopefulness of his books. In his entry in *Dictionary of Literary Biography*, Theodore W. Hipple wrote, "Much of the credit for [the change in adolescent literature] must go . . . especially to Zindel." The critic concluded by placing the author in the "forefront of adolescent novelists. Few other writers match his awareness of teenagers' problems and attitudes. . . . It is not at all surprising—indeed, it is

gratifying—that he is among their most esteemed novelists." James T. Henke, writing in *Children's Literature*, called Zindel "a fine craftsman, a genuine literary artist," while Judith N. Mitchell of *Voice of Youth Advocates* claimed that "he is to the teen novel what [Edward] Albee is to drama." In an essay in *The Lion and the Unicorn*, Stanley Hoffman commented, "Zindel may be the Jekyll and Hyde of modern young adult fiction; his books get better, worse, better, worse, and one never knows what will come next." The critic concluded, "He is absurdly uneven, but so what? Better to have him risk terrible books . . . because somewhere he's bound to come up with another winner." Writing in *Elementary English*, Beverly A. Haley and Kenneth L. Donelson observed that Zindel "examines our society, realizes the pathos and sometimes the bathos of its condition, and finally presents an affirmation of his faith in people and particularly young people of the basic worth of the individual human being and the collective human spirit."

A Difficult Childhood

Zindel often draws his characters and situations from life and from his own background, and his stories are usually underscored with themes derived from lessons that he has learned. Born in Staten Island, New York, to a policeman, Paul, and a homemaker, Beatrice, Zindel came from a broken home. When he was two and his sister Betty was four, his father deserted the family to live with a woman he had met on his daily rounds. Zindel later noted that he only saw his father about ten times before his death in 1957: "There was no room for me in his life," he commented to Jack Jacob Forman in *Presenting Paul Zindel*. In the years following his father's desertion of the family, Zindel's mother, the author remembered in the *Morning Telegraph*, "worked at everything, nursing, real estate, a hot dog stand, and inventions, but we usually lived in a shambles." Beatrice Zindel also had bouts of depression and paranoia. "Our home was a house of fear," Zindel recalled in the *Morning Telegraph*. "Mother never trusted anybody. . . ." He later told Stephen M. Silverman of the *New York Post* that Beatrice "instilled in me the thought that the world was out to get me." His mother's sickness and the family's constant moving led to a solitary childhood for Zindel. "There were no peers, there were no friends, there was no one to talk to," he told Forman. Consequently, Zindel said in the New York *Daily News*, "I felt worthless as a kid, and dared to speak and act my feelings only in fantasy and secret. That's probably what made me a writer." He added in the *Morning Telegraph*, "When I write, I hear the voices of my mother and sister. I'm writing from their voices in a metaphor I know about."

Although the Zindel household contained limited resources—"We had no books, no theatre. We had none of those things," the author told Paul Janeczko in *English Journal*—the future author had an active imagination and found ways to entertain himself: marionettes, some of which he made; cycloramas; movies and comic books; and aquariums, terrariums, and insectariums. "What a great love I had of microcosms, of peering at other worlds framed and separated from me," he declared in the *New York Times*. When he was eleven, Zindel recalled, he grew "tired of eavesdropping on the world and decided to enter it." He added to Jerry Tallmer of the *New York Post*, "I found out there was another world beyond that mother and sister of mine. A world where I learned there were fresh vegetables, and that you raised the seat up to urinate. Because, boy, I was pistol-whipped when I was a boy. So when my aunt says: "You were *really* a good boy," I know "good" means I really was kept under control." After unsuccessful attempts to act in plays, sing in school, and even to be "swung around at 180 rpms by a roller-skating acrobat" at a local movie theater, as he wrote in the *New York Times*, Zindel "decided that even if I could not succeed in the real world, perhaps my appointed role in life was to help other people succeed." In high school, he wrote sketches and skits before contracting tuberculosis at the age of fifteen. Zindel "was whisked off to a sanitorium at Lake Kushaqua, New York, where once again the world became something I could look at only through a frame. Big deal, Paul Zindel—fifteen years old, tubercular, drab, loveless, and desperate." Upon returning to school, he entered a playwriting contest sponsored by the American Cancer Society and won a silver Parker pen for his first full-length play, the story of a stricken pianist who beats his disease and ends up playing Chopin's "Warsaw Concerto" at Carnegie Hall.

After graduating from high school, Zindel attended Wagner College on Staten Island and majored in chemistry. After editing the school newspaper and contributing to its literary magazine, he decided to change his major to literature and drama but was dissuaded when the college threatened to cancel his scholarship if he changed majors. Zindel's interest in theater continued to grow, and after taking a course taught by playwright Edward Albee, he found a mentor for his writing. Zindel told Jerry

Author of THE PIGMAN

PAUL ZINDEL

MY DARLING, MY HAMBURGER

This 1969 novel concerns a teenage couple who must deal with an unwanted pregnancy.

Tallmer of the *New York Post* that Albee "was one of my primary inspirations in writing plays. I felt very grateful because he took time." Under Albee's direction, Zindel wrote the play *Dimensions of Peacocks*, which features a disturbed teenager whose domineering mother is a visiting nurse who steals from her patients; the play is a precursor to the author's YA novel *Confessions of a Teenage Baboon*. He also began attending professional plays by writers such as Kurt Weill, Eugene Ionesco, Tennessee Williams, and Lillian Hellman; Zindel later wrote in the *New York Times* that Hellman "theatrically baptizes me with my first real play, "Toys in the Attic," in 1959. . . . I remember thinking I had at last found what would be my religion, my cathedral." After graduating from Wagner College with a degree in chemistry, Zindel worked for a year as a technical writer at Allied Chemical before deciding to become a teacher. He received a master's degree in education from Wagner College and began teaching chemistry and physics at Tottenville High School on Staten Island. Zindel taught for ten years and continued to write plays in his spare time. In 1963, he wrote *The Effect of Gamma Rays on Man-in-the-Moon Marigolds;* the following year, the play premiered at Houston's Alley Theatre.

Gamma Rays features a bright young girl, Tillie; her abusive mother, Beatrice; and her epileptic sister, Ruth. When Tillie receives recognition for her school science project—from which the title of the play is taken—it becomes clear that she will be able to break away from her dysfunctional family. In his introduction to the play, Zindel recalled the genesis of *Gamma Rays:* "One morning I awoke and discovered the manuscript next to my typewriter. I suspect it is autobiographical, because whenever I see a production of it I laugh and cry harder than anyone else in the audience." The author confirmed that he based the character of Beatrice on his mother. "I've exaggerated, of course," he noted. "It's true that Mother did a lot of the mean things that Beatrice does, but she was also capable of enormous compassion."

Before it appeared on Broadway, was made into a film, and won several major awards, *Gamma Rays* had been adapted for television in 1966. When noted children's book editor Charlotte Zolotow saw the network production, she was touched by the play and impressed by Zindel's depictions of his teenage characters as well as by his creation of realistic dialogue. Zolotow met with Zindel to persuade him to begin writing books for young adults; Zindel told Sidney Fields of the New York *Daily News* that Zolotow "brought me into an area that I never explored before, my own confused, funny, aching teenage days." After their meeting, Zindel began reading adolescent literature. He later told Sean Mitchell of the *Dallas Times Herald,* "I discovered that there weren't many writers who were getting through. . . . What I saw in most of them had no connection to the teenagers I knew. I thought I knew what kids would want in a book, and so I made a list and followed it." The result was *The Pigman.*

Classic Early Novels

In *The Pigman,* Zindel describes how sophomores John Conlan and Lorraine Jensen befriend the lonely widower Angelo Pignati, whom they nickname "The Pigman" because of his cherished collection of pig figurines. Mr. Pignati and his young friends mutually accept and enjoy each other, and the teens find the Pigman's openness and respect to be in

Zindel received the Pulitzer Prize in Drama in 1971 for this work about a dysfunctional family.

refreshing contrast to their usual experiences of adult behavior. When Mr. Pignati suffers a heart attack, he entrusts his house keys to John and Lorraine, who throw a party in his home. Pignati's figurines are smashed just as he returns unexpectedly from the hospital. The old man, who forgives John and Lorraine for their betrayal, has a fatal heart attack. After his death, the teens alternate chapters of their "memorial epic," in which they reflect upon what they learned from Mr. Pignati as well as on their guilt. Writing in *Publishers Weekly,* Lavinia Russ claimed that *The Pigman* is "headline news because, though it is a first book, it is so remarkable that it automatically shows its writer to be a professional. . . . He has written a story that will not be denied. I hope he's very proud of it. He should be."

Horn Book reviewer Diane Farrell concluded, "Few books that have been written about young people are as cruelly truthful about the human condition. Fewer still accord the elderly such serious consideration or perceive that what we term senility may be a symbolic return to youthful honesty and idealism." *The Pigman* became a best-seller and a landmark of YA literature as well as the work against which all of Zindel's subsequent books for young people would be judged.

Twelve years after its publication, Zindel wrote a sequel to his debut novel, *The Pigman's Legacy*. The author picks up the lives of John and Lorraine two years after the death of Mr. Pignati. When the friends return to the Pigman's house, they discover that it is being occupied by another elderly tenant, Colonel Gus Glenville, a former subway builder who is hiding from the IRS. Realizing that the colonel is dying of cancer, John and Lorraine take him to Atlantic City and arrange a marriage with Dolly, a worker in their school cafeteria. At the end of the novel, the colonel passes away, and John and Lorraine, realizing that the legacy of the Pigman is love, declare their affection for each other. Writing in the *New York Times Book Review*, Paxton Davis noted that sequels often merely try to imitate previously successful formulas. "But," the critic concluded, "Zindel is on to something bolder here: Instead of merely tacking it on, he's wrapped his sequel around its precursor, returning to old themes but enlarging and deepening them. The result is a story in which we become involved with recognizable youths who grow and mature. And as they mature, their tale takes on broader implications; it is a surprising, beautiful, and even profound story." *Books for Your Children* reviewer Joyce Wyatt concurred, calling *The Pigman's Legacy* a "profound book. . . . One of the few genuine teenage books of quality, a distinguished sequel to *The Pigman*."

In 1991, Zindel published *The Pigman and Me*, an autobiography for young people that describes a significant period of his youth, the time when he met his own Pigman, Nonno Frankie. The father of Connie Vivona, a single mother who purchases a house on Staten Island with Zindel's mother Beatrice, Nonno Frankie—a font of wisdom and advice who taught young Paul, in the author's words, "the greatest secret of life"—becomes the boy's first positive male role model. When Beatrice Zindel becomes resentful of the Vivona family, she moves Paul and his sister to another residence, but not before Nonno Frankie has given Paul some important tools for living. Writing in *School Library Journal*,

Two fifteen-year-old misfits meet at school and embark on a journey halfway across the country in this work.

Susan R. Farber commented that Zindel "is in rare form here. While's he's not the first to turn teenage angst into humor, he is certainly among the best." Betsy Hearne of *Bulletin of the Center for Children's Books* called *The Pigman and Me* "the freshest writing he's done for a long time. In fact, the Pigman here—and the relationship between him and the author as adolescent—is developed with a depth not always accorded their fictional counterparts."

Along with *The Pigman, My Darling, My Hamburger* is generally considered the best of Zindel's early works for teenagers. In this novel, the author's second, Zindel portrays two couples: the popular and confident Sean and Liz and the sensitive, less secure Maggie and Dennis. Liz is pressured for sex by

Sean; the title of the novel comes from advice that she received from one of her teachers on how to deflect Sean's sexual advances: ask him out for a hamburger. When Liz and Sean make love, she becomes pregnant. When Sean refuses to marry Liz, Maggie takes her for an abortion, and after the experience leads to complications, Maggie tells her mother about it. At the end of the novel, the couples split up, having been "matured and embittered by their experiences," in the words of Theodore W. Hipple in the *Dictionary of Literary Biography*. Hipple concluded that in "many ways *My Darling, My Hamburger* is Zindel's best book for adolescents.... [What] happens in the novel, though it ranges from first-date behavior to a butchered abortion, is well within the experience of teenagers. Although Zindel provides no definitive solutions ... his insights in this novel are informative in positive ways." Writing in the *New York Times Book Review*, John Rowe Townsend called *My Darling, My Hamburger* "a better novel than "The Pigman."" *Publishers Weekly* reviewer Lavinia Russ concurred: "When Paul Zindel's first book "The Pigman" appeared, it was so astonishingly good it made your reviewer feel like some watcher of the skies when a new planet swims into its ken. When his second book arrived and topped his first, even Keats could offer no poetry to express the joy it brought...." The critic concluded that readers are "swept immediately into the illusion that no outsider is recording [the characters's] story: they are talking it out themselves. And that, my friend, is *writing*."

Zindel encountered a decidedly mixed reception for his next novel, *I Never Loved Your Mind*. The story focuses on the relationship between Dewey Daniels, a seventeen-year-old high school dropout whom Jean Stafford of the *New Yorker* called "one of the most offensive young blatherskites to be found in all of fiction," and Yvette Goethals, the eighteen-year-old hippie whom he meets in the autopsy room of the hospital where they both work. *I Never Loved Your Mind* describes the commune where Yvette lives with a rock band as well as the sexual pairing of Yvette and Dewey and includes some antiestablishment jabbing. At the end of the novel, Yvette breaks up with Dewey, telling him that their sexual relationship did not mean that she loved his mind, and heads for New Mexico. Dewey, changed by his experience, decides to become a doctor. Stafford declared that "an honest bookseller should hang over it a placard reading "Caveat Emptor."" Writing in *Publishers Weekly*, Lavinia Russ said, "Paul Zindel's talent is too big to ignore. He has used it this

time to write an ugly book." However, noted Aneurin Rhys of *Junior Bookshelf*, whether "you like the story or despise it, you cannot deny that Zindel lightens the gloom and disgust with the pithiness of his language, if only to remind you that laughing at life is what makes it bearable."

Popular YA Fiction

Confessions of a Teenage Baboon, a YA novel published in 1977 that reworks Zindel's early play *Dimensions of Peacocks*, is generally considered a return to form. Fifteen-year-old Chris Boyd lives with his mother, a visiting nurse, wherever she is caring for one of her terminally ill patients. As the story begins, Chris and his mom are living with the Dipardi family: Mrs. Dipardi, an emotionally unbalanced woman, is dying of cancer; Mr. Dipardi is senile; their son, thirty-year-old Lloyd, fills the house with his teenage friends, including sixteen-year-old Harold, who does the cooking for the family. Lloyd, who is drunk most of the time, sees in Chris a reflection of himself and attempts to toughen him up through badgering and insults. Accused by Chris's mother of homosexual acts with Harold, Lloyd shoots himself in the head. At the end of the novel, Chris realizes what Harold was trying to tell him: that he must take responsibility for his own life. Writing in the *Lion and the Unicorn*, Stanley Hoffman said, "Next to *Pigman*, I think *Baboon* is Zindel's most haunting novel in the best sense of that word. It stays with you long after it's been read and presents the most curious—and believable—adult character in any of his works. ... *Baboon* may be, in fact, Zindel's best novel precisely because it breaks with the formulas of his past books." Isabel Quigley of the *Times Literary Supplement* claimed, "Needless to say, it is not the stuff that teenage novels used to deal with, but then the stuff of teenage life is not what it used to be, either, and what counts is the way Paul Zindel handles it, with a delicacy at once funny and heartfelt, outspoken and sensitive." Writing in *Best Sellers*, Janet P. Benestad concluded that Zindel's treatment of Chris's problem is "sympathetic, realistic, and appropriately written for a young adult audience. It portrays the moral bankruptcy of modern man in the character of Lloyd...." Zindel claimed in *Top of the News* that *Confessions of a Teenage Baboon* "is a story so close to me that I almost had a nervous breakdown writing it. I pushed myself too close to the inner demons that drive me."

In 1973, Zindel married Bonnie Hildebrand, a publicity director whom he had met at the Cleveland

Playhouse during a staging of *Gamma Rays;* the couple has two children, David and Elizabeth. Paul and Bonnie Zindel collaborated on *A Star for the Latecomer,* a novel for young adults published in 1980 that features the first female protagonist to appear without a male counterpart in one of the author's works. Written mostly by Bonnie Zindel, who has continued to write for young adults on her own, the novel outlines how sixteen-year-old Brooke Hillary deals with her mother's terminal illness, experiences first love, and discovers that she does not want to be the dancer that her mother expects her to be. A critic in *Kirkus Reviews* noted that "this is played straight, without the usual bizarre social-satiric enlargements. Still, this being Zindel, the performing-child scenes are just a little sharper, Brooke's typical teenage fantasies just a little bit more convincingly hers, and her relationship with her mother just a lit-

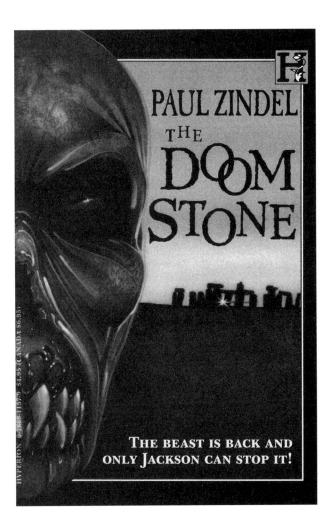

During a visit with his aunt in England, fifteen-year-old Jackson Cawley battles a bloodthirsty hominid that returns to its home every nineteen years to feed.

tle less black-or-white than in other stories of child-star trials or bereavement." Zindel also features a young woman as the main character of *The Girl Who Wanted to Be a Boy,* a novel published the following year about Sibella Cametta, a fifteen-year-old who is determined to snag a boyfriend. She goes after a young man who operates a mini-racetrack, buys him a Surfer van, and loses him. At the end of the book, Sibella realizes that it is better to have loved and lost, and muses that since she is only fifteen she can wait a little longer for love. Judith N. Mitchell of *Voice of Youth Advocates* noted, "Zindel's adolescent novels are not everyone's cup of tea, but I love them. This one, too, is a fun house ride. . . ." Commenting that black comedy "is the key to Zindel's adolescent novels," the critic added, "What is new and compelling is the force with which Sibella's pain is delineated. . . ."

A novel regarded as one of Zindel's most effective is *A Begonia for Miss Applebaum,* a work published in 1989. High-school friends Henry and Zelda become companions to and protectors of Miss Applebaum, their retired science teacher, who is suffering from cancer. Focusing on Miss Applebaum's final months of life, Zindel describes how Miss Applebaum takes the teens around New York City and teaches them to view the world in a new way. The children also become involved in Miss Applebaum's treatment and, at the end of the novel, in her burial; through their experiences, Henry and Zelda learn about living with zest and dying with dignity. Linda Halperin of *Voice of Youth Advocates* called *A Begonia for Miss Applebaum* "another smashing success. . . . YAs who pick up the book will devour it from beginning to end." Writing in *Junior Bookshelf,* M. Hobbs noted that Zindel "has lost none of his persuasiveness and vigour," concluding that, "The story raises a number of uncomfortable questions, which is not a bad thing in the hands of such an accomplished writer."

Pens Suspenseful Novels

In the early 1990s, Zindel added humorous fiction for middle graders to his body of work with the "Wacky Facts Lunch Bunch" series of stories about the exploits of five fifth-grade friends. In the late 1990s, the author began creating fast-paced adventures with fantastic overtones for young adults. In *Loch,* Zindel introduces fifteen-year-old Luke Perkins, nicknamed "Loch" for his claim that he saw the Loch Ness monster at the age of five. The son of an oceanographer, Luke enters into a quest to save the prehistoric inhabitants of a small Vermont lake from an exploitative tabloid publisher who wants them killed. Luke and his younger sister Zaidee have recently lost their mother, and their father appears to have sold himself out to his employer. With the help of the publisher's teenage daughter Sarah, Luke and Zaidee save a stranded young plesiosaur. The novel closes with a showdown between the sea creatures and the hunters; after the battle, in which the siblings's father redeems himself, the plesiosaurs head back to their original—and safer—habitat. Writing in *Bulletin of the Center for Children's Books*, Deborah Stevenson commented, "The characters are pretty stock, the sentimental undertones rather unsubtle. . ., and nobody seems much worried about what will happen to the residents of the bigger lake to which the creatures flee. Still, it's a good, rip-roaring, kids-know-best adventure that would make a terrific beach paperback and has "reluctant reader" written all over it." *School Library Journal* reviewer Connie Tyrrell Burns observed, "The book is really about what makes a family, whether human or creature. . . .."

In *The Doom Stone*, fifteen-year-old Jackson Cawley, an American boy visiting his anthropologist aunt in England, hunts a bloodthirsty mutant hominid that lives beneath Salisbury Plain. The beast, who comes out of his home every nineteen years to feed, has bitten Jackson's aunt and has killed several other people. With the help of his friend Alma, Jackson stops the monster on the roof of Salisbury Cathedral. Writing in *School Library Journal*, Steven Engelfried noted that the "intriguing premise and suspenseful, fast-paced action will surely please readers who like horror stories with a bit more substance than the latest Pike or Stine." Deborah Stevenson of *Bulletin of the Center for Children's Books* noted that *The Doom Stone* "has the same brisk pacing and old-fashioned, satisfyingly kid-driven adventure as *Loch*," while a reviewer in *Publishers Weekly* concluded that Zindel makes "plentiful use of local scenery and Stonehenge lore and, for YA thrill-seekers, there's plenty of gore and creepy-crawly slimy stuff. The final showdown on the roof of Salisbury Cathedral is a spine-tingler."

Reef of Death, an adventure/horror story set along Australia's Great Barrier Reef, received comparisons with Peter Benchley's *Jaws* as well as the books of R. L. Stine and Christopher Pike. The novel describes how young PC McPhee and two aborigines, Maruul, a young girl, and Wally, an elder from Maruul's village, defeat the wicked Dr. Ecenbarger, a German scientist who likes to feed people to the sea creatures she captures. Writing in *Voice of Youth Advocates*,

Suspense and adventure abound in Zindel's 1998 novel about a seventeen-year-old boy who stumbles upon a mad scientist's plot to feed humans to her sea creatures.

Lynn Evans opined that Zindel "has forsaken characterization and plot development for stereotypes and gore," although she claimed that readers of Stine and Pike "will enjoy the vivid descriptions of humans being destroyed by fish, punctuated with plenty of flesh ripping and dismemberment." Joel Shoemaker, writing in *School Library Journal*, called *Reef of Death* a "page-turning, toothy monster story" that is "best read as pure fantasy."

In an interview with Jean Mercier of *Publishers Weekly*, Zindel claimed, "Teenagers *have* to rebel. It's part of their growing process. In effect, I try to show them they aren't alone in condemning parents and teachers as enemies or ciphers. I believe I must convince my readers that I am on their side. I know it's a continuing battle to get through the years between twelve and twenty—an abrasive time. And so I

If you enjoy the works of Paul Zindel, you might want to check out the following books:

Michael Crichton, *Jurassic Park*, 1990.
S. E. Hinton, *The Outsiders*, 1967.
E. L. Konigsburg, *The View from Saturday*, 1996.
Norma Fox Mazer, *After the Rain*, 1987.
Rob Thomas, *Satellite Down*, 1998.

write always from their point of view." In an interview with Paul Janeczko, Zindel said, "I write for the people who don't like to read, as a rule. I found that academic students, the ones from better homes and gardens, so to speak, were able to enjoy a whole range of material. . . . But, as a rule, that left out an enormous body of students. I found even the subject of chemistry becoming too sophisticated and leaving behind a lot of kids, and even those from better homes and gardens weren't able to catch on to the new chemistry. And they had no need for it. They had need for other, more immediate bodies of information." The author concluded, "[What] I think of the world really is reflected through my books. It's in transition and like the motion of being keys on a piano: I just play different ones at different times, but what I do learn now, and what I'm concerned about now, is how to maintain the most sensible level of happiness and fulfillment for myself, while at the same time trying to satisfy the demands of society, which are to bring innovation to civilization, to institutions, to make contributions which make the world a better place to live. So that really I try to satisfy both. I see the world as a problem-solving situation, and the solution of those problems through fiction seems to be the adventure that I've chosen for myself."

■ Works Cited

Benestad, Janet P., review of *Confessions of a Teenage Baboon, Best Sellers*, February, 1978, p. 368.

Burns, Connie Tyrrell, review of *Loch, School Library Journal*, January, 1995, p. 138.

Davis, Paxton, review of *The Pigman's Legacy, New York Times Book Review*, January 25, 1981, p. 27.

Review of *The Doom Stone, Publishers Weekly*, December 4, 1995, p. 63.

Engelfried, Steven, review of *The Doom Stone, School Library Journal*, December, 1995, p. 132.

Evans, Lynn, review of *Reef of Death, Voice of Youth Advocates*, April, 1998, p. 64.

Farber, Susan R., review of *The Pigman and Me, School Library Journal*, September, 1992, p. 288.

Farrell, Diane, review of *The Pigman, Horn Book*, February, 1969, p. 61.

Fields, Sidney, "Author Has Chemistry for Kids," *Daily News* (New York), March 9, 1978.

Forman, Jack Jacob, *Presenting Paul Zindel*, Twayne, 1988.

Haley, Beverly A., and Kenneth L. Donelson, "Pigs and Hamburgers, Cadavers and Gamma Rays: Paul Zindel's Adolescents," *Elementary English*, October, 1974, pp. 941-45.

Halperin, Linda, review of *A Begonia for Miss Applebaum, Voice of Youth Advocates*, June, 1989, p. 109.

Hearne, Betsy, review of *The Pigman and Me, Bulletin of the Center for Children's Books*, December, 1992, p. 129.

Henke, James T., "Six Characters in Search of the Family: The Novels of Paul Zindel," *Children's Literature: Annual of the Modern Language Association Seminar on Children's Literature and the Children's Literature Association*, edited by Francelia Butler, Volume 5, Temple University, 1976, pp. 130-39.

Hipple, Theodore W., entry in *Dictionary of Literary Biography*, Volume 52: *American Writers for Children since 1960: Fiction*, Gale, 1986, pp. 405-10.

Hobbs, M., review of *A Begonia for Miss Applebaum, Junior Bookshelf*, August, 1989, p. 198.

Hoffman, Stanley, "Winning, Losing, But Above All Taking Risks: A Look at the Novels of Paul Zindel," *The Lion and the Unicorn*, fall, 1978, pp. 78-88. Janeczko, Paul, "In Their Own Words, an Interview with Paul Zindel," *English Journal*, October, 1977. Amended by Paul Zindel.

McGrath, Joan, entry in *Twentieth-Century Children's Writers*, 3rd edition, edited by Tracy Chevalier, St. James, 1989.

Mercier, Jean, "Paul Zindel," *Publishers Weekly*, December 5, 1977.

Mitchell, Judith N., review of *The Girl Who Wanted a Boy, Voice of Youth Advocates*, October, 1981, p. 40.

Mitchell, Sean, "Grown-up Author's Insights into Adolescent Struggles," *Dallas Times Herald*, June 27, 1979.

Quigley, Isabel, "Banking on Lloyd," *Times Literary Supplement*, April 7, 1978, p. 383.

Rhys, Aneurin, review of *I Never Loved Your Mind, Junior Bookshelf*, October, 1972, p. 295.

Russ, Lavinia, review of *The Pigman, Publishers Weekly*, September 30, 1968, p. 61.

Russ, Lavinia, review of *My Darling, My Hamburger, Publishers Weekly*, September 27, 1969, p. 85.

Russ, Lavinia, review of *I Never Loved Your Mind*, *Publishers Weekly*, April 13, 1970, p. 85.

Shoemaker, Joel, review of *Reef of Death*, *School Library Journal*, March, 1998, p. 226.

Silverman, Stephen M., "How "Moon's" Zindel Stays Happy in His Work," *New York Post*, March 6, 1978.

Stafford, Jean, review of *I Never Loved Your Mind*, *New Yorker*, December 5, 1970, pp. 218-19.

Review of *A Star for the Latecomer*, *Kirkus Reviews*, April 1, 1980, p. 444.

Stevenson, Deborah, review of *Loch*, *Bulletin of the Center for Children's Books*, November, 1994, p. 110.

Stevenson, Deborah, review of *The Doom Stone*, *Bulletin of the Center for Children's Books*, February, 1996, pp. 210-11.

Tallmer, Jerry, "Hearts and Marigolds," *New York Post*, May 8, 1971.

Townsend, John Rowe, review of *My Darling, My Hamburger*, *New York Times Book Review*, November 9, 1969, p. 2.

Wyatt, Joyce, review of *The Pigman's Legacy*, *Books for Your Children*, spring, 1981, p. 19.

Zindel, Paul, "The Theatre Is Born within Us," *New York Times*, July 26, 1970.

"Zindel Having Problems and Lots of Fun Too," *Morning Telegraph*, July 30, 1970.

Zindel, Paul, foreword to *The Effect of Gamma Rays on Man-in-the-Moon Marigolds*, Bantam, 1971.

Zindel, Paul, commentary in *Top of the News*, winter, 1978.

■ For More Information See

BOOKS

Children's Literature Review, Gale, Volume 3, 1978, Volume 45, 1997.

Dictionary of Literary Biography, Volume 7: *Twentieth-Century American Dramatists*, Gale, 1981, pp. 368-73.

Helbig, Alethea K., and Agnes Reed Perkins, *Dictionary of American Children's Fiction*, Greenwood, 1986.

Holtze, Sally Holmes, editor, *Fifth Book of Junior Authors and Illustrators*, H. W. Wilson, 1983.

Rees, David, *The Marble in the Water: Essays on Contemporary Writers of Fiction for Children and Young Adults*, Horn Book, 1980.

St. James Guide to Young Adult Writers, St. James Press, 1999.

PERIODICALS

Booklist, December 1, 1993, p. 686; March 15, 1996, p. 1296.

Books for Keeps, July, 1995, p. 14.

Children's Literature Association Quarterly, fall, 1992, p. 11.

English Journal, December, 1993, p. 71.

Reading Time, Number 1, 1992, pp. 8-10.

School Library Journal, October, 1998, pp. 148-49; October, 1999, p. 163.

Times Educational Supplement, June 17, 1994, p. 12.

Wilson Library Bulletin, May, 1993, p. 89.

Sketch by Gerard J. Senick

Author/Artist Index

The following index gives the number of the volume in which an author / artist's biographical sketch appears: